HIDEOUS PROGENIES

Dramatizations of *Frankenstein* from Mary Shelley to the Present

STEVEN
EARL
FORRY

upp

UNIVERSITY OF PENNSYLVANIA PRESS

PHILADELPHIA

PRINTED IN THE UNITED STATES OF AMERICA

Library of Congress Cataloging-in-Publication Data

Forry, Steven Earl.
Hideous progenies : dramatizations of Frankenstein from Mary Shelley to the present / Steven Earl Forry.
p. cm.
Bibliography: p.
Includes index.
ISBN 0-8122-8131-4
1. Shelley, Mary Wollstonecraft, 1797–1851. Frankenstein.
2. Shelley, Mary Wollstonecraft, 1797–1851—Adaptations.
3. Frankenstein (Fictitious character) in literature.
4. Frankenstein (Fictitious character)—Drama. 5. Frankenstein films—History and criticism. 6. English drama—19th century.
I. Title.
PR5397.F73F67 1989
823′.7—dc20 89-14628
CIP

Contents

Illustrations

Preface

And now, once again, I bid my hideous
progeny go forth and prosper.
Frankenstein[1]

AFTER READING Mary Shelley's *Frankenstein* upon its publication in 1818, William Beckford turned to the fly-leaf of his copy and wrote: "This is, perhaps, the foulest Toadstool that has yet sprung up from the reeking dunghill of present times."[2] Fortunately not everyone shared Beckford's opinion, and the novel went on to enjoy immediate although not unequivocal success.[3] However, not until the production of Richard Brinsley Peake's *Presumption; or, The Fate of Frankenstein* in 1823 would the tale of Frankenstein again stimulate the general public enough for a publisher to issue a second edition of the novel.[4] Moreover, Peake's melodrama instigated not only the 1823 edition by G. and W. B. Whittaker, but an equal interest in dramatizing Shelley's novel. Within three years of the first performance of Peake's *Presumption,* fourteen other English and French dramatizations had utilized the Frankenstein theme. To date over ninety dramatizations of *Frankenstein* have been undertaken.

This study of *Frankenstein* dramatizations contains an historical introduction and the texts of selected dramatizations. The historical introduction charts the development of the dramas from 1823 to 1930, the dawn of the celluloid image made famous by Universal Studios' 1931 production starring Boris Karloff. These chapters isolate three movements in the dissemination of the myth: 1823 to 1832 are years of transformation and proliferation during which fifteen dramatizations were performed and the myth was mutated for popular consumption; 1832 to 1900 are years of diffusion during which the myth spread among the populace and began appearing regularly in various media; and 1900 to 1930 are years of transition during which dramatic and cinematic interpretations vied for popularity. The last chapter of this section briefly surveys post-Karloffian dramatizations, and concludes with a comprehensive list of dramatizations to 1986.

During the first phase, the early playwrights established nineteenth-century conceptions of the myth, conceptions that were in turn assimilated during the second phase and passed on to the third. As the first interpreters systematically to concentrate on the gothic background of Shelley's novel, these dramatists heightened the demoniacal aspects of the Creature, elaborated the alchemical overtones of Frankenstein's experiments, and expanded the sinister context of the laboratory. Just one month after the premiere of Peake's *Presumption,* the surname "Frankenstein" had already been transformed into a thaumaturgical adjective, as when the *Times* (1 September) described a performance of *The Three Vampires* as "melodramatic, terrific, monstrous, [and] Frankensteinish."[5] In contrast, Shelley's narrative secularized the Faust myth, combined the techniques of romance and realism in one virtually self-destructing narrative, employed the doppelgänger theme to suggest that the created was the creator's double, presented in Frankenstein a portrait of the Byronic hero-villain, and implied tragic analogues between every character (each being both victim and victimizer). The early playwrights charged the tale with alchemy, developed solely the gothic (or romance) roots of the story, abandoned the doppelgänger theme in favor of a simplified Byronic hero-villain (Frankenstein) tormented by a dumb show villain-hero (the Creature), and simplified the plot by removing Walton's narrative, confining the action to twenty-four hours, and reducing the major characters to four types: the hero, the villain, the persecuted heroine, and the comical rustic. By reducing the character of Frankenstein to that of a simple hubristic overreacher condemned for challenging God's order, they transformed the novel into a simplistic moral allegory. A reviewer for the *London Magazine* (September 1823) even complained that the moral of *Presumption* appeared "so glaring, as almost to disturb the mystery and interest of the work."

By simplifying or streamlining the novel, playwrights were simply reducing Shelley's work into formulas established by men like Pixérécourt, Holcroft, Planché, and Lewis. These formulas dictated four characteristic alterations. First, the time frame of the novel was condensed to twenty-four hours and the plot to three acts. In general, the acts focused on the creation of the Creature (act 1); the Creature's adventures with the De Lacey family, culminating in the spectacular conflagration of their cottage and the abduction of Frankenstein's fiancee (act 2); and the Creature's destruction (act 3). Second, the majority of Shelley's characters were eliminated. Walton, the "framing" narrator, never appears in any pre-Karloffian dramatization. The remaining characters, as has been indicated, were cast as melodramatic "types," perhaps the most interesting of which was the low comic character who interjects laughter amid the pathos. As will be seen, this comic character also served an essential role as narrator. Third, wild action, alchemical rituals, and gothic settings replaced the novel's epistolary format, scientific background, and internalized landscape. And fourth, pithy maxims, divine intercession, and human repentance for hubristic transgression replaced the ambiguous moral stance of Shelley, especially in Frankenstein's desperate speech to Walton's sailors, in which he invokes Ulysses' problematic plea from Dante's *Inferno* (XXVI): "I have myself been blasted in these hopes, yet another may succeed."

NOTES

1. Mary Shelley, *Frankenstein; or, The Modern Prometheus,* ed. James Rieger (1974; Chicago: University of Chicago Press, 1982) 229. The quotation derives from the introduction to the 1831 edition printed in London by Colborn and Bentley. Rieger includes the introduction as an appendix to his edition. Subsequent references are to Rieger's edition and will be cited by page number in the text.

2. Howard B. Gotlieb, *William Beckford of Fonthill* (New Haven, Conn.: Yale University Press, 1960) 61.

3. In 1818 nine journals reviewed *Frankenstein*. The novel received four unfavorable reviews (*The British Critic,* ns [1818]: 432–38, reprinted in *Port Folio* [Philadelphia] 6 [1818]: 200–207; *The Quarterly Review* 18 [1818]: 379–85; *The Literary Panorama and National Register* ns 8 [1818]: 411–14; and *The Monthly Review, or Literary Journal,* ns 85 [1818]: 439); three favorable reviews (*La Belle Assemblée, or Court and Fashionable Magazine,* 2nd ser., 17 [1818]: 139–42; *The Edinburgh Magazine and Literary Miscellany* 2 [1818]: 249–53; and Scott's famous review in *Blackwood's Edinburgh Magazine* 2 [1818]: 613–20); and one mixed review—(*The Gentleman's Magazine* 88 [1818]: 334–35). For a discussion of these early reviews see R. Glynn Gryllis, *Mary Shelley: A Biography* (London: Oxford University Press, 1938) 315–18; Muriel Spark, *Child of Light: A Reassessment of Mary Wollstonecraft Shelley* (Hadleigh, Essex: Tower Bridge, 1951), 140; and most especially W. H. Lyles, *Mary Shelley: An Annotated Bibliography* (New York: Garland, 1975), 168–69. My review citations derive from Lyles.

4. Lyles indicates that the Whittaker publication was a reprint of the 1818 edition, "using the same plates" (6). A comparison of the two texts reveals, however, that Whittaker in fact reset the type to produce a new edition.

5. An advertisement in the *Morning Post* (3 September) repeats the adjectival

rendering of Frankenstein's name and embellishes the description of the play: "THIS EVENING . . . will be presented an entirely new Operatic, Melo-Dramatic, Terrific, Vampiric, Monstrous, Frankensteinish, Horrific Romance Burletta, comprising much Moonshine and more Mirth, written under Lunar influence, but not by a Lunatic."

Acknowledgments

IN UNIVERSAL STUDIOS' *The Forbin Project* (1969), Dr. Forbin laments to a friend: "I think your mother was right. *Frankenstein* should be required reading for all scientists." Fortunately, acknowledgments are not required reading, for I fear that my list of indebtedness lacks trenchant analysis or even an engaging plot. Nonetheless, debt has been incurred and debt must be repaid. Indeed, my sparse remarks bode little of the true sense of gratitude I bear for those acknowledged—and especially for those whom I have inadvertently failed to acknowledge.

Of those who shed the most blood during this project, my wife, Mary, must be noted first. My teacher and always my friend, she will receive a more lengthy mention below. Of teachers, G. Thomas Tanselle and Karl Kroeber have earned my lasting gratitude. Special mention must also be made of the timely support of Professors Michael R. Booth, Coral Lansbury, Donald Stone, Genevieve Delattre, and the late Bernard Beckerman. Anaïs Nin should also be mentioned because her encouragement pulled me through the dog days of Paris. Those who knew her will understand. Others intimately—although at times unknowingly—contributing to this project include Mark Jones, Jack Reider, Yvonne Corothers, Mark Haselfeld, Gail Brower, David Toole, Sanford Koufax, Mark Langlet, Dan Strauss, Van Tibbles, C. Allen and Elizabeth Parker, Michael and Kim Cosack, Bertie and Rachel Laddie, Larry and Brenda Moore, James Morrison, and Mary Ann Fisher. Forrest J. Ackerman, Ted Newsom, and Alios F. Dettlaff must be mentioned in the same breath because their efforts facilitated what was for me one of the most interesting aspects of this project: the hunt for the putatively lost copy of the Thomas Edison film *Frankenstein* (1910). I must also acknowledge Mr. D. A. King, who, from his home in Surrey, directed my attention to several important developments in regard to the work of Henry M. Milner. Last of all, I wish to extend a special remark to John Balderston, Jr. and to Edward L. Webling. Mr. Balderston's efforts to procure for me the rights to reproduce his father's play were truly Herculean. And Mr. Webling's speedy response to my never-ending requests to reproduce his late aunt's material will always be appreciated.

Thank heaven for libraries and their librarians. Contributors to the present study include Sara S. Hodson, whose speedy work at the Huntington Library belied my endeavors to procrastinate; Raymond Mander and Joe Mitchenson, whose theatre collection is a blessing to their homeland; Terri Mastrorocco of the Library of Congress; Jane Broghton-Perry of the Victoria and Albert Museum; Andrée L'Heritier of the Bibliothèque Nationale; M. A. E. Nickson of the British Library; Mena Williams, District Librarian of the Lancashire County Council; Nesta Jenkins of the Birmingham Public Library; and D. J. Foskett of the University of London Library. Librarians at the following institutions have also contributed splendid assistance: the Harvard College Library; the Lilly Library of Indiana University; the Beinecke Rare Book and Manuscript Library of Yale University; the Bodleian Library at Oxford; the Cambridge University Library; the Billy Rose Theatre Collection of the New York Public Library; and the libraries of Cornell and Columbia Universities. I would never have been able to work in London without the support of Columbia University. And upon returning from London, I would not have completed this seemingly interminable project without a grant from the Mrs. Giles Whiting Foundation.

Members of my family have never provided a more stable platform from which to work. They have learned to put up with my quirks, my unexpected visits, and my seemingly endless nagging—all the while extending sympathy and encouragement, especially Sandy and Mike. Earl Forry and Darlys Weiss must come first on this list. As parents, they provided love and encouragement—even when I proved a most obstreperous and hideous progeny. Best of all, they somehow managed to see to it that I was born on Mary Shelley's birthday. Thank you. Robert Weiss and Eva Forry came into and transformed my life at an early age. Paul and Henriette Caner and their daughters, Patricia and Marie-Laure, must also be remembered. Cezanne Dawa Cartier and Sandy and David Dilling have helped immeasurably to fill voids that only they knew existed, as has Mike Forry. Harry and Alma Forry and William and Dorothy Gallagher as well as Ray and Mary Gallagher, Jack and Marvel Schuler, Donald and Laverne Robinson, and William Gallagher, Jr. have taught me tenacity and pride.

Their children have taught me unity. The Trotechaud family taught me faith. And finally, the greatest debt I owe is to Mary. Nothing here would have been accomplished without her. To her, to our daughter Sarah, and to all our future progenies I dedicate this book.

PART I

Historical Introduction

O brave monster! lead the way.
The Tempest II.ii

1

Melodrama and Burlesque: 1823 to 1826

On 22 July 1823 William Godwin addressed the following in a letter to Mary Shelley, who was returning to London after five years on the Continent:

> It is a curious circumstance that a play is just announced, to be performed at the English Opera House in the Strand next Monday, entitled, Presumption, or the Fate of Frankenstein. I know not whether it will succeed. If it does, it will be some sort of feather in the cap of the author of the novel, a recommendation in your future negociacions with booksellers.[1]

The first performance of the dramatization occurred six days later. As Godwin had hoped, Richard Brinsley Peake's melodrama initiated enough interest in Mary Shelley's novel that less than one month after its debut a second edition had been published.[2] Godwin did not foresee, however, that *Presumption* would inspire fourteen other dramatizations within three years of its premiere. To a large degree three early gothic melodramas, Peake's *Presumption* (1823), Jean-Toussaint Merle and Béraud Antony's *Le Monstre et le magicien* (1826), and Henry Milner's *The Man and the Monster* (1826), share the responsibility for shaping the destiny not only of subsequent dramatizations, but of popular conceptions of the novel. Indeed in the three years that succeeded the first performance of the melodrama by Peake, dramatizations of Shelley's novel effectively transformed for the general public the author's original conception of the Frankenstein myth.

* * *

In 1823 *Presumption; or, The Fate of Frankenstein* enjoyed enormous popularity, being performed thirty-seven times in its first season, despite—or perhaps because of—complaints in *Gentleman's Magazine* (93 [1823]: 174) that it "was replete with too many horrors." While lauding the performance of T. P. Cooke as the Creature, London newspapers were of mixed opinion on the merits of the play. For example, of Cooke's performance the *Examiner* (3 August) remarked that he "exhibited the preternatural with much imagination, and the natural with truth"; however, it also lamented: "The dialogue, except for the part of *Frankenstein,* and probably his servant, is miserable prattle, and so divested of a judicious connexion with the main incident . . . nobody cares a tittle about hearing it." Mary Shelley agreed with this assessment when, of a performance she attended the day before her twenty-sixth birthday, she wrote to Leigh Hunt: "The story is not well managed—but Cooke played ———'s part extremely well. . . . I was much amused, & it appeared to excite a breathless eagerness in the audience" (1:378). In contrast, the *Morning Post* (30 July) approved of both performance and performer: "As it stands, however, as a drama, it is most effective; and T. P. COOKE well pourtrays what indeed it is a proof of his extraordinary genius so well to pourtray. . . . Too much cannot be said in praise of T. P. COOKE." On the other hand, the *Times* (29 July) found the whole situation a bit contemptible: "Mr. Cooke threw some energetic pantomimic acting into the character of the *Monster,* but *Frankenstein* had little opportunity. . . . The piece upon the whole has little to recommend it; but that, as times go, will be no great obstacle to its success." Nevertheless, the *Drama* (August 1823) described the premiere quite differently:

> There was much boisterous applause throughout the whole of the performance, especially where the "walking pestilence" deals death and destruction around. It has been repeated several times since with varied success, and we cannot but deny that this strange melo-drame has excited a very considerable degree of curiosity in the town.

In 1823 *Presumption* also inspired one melodrama, three burlesques, and a series of protests mounted by the London Society for the Prevention of Vice. As early as the first performance of *Presumption,* scattered protests could be heard, although at this early stage they can probably be regarded as "puffs." "Though the progress of the performance was frequently marked with much boisterous applause," remarked *The News* (29 July) "there was considerable opposition on the falling of the curtain, so much so, that it was a long time before Mr. BARTLEY could announce it for repetition." And in the *Theatrical Observer* (3 July) the ever present "John Brown," referring to the greasepaint color of the Creature, complained: "I would not take my wife . . . to see this blue-devil."

No specific charges are leveled in these complaints; however, the most likely source of conflict was the longstanding animosity that existed between certain members of the public and the Shelley circle. For example, virtually every review of *Presumption* prefaced its comments with allusions to Percy Shelley, et al. The *Morning Post* sounded the alarm when on 29 July it warned: "To Lord Byron, the late Mr. Shelley, and philosophers of that stamp, it might appear a very fine thing to attack the Christian faith . . . and burlesque the resurrection of the dead . . . but we would prefer the comparatively noble assaults of VOLNEY, VOLTAIRE, and PAINE." The *SundayTimes* (3 August) reminded its audience that the play's inspiration could be "laid at the door of Mary Ann Wollstoncroft [sic] Godwin, who erewhile drew in the yoke of matrimony along with the tuneful and lamented, but somehow eccentric Mr. Percy Shelley." Even the normally equable *Drama* (August 1823) noted that Mary Shelley was "the widow of PERCY BYSSHE SHELLEY, and daughter of Mr. GODWIN, the author of '*Political Justice,*' and other celebrated works. The novel itself is one of the *boldest* of fictions; and did not the authoress, in a short preface, make a kind of apology, we should almost pronounce it *impious*." Finally, when in 1824 *Presumption* appeared in Birmingham, the *Theatrical John Bull* (3 July) recalled the protests in London with the statement: *Presumption* "is taken from a Novel, by a woman who . . . is one of the *coterie* of that self-acknowledged Atheist, Percy B. Shelley, and the daughter too of the well-known Godwin—a precious breed and association."

Hence *Presumption* suffered from what can only be called guilt by association, despite its playbills, which fervently asserted: *"The striking moral exhibited in this story, is the fatal consequence of that presumption which attempts to penetrate, beyond prescribed depths, into the mysteries of nature."* Heated thus by reviews and by their own preconceptions, a small section of the London public mounted a protest centered on the supposed immorality of Peake's dramatization. Within one week of the play's debut, leaflets began to appear throughout the metropolis warning potential theatregoers against attending performances. One leaflet read:

> Do not go to the Lyceum to see the monstrous Drama, founded on the improper work called *"Frankenstein."*—Do not take your wives and families—The novel itself is of a decidedly immoral tendency; it treats of a subject which in nature cannot occur. This subject is pregnant with mischief; and to prevent the ill-consequences which may result from the promulgation of such dangerous doctrines, a few zealous friends of morality, and promoters of this Posting-bill, (and who are ready to meet the consequences thereof) are using their strongest endeavours.

The protests continued, despite the assurances of the *Theatrical Observer*, which informed readers (11 August): "The romance of *Presumption* thus has proved as attractive as ever, notwithstanding the extraordinary efforts of some puritanical zealots, who have attempted to persuade the public that it contains matter unfit for them in a moral point of view." This assurance did nothing to stop the flow of leaflets, and the management of the English Opera House was forced to act. In a letter dated 9 August and published in the *Theatrical Observer* on the 12th, Samuel James Arnold countered the protests on three fronts: first, the Lord Chamberlain would not have licensed an immoral play; second, fashionable (i.e., morally sound) audiences attended performances of *Presumption;* and third, not a single critic had protested the immorality of the piece. The text of Arnold's letter reads:

TO THE PLAY-GOING PUBLIC!

WHEREAS a scurrilous Posting-bill has been industriously circulated throughout the Metropolis, intended to injure the interests of *The English Opera-House,* by gross misrepresentations respecting the new Romantic Drama, entitled "PRESUMPTION! or, the FATE OF FRANKENSTEIN." The Public is respectfully requested not to suffer their judgments to be influenced by this malignant and unjust attack.

It is to be remembered that the *Right Honorable the Lord Chamberlain* sanctioned the Piece by granting his License, which License would certainly *have been withheld,* had the Drama been of an IMMORAL TENDENCY. The piece also continues to be performed to crowded and fashionable Audiences; and whatever difference of opinion may exist respecting its merits as a dramatic work, not one Critic has objected to it on the score of morality.

The *"Few zealous friends of Morality"* are CAUTIONED, (under legal opinions) that although there may not be grounds on the part of the Theatre for a Prosecution for a Libel, yet an Action for a *Con[s]piracy* will perhaps effectually silence *"the Promoters of a Posting-bill,"* distinguished by falsehood and hypocritical cant.

By seizing the initiative in a public forum, the English Opera House not only gained the moral high ground, but manipulated the protests to its own best advantage. The theatre's strategy prevailed, the protests immediately ceased, and box office receipts soared.[3]

Protests eventually abated in the Capital, but the lessons of London were not lost on Alfred Bunn, "Poet Bunn" as *Punch* would have it, who in 1819 had succeeded Elliston as the manager of the Theatre Royal, Birmingham. When in 1824 Bunn wished to produce a benefit for the actor Power, he took to heart a comment made by a London journal in 1823 at the height of the furor over *Presumption*. In response to one of the leaflets circulated in London, the *Theatrical Observer* (5 August) questioned: "What wise-acres could have been at the trouble and expense of such a tissue of nonsense? It will serve the house." Indeed, Bunn planned a campaign that would, he hoped, fill his theatre while it filled the town with controversy. As the *Theatrical John Bull* would later comment (3 July 1824): "You have only to tell a Cockney that an Exhibition is shocking—abominable—impious, and off he starts to bear witness to the fact, without even staying to wash his face!"

One week before the debut of *Presumption* on 28 June, leaflets mysteriously began appearing throughout Birmingham warning potential patrons of the impiety of the production (figure 1). It was rumored that a certain Reverend J. A. James was the author of the leaflets, but as the *Theatrical John Bull* again inveighed: "It was certainly not Mr. JAMES!" The review goes on to state in unequivocal terms its own opinion that whereas in London the protests succeeded as a form of publicity, they would not serve the same function in Birmingham: "Some of the knowing ones tried the same Trick here, *but it was no go!* Power offered Ten Guineas reward for the discovery of the rogues; ah! ah! we *calculate* that we could help him to *guess* a little!" (figure 2). Indeed, rather than attracting audiences, Bunn seems to have alienated them. The theatre "was but thinly attended" we read in the same review, while on the same day the *Birmingham Spectator* lamented: "We are absolutely angry with Mr. Power for selecting such a Piece, and angry with ourselves for losing our time in witnessing it."

In truth, Bunn's production was doomed from the outset. Not only were costumes lacking for the cast (O. Smith, who played the Creature, was forced to wear a dress shirt with a plaid coat pinned to his shoulders), but the theatre did not have enough white canvas to stage the elaborate avalanche in which, at the play's conclusion, Frankenstein and his "unhallowed abortion" are destroyed. Rather, a large canvas elephant, which earlier that year had been commissioned for a performance of *Thalaba the Destroyer*, was white-washed and shoved over the flies followed by a quick curtain. Even this expedient miscarried, however, as a review for the *Birmingham Spectator* (3 July) notes: "*Thunder* and *Lightning* would have done better, had they been less metallic and smoky; and *Avalanche* (the Stage Elephant) came down before the cue was given him, so that *Franky* and his *Demon* were obliged to seek death from some other source than excessive *snow-ball*." O. Smith later recalled the scene in his memoirs:

> before we reached our elevation a pistol was fired behind the scenes, when the Master Carpenter being over anxious for the success of the experiment let go—when down came the elephant with a tremendous crash, knocked down the platform and scenery and came rolling down the stage to the footlights where it ran some danger of being roasted till it was dragged off the stage by the green-coat men, and the curtain dropped upon Frankenstein amid the laughter and applause of a good natured audience.[4]

Peake in London learned of Bunn's catastrophe. From the English Opera House on 10 December 1824 he posted to Charles Mathews a letter in which he comically detailed the production. His letter reads in part:

CAUTION

TO

Playhouse Frequenters.

A sincere well-wisher to the Moral and Religious Conduct of the Population of Birmingham, has witnessed with much regret the announcement of a Piece named "FRANKENSTEIN, or PRESUMPTION," for representation on Monday next. As if the impious description of the NOVEL were not enough, we must here have the very horrid and unnatural details it contains embodied and presented to the view. This Piece, when acted in London, drew down the indignation of every devout and moral man, and was publicly exposed by the Society for the Suppression of Vice and Immorality. In giving this Caution, the Author has but the best feeling towards his Fellow Townsmen, and he will be amply rewarded by observing it attended to.

WHY do not the Proprietors of the Theatre interfere to prevent this impiety?---it reflects highly on them! They should remember "The Wages of Sin are Death," and that the rent of *such* a place will poorly compensate them for the Sin and Sorrow they are daily heaping on the deluded frequenters of this "Grave of the Soul."

Figure 1. "Caution to Playhouse Frequenters," Birmingham, 1824 (London, British Museum).

THEATRE ROYAL, BIRMINGHAM.

10 Guineas Reward.

Mr. POWER

THINKS it a duty he owes himself to call the attention of his Friends and Patrons to the insidious circulation of a Handbill, headed,

"*Caution to Playhouse Frequenters,*"

decrying, in the most specious terms, the representation of FRANKENSTEIN, which he selected for his Benefit on *Monday next, June* 28. Mr. POWER hereby pledges his own reputation that there is not the slightest tendency in the Piece to that false character wich the libellous handbill in question has endeavoured to convey—an assertion borne out by the fact of its having drawn 109 full houses last year at the English Opera House; and in announcing the ABOVE REWARD for the apprehension of the infamous Slanderer, Mr. POWER has the gratification of being backed by the Manager, Mr. BUNN, in the view of protecting his own vast property in the Theatre, while Mr. POWER is also desirous of rescuing from prejudgment a Drama which he has deemed so essential to his own interest, and which has stood with such success the test of a London Audience.

Figure 2. "10 Guineas Reward," Theatre Royal, Birmingham, 1824 (London, British Museum).

Under the head of *"Provincial Theatricals—"* I send the following, *Theatre Royal Birmingham—for the Benefit of Mr. Power*—(the new & clever Irishman)—amongst other entertainments Power announced the performance (for that night only) of my abortive, tho' successful Piece called *"Presumption, or the Fate of Frankenstein"*—You know how these things are got up out of London—one rehearsal—vamped scenery—properties not forthcoming; . . .

Power waited on Mr. Bunn, the Lessee & Manager in the morning & the following conversation ensued

Power—My dear Bunn, I take that d———d piece of Dick Peake's to-night, as the farce
Bunn—And a precious farce it is!
Power—There is no dress in the Wardrobe for the Monster, the Blue man
Bunn—You wont get one out of me for such rubbish—ask for Touchstone's dress, that will do . . .
Power—Red & Yellow wont accord at all for the Monster
Bunn—Who plays the Monster—aye—O. Smith—O. Smith has looked black at me often enough, now he may *look blue* if he likes—Will that answer your purpose?
Power—Well! if I contrive the dress (there's a blue smock frock up stairs), What shall we do for the last scene, the Avalanche?
Bunn—Do without!
Power—But have you looked at the Play-bill? the fall of the avalanche destroying Frankenstein & the Monster, is particularly described
Bunn—That is your fault—I dined out yesterday, was late at the Theatre
Power—Very: so late that you didn't come at all—but the avalanche! What the divel is to be done?—I think that the credit of both of us is at stake in Birmingham
Bunn—I don't know what your credit may be in Birmingham my dear Power—but depend upon it, I sh'ant go in debt for an avalanche; that would be *overwhelming!*
Power (winking) Couldn't you give me a cheque on *Snow's* in London, for it?
Bunn—Ha! ha! ha!—but come, business is business—I am accustomed to meet theatrical difficulties
Power—Yes; but the avalanche
Bunn—I have hit it—yes—that will do—but mind, they must let down the green curtain rapidly on the extraordinary effect
Power—How—what do you propose?
Bunn—Hanging up in the *Flys* is the large Elephant I had made for Blue-Beard
Power—What has that to do with it?
Bunn—We'll have that Elephant white-washed
Power—Eh?
Bunn—White-washed—a mass of white . . . What is an avalanche but a vast mass of white?—When Frankenstein is to be annihilated, the carpenters shall shove the whitened Elephant over the Flys—destroy you both in a moment, & down comes the curtain . . .

N.B. This expedient was actually carried into *effect.*[5]

In July of 1824 *Presumption* was revived five times in London, three times at Covent Garden and twice at the English Opera House. The performances proved to be as successful as in their first season, although the *Theatrical Observer* (13 July) seemed to be tiring of the play. As it snidely noted of the Opera House production: "*Presumption* has succeeded here in an uncommon degree; although we think *modesty* is as prevalent in this theatre as anyone." In 1825 the *New York Evening Post* (5 January) reported that at the Park Theatre a performance of the "grand melodrama Presumption, or Frankenstein" was "received with the most unbounded applause."[6] That summer the play returned to London where it reopened on 25 July at the English Opera House. *Presumption* still held the stage throughout the 1820s and into the 1830s. An English Opera House playbill for 14 August 1835 announced that "each succeeding Scene was hailed with increased enthusiasm." And although in 1837 *Presumption* was termed "all threadbare and begrimed," and by 1840 a "now somewhat antique drama,"[7] in February of 1843 it was still being performed in New York City (at the Chetham Theatre). The *Illustrated London News* (15 October 1853) estimated that by the half-century T. P. Cooke had played the role of the Creature at least 365 times.

Le Monstre et le magicien and *The Man and the Monster* achieved almost as much popularity as *Presumption*. *Le Monstre et le magicien* opened in Paris at the Théâtre de la Porte Saint-Martin on 10 June 1826 with the gout-ridden T. P. Cooke playing the role of the Creature.[8] The melodrama enjoyed an extraordinary success due, in part at least, to its fantastic special effects, which it borrowed from the British stage. As Maurice Albert notes: "Jamais, avant la représentation anglaise à la Porte-Saint-Martin de Monstre et le magicien, on n'avait vu chez nous machinerie plus compliquée et plus extraordinaire."[9] In its first season the French melodrama recorded ninety-four performances before closing on 25 November. Crowds packed the theatre even during one of the hottest summers of the decade. As *La Quotidienne* (10 July) noted:

> Le succès du *Monstre* est monstrueux comme lui-même. Toutes les loges sont louées pour six représentations à l'avance, et les plébéiens du parterre et des galeries se font assommer pendant deux ou trois bonnes heures avant d'être placés; on se bat maintenant, on se tuera dans quelques jours. . . .

Eventually it became necessary to purchase tickets three weeks in advance, with extra police being called in to control the crowds. And while the managers of the Gaîté, Variétés, and Vaudeville struggled with daily receipts of 280, 100, and 50 francs respectively, *Le Figaro* (29 June) reports that the Porte Saint-Martin grossed 1,300 francs. On 2 September a benefit performance earned as much as 3,600 francs.[10]

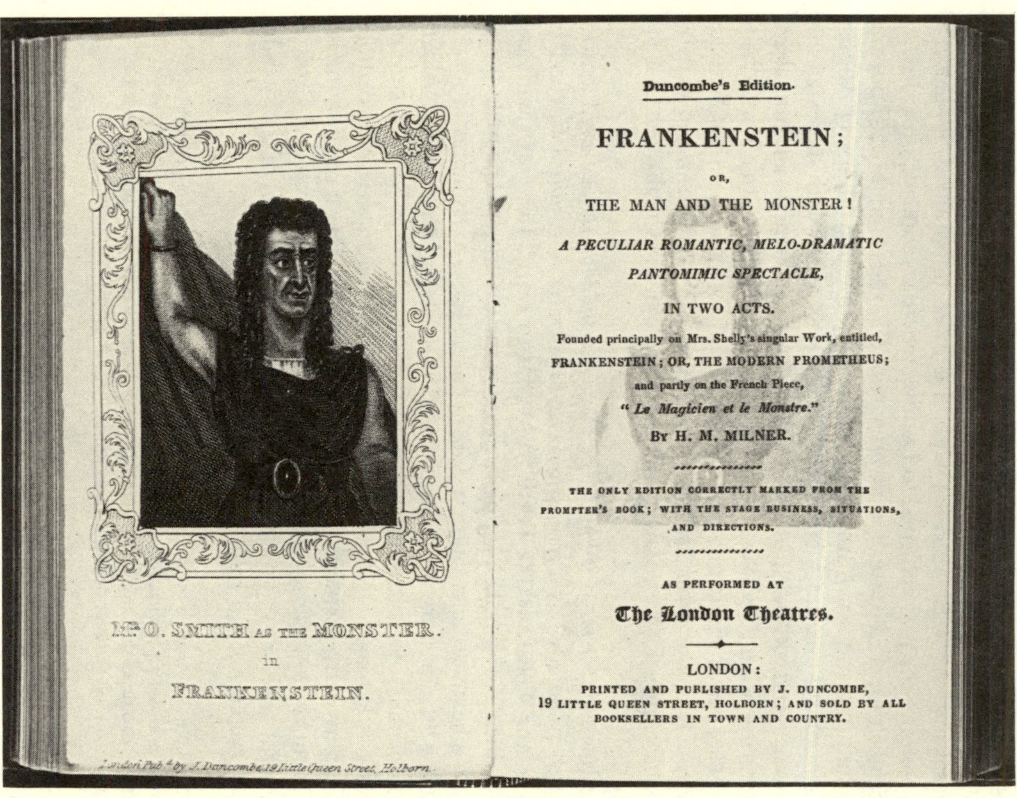

M^r. O. SMITH as the MONSTER.

in

FRANKENSTEIN.

London Pub^d by J. Duncombe, 19 Little Queen Street, Holborn.

Duncombe's Edition.

FRANKENSTEIN;

OR,

THE MAN AND THE MONSTER!

A PECULIAR ROMANTIC, MELO-DRAMATIC PANTOMIMIC SPECTACLE,

IN TWO ACTS.

Founded principally on Mrs. Shelly's singular Work, entitled, FRANKENSTEIN; OR, THE MODERN PROMETHEUS; and partly on the French Piece, "*Le Magicien et le Monstre.*"

BY H. M. MILNER.

THE ONLY EDITION CORRECTLY MARKED FROM THE PROMPTER'S BOOK; WITH THE STAGE BUSINESS, SITUATIONS, AND DIRECTIONS.

AS PERFORMED AT

The London Theatres.

LONDON:

PRINTED AND PUBLISHED BY J. DUNCOMBE, 19 LITTLE QUEEN STREET, HOLBORN; AND SOLD BY ALL BOOKSELLERS IN TOWN AND COUNTRY.

Figure 3. O. Smith as the Creature in *The Man and the Monster* (Cambridge, Mass., Harvard Theatre Collection).

Le Monstre et le magicien also exerted a tremendous influence on other dramatizations of *Frankenstein* both in England and in France. For example, the 1826 English Opera House revival of *Presumption* borrowed its nautical conclusion from Merle and Antony wherein, instead of Frankenstein and the Creature being killed in an avalanche, the two die aboard a schooner tossed in a storm. In the following quotation, Zametti is the Parisian Frankenstein:

(On aperçoit dans le fond sur un frêle esquif, le Monstre qui cherche à aborder le vaisseau. Cri d'épouvante de tout l'équipage.)

Voicc le Monstre!

(Malgré une vive résistance, le Monstre parvient à s'élancer sur le naivre; à peine y a-t-il mis le pied, que tous les matelots s'écartent épouvantes; la tempête redouble; des figures fantastiques paraissent à travers les nuages, le Monstre terrasse Zametti, l'immole, et tombe lui-même frappé de la foudre.)

Le Monstre et le magicien also initiated John Kerr's translation, *Frankenstein; or, The Monster and the Magician,* which opened at the West London Theatre on 9 October 1826; inspired Henry Milner to write *The Man and the Monster,* the only serious long-term rival of *Presumption;* and in 1861 was adapted by Ferdinand Dugué.

Milner's *The Man and the Monster* premiered at the Royal Coburg Theatre on 3 July 1826 and quickly established O. Smith as the rival of T. P. Cooke in the role of the Creature (figure 3).[11] The year after Milner's play premiered at the Coburg, Elliston at the Surrey capitalized on its popularity by retitling it *Frankenstein; or, The Monster* and staging it on 4 August—two days before the Coburg revival. Elliston's coup proved unsuccessful, however, as the next week a reviewer for the *Theatrical Observer* remarked that the Surrey production "dwindles into a mere burlesque, and we are quite sure that its talented author [Mary Shelley] would not recognize her own offspring." Like *Presumption,* Milner's play regularly held the stage until the 1840s. Sadler's Wells staged a performance on 6 November 1843; on 2 December 1857 Sir William Don played the Creature in Birmingham;[12] and as late as 1859 Henry Irving could be seen in Edinburgh playing the role of the Prince del Piombino, Frankenstein's benefactor.[13] Ultimately the popularity of *The Man and the Monster* may be judged by its early appearance in print. In contrast to *Presumption,* which was not published until after 1865 (as number 431 in *Dicks' Standard Editions*), *The Man and the Monster* was published by John Duncombe in 1826 in an edition that eventually went through five impressions before 1840. Moreover, attesting to its continuing popularity, in 1867 *The Man and the Monster* was reprinted in a second edition by Thomas Hailes Lacey.

* * *

The early melodramatizations of *Frankenstein* combined the conventions of the gothic novel with three popular melodramatic influences—nautical, Oriental or Eastern, and gothic. Nautical melodrama, which had been in existence since 1798 when John Cross introduced Jolly Jack Tar in *Blackbeard the Pirate,* reached a peak in popularity during the 1820s with the production of Moncrieff's *The Shipwreck of the Medusa* (1820), Fitzball's *The Pilot* (1825), and Jerrold's *Black-Eyed Susan* (1829). This influence can be seen in John Kerr's translation of *Le Monstre et le magicien,* which followed the French conclusion while including a more demoniacal portrait of the Creature and deleting dialogue in favor of nautical action. In his conclusion, Frankenstein is again trapped in a violent storm.

The boat is again compelled towards the ship and Jansken endeavours a second time to convey a rope to Frankenstein, but is again disappointed—at this moment the Monster appears on the rock uttering a shout of demoniac joy on beholding him, Frankenstein utters a shriek of despair.

The Monster darts from the rock into the boat, seizes Frankenstein—a moment after a thunder bolt descends and severs the bark, the waves vomit forth a mass of fire and the Magician and his unhallowed abortion are with the boat engulphed in the waves.

After 1826 this conclusion became a permanent feature of *Presumption;*[14] by 1827 it dominated the stage. In July of that year, according to the *Morning Post,* we are presented with the following:

The stage appears covered with waves, a vessel of considerable size is represented as in a dreadful seaway, and the monster is seen with a torch plunging in the waves until he gains her side, when he rapidly mounts the deck, fires the canvas and cordage, and the conflagration being at the height, the curtain falls.

Oriental or Eastern literature may account for the exotic wardrobes, but most importantly, it displaced the settings of the novel from its late eighteenth-century context.[15] Judith Wilts has already observed that Mary Shelley "moved the English gothic out of the God-haunted Mediterranean into the Swiss republic."[16] By contrast, *Frankenstein* melodramas returned the story to the God-haunted Mediterranean. *Le Monstre et le magicien* has a Venetian atmosphere similar to that in *The Castle of Udolpho* and the sixteenth-century time similar to that in *The Sicilian Romance*. A playbill for *The Man and the Monster* (10 July 1826) advertises a "SICILIAN LANDSCAPE," with the climax of the play occurring on the edge of the crater of Mount Etna, into which the Creature leaps after killing Frankenstein.[17] Lavish exoticism may also be witnessed in the villa of the Prince del Piombino. Mayer notes (157) that the standard eastern costume on the Regency stage consisted of "ballooning trousers, brocaded coats falling almost to the knee, turbans, veils, shawls, and turned-up slippers." Piombino dresses in a "Green Italian tunic, richly embroidered with silver, crimson sash, white pantaloons, [and] yellow boots," while in *Presumption,* one female lead wears a turban, red shoes, and a "large silk shawl or scarf to give an Oriental appearance." The comic woman, Ninon, wears a "showy Italian peasant's dress," while the comic man, Fritz, wears a "Buff jacket and trunks, trimmed with orange-blue stockings . . . [and a] small three-cornered drab hat." The Creature is dressed *"à la Octavian,"* presumably a reference to the wild dress of the Spaniard Octavian in Colman's *The Mountaineers* (1794). For his part, Frankenstein appears dressed *"à la Rolla,"* a reference to the heroic Peruvian Rolla in Sheridan's *Pizarro.*

The dramas also exercise care in the selection of exotic names for their dramatis personae, names evocative of the characters of Walpole and Radcliffe, such as Manfred, Alfonzo, Schedoni, Montoni, and Vincento de Vivaldi. In *The Man and the Monster* we encounter Prince del Piombino, Quadro, Rosaura, and Emmeline, a name perhaps derived from the heroine of Charlotte Smith's *Emmeline, or, The Orphan of the Castle* (1788) or from Emily, the heroine of *Udolpho.* Merle and Antony's characters include Pietro, Antonio, and Zametti (a name reminiscent of Zamiel, Zastrozzi, and even Zamoski, the villain of Pixérécourt's *Les Mines de Pologne*). Kerr adds in his translation Malfino and the banditti Litolf, Gontram, Zomar, and Swendor. Later burlesques parody these names, as in *Frankenstein; or, The Model Man* (1849) with characters like Ratzbaen (*"an Evil as well as a Pantomimic Genius"*), Tiddliwincz, Otto of Rosenberg, and Bobinetta, and in *Frankenstein; or, The Vampire's Victim* (1887), with Visconti, Mondelico, Il Capitano Maraschino, Risotto, and Caramella.

Not surprisingly, gothicism exerted the most important and pervasive influence on the *Frankenstein* dramatizations. In *The Man and the Monster,* characters wander between the "craggy precipices" of Mount Etna and the "heart of a gloomy and intricate Forest." *Le Monstre et le magicien* opens in a somber forest—*"Au lever du rideau le tonnerre gronde, et l'on voit briller les éclairs à travers le feuillage épais de la forêt"*—but the principal action and penultimate scene takes place in and around the castle of Zametti. *Presumption* opens in a *"Gothic Chamber in the House of Frankenstein"* where we encounter the sleeping Fritz in a *"Gothic arm-chair."* Kerr's translation opens up on "a Gothic Tomb." The treatment of De Lacey's forest cottage in the melodramas derives from the numerous "cottage-forest" melodramas such as *The Foundling in the Forest* (1809) and *The Miller and His Men* (1814), although both Arnold's *The Woodman's Hut* (1814) and Dibdin's *The Vicar of Wakefield* (1817) featured burning cottages.

The supernatural aspects of Frankenstein's undertaking were immediately seized upon by the melodramatists, especially in France where, as

Paul Ginisty points out, the same playwrights regularly composed both melodramas and *féeries.*[18] Thus, *Le Monstre et le magicien* is described on its title page as a "MÉLODRAME FÉERIE," or an enchanted melodrama. Furthermore, *Frankenstein* melodramas freely employed the Rosicrucian theme of the elixir vitae, which had figured prominently in the gothic novel from St. Leon in Godwin's *St. Leon: A Tale of the Sixteenth Century* (1799), through Ginotti in Percy Shelley's *St. Irvyne; or, The Rosicrucian* and Maturin's *Melmoth the Wanderer* (1820). Mary Shelley certainly was aware of the Rosicrucian theme in *Frankenstein,* and in 1843 would comically employ it in "The Mortal Immortal," in which Winzy, the assistant of Cornelius Agrippa, drinks an elixir of life thinking it is a love potion.

The early melodramas absorb the Rosicrucian influence while they eliminate Shelley's references to Erasmus Darwin and Luigi Galvani. In *The Monster and the Magician* Jansken says that "the abstruse compositions of Albert[us Magnus] and Faustus, have inflamed [Frankenstein] with guilty pretensions." "Your master is a studious chemist—nay, as I sometimes suspect, an alchemist," Clerval exclaims to Fritz in *Presumption.* "Did you never hear him make mention of the grand elixir which can prolong life to immortality?" Later, in response, Fritz tells Clerval: "there [Frankenstein] goes again, amongst otamies and phials, and crucibles, and retorts, and charcoal, and fire, and the Devil—for I'm sure he's at the bottom of it." Frizzy warns in *Another Piece of Presumption* (1823), Peake's burlesque of *Presumption:* "Master's like Dr. Faustus, he is raising the Devil!" And in the burlesque *Frank-in-Steam; or, The Modern Promise to Pay* (1824), Fritz turns to Pontie and says: "Why, Sir, [Frank-in-Steam] has been locked up in his study for the last three hours poring over the big books with Skeleton figures. He's certainly going to raise the devil or Doctor Foster."

These alchemical aspects culminate in the most thrilling scene in *Presumption:* the vivification of the Creature. Although the actual process transpires behind the closed doors of Frankenstein's laboratory, the changing colors of the window and Fritz's narration clearly suggest alchemy as well as a portent of the pyrotechnic emphasis of later adaptations. Peake employs these archetypal scenes early in the first act when Fritz, the servant, enters Frankenstein's laboratory and drops his candle—his only source of light.

> *Fritz.* Master isn't here—dare I peep . . . My candle burns all manner of colours, and spits like a roasted apple. *(Runs against the chair and drops his light, which goes out.)* There, now, I'm in the dark . . . *(A blue flame appears at the small lattice window above, as from the laboratory.)* What's that? Oh, lauk; there he is, kicking up the devil's own flame! . . .

(Music.—Fritz takes up a footstool . . . he stands on the footstool tiptoe to look through the small high lattice window of the laboratory, a sudden combustion is heard within. The blue flame changes to one of a reddish hue.)

Frank. *(Within)* It lives! it lives! . . .

Fritz. There's a hob-hob-goblin, seven-and-twenty feet high!

Fritz escapes just as a distraught Frankenstein appears at the door of the laboratory. He descends a stairway and faints in a chair. The Creature then bursts through the laboratory door (figure 4). Descending the stairs, he breaks through the balustrade (figure 5) and confronts Frankenstein, who draws a sword, which the Creature seizes and snaps in half (figure 6). The Creature then throws Frankenstein to the ground and exits out the parlor window.[19]

The first "on stage" creation scene occurred in Milner's *The Man and the Monster.* In a variation on Peake and amid a laboratory cluttered "with Bottles, and Chemical Apparatus—and a brazier with fire," Frankenstein steps back to "enjoy a triumph never yet attained by mortal man!"

(Music.)

As the cool night breeze plays upon its brow, it will awake to sense and motion. (*Music.—He rolls back the black covering, which discovers a colossal human figure, of a cadaverous livid complexion; it slowly begins to rise, gradually attaining an erect posture, Frankenstein observing with intense anxiety. When it has attained a perpendicular position, and glares its eyes upon him, he starts back with horror.*) Merciful Heaven! And has the fondest visions of my fancy awakened to this terrible reality; a form of horror, which I scarcely dare to look upon:—instead of the fresh colour of humanity, he wears the livid hue of the damp grave. Oh, horror! horror!—let me fly this dreadful monster of my own creation!

(He hides his face in his hands; the Monster, meantime, springs from the table, and gradually gains the use of his limbs; he is surprized at the appearance of Frankenstein,—advances towards him and touches him; the latter starts back in disgust and horror, draws his sword and rushes on the Monster, who with the utmost care takes the sword from him, snaps it in two, and throws it down. Frankenstein then attempts to seize it by the throat, but by a very slight exertion of its powers, it throws him off to a considerable distance; in shame, confusion, and despair, Frankenstein rushes out of the Apartment, locking the doors after him. The Monster gazes about it in wonder, traverses the Apartment; hearing the sound of Frankenstein's footsteps, without, wishes to follow him; finds the opposition of the door, with one blow strikes it from its hinges, and rushes out.)

Shortly after the phenomenal success in 1824 of Kind and Weber's *Der Freischutz*—in which T. P. Cooke played Zamiel—alchemy became a permanent part of *Frankenstein* adaptations. As far as the dramatizations of Shelley's novel are concerned, the most influential scene from this play was that in which Caspar leads Max to the Wolf's glen in order to cast the seven magic bullets. In this scene Caspar calls forth Zamiel: "A subterranean noise is heard—a rock on Right splits asunder, and ZAMIEL ap-

Figure 4. T. P. Cooke as the Creature in *Le Monstre et le magicien*, Théâtre de la Porte Saint-Martin, 1826 (Paris, Bibliothèque Nationale).

DICKS' STANDARD PLAYS.

FRANKENSTEIN.

BY R. B. PEAKE.

ORIGINAL COMPLETE EDITION.—PRICE ONE PENNY.

*** THIS PLAY CAN BE PERFORMED WITHOUT RISK OF INFRINGING ANY RIGHTS.

LONDON: JOHN DICKS, 313, STRAND.

Figure 5. T. P. Cooke as the Creature in *Presumption* (Oxford, Bodleian Library).

Figure 6. T. P. Cooke as the Creature in *Presumption* (Cambridge, Mass., Harvard Theatre Collection).

pears in the opening." Merle and Antony steal Peake's creation scene, rename Frankenstein Zametti, transform Zamiel into a genie, and set their play in the century of Paracelsus and Agrippa. The results are as follows:

A la voix de Zametti, le bruit souterrain augmente. Le tonnerre et les éclairs redoublent, le Monument s'ébranle: au milieu des flammes qui l'entourent, un génie apparaît.

Le Génie, d'une voix sombre, un vase à la main. Que me veux-tu?

Zametti. Tu le sais. Ce vase que tu tiens renferme le prix de mes efforts.

Le Génie. Insensé! qu'exiges-tu de moi.

Zametti. Donne!

Le Génie. Je sais à quelles bisarres [*sic*] espérances ta présomption s'est livrée. Mais tremble, malheureux!

Zametti. Ne crains rien pour moi . . . Donne, je le veux.

Le Génie, donnant le vase à Zametti. Prends donc; je dois t'obéir. Ton bonheur est passé sans retour; tu ne me reverras plus. Adieu!

(Tonnerre, éclairs. Le génie s'abyme au milieu des flammes . . . Zametti, maître du vase mystérieux, s'éloigne, saisi à-la-fois de joie et d'une horreur profonde.)

As if to confirm the opinion of those who view *Frankenstein* in the Realist tradition or as anti-gothic, the novel predates by thirty years Thackeray's claim to have produced a novel without a hero; moreover, *Frankenstein* also contains no pure villain. Rather, Frankenstein and the Creature are aspects of one another, doppelgängers as it were. As such, the Creature and Frankenstein present no clearly defined moral antagonisms: Frankenstein is no more the "protagonist" than the Creature is the "antagonist." The novel's lack of diametrically opposed characters presents obvious difficulties for the Manichaean world of melodrama, for how could a melodrama portray the triumph of virtue when the supposed hero perishes with the supposed villain? Peake and the other playwrights solve their dilemma by substituting for an incarnated moral order (the hero) a divine moral code.[20] In the dramas, Frankenstein becomes a fallen protagonist, a modern hero-villain whose crimes we exonerate because of his exaggerated remorse. Having cast Frankenstein as the hero-villain, the melodramas then cast the Creature in the role of the typical villain-hero. They accomplish the transformation by combining two popular character types: the black villain such as Lord Ruthven in *The Vampire* and Grindoff in *The Miller and His Men,* and the heretofore benign dumb show character.[21] Thus, the Creature displays the sympathetic emotions of a criminal-hero or a dumb show character like Francisco in *A Tale of Mystery,* while simultaneously incarnating all the evil of a typical early-gothic villain. These dual roles illustrate themselves upon the first stage entrance of the Creature. For example, in *Presumption,* the Creature enters and "approaches [Frankenstein] with gestures of conciliation." But rather than accepting this kind overture, Frankenstein rejects him forthwith, thereby triggering a violent reaction on the part of the Creature:

Frank. The horrid corpse to which I have given life! . . . Fiend! dare not to approach me—avaunt, or dread the fierce vengeance of my arm.

(Music.—Frankenstein takes the sword from off nail . . . points with it at Monster, who snatches the sword, snaps it in two and throws it on stage. The Monster then seizes Frankenstein—loud thunder heard—throws him violently on the floor, ascends the staircase, opens the large window on [the left], and disappears through the casement. Frankenstein remains motionless on the ground—Thunder and lightning until the drop falls.)

Perhaps the most formidable influence on this role is that of Caliban in *The Tempest*. Like Caliban, the Creature represents nature devoid of nurture, the senses devoid of mind, a creature, in Prospero's words, "on whose nature nurture can never stick," and in the words of Miranda, an "Abhorred Slave which any print of goodness wilt not take." Like Caliban, too, the Creature's deformed body mirrors an evil nature. For his part, Frankenstein plays a Prospero whose white magic has been corrupted into the black magic of Sycorax. Thus, as opposed to Prospero who can redeem the Creature by claiming "this thing of darkness I acknowledge mine," Frankenstein can never reclaim the image of darkness that he has unleashed.

Melodramatizations, concerned as they were with action, did not really desire to exhibit the mind of the Creature coming into Lockean awareness. Nevertheless, the melodramas transferred from the novel a few of the Creature's characteristic actions, including viewing his reflection, burning his fingers in a fire, and experiencing for the first time sunlight and the beauties of nature. As an example of the Creature's depth of emotion, and as if to prove that music tames the savage breast, every melodrama relentlessly exploited the Creature's reaction to music. Obviously, Shakespeare's Caliban served as an influence. For example, in *Presumption,* to the sound of Felix's flute, the Creature "stands amazed and pleased, looks around him, [and] snatches at the empty air." In *Le Monstre et le magicien,* he listens to music *"avec extasie, et suit attentivement tous les sons."* Thomas Morton's *Zorinski* (1795) serves as a precursor for this conquest of the beast by music. In Morton's melodrama, the beautiful Rosolia subdues with a lute the savage desires of Zorinski. For *Frankenstein* dramatizations, the scene receives its most extravagant treatment in *The Man and the Monster,* where, like most villains of melodrama, the Creature abducts the heroine and her child. Pursued to the summit of Mount Etna, the Creature turns to the crowd:

(The Monster points to his wounds—expresses that he would willingly have served Frankenstein and befriended him, but that all his overtures were repelled with scorn and abhorrence—then, with malignant exultation seizes on the Child, and whirls it aloft, as if about to dash it down the

rock—Emmeline screams, Frankenstein, with a cry of horror, covers his eyes—at this moment a thought occurs to Emmeline—she pulls from under her dress a small flageolet, and begins to play an air—its effect on the Monster is instantaneous—he is at once astonished and delighted—he places the Child on the ground—his feelings become more powerfully affected by the music, and his attention absorbed by it—the Child escapes to its father—Emmeline continues to play and Frankenstein intently to watch its effect on the Monster. As the air proceeds his feelings become more powerfully excited—he is moved to tears; afterwards, on the music assuming a lively character, he is worked up to a paroxysm of delight—and on its again becoming mournful, is quite subdued, till he lays down exhausted at the foot of the rock to which Emmeline is attached.)

One of the most interesting alterations of the novel by the adaptors involves the introduction of the laboratory assistant. As a comic foil, he may be traced back to Sancho Panza through such comic gothic predecessors as Bianca in *Castle of Otranto,* Annette and Ludovico in *Mysteries of Udolpho,* Peter in *The Romance of the Forest,* and the garrulous rustics of *The Italian,* Paulo and Beatrice. Boden's *Fontainville Forest* (1794), a dramatic adaptation of *Romance of the Forest,* opens in "A Gothic Hall of an Abbey, the whole much dilapidated." Peter, the servant, steps down stage and—in a tone much like that of Peake's Fritz—moans:

Heaven send my master back! On my old knees
I begg'd him not to explore that dismal wood! . . .
He went at dusk; by the same token then
the owl shriek'd from the porch—He started back;
But recollected, smote his forehead, and advanced.
I clos'd the Abbey gate, which grated sadly.

Possible melodramatic sources for the comical laboratory assistant include Karl in *The Miller and his Men,* Robinson in *Cataract of the Ganges,* and especially Martin in *The Sicilian Romance,* Henry Siddon's 1794 dramatization of *Castle of Otranto,* which he later retitled to capitalize on the popularity of Radcliffe's novel.[22] Compare, for example, Martin's speech in Act 3—"od—od—od! how my teeth chatter! Every whisper of the wind, and every crack of this damn'd rotten old mansion, makes me feel as if I had an icicle in my belly—I'm afraid to look round for fear of saluting a tall skeleton"—with the opening lines of Fritz in *Presumption:* "Oh, Fritz, Fritz, Fritz! what is it come to! You are frightened out of your wits . . . Oh, anything frightens me now—I'm so nervous! . . . I jump like a maggot out of cheese! How my heart beats!" The laboratory assistant also shares characteristics of Leporello in Mozart's *Don Giovanni,* which in 1817 experienced the height of its popularity in London, especially with pantomimes such as *Harlequin's Vision; or, The Feast of the Statute* and *Don Giovanni in London,* in which Leporello figured prominently as Clown. Leporello also figures as the valet of Giovanni in Planché's *Giovanni the Vampire; or, How Shall We Get Rid of Him?* (Adelphi, 1821). Finally, since the laboratory assistant shares characteristics of the harlequin clown, we may perhaps also include the influence of Joseph Grimaldi, who, between 1806 and 1823 transformed the harlequinade of John Rich into a harlequinade dominated by Clown.[23] Certainly the *Morning Post* (21 September 1826) agrees with this assessment when of Milner's melodrama it observed: "The veteran GRIMALDI it must be admitted had before ably delineated many of the workings of feeling and excellencies concentrated in this piece, particularly the effect of music on the senses of the Monster."

The most popular laboratory assistant is, of course, Fritz, who makes his first appearance in *Presumption*. Peake may have derived the character and indeed the name "Fritz" from John Poole's burlesque *The Sorrows of Werther,* which appeared at the English Opera House in April of 1822 and in which Peake played Fritz, Werther's comic servant.[24] Other laboratory assistants include Pietro, in *Le Monstre et le magicien* and its English translation, and Strutt, in *The Man and the Monster,* with burlesque assistants variously named Frizzy (*Another Piece of Presumption*), Fritz (*Frank-in-Steam; or, The Modern Promise to Pay*), and Frightz (*The Model Man*). In *Frankenstein: An Adventure in the Macabre,* both Waldman and Frankenstein's best friend assist; however, when the drama was rewritten as a screenplay, the character of Fritz was reintroduced—possibly because the screenwriters had read a copy of *Presumption*.

In a final analysis, the laboratory assistant provides much more than comic relief. Like M'Swill in *The Vampire,* a comic character who in Act 1 supplies much of the background information concerning the nature of vampires, the laboratory assistant in *Frankenstein* adaptations figures as the low character who presents the initial exposition and much of the necessary background information.[25] He therefore substitutes for the first-person narratives of the novel. For example, in *The Man and the Monster* Strutt informs two companions:

> My master is the most profound philosopher, and consequently the greatest man that ever lived; to tell you what he can do is impossible; but what he cannot do, it would be still more difficult to mention.

We have already witnessed how, from his perch outside Frankenstein's laboratory, Fritz narrates the Creation scene for the audience. As early as Act 1, however, his role as narrator defines itself when Fritz faces the audience and explains the background of the story:

> Why did you ever leave your native village . . . instead of coming here to the city of Geneva to be hired as a servant! . . . To be sure Mr. Frankenstein is a kind man, and I should respect him, but that I thinks he holds converse with somebody below with a long tail, horns, and hoofs, who shall be nameless.

The above informs us that the action occurs in Geneva; Fritz is a servant in the household of Frankenstein; and Frankenstein has associations with the devil and alchemy. In less than three months Peake would burlesque his own character in *Another Piece of Presumption*, where Fritz is discovered in Act 1:

> Why did you ever leave Whitechapel? What a situation for a Tailor! . . . you must come here you spooney, and hire yourself as a light porter to a first rate clothier! . . . Mr Frankinstitch is my Master and a good sort of body, but that he is always wrapt up in his thoughts like a pair of breeches in brown paper.

And by 1824 Fritz was lamenting in the burlesque *Frank-in-Steam; or, The Modern Promise to Pay:*

> Why did I ever leave the County where I sold asses milk to all the neighbours around me? Why did I ever come up to town to live with a wild young medical Student who I believe deals with somebody with horns? he's over head-and-ears in debt and has tired out all of his friends and relations. He expects the Bailiffs to nab him every hour . . .

In his *Le Monstre et le magicien* (1861), Ferdinand Dugué borrowed the plot and much of his dialogue from Merle and Antony;[26] it therefore seems appropriate here to discuss the last nineteenth-century melodramatization of Shelley's novel. Dugué's version, which premiered on 22 June at the Ambigu Comique, contains two new characters: Paula, the ghost of Zametti's first wife, and Faustus-le-damné. The melodrama received elaborate preproduction treatment. The Ambigu Comique hired special musicians and, according to *Le Temps* (10 June 1861), closed its production of Alexander Dumas's *Angèle; ou, l'Échelle des femmes* six days early in order to prepare for the spectacle, which, according to *Journal des Débats* (22 June) the theatre promoted by distributing 25,000 "éventails-programmes" to all ladies in attendance. These preparations proved successful. For example, *Le Temps* continually refers to the play as a "grand drame fantastique" (20 June), as "l'immense succès du jour" (5 July), and as "ce drame, si varié, si magnifique" (17 July). On 3 August *Le Temps* even advertised the following timetable for those who wished to arrive in time for their favorite scene:

À	9	heures,	la Naissance du Monstre.
	9 1/2	———,	le Ballet.
	10	———,	l'Incendie.
	10 1/2	———,	le Ravin des Torrents.

Dugué's melodrama represents the farthest extension of the direct influence of Merle and Antony into the nineteenth century and the first time that the Faust myth would be represented in a Frankenstein play by Faust himself, who appears as a tutelary genius for Zamiel. In Dugué's play,

Faust proves to be a wandering demon, "le damné," of the otherworld. The appearance of Paula, a ghostly saint, complements the demonic figure of Faust and culminates the Manichaean influence: good and bad vie for Frankenstein's soul. These themes resolve themselves when Dugué borrows from Merle and Antony the boating conclusion, which here becomes a cheap vehicle for divine intervention and moralistic caveat. In the closing scene Zametti attempts to flee with his son, his second wife, and a servant named Pietro. The Creature dives into the water and is about to reach their boat:

> *Pietro.* Nous sommes perdus!
>
> *Zametti.* Cécilia, Antonio, il faut mourir! . . . Oh! dans mes bras, du moins, dur mon coeur! . . . Prions, amis.
>
> *Antonio.* Oui, prions.
>
> *Pietro.* Ah! maître, voyez la-bas.
>
> *Zametti.* Quoi donc?
>
> *Pietro.* Cette forme humaine qui se dirige vers nous à la nage!
>
> *Zametti.* Ah! c'est le Monstre!
>
> *Tous.* Le Monstre! . . .
>
> *Antonio.* Sauve-nous, ma mère!
>
> *Zametti.* Ah! Monstre, tu n'arriveras pas jusqu'à eux! *(La foudre sillonne le ciel et vient frapper le Monstre, qui tourbillonne sur lui-même et tombe au fond de l'abîme. La mer se calme, le tonnerre cesse, l'horizon redevient bleu, et Paula apparait dans une auréole de lumière. Les naufragés sont agenouillés et prient.)*
>
> *Paula.* Réconcilie-toi avec Dieu, Zametti; et, après avoir été heureux sur la terre, vous viendrez tous me retrouver dans le ciel!

Melodrama was rarely so "melodramatic!"

* * *

The less popular melodramas and burlesques produced between 1823 and 1826 suffer from an obscurity that has been enhanced by many critical misstatements.[27] Despite some problematic observations, Elizabeth Nitchie provides a valuable point of departure for any discussion of the dramatizations in that her research represents the first extensive attempt to grapple with their convoluted history. Given the seminal influence of her article, it is a shame that some of her evidence is couched in vague terms that at times perpetuate confusion. For example, at one point she writes:

> Had she wished, Mrs. Shelley might have gone [in 1823] . . . to see two other serious melodramatic versions of the story at the Coburg [*Frankenstein; or, The Demon of Switzerland*], and at the Royalty [*Frankenstein; or, The Danger of Presumption*] and three burlesques at the Surrey [*Humgumption; or, Dr. Frankenstein and the Hobgoblin of Hoxton*], at the Adelphi [*Another Piece of Presumption*], and Davis's Royal Amphitheatre [*Presumption and the Blue Demon*]. (219)

Rather than the estimated six dramatizations, only five were written in the months immediately following the production of *Presumption*. The melodrama *Frankenstein; or, The Danger of Presumption* is actually a retitling of Peake's play, which was presented, as Summers notes (330), at the Royalty in an effort to capitalize on the success of *Presumption* at the end of the season. More to the point, Nitchie's failure to acknowledge the title of the burlesque at Davis's Royal Amphitheatre leads Donald Glut, a most enthusiastic Frankenstein sleuth, to write in *The Frankenstein Legend:* "The third of these comic plays [of 1823], presented at the David-Royal [sic] Amphitheatre, had a Parisian sculptor give life to a statue of Aesop, which ran about the stage in the person of a dwarf actor" (34). Here it appears that Glut has misunderstood Nitchie's observation about the various burlesque manifestations of the Creature:

> The Monster appeared as a Hobgoblin [in *Humgumption* (1823)], as the "Blue Demon of the Strand and the Cut" [in *Presumption and the Blue Demon* (1823)], as the composite product of "the Promethean bodkin of Mr. Frankinstitch" [in *Another Piece of Presumption* (1823)], as a resuscitated bailiff, dug writ in hand by Frank-in-Steam from the grave where he had been buried in a trance [in *Frank-in-Steam* (1824)], [and] as the dwarf who impersonates the statue of Aesop . . . (228)

This last description refers to a burlesque of *Le Monstre et le magicien* entitled *Le Petit monstre et l'escamoteur,* written by Jules-Henri Vernoy de Saint-Georges and Antoine-Jean-Baptiste Simonnin and presented at the Gaîté on 7 July 1826.[28] Glut advances the performance date by three years while translating it into English. Although Glut apparently never read the play, he is surprisingly correct when he imagines the actions of the dwarf. The play in fact concludes with a dwarf (Narcisse) pursuing a sculptor (Beaumodèle) in a parody of the boating conclusion of *Le Monstre et le magicien*. In this scene, Victoire is Beaumodèle's new bride:

> *(Le théâtre change à vue, et représente la rivière: on voit le bateau à vapeur sur lequel sont . . . Beaumodèle et Victoire; bientôt la rivière déborde et vient jusqu'à l'avant-scène: Narcisse s'y jette à la nage; les flots se soulevent comme pendant un fort orage; Narcisse lutte contre les flots pour gagner le bateau à vapeur, où il arrive enfin.)*
>
> *Narcisse, criant de dessus le bateau.* Adieu! . . .

Like many critics, Glut errs in assuming that *Frankenstein; or, The Demon of Switzerland,* written by Henry Milner in 1823, is simply an early version of *The Man and the Monster.*[29] The two plays bear little resemblance beyond their source (Mary Shelley's novel) and genre (melodrama). In the conclusion of *The Man and the Monster* the mute and angry Creature attacks and stabs Frankenstein before leaping into the crater of Mount Etna, "now vomiting burning lava." No such scene exists in *Demon of Switzerland,* a play in which the Creature speaks and has a somewhat benign temperament. According to the *Morning Post* (19 August 1823), the play also contained several characters that bore no relationship to the novel, including Mr. Theodosius Cornelius Maximan Lightbody, Clara and her brother Clariville, and Lightbody's sister, Eliza. The play was probably unsuccessful because, in Milner's first attempt at dramatizing the novel, he seems to have misjudged the audience's desire for violent destruction over sympathetic communication. As the *Theatrical Observer* (23 August 1823) commented: "As to *Frankenstein* [*or, The Demon of Switzerland*], it had better be put aside." No form of the script of Milner's first dramatization is known to exist, but *The Drama* (August 1823) contains a review that characterizes both the nature of *Demon of Switzerland* and its thorough dissimilarities to *The Man and the Monster. The Drama* observes:

> The *Daemon,* in the present piece, is endowed with speech, and holds a long conversation with his maker *"all about nothing."* The present *Daemon,* however, is so much endowed with the milk of human kindness, that he preserves his creator twice from destruction, and is at last destroyed himself by the fall of part of the burning ruins of a church, to which he had fled for refuge, from the mad pursuit of the peasantry, leaving his creator in "this wide world alone."

In another misreading of Nitchie, Glut creates a play that never existed. In her article, Nitchie refers to "a poem of ten stanzas on 'The Devil among the Players'—*Faustus, Frankenstein,* and *The Vampyre*" (220). Appearing in the *Opera Glass* magazine for 9 October 1826, the poem contains two stanzas of particular interest to the present discussion:

> What shall I say of FRANKENSTEIN,
> Such crowds each night attracting?
> The devil's in it, I maintain;
> And as for COOKE—why his, 'tis plain,
> Is *monstrous* clever acting!
>
> In PARIS how he made them stare,
> While looking fierce this part in!
> 'Twas voted by the gay PARTERRE
> Fit for the BARRIÈRE D'ENFER,
> Rather than PORTE ST. MARTIN!

Glut transforms the magazine into a theatre and the "poem of ten stanzas" into a full-length play when he writes (38): "A third play using the Frankenstein theme in 1826 was first presented on October 9 at the Opera Glass.[30] Titled *The Devil Among the Players,* this poetic dramatization featured three characters of horror—Frankenstein (probably the Monster, as

Cooke fostered the mistake in calling the creature by its creator's name), Faust, and the Vampire."[31] Radu Florescu, who usually repeats Glut's errors, also places the poem among his list of dramatizations when he writes (166): "Another 1826 dramatization of Mary's story was *The Devil Among the Players,* and featured a trio of monsters: Frankenstein, Faust, and the Vampire."

Elsewhere Nitchie writes of Peake's burlesque *Another Piece of Presumption:* "Frankenstein was variously transformed into Frankenstitch, a tailor who in accordance with the proverb makes a Man out of nine of his journeyman tailors . . ." (228). Glut (33), Florescu (166), and LaValley (247) wrongly assume that here Nitchie refers to the Surrey Theatre production of *Humgumption; or, Dr. Frankenstein and the Hobgoblin of Hoxton.* No script of *Humgumption* is known to exist; however, a squib in the *Morning Post* (5 September 1823) provides a description of the play that is clear enough to distinguish the two plays; it is also the only printed plot summary of this melodramatic-burlesque:

> THIS PRESENT EVENING . . . will be presented an entirely New and Original Romance, founded partly on the celebrated Novel, partly on ancient legends, and principally upon modern Dramas, called HUMGUMPTION, or Dr. Frankenstein and the Hobgoblin of Hoxton; in the course of the Piece will be exhibited a well known imaginary view of Dr. Frankenstein's House at Hoxton, painted on the spot where it now stands; a characteristic barbarous Interior; the Doctor's Study with the marvelously mysterious animation of his handy work; Peerless Pool, as it appeared A.D. 1267; exclusive facsimile of a celebrated Starch and Powder Factory, with Mill &c.; the Piece to conclude with an awful Avalanche of Earthenware, and a tremendous Shower of Starch, and an overwhelming explosion of Hair Powder!

The conclusion, of course, mocks that of *Presumption.* The burlesque evidently proved quite satisfying. "We had buoyed our expectation not a little high," commented the *Theatrical Observer* on 2 September, "nor were we disappointed; 'tis one broad laugh from the commencement to the finish, and it was extremely well acted." Three days later the same journal continued: "*'Humgumption'* continues a favorite. The scenery, by TOMKINS, after some trifling alteration, is excellent. Miss TUNSTALL, as *Miss Agatha deLazy,* played the character in a truly burlesque style, and the loudest applause was bestowed on her whole performance." A few days later, the play closed. As the *Theatrical Observer* noted on September 8: "*Dr. Frankenstein* has, with filial pity and regard for the future interests of his bantling, put him out to nurse for a short time. Perchance we may see him again, with renovated strength and vigour."

Nothing like the action of *Humgumption* transpires in Peake's *Another*

Piece of Presumption, which begins in the mode of a rehearsal-burlesque, such as *Vampire Giovanni* (1821), *Quadrupeds of Quedlinburgh* (1811), Sheridan's *The Critic* (1779), or even as far back as George Villier's *The Rehearsal* (1671). In fact, Peake seems to have patterned his opening after Villier's burlesque. In the first scene of *The Rehearsal,* Smith entreats Bayes the playwright to tell Johnson about his last play. In response Bayes says:

> Faith, Sir, the Intrigue's now quite out of my head; but I have a new one, in my pocket, that I may say is a Virgin; 't has never yet been blown upon . . . I think it is in this pocket . . . Yes, here it is. No, cry you mercy: this is my book of *Drama Common Places;* the Mother of many other Plays.[32]

In *Another Piece of Presumption* the hack playwright Dramaticus Devildum explains to Mr. Lee, the (actual) stage manager of the Adelphi:

> I don't know much about money—but I have a great many *pocket pieces*—here it is—no that is not that—that is the *"Mysterious Rat-Catcher"* and I flatter myself that's a very taking title that is if you understand trap—if you bring out the *Mysterious Rat-Catcher* I shall want every trap on the stage—here it is—no that's the *Gloom Grand-father; or, The Sorrows of Three Generations,* in five acts . . . Here it is at last—here—bless you—(*kisses it*) you darling—here it is—*"Another Piece of Presumption."*

The play then strikes out at its intended target: gothic melodrama, *Presumption* in particular. However, like Dibdin in *Bonifacio and Bridgetina* (1808), which also contained a play within a play, Peake sets about to burlesque a melodrama but instead reveals his affection for it. (He was after all burlesquing his own play.) Peake's enjoyment is most evident in the Creation scene. Here the tailor Frankenstein rushes on stage after animating the Creature:

> *Frank.* I have lock'd the workshop up—What a wretch have I form'd—There's Jemmy Wilson's hair—Billy Boroughs's head—Bobby Bluethread's arms—Old Nicholas's neck—Christopher Cabbage's back—Ben Baste's one leg, and Patrick Longmeasure's tother—Dreadful incorporation of nine Tailors . . . the beauty of my dream has vanish'd! and melodramatic horrors assail me . . .
>
> *Music—(sinks into a chair)*
>
> *Shop window is smashed—The Hobgoblin jumps out—& sits upon a Table cross-leg'd.*
>
> *Hob.* How are you?
>
> *Frank.* Thou thing of threads & patches—avaunt!
>
> *Hob.* But where am I to go?
>
> *Frank.* Go to the Devil—anywhere!
>
> *Hob. (Getting off the Table)*
>
> *Frank.* Approach not—you Tom Tawdry!—Would that I had never put you together—
>
> *Hob.* Then you are the Gentleman that I have to thank—It is quite a new sensation!
>
> *Lee.* I beg pardon for interrupting—but the Demon or Hobgoblin appears to speak English very well for a new made man!
>
> *Devild.* Why he has got Billy Burrows's head on—that's the reason.

Lee. Oh.

Hob. You should have an affection for me . . .

Frank. Never!—This poor unletter'd creature will be quite at a loss for want of words. I'll give him an Enticks' Dictionary—here—(*gives a Book*)

Hob. What's this?

Frank. A Volume of words which will find you meat, drink, washing, and lodging—let me put it in your pocket—there—!

Hob. Pocket—thank you. (*snuff box upset—Hob sneezes*) that is a new sensation—how nice—I'll do it again—No—I can't—tell me, why am I manufactured?

Frank. Do not grumble—you are a *made* man!—How wildly he looks—he has never yet been out of the room—and knows not how to conduct himself—he moves.

Hob. *(Walks—runs his head against Wall)* Oh, damn it!

Frank. What's the matter?

Hob. *(rubbing his head)* That's a new sensation! What was that I knock'd my forehead against?

Frank. The Wall.

Hob. I shall have a *Wall* Eye?

Frank. Now he is rolling his Billy Burrows's twinklers at me—don't come near me—Dreadful Monster in a human form—keep off—*(Strikes Hob with a pair of sheers)* . . .

Hob. *(Seizing & pulling them in two)* I'm a cut above them—and now my old cock—for a bit of fun with you. *(takes hold of him)*

Frank. Hold—hold—wretched professional man that I am!

Music—they are in an attitude.

Devild. Stop—Stop—here's the place for a little thunder—have you no thunder in the House?

Hob. How long am I to hold this heavy back'd Christian in this position, Mr. Author?

Devild. Now thunder—thund away & bundle old Frankinstich by his waistband out of the window—bravo—bravo

Violent Music—the Hobgoblin struggles with Frankinstitch & succeeds in putting him out of the broken window.

(ACT DROP FALLS)

Whereas *Presumption* inspired four burlesques between 1823 and 1824, within three months of its premier, *Le Monstre et le magicien* had inspired six comic adaptations—one *revue* or *pièce de circonstance,* two burlesques, and three classical extravaganzas. The extravaganzas derive their comedy from the domestication of gods and goddesses—from the incongruity of action and idiom when commonplace dialogue is set in the mouths of mythical characters. The style may be traced back through the fairy stories of Charles Perrault and Madame d'Aulnoy in France, and in England through Charles Dibdin's *Poor Vulcain* (1778), G. A. Stevens's *The Court of Alexander* (1770), and especially Kane O'Hara's *Midas* (1762) and Fielding's *Tragedy of Tragedies* (1730).[33] The French burlesque influence may be traced forward through Planché, whose classical burlesques, with two exceptions, were all produced at the Olympic Theatre between 1831 and 1834.[34] In *Frankenstein* adaptations the fairy-tale story is carried forth in *Franken-*

stein; or, The Model Man, whose atmosphere resembles, as we shall see in the next chapter, the *folies féeries* and whose plot, the harlequinade.

The first extravaganza, *Les Filets de Vulcain, ou La Vénus de Neuilly,* takes its title from *Mars et Vénus,* a recent production at the Paris Opéra. The play opened on 5 July at the Théâtre des Variétés and was written by Guillaume Dumersan, Gabriel-Jules-Joseph de Lurien, and Nicolas Brazier, who with Saurin wrote *Riquet à la Houppe,* which Planché viewed at the Porte Saint-Martin in 1821 and which he translated in 1836 as *Riquet with the Tuft,* "the first of those fairy extravaganzas."[35] *Filets de Vulcain* evinces the harlequinade tradition in which an elderly guardian threatens to marry his ward to a hideous old man. In this production the Creature plays the part of Clown, the figure of anarchy and the butt of all humor. The title of the play juxtaposes pompous Olympus with prosaic Neuilly, located in the suburbs of Paris. In the play Caramel (a comical Pantaloon) intends to force his ward, Jeanneton (the Venus-Columbine figure), to marry the lame and hideous ironmonger named Clopineau (Vulcan/Lover), even though Jeanneton loves La Valeur (the figure of Mars and Harlequin). As part of the wedding festivities Caramel invites the Creature, played by Charles Odry and appropriately named "Quoique," to perform a pantomime. In a parody of T. P. Cooke, Odry enters the stage *"Seul en monstre"* and *"habillé comme celui de la Porte Saint-Martin":*

> *Il s'avance avec précaution, fait plusieurs fois le tour du théâtre et s'arrête: Un air de romance frappe d'abord le premier de ses sens; ses yeux brillent de joie et d'étonnement. Il lève les bras comme s'il pouvait atteindre les sons qu'il entend. Ici un grand charivari succède à cette douce harmonie, le Monstre se ferme les oreilles en marchant à grands pas. Bientôt il s'approche de la rampe, il se baisse, met la main au dessus d'un quinquet et se brule les doigts, sa fureur redouble.*
>
> *Quoiq[ue].* Ah! diable je me avais brulé; rien ne brule comme le feu . . .

Two days later, on 7 July, the Théâtre de la Gaîté presented *Le Petit monstre et l'escamoteur,* which contains the best early burlesque of this scene. In the play Narcisse, who as a prank replaces a statue of Aesop with himself, comes to life before the alchemist Beaumodèle and his friend, Doigts-Légers:

> *Beaumodèle, se levant et marchant à grands pas.* O bouteille précieuse! ce n'est pas sans peine que je t'ai trouvée . . . cette cave est si sombre! . . . mais le petit vin du beau-père a ranimé mon courage . . .
>
> *Narcisse, à part, sans etre entendu.* Ah ça, mais j'vas descendre moi! . . . s'il ne me regarde pas! . . .
>
> *Beaumodèle, avec force.* Et dire que ce trésor était caché sous un tonneau vide!
>
> *Doigts-Légers, à part.* En v'là une bonne . . . la dernière bouteille de Champagne . . .
>
> *Beaumodèle, regardent Narcisse qu'il prend pour la statue.* O Esope! c'est pour toi seul cette liqueur bienfaisante! . . .

Narcisse, à part. Tiens! il paraît qu'il fait boire la goutte à ses statues! . . .
Beaumodèle. Oui, c'est pour toi! . . . pour toi seul! . . .
Doigts-Légers, à part. Est-il bête! il s'imagine que ça va faire remuer cette statue.
Beaumodèle, à Narcisse qu'il prend pour la statue. O toi! le plus parfait de mes ouvrages! toi le mieux fait des bossus! . . . (*il reste en extase.*)
Narcisse, à part. Merci!
Beaumodèle, se retournant vivement. Hein! . . . j'ai cru entendre. *(regardant Narcisse.)* Cette figure qui ne dit rien, demande la parole . . . eh bien . . . *(Il met la bouteille sous le nez de Narcisse, et lui fait sauter le bouchon au nez avec explosion, un feu d'artifice sort de la bouteille.)*
Narcisse, criant et se levant en tenant son nez. Ah! la la! ah! la la! . . . c'est des bêtises ça! c'est des bêtises! . . .
Beaumodèle, se sauvant de Narcisse. O ciel . . .
Doigts-Légers, effrayé. Ça remue! ah bon dieu! ça remue! au secours! . . .
Tous, dans le plus grand effroi. Au secours! . . . au secours! . . .

On 10 July the Théâtre du Vaudeville premiered *La Pêche de Vulcain, ou L'île des fleuves,* whose title ironically alludes both to Vulcan's innocent fishing expedition—to "pêcher à la ligne"—and to his sinful seductions—to "péché contre quelque chose." The play parodied not only the production at the Opéra, but three other recent Parisian productions: *L'Intrigue et l'amour,* Alexandre Dumas's translation of Schiller's *Kabale und liebe,* Charles Arlincourt's five-act verse tragedy *Le Siège de Paris,* and of course *Le Monstre et le magicien.* In *La Pêche de Vulcain,* Vulcan has been sent to Earth in search of Apollo, who has deserted Olympus. After a fruitless search of cities, fields, and theatres, Vulcan addresses himself to the river Danube, from which he pulls Ferdinand, the hero of Schiller's play, and to the river Seine, from which he pulls Ordamant, the hero of the play by Arlincourt. Finally, Vulcan addresses the Thames, from which he pulls the Creature of the Porte Saint-Martin:

Tous. C'est un monstre!
Vulcain. Quelle horreur! ne l'amenez pas! . . .

Air: Des guerriers honneur de la France.
Ah! repoussons dans la Tamise
Ces fruits d'un cerveau délirant;
  Au bon goût la raison soumise
  Vous offre un assez vaste champ.
Pourquoi chercher, dépassant ses limites,
  Des monstres qui n'exitent pas . . .
Pour les siffler n'est-il plus d'hypocrites;
Pour les flétrir n'avez-vous plus d'ingrats?

(Le Monstre disparaît sous une trappe.)

At the Creature's next appearance (*"avec un roulement de tonnerre"*), he is momentarily seduced by the sound of music and burns his fingers in a gas jet. He then attempts to abduct the goddess of the Thames, and Venus, who has descended to Earth to avoid housework on Olympus. Vulcan averts the abduction by promising to present the Creature to Jupiter in place of Apollo. As *Le Journal des Débats* (11 July) observed: "s'il n'est point en effet le dieu des beaux-arts, il est du moins le dieu du jour."

In answer to its rivals, the Porte Saint-Martin mounted on 15 July a revue entitled *Les filets de Vulcain, ou le lendemain d'un succès*. In this play Vulcan, the Manager of the Porte Saint-Martin, gathers around him managers from those Parisian theatres that have in the past months attempted to rival his theatre. Vulcan pompously instructs them on the art of producing a good play—for example, *Le Monstre et le magicien*. Cooke's appearance proved to be the only interesting aspect of this production. As *Le Journal des Débats* (18 July) described him:

> M. Cooke a paru dans cette pièce sous costume bourgeois, et l'on a vu avec plaisir que le monstre si effrayant avec sa peau verte et sa perruque à la conseillère, avait de très-bonnes manières à la titus et en franc bleu.
>
> L'étrangeté de son accent, et ses efforts pour prononcer le français, avaient une sorte de charme qu'augmentait encore la modestie avec laquelle il s'est présenté.[36]

On 11 July and 3 August, Louis-Christian Comte presented, respectively, *Le Présomptueux* and *Le Monstre et le physicien*. Both plays mark the extent to which the story of Frankenstein permeated French theatre from the Théâtre des Boulevards to the minor playhouses such as the Théâtre de M. Comte, a playhouse originally named Le Théâtre des Jeunes Acteurs because it specialized in short topical pieces presented by child actors.

* * *

In the course of three years, from 1823 to 1826, at least fifteen dramas employed characters and themes from Shelley's novel. Whether in burlesque or melodrama, things Frankensteinian were all the rage on stages in England and France. Aside from the intense interest generated by T. P. Cooke in the role of the Creature in both *Presumption* and *Frankenstein; ou, Le Monstre et le magicien*,[37] it is difficult to pinpoint exactly why audiences seized so quickly on themes dramatized from the novel. That Peake chose to dramatize Shelley's work at the height of the popularity of Gothic melodrama accounts for its selection as a subject but fails to explain completely the play's immediate success and the continual outpouring of other dramatizations. A case in point would be James Robinson Planché's *The Vampyre* (1820), which triumphed upon its debut at the English Opera House. Nonetheless, its only lasting contributions to the stage were an impetus for other dramas of the supernatural and a new kind of trap door.

Clearly, Frankenstein and his Creature touched a raw nerve in France, a nation in which the anti-tyrannical or "Bastille" drama evolved in response to the post-Revolutionary maelstrom. Reviewers of *Le Monstre et le magicien* immediately equated the Creature with mob violence. As *La Quotidienne* remarked on 10 July: "Le succès du Monstre est monstreux comme lui-même." The observation brings to mind an important point: by 1826, the Creature was an amalgam of popular conceptions—"monstreux comme lui-meme." He could represent anything violent, in particular mob rule and man-made catastrophe.

The point would not be lost in England, where conservatives ever since the reign of the Sanscoulottes had linked social reform and mob rule. The times themselves proved ripe for such a symbol, especially since between 1815 and the mid-century the country stood on the verge of its own revolution.[38] Therefore, on the English stage—to say nothing of the novel's reputation in print—Frankenstein immediately became associated with unbridled revolution, atheism, and blind progress in science and technology. Richard Yeo has recently discussed early nineteenth-century distrust of science and scientists, emphasizing popular fears of "the spectre of French materialism and its radical connotations" as well as the "political implications in the aftermath of the French Revolution."[39] Quite logically, therefore, in a country where Bentham's "felicific calculus" had helped to unleash a crushing and mechanistic revolution, which followed on the heels of the French Revolution and post-Waterloo Depression, themes of hubris and self-engendered destruction found fertile soil. Percy Shelley's reputation as a revolutionary and atheist certainly preceded and tainted the reception of his wife's first novel. Fears of this radical group also helped to fan the flames of controversy surrounding dramatizations of *Frankenstein*. As I noted at the beginning of this chapter, during the premier of *Presumption* the London Society for the Prevention of Vice protested the supposed immorality of Peake's melodrama as well as its association with the Shelley circle.

Shortly after the triumph of T. P. Cooke in *Le Monstre et le magicien,* the managers of the English Opera House wisked him home to London where he reopened *Presumption* on 20 September.[40] Comparing *Presumption* to its French competition, the *New Monthly Magazine and Literary Journal* (1 November) observed: "It is a very striking piece of ghastly pantomime, but will never produce the effect here which it did in France, where pamphlets, ribands and sweetmeats, were called by its name." As early as 1826, therefore, the hero of Shelley's novel had become so popular that his name, like that of Babe Ruth in our own century, could be invoked to retail commercial products. Throughout the decade these misconceptions worked themselves into the fiber of popular thought. With the rise of enfranchisement during the 1830s in England, popular references to *Frankenstein* increasingly assumed not only melodramatic but political overtones as well. For example, in 1832 the *Episcopal Gazette,* a satirical miscellany that criticized the Church of England, "announced by desire of John Bull" a performance of *Presumption; or, The Fate of the Episcopals*. Comic allusions figured in a number of media, perhaps most effectively in a journal called *The Man in the Moon,* which in 1847 printed a sixth act to *Hamlet* in which all of the characters return to life only to slay themselves in sorrow after Laertes dies from drinking poisoned beer. The act concludes with the return of the ghost of Hamlet's father and the Frankenstein Creature, listed as simply "———":

Enter Ghost of Hamlet's Father.

Ghost. As I'm a ghost I can't be poisoned—so I'll drink the beer. *(Sits down and drinks.)*

Enter—through a trap—a strong sulphorous smell perceived.

———. Oh ghost what dost thou—revelling on beer when thou should'st be, as well thou know'st, below?

Ghost. There's lots of time—just take a pull yourself.

———. Thou speakest sooth—we've yet until the dawn.

Ghost. So as the song says—?

———. Sing it—bully Ghost!

Ghost and———in chorus.

We wo'nt go home till morning,
We wo'nt go home till morning,
We wo'nt go home till morning,
Till daylight doth appear.

CURTAIN FALL

Less than thirty years later book reviews would allude to *Frankenstein* as a kind of monstrous common denominator. For example, in 1871 *Punch* (29 July) placed under the heading "Frankenstein's Chemistry" a commentary on Tyndall's recently published *Fragments of Science for Unscientific People*.

Concurrent with this trend, the name of the creator and created began to be confused. In reference to the actor who had assumed the mantle of Cooke as the Creature in 1826, *Punch in London* (14 January 1832) nominated in a satirical peerage "MR. O. SMITH, as *Lord Frankenstein.*—I am induced to create this gentleman a Peer, inasmuch as I do not think it fair that the Marquis of L——— should continue to *play the devil* by himself."[41] During his visit to Sicily in 1838, William Gladstone wrote in his diary that mules, his mode of transportation on the island, "really seem like Frankensteins of the animal creation."[42] Nine years later Elizabeth Gaskell repeated the confusion in *Mary Barton* when she wrote: "The actions of the uneducated seem to me typified in those of Frankenstein, that monster of so many human qualities, ungifted with a soul, or a knowledge of the difference between good and evil."[43] By 1869 Edward Trelawny would write to Clair Clairmont regarding her daughter:

> If I was in Italy I would cure you of your wild fancy regarding Allegra: I would go to the Convent—and select some plausible cranky old dried-up hanger-on of the convent about the age of your child would be, fifty-two, with story and documents properly drawn up, and bring her to you—she would follow you about like a feminine Frankenstein—I cannot conceive a greater horror than an old man or woman that I had never seen for forty-three years claiming me as Father.[44]

These references are typical, but they fail to evoke in the mind visual images of the kind that we in the twentieth century have grown to know, the kinds of images first brought to public attention via drama and then expanded in illustrations. In point of fact, it was not until the first decade of enfranchisement, specifically during the turmoil of the First Reform Bill, that the spectre of Frankenstein's creation received wide dissemination in the form of political cartoons. These developments form the topic of the next chapter, for it was during the last half of the nineteenth century that the widest dissemination took place.

NOTES

1. William Godwin, Letter to Mary Shelley, Huntington Library (HM 11634). I am indebted to Professor Betty Bennett for directing my attention to this letter in her invaluable *The Letters of Mary Wollstonecraft Shelley* (Baltimore: Johns Hopkins University Press, 1981) 1:372, n. 8.

2. An advertisement on the first page of the *Morning Post* (23 August) reads: "This day is published, in two vols., 12 mo., price 14s. in boards, a New Edition of FRANKENSTEIN; or, The Modern Prometheus. By MARY WOLLSTONECRAFT SHELLEY."

3. In his burlesque of *Presumption* entitled *Another Piece of Presumption* (1823), Peake even mocked the protestors in Devildum's comment to Mr. Lee, the manager of the Adelphi Theatre: "Bring my [*Another Piece of*] *Presumption* out, Sir—and you'll probably set the zealous friends of morality to work."

4. George C. Odell in *Annals of the New York Stage* (New York: Columbia University Press, 1927; reprint AMS Press, 1977) 3:145, tempers this opinion when he writes of the same production: "A season so rich in novelty of superior quality signalized the first of January with a trying gift—a melodrama founded on Mrs. Shelley's gruesome story of Frankenstein. . . . Assuredly they supped full of horrors in 1825."

5. Anonymous review in the Enthoven Collection of the Victoria and Albert Museum [18 September ?] 1837; *Theatrical Journal*, 14 March 1840.

6. Mary C. Henderson, ed., *Performing Arts Resources, Vol. 5: Recollections of O. Smith: Comedian* (New York: Theatre Library, 1978), 57.

7. Richard Brinsley Peake, Letter to Charles Mathews, 10 December 1824, Enthoven Collection, Victoria and Albert Museum. Quoted by permission. Anne Mathews published a greatly expurgated form of this letter in which all references to Bunn were removed. See *Memoirs of Charles Mathews, Comedian* (London: Bentley, 1838–39) 3:460–67.

8. James Robinson Planché, *Recollections and Reflections* (London: Tinsley, 1872) 1, 89.

9. Albert, *Les Théâtres des boulevards* (1789–1848) (Paris: Société Française, 1902) 306–07.

10. Victor Leathers, *British Entertainers in France* (Toronto: University of Toronto Press, 1959) 56.

11. Like Cooke, Smith achieved much notoriety in the role. In a letter written in 1827, the comedian Charles Mathews commented: "I am happy to have it in my perfect belief that Mr. Smith is a most respectable character in private life—though a *great* Ruffian on the stage." (Letter from Mathews dated 21 August 1827, Enthoven Collection, Victoria and Albert Museum.) By 1828 the *Drama* (11 September) had to announce: "We really fear that poor Mr. O. Smith will lose all the attributes of humanity, unless they occasionally give him a mere mortal character to represent."

12. W. H. Lyles, *Mary Shelley: An Annotated Bibliography* (New York: Garland, 1975) 221.

13. Laurence Irving, *Henry Irving: The Actor and His World* (London: Faber, 1951) 687.

14. A playbill for a performance at Covent Garden on 13 December 1830 advertises: "Among the many striking effects . . . A SCHOONER in a VIOLENT STORM, In which Frankenstein and the Monster are destroyed." However, the avalanche conclusion may have returned in 1835 when, for a performance on 13 August at the English Opera House, a playbill curtly announces that the play concludes with the "Pursuit and Utter Annihilation of Frankenstein and the Monster!" *Dicks* prints only the avalanche conclusion of *Presumption* because it probably employed as copy-text the Lord Chamberlain manuscript (now located in the Huntington Library) or a copy thereof.

15. For the influence of the Eastern style on pantomime productions see David Mayer, *Harlequin in His Element: The English Pantomime, 1806–1836* (Cambridge, Mass.: Harvard University Press, 1969) 142–56.

16. Wilt, "*Frankenstein* as Mystery Play," in Levine, *Endurance* 31.

17. Another possible influence on this scene may have been Pixérécourt's *Le Belvedere ou la vallée de l'Etna* (1818), which concludes beneath the beneficent image of Etna after Emilia and Loredan are finally united: "Le ciel s'éclaircit et laisse voir dans toute sa beauté, la vue majesteuse de l'Etna, don't la furie s'est apaisée en ce moment." (Pixérécourt, *Théâtre choisi de G. de Pixérécourt* (Paris: 1842) 3:576). Finally, the conclusion of *The Man and the Monster* may have also been modelled on

Planché's 1821 melodrama *The Corsair's Bride,* at the conclusion of which the corsair meets his death by jumping into Etna.

18. Ginisty, *La Féerie* (Paris: Louis-Michaud, 1910) 66.

19. The frontispiece for the *Monstre et le magicien* pamphlet presents an engraving of the Creature in a pose similar to figure 12. I have located only one source that reproduces this frontispiece: a microprint of the play. The original microprint was made from a copy of the play held in the Library of Congress. Unfortunately, after the microprint was made, the Library of Congress destroyed its copy of the pamphlet.

20. Actually, Shelley's novel argues very ambiguously for the moral code adopted by the dramas. "Learn from me, if not by my precepts," Frankenstein tells Walton, ". . . how dangerous is the acquirement of knowledge, and how much happier that man who believes his native town to be the world, than he who is aspiring to become greater than his nature will allow" (48). Yet in the conclusion of the novel, Frankenstein's final statement—"yet another may succeed"—belies any return to or substantiation of a moral order. The dramatizations ignore these ambiguities and take at face value Frankenstein's earlier statement to Walton.

21. In several traits the Creature also resembles the criminal-hero who, like Dick Turpin and Jack Sheppard, is not born evil, but is thrust into a life of crime by the injustices that surround him. But because the Creature cannot vow, as does the hero in Fitzball's *Paul Clifford,* "my hand is free from bloodshed—I never wronged, but always defended the unfortunate," his true predecessor lies in villain-heroes such as Schedoni, Manfred, and Montoni.

22. See Evans's discussion in *Gothic Drama from Walpole to Shelley* (Millwood, N.Y.: Kraus, 1977) 103–04.

23. David Mayer, *Harlequin in His Element* 6. Dalton Gosse and Mary J. H. Gosse suggest that Grimaldi's famous Covent Garden performance in the first of the Regency pantomimes *Harlequin and Asmodeus*—in which "Grimaldi constructed a monster from vegetables—only to have the monster come alive, fight with him, and drive him off the stage"—served as a possible inspiration for Mary Shelley. (See *Notes and Queries,* 226 (1981): 403–04.) Certainly Grimaldi was aware of his "Frankensteinish" undertaking when in a poem he recited upon his retirement from the stage in 1824 he called his vegetable-man "Joe Frankenstein":

> Ne'er shall I build the wondrous verdant man,
>   Tall, turnip-headed,—carrot-finger'd,—lean; . . .
> Ne'er shall I, on the very newest plan,
>   Cabbage a body;—old *Joe Frankenstein.*

For the complete poem see *The Drama* (January 1824) 300.

24. Charles Mathews describes Peake's performance in *Memoirs of Charles Mathews, Comedian* 1:50–53.

25. See A. Owen Aldridge, "The Vampire Theme: Dumas Père and the English Stage," *Revue des Langues Vivantes* 39 (1973/74): 316. Compare M'Swill's lines to Lord Ronald:

M'Swill. Well, they were seen to enter the grotto, and . . .
Ron. And what?
M'Swill. They never came out again.

with Frizzy's lines to Cleaver in *Another Piece of Presumption:*

Friz. I have something wonderful to communicate; the other night he went to bed . . .
Cleav. Wonderful!
Friz. And something more astonishing, he got up again!

26. For example, juxtapose the Merle and Antony Creation scene, in which the creator rushes on stage to announce:

Qu'ai-je fait? qu'ai-je fait [. . .] Quel monstre l'enfer a-t-il livré? Il respire! son regard s'est fixe sur moi! . . . O ciel! quelle oeuvre ai-je accomplie! quel objet d'horreur! et c'est pour arriver à ce résultat fatal que je me suis privé du repos? une lumière affreuse a pénétré dans mon [â]me . . . Déjà ma punition commence; déjà tout me dit que j'ai mérité les châtiments du ciel! . . . *(Il écoute.)* tout est tranquille . . . le monstre est peut-être rentré dans le néant! . . . S'il que je suis! . . . Olben, mon fils, chère Cécilia, je n'oserai plus m'approcher de vous! . . . Je suis perdu, perdu pour jamais!

with the Creation scene as found in Dugué:

Qu'ai-je fait? . . . qu'ai-je fait? [. . .] Quel monstre l'enfer a-t-il créé! . . . Il respire! son regard de cadavre s'est fixe sur moi! Malheureux! Quelle oeuvre ai-je accomplie! . . . Et c'est pour arriver à ce résultat fatal que j'ai usé ma jeunesse dans les veilles et abreuvé mon âme de poisons! . . . Ah! c'en est fait de moi! je sens que ma punition commence déjà, et que la vengeance du ciel va éclater sur moi comme la foudre! . . . *(Il écoute.)* Tout est redevenu tranquille . . . si le monstre était rentré dans le néant! Oh! c'est qu'aucun mortel ne pourait supporter sa présence! . . . Et c'est moi, moi, qui ai jeté ce démon sur la terre! . . . Misérable que je suis! . . . Antonio! Cécilia! tout ce que j'aimais est à jamais perdu pour moi! . . . Ah! si je priais . . . si j'essayais de prier . . .

27. See the following discussions: Elizabeth Nitchie, *Mary Shelley: Author of Frankenstein* (New Brunswick, N.J.: Rutgers University Press); Donald Glut, *The Frankenstein Legend* (Metuchen, N.J.: Scarecrow, 1973) and *The Frankenstein Catalog* (Jefferson, N.C.: McFarland, 1984); Radu Florescu, *In Search of Frankenstein* (Boston: New York Graphic Society, 1975); Albert La Valley, "The Stage and Film Children of *Frankenstein,*" in Levine *Endurance;* Gordon Hitchens, "Breathless Eagerness: Historical Notes on Dr. Frankenstein and His Monster," *Film Comment* 6 (1970): 49–51; and Douglas William Hoehn, "The First Season of *Presumption!; or, The Fate of Frankenstein,*" *Theatre Studies* 26–27 (1979–81); 79–88.

28. In *British Entertainers in France,* Leathers incorrectly notes that "*Le Petit monstre* . . . was not a parody since it had been given two years earlier although its revival was obviously an attempt to catch popular attention by the title" (57). Perhaps, like Glut and the others, Leathers derives his information from Nitchie. He might also be confusing the Gaîté burlesque of 1826 with a one-act comedy by Merle, Simon, and Brazier entitled *Le Petit monstre de la Rue Plumet, ou est-elle laide*

ou est-elle jolie?, which antedates the production of *Presumption* by six years, being performed in 1817.

29. See Glut 34; Nicoll 4:356; *The New Cambridge Bibliography of English Literature* (Cambridge: Cambridge University Press, 1969) 3:1134; and L. W. Conolly and J. P. Wearing, *English Drama and Theatre, 1800–1900: A Guide to Information Sources* (Detroit: Gale, 1978) 222.

30. This is not the only time Glut transforms a poem into a play. Later in the same chapter he commits a similar error when he writes (45): "A one-act satirical play entitled *Frank and Mr. Frankenstein* was written by Alfred Kreymborg and performed in 1935. The nature of this play is not known." The publication is actually a one hundred and twelve line poem, available in the collection of most major libraries. To my knowledge the poem was never "performed."

31. Here Glut embellishes Nitchie's observation (224): "It almost seems as if he [Cooke] might have been responsible for the common confusion that transformed 'the Frankenstein monster' into 'the monster Frankenstein.'" As far as I know, Cooke never publicly called the Creature by any name, although in a satirical peerage, *Punch in London* (14 January 1832) labeled O. Smith "Lord Frankenstein." On the subject of a name for the Creature, David Ketterer contributes a concise overview in his excellent *Frankenstein's Creation* (118–19, n. 10), while on Mary Shelley's selection of "Frankenstein" as the surname of Victor, see Jean de Palacio, *Mary Shelley dans son oeuvre* (Paris: Editions Klincksieck, 1969) 93–94, n. 5.

32. *Burlesque Plays of the Eighteenth Century,* ed. Simon Trussler (London: Oxford University Press, 1969) 8–9.

33. Michael R. Booth, *Prefaces to English Nineteenth-Century Theatre* (Manchester: Manchester University Press 1981) 159; Phillis T. Dircks, "James Robinson Planché and the British Burletta Tradition," *Theatre Survey* 17 (1976): 68.

34. See Dougald MacMillan, "Planché's Early Classical Burlesques," *Studies in Philology* 25(1928): 340.

35. J. R. Planché, *Recollections and Reflections* I:44.

36. In answer to *Le Lendemain d'un succès,* the Théâtre des Variétés mounted a revue entitled *Le Médicin des théâtres,* summarized in *La Quotidienne* (15 August) as follows:

> C'est un de ces docteurs . . . qui étudient l'anatomie à l'amphithéâtre de l'Opéra et qui donnent leurs consultations à Tortony ou au café Anglais. Tous les théâtres viennent tour à tour demander des remèdes contre le malaise qu'ils éprouvent. Ce cadre était très-ingénieux pour donner en plaisantant des conseils utiles.

37. Jean-Toussaint Merle, director of the Théâtre de la Porte Saint-Martin, recruited Cooke and was quite pleased with his accomplishment. See his letter to the *Courier des théâtres* for 20 July 1827.

38. Thompson, *The Making of the English Working Class* (1963; rev. ed., Harmondsworth: Penguin, 1983) 898.

39. Yeo, "Science and Intellectual Authority in Mid-Nineteenth-Century Britain: Robert Chambers and *Vestiges of the Natural History of Creation,*" *Victorian*

Studies 28 (1984): 10. For book-length studies, see Mario A. di Gregorio, *T. H. Huxley's Place in Natural Science* (New Haven, Conn.: Yale University Press, 1984), Robert Bud and Gerrylynn K. Roberts, *Science versus Practice: Chemistry in Victorian Britain* (Dover: Manchester University Press, 1984), and Peter Mortion, *The Vital Science: Biology and the Literary Imagination, 1860–1900* (London: George Allen, 1984).

40. *Le Monstre et le magicien* closed on 10 September. The demand for continued performances, however, was so great that the Porte Saint-Martin recruited a new Creature and reopened in late October for a run of one month.

41. The perfect inheritor of Cooke's role, Smith by 1827 had achieved such notoriety that Charles Mathews was prompted to quip: "I am happy to have it in my power to express my perfect belief that Mr. Smith is a most respectable character in private life—though a great Ruffian on the stage." (Letter from English Opera House, 21 August 1827. London, Enthoven Collection, Victoria and Albert Museum.) One year later, on 11 September, *The Drama* commented: "We really fear that poor Mr. O. Smith will lose all the attributes of humanity, unless they occasionally give him a mere mortal character to present." The remark was prompted by Smith's performance in *Presumption* the previous evening.

42. *The Gladstone Diaries,* ed. M. R. D. Foot (Oxford: Clarendon, 1968) 2:481. See also John Murray, *A Handbook for Travellers in Sicily* (London: 1864) xlvi and David Ketterer, *Frankenstein's Creature: The Book, The Monster, and Human Reality,* ELS, no. 16 (University of Victoria, B. C., 1979) 118, n. 10. Ketterer first directed my attention to this quotation, which he located in *A Supplement to the Oxford English Dictionary* (1972).

43. Gaskell, *Mary Barton* (1958; rev. ed. Harmondsworth, Middlesex: Penguin, 1984) 219–20. Discussions of this quotation are numerous and include the following: Ketterer's *Frankenstein's Creature* 118, n. 10; George Levine's *The Realistic Imagination: English Fiction from Frankenstein to Lady Chatterly* (Chicago: University of Chicago Press, 1981) 25; and Lee Sterrenburg's excellent "Mary Shelley's Monster: Politics and Psyche in *Frankenstein*" in Levine, *Endurance* 167–68.

44. *The Letters of Edward John Trelawny,* ed. Henry Fronde (London: Oxford University Press, 1910) 222–23. See also R. Glynn Gryllis, *Mary Shelley: A Biography* (London: Oxford University Press, 1938) 319, n. 2.

2

Frankenstein Amid the Populace: Victorian Renderings of Shelley's Novel, 1832–1900

As WE HAVE SEEN, the years between 1823 and 1832 were years of proliferation during which the Frankenstein myth was transformed for popular consumption. From the passage of the first Reform Bill to the turn of the century, however, the myth spread among the populace, taking on new media, the most important of which was the political cartoon. As it turns out, political cartoons lambasting the passage of the Reform Bill, labor unrest, and the Irish Question were the most important mid-century influences on the myth before Boris Karloff donned cement boots to play the Creature for Universal Studios.[1]

* * *

The first cartoon resulting from the Reform Bill appeared in *McLean's Monthly Sheet of Characters* on 1 March 1832 (figure 7).[2] Entitled "Frankenstein's Creating Peers," the cartoon concerned the creation of peers to ensure the passage of the Bill and referred to January 15th when, under pressure from Earl Grey and Henry Brougham, William IV consented to the creation of peers. In February the list was drawn up. The cartoon presents a Gothic table laden with lifeless peers. Brougham presides over the table and Grey holds an elixir vitae labeled "Royal Assent." Reminiscent of *Presumption,* where Fritz gazes through a window and into Frankenstein's laboratory, an angry Duke stares through a leaded window.

Grey also serves as the subject of a second cartoon, published on 28 April in *Figaro in London*. In "The Political Frankenstein" (figure 8), Grey,

Figure 7. "Frankenstein's Creating Peers," *McLean's Monthly Sheet of Characters* (1 March 1832).

Figure 8. "The Political Frankenstein," *Figaro in London* (28 April 1832).

Figure 9. James Parry, "Reform Bill's First Step Amongst His Political Frankensteins" (1833), Michael W. Jones, *The Cartoon History of Britain* (New York: Macmillan, 1971), 140.

"a student of political alchemy," stands over the Creature, whose arms are labeled "Schedule A" and "Schedule B," and whose legs are labeled "[Prope]rty" and "Population." Brougham stokes a bellows that warms a retort from which the elixir runs into the Creature's mouth. Again, a frightened servant (Wetherell) gazes through a casement.[3]

In "Reform Bill's First Step Amongst his Political Frankensteins" (1833), a final cartoon aimed at the Reform Bill, James Parry denigrates those who would place the extension of the franchise above the abolition of slavery and free trade (figure 9).[4] In the lithograph, the devilish Creature thumbs his nose at his creators while trampling worthier "Bills." In retrospect, how violent these images seem in contrast to *Frankenstein's* first appearance in a cartoon, the rather domestic "Tugging at a ~~High~~ Eye-Tooth" (1821) (figure 10), in which a chubby dentist pulls an elderly patient's tooth. On the dentist's bookshelf may be found several books, among them "Frankensteiv" [sic].[5]

Distrust of enfranchisement can also be viewed in cartoons that portray labor and its disputes. In 1866 Birmingham labor demonstrations and the speeches of reformer John Bright served John Tenniel for the satirical "The Brummagem Frankenstein," in which a timorous Bright tiptoes past a member of his Birmingham constituency—a politically rampageous monster that he had stirred into action but now could not control (figure 11).[6] Dissolute and unbridled forces also form the subject of "The Russian Frankenstein and his Monster," which appeared in *Punch* on 15 July 1854 and in which Tenniel, who during this period had lambasted British incompetence in the Crimea, cited the fatuous Tzars and the havoc they had wreaked (figure 12). The metal-munching cossack bears a bloody sword through the ravaged fields of his homeland and serves as a reminder that the Creature could serve both provincial and cosmopolitan themes.

After the Reform Bill and labor disputes, disturbances in Ireland were to form the next target of attack. Early in 1843, *Punch* (5:199) published "The Irish Frankenstein," in which an Irish hooligan brandishing a shillelagh attacks a respectable British gentleman (figure 13). Irish troubles again raised their head in a Frankenstein cartoon when on 18 December 1869 Irish Fenianism filtered into the myth with the conservative *Tomahawk*'s publication of Matt Morgan's "The Irish Frankenstein" (figure 14).[7] The *Tomahawk* illustrated its revulsion at John O'Mahony's Fenian Brotherhood by publishing along with its Frankenstein cartoon a story entitled "The Monstrous Legacy" in which a "wicked, violent man" named Maloreux (read "Malheureux") constructs Fenianism. The tale presents an interesting portrait of what the popular image of Frankenstein had become by the late 1860s:

Figure 10. George Cruikshank, "Tugging at a ~~High~~ Eye Tooth," published on 1 November 1821 by George Humphrey (London, British Museum).

Figure 11. John Tenniel, "The Brummagem Frankenstein," *Punch* (8 September 1866).

Figure 12. John Tenniel, "The Russian Frankenstein and his Monster," *Punch* (15 July 1854).

Figure 13. "The Irish Frankenstein," *Punch* 5 (1843): 199.

Figure 14. Matt Morgan, "The Irish Frankenstein," *The Tomahawk* (18 December 1869).

Figure 15. John Tenniel, "The Irish Frankenstein," *Punch* (20 May 1882).

> So he consulted all his books of evil lore, and he set to work, he and his sons and grandsons; and he took the blood of brave and good men, and he took the hearts of gentle women, and he took the bones of helpless babes, and he ground them all down together with a very great millstone, and he poured in the blood; and when he had made a cement thereof, he began to fashion the body of a monster after the form of a man, but so vast, and so horrible, and so hideous, and so mighty, that no man could withstand the sight thereof, but would fly away in terror. (273)

Tennial returned to the Irish theme in 1882 when in "The Irish Frankenstein," a cartoon published on 20 May in *Punch,* he intimated an analogy between Parnell's efforts on behalf of Irish nationalism and the creation by Frankenstein of an uncontrollable and ferocious beast (figure 15). The cartoon is accompanied by supposed quotations from the novel, quotations that employ a sentence of Mary Shelley's as the basis for a lurid description in an effort to heighten the horrors of the original story. Obviously then, by 1882 the myth had become so trammelled by popular interpretation that direct quotations from the novel had to be embellished in order not to disappoint readers.[8]

* * *

In the caldron of literary activity that characterized the early and mid-Victorian period, one would expect the theatre to thrive. Such was not the case. Rather, during the early part of the century the stage had been taken over by conceited actor-managers, playwriting by poorly paid hacks, and the theatre itself by assorted ruffians. Perhaps the major writers were simply too preoccupied with more lucrative and respected endeavors, for one cannot say that major talents ignored the stage altogether. Browning, Tennyson, and Swinburn all produced dramas, but like the Romantics that preceded them, they produced no lasting achievements.[9] As George Rowell notes in *The Victorian Theatre:* "From the immense output of a hundred years of English drama only *Caste* (1867) retains a hold on the modern repertory."[10]

Despite Thomas Robertson's work for the Bancrofts at the Prince of Wales's and Henry Irving's efforts at the Lyceum, it was not until the first performances of Pinero's *The Second Mrs. Tanqueray* (1893) that the Victorian theatre was on the road to recovery. Into this gulf fell two dramatizations of *Frankenstein: Frankenstein; or, The Model Man* (1849) and *Frankenstein; or, The Vampire's Victim* (1887). But where the former appeared at the height of the popularity of burlesque-extravaganza and certainly represents one of the best nineteenth-century dramatizations of the novel, the latter appeared during the last gasps of burlesque-extravaganza and represents one of the weakest versions of the myth, albeit one of the slickest pieces of Frankensteinian entertainment.[11] For where *Model Man* harbingers the popularity of burlesque-extravaganza in the 1860s, *Vampire's Victim* represents its final demise under the assault of opera bouffe and opera comique.[12]

Following the tradition established by Planché in his Olympic productions of the 1830s, both *Model Man* and *Vampire's Victim* were conceived of as Christmas entertainment. *Model Man* opened at the Adelphi on Boxing Day 1849 and closed on 27 February 1850 after fifty-four performances and very good reviews. As *Punch* hyperbolically observed in its first issue of 1850: during one "killingly droll" production "six children in arms were taken from the pit to the nearest apothecary's, in convulsions of laughter." *Vampire's Victim,* which opened on 24 December 1887, was orchestrated to capitalize on the Christmas crowds. As the manager of the Gaiety Theatre, John Hollingshead, later remarked: "the return of Fred Leslie and Miss Ellen Farren from their American and Australian trip, necessitated the production of a strong bill for Christmas, 1887–8."[13] The play enjoyed 106 performances, the longest run of any British dramatization of the novel, before closing on 27 April 1888.[14]

Produced only six years after the breaking of the monopoly of the Theatres Royal with the passage of the Theatre Regulation Act, *Model Man* shares many ties with the early days of the theatre. Its plot combines the *Frankenstein* myth with the harlequinade of pantomime.[15] Otto of Rosenberg takes the role of Harlequin and Agatha Von Donnerundblitzen, the unhappy heroine whose boorish father has betrothed her to Frankenstein, assumes that of Columbine. Baron Von Donnerundblitzen, Agatha's father, appears as a bungling Pantaloon while Frankenstein, a pompous dandy, appears as Lover. Of her student-scientist fiance, Agatha laments: "He's to his work so wedded by the wig-o-me/That if he marries me as well, 'tis bigamy." Undine, the benevolent water-spirit, takes lovers Otto and Agatha into her protection. She provides Otto with a magic flute that tames the wild Creature, condemns the evil wizard Zamiel for concocting Frankenstein's elixir vitae, and reconciles the wayward daughter with her father. The Creature plays the part of Clown by wreaking havoc until the end of the play when, having been tamed by music from Otto's flute (the bat of the harlequinade), he dances on stage. As in the harlequinade, a transformation scene occurs; but rather than transpiring in the first half of the play, it takes place at the play's conclusion when the curtain descends on a fairy grotto.[16]

Und. Now what?
Fran. Why you're the Fairy Queen,
So it's your place to settle the last scene.
Und. I never thought of that the part's so strange

Figure 16. Fred Leslie as the Creature in *The Vampire's Victim,* Gaiety Theatre, 1887 (London, Mander and Mitchenson Theatre Collection).

To me. Let's see whom I have got to change
To Clown & Pantaloon.
Fran. That's not the way.
Und. Is'nt it? oh! well then suppose we say
I take you all to see me at my quarters
And introduce you to Rhine's fairy daughters.

By contrast, in typical Gaiety fashion *Vampire's Victim* exaggerates every role. Fred Leslie as the Creature makes his first entrance dressed like Galatea, and the role of Frankenstein is transformed into a "breeches part" for Nellie Farren. Most interesting, as in Gilbert and Sullivan's *Patience* (1881), where Bunthorne appears as a satirical portrait of Oscar Wilde, in *Vampire's Victim* Fred Leslie satirizes Wilde in a solo, which was dubbed his "special police number" by the press. The allusions to Wilde are made even more outrageous in the Creature's sartorial appearance (figure 16). The extravagance is carried farthest in the character called the Model, a terra cotta progenitor of the Creature. A comic lackey, he attempts to mimic the actions of the more physically and mentally agile Creature, but he always falls short. Upon coming to life, for example, the Creature asks:

Monster (to Model).
I say can you speak?
Model (Grinning). I think so.
Monster. What's your name?
Model. I dunno . . .
Monster (wondering). I dunno?
Model. What's yours?
Monster (With a happy thought). The same! Perhaps they'll christen soon to give us status.
Model. And later on perhaps they'll vaccinate us.
Monster (Derisively).
Well, while they're doing you, if they remove
Those lumps of yours—your figure 'twould improve.
Model (surly).
My figure may be lumpy—lacking grace
But were I you, I'd amputate my face.

But the difference between these two plays runs much deeper. Like any successful burlesque, *Model Man* obviously targets more than its main source, *Frankenstein*. Throughout the piece, the playwrights lampoon what by 1850 had come to be known as the "Adelphi melodrama"—those melodramas of the 1820s that, in the words of Henry Morley, combined "mystery, villainy, comic business, smugglers, caves, crossing of swords, firing of guns, lost daughters mysteriously recovered, shrieking their way into their father's arms, hairbreadth perils, executions, and reprieves."[17] A fine example of this type of burlesque may be found in the first scene where Frankenstein rudely threatens Otto and his group of friends.

Blockheads, are'nt I the hero of the piece?
And have'nt I a right to clear the stage
When in soliloquy I would engage?

Otto defies him in a tone befitting a true gothic hero:

If on that footing you're inclined to put it,
There's no alternative but we must cut it,
(melodramatically to Frankenstein)
But villain we shall meet again!

In the next scene Otto enters dramatically to save the heroine from lamenting her bondage to Frankenstein.

Aga. For my unhappy fate I can't discover
A single precedent, a learned lover.
Why it's in flat defiance of all rules
Of ancient, modern or medieval schools.
Search Opera, Drama, tragedy or play,
Lovers are always careless, dashing, gay,
Studying nothing but to please the fair,
Dress well, make love and fight.
(Otto jumps in at window) Huh who goes there?
Otto. My love, my life, my soul, my fancy's Queen.
Aga. Yes, that's more like the sort of thing I mean.
Otto. I've risked my neck, I've braved—no matter what.
Aga. Lor! how extremely nice!
Otto. To reach this spot
Dangers enough the boldest heart to scare,
I've dared to grapple with—no matter where,
And overcome them all, no matter how,
To ask you "Will you love me then as now?"
Aga. Momentous question, will I love you then.
By Juno's vow, she breathes no matter when
Whose echo, piercing the Olympian sky,
Incensed the mighty Jove no matter why.
I'd gladly swear—if ladies ever swore,
An oath that "Dearest, then I'll love them more."

One of *Model Man*'s finest burlesques occurs when Frankenstein receives the elixir vitae from Zamiel. The scene brilliantly parodies Weber and Kind's *Der Freischutz,* in which at the Wolf's Glen Caspar casts the magic bullets for Max. The scene also parodies *Le Monstre et le magicien,* where Zametti, the French Frankenstein, accepts the elixir from an evil spirit of the underworld.[18] In *Der Freischutz* Caspar cries out:

Probatum est!—and now, the blessing of the balls.
(During three pauses, he bows his head thrice to the earth.)
Thou the "Mighty Hunger" height,
Zamiel! aid me with thy might!

Stand by me this fearful night,
'Tis the charm be weaved quite
Bid the lead with Fate agree,
Blest be seven, nine, and three,
Pow'rful that each bullet be!
Zamiel! stand this night by me!

In *Model Man* the evil Zamiel concocts the elixir for Frankenstein out of a farrago of popular nostrums:

Those who serve me had always best be stirring.

Takes ingredients out of the basket speaking as he throws the various ones into the mortar.

Macassar oil of virtues rare,
Give a nobby head of hair.
Grimstone's eye snuff give him sight,
Odonto, teeth of pearly white.
Slolberg's lozenge! for the voice,
Make him speak a language choice.
Cockel's pills your warmth impart,
To the cockels of his heart.
Last & greater than the whole,
All the others to control,
Charm vitality to give,
Charm to bid the patient live,
Charm of every power rife,
Parr's life pills shall give him life.

As Zamiel throws Parr's pills in the mortar Thunder Crash, Noise &c. A flash of fire out of the mortar . . .

Probatum est! *(pours liquid from the mortar into a labelled vial with a punch ladle.)*

You may with this Elixir
Make your Automation both live & kick sir.

As has already been pointed out, at the conclusion of the play Undine appears to denounce Zamiel as accountable for the commotion. Therefore, unlike the situation of previous melodramas—and especially that of the novel—Frankenstein remains unpunished for his hubris. As Undine clarifies:

Hold, to be blamed for [damages Frankenstein's] not the one,
The true cause of the mischief I've found out.
Too long this neighborhood he's prow'll'd about,
But I'm resolved he shall no longer stay.
Notice to quite I've served on him to-day,
Behold him.

(Enter Zamiel very miserably in travelling costume.)

The central scene of any *Frankenstein* dramatization is, of course, the Creation scene. In a swipe at the blue complexion that characterized all previous stage Creatures—and I think particularly of the burlesque *Pre-*

Figure 17. Paul Bedford as the Creature and Edward Wright as Frankenstein in *The Model Man, Illustrated London News* (January 1850).

sumption; or, The Blue Demon (1823)—the third scene of *Model Man* opens with the following laboratory scene (figure 17):

Frankenstein's laboratory. A gothic chamber strewn about with chemical apparatus, books &c. Frankenstein at work putting the finishing touches on to the monster with a paint brush. The monster, as yet inanimate, stands on a pedestal in a statuesque attitude. Frankenstein sings as he paints.

I've put him together with joint & screw
And to finish him off a touch or two
Of red just here—and a tinge of blue
And I don't mind saying I think he'll do.

Having finished with the Creature, Frankenstein pours the elixir down its throat:

The Monster . . . suddenly turns round and sees him for the first time and makes a threatening movement towards him. Frank starts away frightened. Tableau. Music.

Frank. Ah would you! *(The Monster approaches him)*

(Frankenstein holds up a chair) . . .

Frank. Oh I fear I've made a trifling error,
Oh I can't control my fright.
His movements make me quake with terror,
Avaunt and quit my sight.
I've made, oh gracious goodness,
A mull despite my shrewdness.
Sorry to have recourse to rudeness.

(At the last line Frank has approached the door which he suddenly disappears through, slamming it in the monster's face who looks in astonishment after him, standing still during the last bar of music—Music changes to the hurried melodramatic style. The monster rubs his nose and goes through pantomime indicative of revenge to express a sense of insult & injury at Frank's treatment.)

Brilliantly parodying the stage antics of his predecessors, Paul Bedford, as the Creature, turns the scene on its head when he steps downstage to ponder his fate:

Monster. Well though I have'nt mixed much in society,
That seems to me an outrage on propriety . . .
But stop. Where am I, aye & likewise who?
How did I get here? that's a poser too.
How is it too that in my situation,
With no advantages of education,
My thoughts in words an utterance are seeking,
Though unaccustomed quite to public speaking?

In this play Zamiel's bumbling servant, Ratzbaen, plays the role of dumb show character, thereby embodying the antics of both the mute Creature and comical servants of earlier melodramas. Ratzbaen's comic role and mute heritage announce themselves at his first entrance. In this scene, Frankenstein summons the spirits of the underworld:

(Rain & Thunder. Ratzbaen rises from a shooting trap. Frank starts frightened.)

[Frank.] Come I say don't do that again young feller.
(Ratzbaen pantomimes extravagantly)
Oh who can understand those fits & starts?
(to Audience)
I see he's not engaged for talking parts.
(Pantomime repeated)
What do you mean you aggravating elf?

(Gong Music. The bush opens & Zamiel appears suddenly pushing Ratzbaen aside.)

Zam. Here, never mind, I'll introduce myself.

The play has many other ties to an earlier age and especially to *Presumption,* whose author died only three years prior to its production. To begin with, playbills for the production of *Model Man* alluded to Peake's melodrama when they described the burlesque as "a Gross Piece of 'Presumption.'" These playbills and the dramatis personae also listed the Creature as simply "———." Furthermore, early reviews of *Model Man* quickly noted the debt owed by that play to the *Frankenstein* dramatizations of the 1820s. One reviewer remarked: "The Christmas extravaganza at this theatre is from the melodrama of 'Frankenstein,' which many years since attracted large audiences of those who woo terror to delight themselves in the old Lyceum theatre." But O. Smith, who debuted as the Creature in Henry Milner's *The Man and the Monster,* represents the most obvious reminder of ties to the early melodramas by Peake and Milner. Although his advancing age forced him to relinquish the role of the Creature to comedian Paul Bedford, Smith proved ideal for the role of the aged and unemployed Zamiel. As he tells Frankenstein:

There ne'er was known such a depression;
Knowledge has played the deuce with our profession.
Magic completely burked by facts and figures,
Charmed bullets superseded by hair triggers.
My celebrated gun trick what's it worth
When ev'ry juggling wizard of the north
Will coolly take a supercilious view of it
And tell you he can do a trick worth two of it?

And when he introduces himself to Frankenstein—in a swipe at the now dead tradition of Gothic melodrama—Zamiel can only be recognized by his famous laugh:

Frank. Zamiel eh; the deuce you are.
Zam. Just listen if you doubt it. Hah! Hah! Hah!

Frank. The old original if folks should doubt it,
Do that & there'll be no mistake about it.[19]

* * *

According to John Hollingshead, *Vampire's Victim* was based on *Model Man,* "the old Adelphi drama" founded, in his words, on Mary Shelley's "not very thrilling novel."[20] In truth, his comment misjudges Shelley's novel and overestimates the influence of *Model Man* on *Vampire's Victim*. As has probably become evident, the plots and characters of each play are quite different. Moreover, only two verbal echoes exist between the two plays. In the first instance, each Creature speaks a snippet of similar dialogue. In *The Model Man* the Creature says upon being animated:

But stop. Where am I, aye & likewise who?
How did I get here? that's a poser too.

The Creature of *Vampire's Victim* also asks:

Where am I? also what—or which—or who?
What is this feeling that is running through my springs—or rather joints?

Another echo occurs when Frankenstein encounters the Creature for the first time. In both plays Frankenstein repeats the ejaculation of Macbeth upon beholding the ghost of Banquo: "Avaunt and quit my sight." The two examples are probably coincidental, especially the latter, which during the course of the nineteenth century had been popularized by many gothic melodramas. In fact, so removed is *Vampire's Victim* from Shelley's story that the reader has the impression that neither of its two playwrights ever read the novel. And where Shelley's name never appears in the text of *Vampire's Victim,* it surfaces continually in *Model Man*. In one scene Zamiel announces that the "Authoress of *Frankenstein*" and he have permitted the Creature's evil actions. And in another, Otto apologizes to the audience:

You must excuse a trifling deviation
From Mrs. Shelley's marvelous narration.
You know a piece could never hope to go on
Without love, Rivals, tyrant pa's and so on.
Therefore to let you know our altered plan,
I'm here to represent the "nice young man,"
And in the hero's person you'll discover,
On this occasion the obnoxious lover.
So in my character I beg to say,
(tragically) Heigho, alas, ah me! & welladay,
And every interjection now in fashion
Indicative of wild and hopeless passion.

In *Vampire's Victim* the Creature never becomes the object of tuition. And in sharp contrast to the highly polemical themes of *Model Man,* which probably derived from Robert rather than from William Brough,[21] contemporary political allusions in *Vampire's Victim* assume the status of flippant, jingoistic asides. At one point an unemployed villager remarks of Frankenstein and his mysterious village business:

What has he done? Why all our trade he's undone,
Just as his fellow Germans have in London.
We're as unemployed as some in London.

A similar allusion is made to the unemployment demonstrations that took place in Trafalgar Square throughout October and into December of 1887. In this instance Capitano Maraschino informs his ragged band of soldiers:

Silence in the ranks . . .
I'll order you to shoot each other.
(Consternation of SOLDIERS)
Or, maybe you to England shall repair
To face the rioters in Trafalgar square!

Vampire's Victim includes only one major scene from the novel: the demand for a mate. In the first act the Creature turns to Frankenstein and pleads:

Mons. *(Pathetically)*
But! I'm a lonely Monster—and I yearn
To love, and to be loved in return.
I see all things around me made in pairs
You have *your* sweetheart—other folks have theirs
Then why have you made me without a mate?

But whereas in the novel the Creature's demand poses the problem of self-propagating evil, in *Vampire's Victim* it initiates a sideshow antic involving Mary Ann, the Creature's obnoxious vampire-mate: because he is made of clay and therefore has no circulatory system, the Creature continually thwarts all attempts by Mary Ann to turn him into a vampire. The liaison also serves to antagonize Visconti, a vampire who loves Mary Ann. These themes climax in the abduction scene that concludes the play. In this scene the Creature rejects the love of Mary Ann for that of Tartina, Frankenstein's fiancée, whom he steals in the second act. In the climax of the last act, Frankenstein and the rest of the cast descend upon a pirate ship caught in an arctic ice floe. The arrival of the Sun Goddess represents the last vestiges of the harlequinade tradition:

Frank (tragically).
Monster! prepare to meet your doom! your crimes
Are quite too dreadful for these quiet times!
Your deeds of terror now shall end—You die!
Where will you have it? *(pointing a pistol).*
Monster (cowering). Kill me by and by!
Frank Can't wait! I'm busy—come, your doom is sealed!
Produce TARTINA! *(about to shoot him)*
Monster. Fain it's! I will yield
Providing you won't send me to my bride.
M.Ann (stepping down). Don't worry, dear! Your darling's by your side!
Visc. (seeing her). You! O, if I were but thawed, from him I'd tear her
Model (to Visconti).
If I were you I cheerfully would spare her.
Monster. Bah! Now I *won't* restore your sweetheart; see!
Frank (furious). Release my girl at once.
(SUN GODDESS ENTERS suddenly at back bringing down TARTINA)
Sun G. Leave that to me!
Tart. My love! and am I once more free?
Frank You are, dear!
Tart. Then from these regions let us wander far dear?
(To SUN GODDESS)
But who are you—young lady? I don't know you!
(Crash heard. Ice melts. Ship disappears &c.)
Sun G. Don't be alarmed! I've something nice to show you!
I am the Goddess of the Sun and Moon
So please retire awhile.

Stepping out of character to respond, Frankenstein concludes the play with a pun on the surname of Wilhelm Meyer Lutz, orchestra conductor of the Gaiety and composer of the libretto of *Vampire's Victim.*

Frank (To Tart). Let's go and spoon.
I understand that ere we go away
The management will give some grand display.
(To leader of band)
Not to have music—during these pursuits
Would be a little rift within the Lutz.

As already noted, *Model Man* contains a level of political satire that is absent from *Vampire's Victim.* In fact, produced between the cartoons of James Parry and those of Tenniel and Morgan, *Model Man* was the first dramatic adaptation in *Frankenstein* to explore the novel's political ramifications. Although many burlesques of this period indulged in political digression,[22] the Broughs extended political commentary by casting their plot as an allegory on unbridled revolution. At one point, Frankenstein steps downstage and alludes to contemporary events in France:

Well I declare my brains & senses dance
In worse confusion than affairs in France.

And later, at his trial for creating the Creature, Frankenstein protests:

But take down my defense. I'll soon be showing
I'm not the only man who's set agoing
A horrid monster that he could'nt stop.
For precedents across the channel pop.

But rather than a cartoon-image brute, in this allegorical setting the Creature appears as a figure of potential reform, his destruction the consequence of society's misdirected or abandoned responsibilities. Quite simply, the Creature's anarchy can only be tamed when he receives an education, which is supplied at the end of the play in the notes of the hero's magic flute. As Undine indicates when she gives the flute to Otto:

Here take this magic flute
And seek him out, the most ferocious brute.
Its notes will bring to calm subordination,
It plays a simple tune called Education.

Hence, as opposed to earlier dramatizations where music served as a temporary panacea for the Creature's rage, in *Model Man* it restores and rehabilitates him. This triumph occurs at the climax of the play when Otto rushes on stage to claim the hand of Agatha:

Otto. The world grows wiser and begins to find
That to its erring sons it should be kind,
And stead of scaring them with jail & fetter,
The proper way is to teach them to grow better.
I've tamed him.
All. Ha.
Otto. Yes, by this weapon small,
Whose unobtrusive power would conquer all
The ills that o'er the earth hold dominion
If people understood its application.
Behold its charm to soothe the savage breast,
And lull the—everybody knows the rest.

Goes to wing R & commences playing "In My Cottage" very slowly. The monster, neatly dressed à la happy Villager with his hair moustaches curled, enters smiling & following the music. Otto leads him round the Stage changing his tune to the original Polka. The monster dances pleased.

Frank. Come to my arms you wild young rascal do,
I don't mind saying now I'm proud of you.

Frankenstein & Monster embrace.

* * *

The one-act structure of *Model Man* is typical of the majority of early burlesque-extravaganzas. As Harley Granville-Baker specifies: "the typical burlesque was the affair of an hour, not more, split into five or six scenes for variety's sake (front cloths alternating with full sets, and nothing very elaborate even about these) played through without any interval—this was most important—for reflection."[23] Like the early melodramas, the action of the play was compressed into twenty-four hours, with three principal scenes from previous dramatizations providing the catalyst: the creation of the Creature; the conclusion of a major scene with a violent conflagration; and the conquest of the Creature with music. Its boldly drawn parody of the *Frankenstein* myth, lightning action, splendid acting and characterizations, witty repartee, and adeptly composed verse distinguished *Model Man* as a high point in burlesque-extravaganza.

By contrast *Vampire's Victim* was a lengthy affair, reflecting the three-act formula introduced in 1878 by Hollingshead in *The Forty Thieves,* called by Macqueen-Pope "the true beginning of a series which paved the way for musical comedy" (200). "Extravagance" would be the word to describe *Vampire's Victim.* Not content with one Creature, it also includes a terra cotta model and two vampires. Thus, it is the first dramatization to place on stage the creations of Mary Shelley and John Polidori. Like its flashy costumes, *Vampire's Victim* emphasized staging over the plot, prompting critics to lament the earlier, purer style of burlesque-extravaganza as practiced by Planché and Vestris.[24]

The three acts contain four important scenes, which were planned more for scenic splendor than for the development of the story line. The first scene is calculated for its sheer splendor:

SCENE: The village of Villasuburba, at the foot of the Pass of Pizzicatto, in the Tyrol. Mountains all around. Descending runs. Roadside tavern L. Everything very bright and picturesque. As the curtain rises Peasants descend the mountain paths, singing somewhat sorrowfully as they come . . .

PEASANTS.

We've done our daily labour
and now to pipe and tabour
Fain we would dance till dewy eve
But Ah, we've cause to grieve.
Alas, our local trade
Is much inclined to fade
And gladly would we roam
From this our mountain home!

"Picturesque" keys the reader to the desired effect, as it does in the opening scene of act 2:

Snow-covered mountains in the distance. River at back. Picturesque bridge over waterfall or torrent. Fine afternoon. The sun is shining . . . Then Enter a picturesque procession—of robber band; pack of mules laden with plunder, Captives (board) following on foot.

Henry and Newton place the climax of their play in the Arctic not so much because Mary Shelley opens and concludes her novel in this region, but because of the dazzling effect that could be created by such a scene. The *Pall Mall Budget* (29 December 1887) enthusiastically endorsed the scene as "as pretty a picture as has ever been put on the stage, representing a Christmassy scene in the Arctic regions, with the monster ship, shining with icicles, half embedded in snow, and surrounded by ice floes." The description of the scene reads:

SCENE.—The Arctic regions. In the foreground a ship is seen embedded in the ice. Centre of stage clear for BUSINESS. Sailors discovered hauling on a rope, endeavouring to extricate ship from its position. At intervals they dance around grotesquely in order to keep themselves warm—Their short ballet of action is accompanied by a short chorus. Sailors are suddenly alarmed by the appearance of four Bears—Sailors run off. Bears come down and dance—After which the Bears are frightened away by a bigger Bear, which is the Monster in disguise. Monster roars and wags his tail with delight. Jumps about &c. Then walks restlessly to and fro like the Polar Bears in the Zoo. Suddenly he stops C. roars at audience then:

Monster. Don't be frightened, please—*(taking off Bear's Head)*
It's only me,
A poor benighted Monster here you see,
This is a neat disguise of double form
It serves to hide me, and to keep me warm.
Besides it is in the fashion in these times . . .

The center of the stage remains "clear for BUSINESS" rather than for acting; Fred Leslie as the chubby, avuncular Creature is a weak parody of his prototypes; the sailors are dreamy Gaiety girls dressed in neat blue pinafores. The allusion to contemporary fashion, the incongruity of rugged sailors doing a "ballet of action," the spectacle of dancing bears—these elements skew the plot in order to highlight the entertainment. The character of Frankenstein serves as a good example of the type of broad liberty taken with Shelley's novel. In the production, Frankenstein is played by leggy and dimpled Nellie Farren because audiences were drawn to the Gaiety for glamorous and sensual diversion. Travesty replaces parody; brash three-act spectacle replaces sleek one-act burlesque; thespianizing replaces acting.

In the context of nineteenth-century burlesque-extravaganza, the last point is the most evident and characteristic. All early melodramatizations of Shelley's novel rearranged the characters into "types": the villain (the Creature), the hero (Frankenstein), the heroine (Frankenstein's fiancée), and the rustic man and woman for comic relief. Culminating and reflecting this division in the dramatis personae, playbills for *Model Man* placed the characters into three groups. The first group consisted of "Characters which, properly speaking, belong to the Story, being in the Original Legend." This category consisted of two characters: the Creature, "THE WHAT IS IT?—a singular being who may be most aptly and expressively described as '———' a curious compound of many qualities—an animated character"—and Frankenstein, "The Student Senior Wrangler of Brazenface College, in the University of Krackenjausen." Interestingly enough, Agatha, the only other character in the play from the novel, did not figure in this first group; rather, she was placed in group two: "Characters which do not exactly belong to the Story, but which, being creations of the Authors' own, they maintain they have a right to do what they like with." This second category also includes Baron Von Donnerundblitzen, Otto of Rosenberg, Tiddliwincz, Ratzbaen, Frightz, and Bobinetta. Obviously, then, by 1849 the story of Frankenstein had become so distorted that even characters from the pen of Mary Shelley were lost amid those like Frightz, who had been created by previous playwrights. That Agatha figures as the heroine of *Model Man* completes an ascendancy that began in *Presumption*, where she appeared as Frankenstein's fiancée. The third group consisted of "Characters with which, honestly speaking, the Authors have no business at all, and like their impudence to make use of them, being other people's property." This category contained Undine, "the Spirit of the Flood & Management Directoress of the Water-works of Germany," and Zamiel, "The Demon of Hartz and Sciences—a victim of the March of Intellect."

Music always played an essential role in melodrama. The backbone of the earlier dramatizations, music plays central (albeit significantly different) roles in the two present plays. In *Vampire's Victim* music highlights itself rather than emerging as an organic part of the plot. For example, Visconti's solo "The Man Who Could'nt Keep Warm" halts the action for the Vampire's aside on his trick wig:

Visconti. Since Mary Ann's flown from her owniest own
I'm a Vampire who can't keep his hair on.
Chorus. Ha! ha! ho! Ha! ha! ho! ho!
It's really so I'm a Vampire who can't keep his hair on
Ho, ho, ho, ho, ho, ho

Such also is the case with "Sworn In," Fred Leslie's "special police" number. The song, which audiences jammed the Gaiety specifically to hear, concerns the merits of London police. Sung at the Vampire Club in Act 3, its main attributes are Lutz's fine music, its contemporary allusions, and Leslie's antics with a walking stick (figure 18):

Figure 18. Fred Leslie as the Creature in *The Vampire's Victim,* Gaiety Theatre, 1887 (London, Mander and Mitchenson Theatre Collection).

I'd have quelled the foe with my baton—so!
   But the foe would'nt come to be quelled;
And, freezing with cold, I made somewhat bold
   With this *(The staff contains liquor, and*
the top, which unscrews, forms a drinking cup.)
   and with what it held.

Music in *Model Man* develops the plot. To the tune of "Mary Blane," Otto describes his past life:

Oh once I loved a lark & led a roaring college life;
'Mongst all my college chums, not one for mischief was more rife.
In town & gown rows then I always entered might & main
But now I'm sad as that dark child who lost his Mary Blane.

And to Mozart's "La ci dareme la mano," from *Don Giovanni,* he sings of his love for Agatha:

Law she's a gem; there are no
Dangers that now need be
Dreaded—we'll let your pa know
We're not afraid of he!

Elsewhere, Frankenstein describes his creation of the Creature in a song entitled "The Steam Arm":

I've managed to make, strange it may seem,
A mechanical man with skill supreme
Each joint is as strong as an iron beam
And the springs are a compound of clock-work & steam.

As these contemporary references indicate, the English public loved seeing and hearing about itself on stage. Like all good burlesques, both *Vampire's Victim* and *Model Man* are replete with topical references. For example in the second act of *Vampire's Victim* the Model sings a song based on "The Toreador" from Bizet's *Carmen;* in the same act the orchestra plays the theme from Il Commendatore's entrance in *Don Giovanni* as Frankenstein nervously awaits the entrance of the Creature; and later, Visconti assumes the "Attitude of Irving as Mephistopheles"—a reference to Irving's tremendous Lyceum performance in W. G. Will's *Faust* (1885). Mary Ann alludes to the morrow's bank holiday, and Frankenstein reads to the Clay Model from Palmer's *ABC Railway Guide.* But whereas in *Vampire's Victim* these topicalities exist as independent entities, as set pieces of comedy that usually have no relation to the plot, in *Model Man* they function within and emerge from the play's context. Because of the expanding railways, Zamiel finds himself without a home. "What can I do? I've no accommodations," he tells Frankenstein. "They've built a railway over the Wolf's Glen." Zamiel also laments that he has nowhere to flee where evil has not preceded him—even to the recently discovered gold fields of California: "In California too my chance is small," he whines to Undine, "there the fiend gold monopolises all the mischief." Earlier Frankenstein sings of Gretna Green and the invention of the telegraph, a cable for which had just been installed between France and England. In the middle of his solo he abruptly stops to call attention to the song's artificiality:

> The invention of the Telegraph has been
> A dreadful blow to poor old Gretna Green.
> Now self-willed heiresses who quit their sires,
> Ere they've got far are caught like hares by wires.
> But pshaw! an end to sorrow and invective,
> 'Twas but to make my entrance more effective.

Contemporary exhibition halls are noted when, upon bringing the Creature to life, Frankenstein's desires to present him to the public in a flurry of playbills and publicity:

> Hurray he moves! he acts! my work's completed!
> Although that he should act might be expected.
> I'll get out bills at once, a cab I'll call
> To hire a room at the Egyptian Hall.
> Or pr'aps he'd make more powerful sensations
> At the art exposition of all nations.

Vampire's Victim also alludes to the telegraph, but the scene exists solely to mock the accent and grammar of the telegraph sprite who delivers the message:

> *GUS*. *(With a strong American accent)* Did you
> ring up a New York messenger sir—because
> that's me.
> *VIS*. *(scornfully)* "That's me" indeed. Is this
> your tele-grammar?

Vampire's Victim employs a literary allusion for popular appeal, as in the references to Henry Rider Haggard's *King Solomon's Mines* (1885):

> *VIS*. *(Boy hands telegram)* What's this?
> *(Reads)* "handed in at the Witch's Head,
> near King Solomon's Mines. No sign of Mary
> Ann in South Africa. Is it a She?
> Love to Stead. Hider Raggard."

By contrast, *Model Man* employs one to define an aspect of the play. For example, an allusion to the recently published *Dombey and Son* characterizes Frankenstein's personality:

Baron *(to Agatha)*
Is'nt the man I've picked for your alliance
As Capt. Cuttle says, "chock full of science".

* * *

Chock full of science Shelley's hero may have been, but through the course of the nineteenth century his scientific quest gave way to alchemical rituals and his Romantic ardor to Victorian censure. So, too, his creation was transformed. Late in Shelley's novel, the frustrated Creature turns to his maker and demands a mate: "You are my creator, but I am your master—obey!"[25] Few nineteenth-century interpretations of *Frankenstein* transcend this conception of the Creature. Cruel, arrogant, despotic—he usurped and conquered man's rightful prerogatives and punished man's foolish quests. In all, he proved the perfect symbol for the age of steam, as Thackeray characterized it. In the *Episcopal Gazette* the Creature symbolized the self-destructing Church of England; to *The Man in the Moon* he frolicked as a drunken companion of King Hamlet. The name of his maker could be adopted to hawk souvenirs, misappropriated to characterize beasts of burden, or invoked to censure a fractious crowd. Cartoonists linked the myth to anything from Reform Bills to John Bright and Fenianism. The Creature appeared as a terra cotta lampoon of Oscar Wilde in *Vampire's Victim* and as an uneducated lout in *Model Man*. His maker usually appeared as a "mad" alchemist, but could also assume any desired role, from foppish dandy to curly-haired Gaiety Girl. By the end of the century, concerned Fabians would warn landlords and capitalists that the steam-engine was "a Frankenstein which they had better not have raised."[26] The spectre of Shelley's novel would even appear in novels as diverse as Wells's *Island of Dr. Moreau* and earlier in Stevenson's *Dr. Jekyll and Mr. Hyde* (1886)—especially in Dr. Jekyll's mysterious "ebullition," in the narrative "Henry Jekyll's Full Statement of the Case," and in Mr. Utterson's dream of the human Juggernaut:

> [H]e would see a room in a rich house, where his friend lay asleep, dreaming and smiling at his dreams; and then the door of that room would be opened, the curtains of the bed plucked apart, the sleeper recalled, and lo! there would stand by his side a figure to whom power was given, and even at that dead hour, he must rise and do its bidding.[27]

Most importantly, without these distortions, Shelley's novel would never have been reduced to the mute and torpid Creature portrayed by Boris Karloff.

NOTES

1. Conspicuously absent from this study is a discussion of illustrated editions of *Frankenstein*. Strangely enough, however, until the twentieth century, few editions of the novel were illustrated. In fact, before 1932, when Nino Carbe's dramatic woodcuts appeared in the Illustrated Editions publication, only two previous editions contained illustrations: the revised edition of 1831, published by Colburn and Bentley and containing Chevalier's engravings, and that of 1849, which reproduced Chevalier's work. As Leonard Wolf has commented in *The Annotated Frankenstein* (New York: Potter, 1977): "The heavy period of *Frankenstein* illustration comes in the 1930s, no doubt as a consequence of the popularity of the 1931 Universal Pictures film" (374). Nonetheless, in the context of the present discussion it must be remarked that anyone who has viewed the magnificent Chevalier frontispiece that appeared in Shelley's revised edition of the novel will immediately be struck with the influence that dramatizations exerted over the artist.

2. See M. Dorothy George, *Catalogue of Political and Personal Satires Preserved in the Department of Prints and Drawings in the British Museum, 1828–1832* (London: Trustees of the British Museum, 1954) 11:586–87. All eleven volumes of this publication have recently become available on microfilm from Chadwyck-Healey. See also Michael W. Jones, *The Cartoon History of Britain* (New York: Macmillan, 1971) 140. Surprisingly, Michael Duffy's superbly edited volumes of *The English Satirical Print, 1600–1832* (Cambridge: Chadwyck-Healy, 1986) fail to list any Frankenstein cartoons. For later political cartoons see Thomas Milton Kemnitz, "Matt Morgan of 'Tomahawk' and English Cartooning, 1867–1870," *Victorian Studies* 19 (1975): 5–34 and Lee Sterrenburg, "Mary Shelley's Monster: Politics and Psyche in *Frankenstein*" in Levine, *Endurance*, 166–71.

3. For a full description, see George, *Catalogue*, 11:601.

4. Reproduced from Michael W. Jones, *The Cartoon History of Britain* 140. See also Sterrenburg's discussion, 166–71, which reproduces figures 9, 11, and 14.

5. For a description of this cartoon, see George, *Catalogue*, 10:273.

6. *Punch*, 8 September 1866, p. 103. The cartoon is accompanied by a poem of four stanzas, entitled "The Brummagem Rough to the Totness Respectable." The first stanza of the poem reads:

> COME down, Respectability—Come down out of that gig, Sir;
> At Yarmouth, Reigate, Totness,
>   We've seen you run your rig, Sir.
> You're a nice chap, *you* are, to scoff
>   At radical and rough, Sir;
> Pitch left and right into JOHN BRIGHT,
>   And middle-class rights puff, Sir.

7. For a brief discussion of this cartoon and Morgan's work in general see Kemnitz, "Matt Morgan of 'Tomahawk' and English Cartooning, 1867–1870," which reproduces this cartoon.

8. For example, the passage from Shelley's novel beginning "He approached; his countenance bespoke bitter anguish" (94), becomes in *Punch:*

> It approached, its countenance bespoke bold defiance, combined with disdain and malignity, while its unearthly ugliness rendered it almost too horrible for human. And yet—yet was it not my Master to the very extent of that it was my Creature? Hideous fatality; inenviable NEMESIS of the shapers of ill! . . . Shaken to the soul, I addressed it, yet faintly and falteringly, in words weakly expressive of disavowal and detestation. It met my late reproach, my tardy denunciation, with mockery and defiance. Hideous, blood-stained, bestial, ruthless in its rage, implacable in its revengefulness, cynical in its contemptuous challenge to my authority, it seemed another and a fouler *Caliban* in revolt, and successful revolt, against the framer and fosterer of its maleficent existence. (234)

9. Browning composed four plays for the Victorian stage: *Stafford* (1837), *A Blot in the 'Scutcheon* (1843), *King Victor and King Charles* (1842) and *Sordello* (1840). Tennyson produced seven pieces: *Queen Mary* (1875), *Harold* (1876), *The Falcon* (1879), *The Cup* (1881), *The Promise of May* (1882), *Becket* (1884), and *The Foresters* (1893). Swinburn, the most successful and prolific of the group, wrote ten plays: *The Queen Mother* (1861), *Atlanta in Calydon* (1865), *Chastelard* (1865), *Bothwell* (1874), *Erectheus* (1876), *Mary Stuart* (1881), *Marino Faliero* (1885), *Locrine* (1887), *The Sisters* (1892), and *Rosamund, Queen of the Lombards* (1899).

10. Rowell, *The Victorian Theatre, 1792–1914,* 2nd ed. (Cambridge: Cambridge University Press, 1978) 75. Rowell also has a brief discussion (pp. 32–38) of the dramatic compositions of the Romantic and Victorian poets. For an extended discussion see Allardyce Nicoll, *A History of English Drama, 1660–1900* (Cambridge: Cambridge University Press, 1959) vols. 4 and 5.

11. Burlesque-extravaganza may roughly be circumscribed by the dates 3 January 1831—when Eliza Vestris presented as an afterpiece at the Olympic Theatre James Robinson Planché and Charles Dance's *Olympic Revels; or, Prometheus and Pandora*—and 24 November 1894, when George Edwards presented at the Gaiety H. J. W. Dam and Ivan Caryll's *The Shop Girl,* called by Macqueen-Pope in *Gaiety: Theatre of Enchantment,* "no less than the very first real musical comedy" (318). In "Political Extravaganza: A Phase of Nineteenth-Century British Theatre," *Theatre Survey* 3 (1962): 19–31, Martin Meisel has already delineated the problems of using "burlesque" and "extravaganza" interchangeably. Certainly Planché distinguished the two when he announced in the Preface to *The Sleeping Beauty in the Wood* (1853) that extravaganza emphasized "the whimsical treatment of a poetical subject," while burlesque emphasized "the broad caricature of a tragedy or serious opera" (*The Extravaganzas of J. R. Planché* (London: 1870) 2:66). Nevertheless, I purposely link the two terms in order to specify those plays created by Planché at the Olympic Theatre in the 1830s, and which made their last appearance at the Gaiety Theatre in the 1890s. For backgrounds of this discussion I am indebted to three studies: V. C. Clinton-Baddeley's *The Burlesque Tradition in the English Theatre After 1660* (London: Methuen, 1952); Winton Tolles' *Tom Taylor and the Victorian*

Drama (New York: AMS, 1966); and John Degen's "A History of Burlesque-Extravaganza in Nineteenth-Century England," Dissertation, Indiana University, 1977.

12. In the present context the term "burlesque-extravaganza" will be employed to distinguish a play whose dialogue is written in doggerel couplets, whose plot concerns classical or mythical figures degenerated through familiarization, whose songs consist of new words set to pre-existing airs, and whose comedy relies on topical allusion, puns, popular slang and extravagant effects. The term "musical comedy" will be employed here to indicate a dramatic production that relies on a relatively original plot (usually set in a modern context), utilizes prose dialogue and original songs set to an original musical score, and eliminates the grotesque or the absurdly burlesque in favor of elaborate dances.

13. Hollingshead, *"Good Old Gaiety"* (London: Gaiety Theatre, 1903) 54.

14. Apparently Richard Butler and Henry Chance Newton, respectively the editor and the theatrical correspondent of *The Referee,* did not originate the idea of a burlesque of *Frankenstein.* Macqueen-Pope indicates that after completing *Miss Esmerelda* (1887) with Horace Mills, Fred Leslie "was already thinking ahead for another new burlesque. His ideas ran upon the story of Frankenstein" (258). Although he seems to have originated the idea, Leslie probably did not contribute to the composition of *Vampire's Victim.* Rather, he most likely mentioned it to Butler and Newton, who had just experienced a tremendous hit with *Monte Cristo, Jr.* (1886), their first production at the Gaiety and the first solo venture of George Edwardes.

15. As Mayer notes in regard to the plot of pantomime:

> We need only to recall the convention of the pantomime to prove its debt to Gothic drama: the girl compelled by her father or guardian to give up her preferred suitor for someone far less appealing; the help that the ugly rival suitor obtains from a wizard; the intervention of the benevolent agent to transform the heroine to Columbine and the hero to Harlequin; and the appearance of a complementary hostile agent to transform the father to Pantaloon and the suitor to Clown or Dandy Lover; and last the moment of the harlequinade when Harlequin's bat passes into the hands of Pantaloon or the hostile agent and Columbine is again threatened.

David Mayer, *Harlequin in his Element: The English Pantomime, 1806–1836* (Cambridge, Mass.: Harvard University Press, 1969) 90.

16. *Vampire's Victim* also concludes in a transformation scene. As the *Pall Mall Budget* (29 December 1887) observed: "The lights go down, and then the picture changes to a lovely transformation scene, representing the land of the Sun, peopled by gods and their satellites in brilliant attire. There is a glowing procession of Northern Lights and Planets, and the Stars and their satellites dance."

17. Morley, *The Journal of a London Playgoer from 1851 to 1866* (London: 1866) 82.

18. For a discussion of this scene in the context of the early dramatizations, see chapter 1, pp. 000.

19. Smith's laugh became a centerpiece of the play. As one review commented: "Mr. O. Smith, as *Zamiel,* with his unforgettable 'Ha! ha! ha!' in 'Freischutz,' [is]

comic in the extreme." Anonymous review from the Enthoven Collection (Adelphi Box 1848–50). The decade itself had many ties to *Presumption*. James Bland, who played Clerval in Peake's melodrama, had become the leading burlesque actor of the day. Robert and Mary Keeley, who played Fritz and Safie in *Presumption*, managed the Lyceum from 1847 to 1856. And only six months before the premier of *Model Man*, Bland and the Kelleys played lead roles in William and Robert Brough's *The Sphinx*. Therefore, perhaps the reunion provided the two playwrights with the idea of burlesquing *Presumption*.

20. Hollingshead, "Good Old Gaiety" 55.

21. Best remembered in his day for the satirical *Songs of the Governing Classes* (1858), Robert Brough was termed in Edmund Yates's *Recollections and Experiences* (London: 1884) 1:315 a "Radical" and a "Republican." In *The Poets and Poetry of the Nineteenth Century: Charles Kingsley to James Thompson* (London: Routledge, 1905) 5:332–33, Alfred Miles distinguished Robert for his "hatred of shams, his detestation of Political self-seeking, [and] his scorn of hereditary claims to govern or to oppress mankind."

22. Planché intended *The Seven Champions of Christendom* (1849) as a political allegory, and in Brough's *The Enchanted Isle* (1848) Caliban marches on stage to the "Marseillaise" and wearing a Cap of Liberty while carrying a red flag in one hand and a small bundle of firewood in the other—presumably to set fire to the barricades of Paris. See Meisel, "Political Extravaganza" 26.

23. Granville-Barker, "Exit Planché—Enter Gilbert," *London Mercury* 25 (1931–32): 568.

24. A critic for the *Saturday Review* (31 December 1887) complained:

> If the author had read some of those delightful extravaganzas which Planché and Mme. Vestris produced many years ago at the Lyceum, he would at once have perceived that, however light and amusing were those exquisite productions, however clever the allusions which they contained to political and other passing events, nothing was introduced which did not in some way bear directly upon the plot. This certainly was not the case in Mr. "Richard Henry's" last work, in which there is scarcely a song, duet, or chorus which contains a line concerning the dramatic situation in which it is sung. The actors sing about the riots in Trafalgar Square, the "Specials" [Metropolitan Police], Mr. Gladstone, the Jubilee, and the Irish question, but say little or nothing about poor Frankenstein and the uncanny work of art which he has, to his sorrow, endowed with life.

25. Shelley, *Frankenstein; or, The Modern Prometheus*, ed. James Rieger (1974; Chicago: University of Chicago Press, 1982) 165.

26. *Fabian Essays in Socialism*, ed. G. B. Shaw (London: 1889) 38.

27. Robert Louis Stevenson, *Dr. Jekyll and Mr. Hyde* (New York: Bantam, 1981) 13–14.

3

Reviving *Frankenstein* in the Twentieth Century: Drama and Cinema, 1900–1930

"Melodrama," remarked the actor, leaning tragically upon his carefully folded gloves and cane, "melodrama is ruined! . . . Blessings upon the head of whoever first invented moving pictures."
New York Times 20 March 1919

AFTER 106 performances at the Gaiety Theatre in London, *Frankenstein; or, The Vampire's Victim* closed on 27 April 1888. *Vampire's Victim* proved to be the last dramatization of Shelley's novel undertaken in the nineteenth century. Twenty-seven years would pass before drama again took up the themes of *Frankenstein*.[1] With the advent of the twentieth century, moving pictures increasingly encroached upon the heretofore unchallenged domination of the theatre. As early as 1873 photographic methods were used in New York City to entertain audiences with images of Frankenstein.[2] Perhaps it is not surprising, therefore, that the first twentieth-century adaptation of Shelley's novel would occur in film. Its adaptation in 1910 revived interest in the novel and led indirectly to the filming in 1931 of Universal Studios' *Frankenstein*, starring Boris Karloff. The circuitous road to Karloff, however, wends through three early films, a farcical drama, and a melodrama that was rewritten twice by one author and once by a second before ultimately forming part of the Universal film—which itself went through two directors, two conclusions, an unsuccessful two-reel test film, and at least three screenplays. The present chapter focuses on three twentieth-century pre-Karloffian treatments of the Frankenstein myth—one cinematic and two dramatic—in an effort to elucidate its transformation from a grotesque travesty of nineteenth-century prototypes to a powerful cult image that eclipsed all previous interpretations.[3]

* * *

The perfect medium of interpreting the Sensation dramas of the 1880s and 1890s, cinema unveiled special effects impossible to duplicate on the stage. Cinema also proved the perfect medium for terror. For example, audiences viewed a beheading in Alfred Clark's *The Execution of Mary, Queen of Scots* (1895), and Edwin Porter's *The Great Train Robbery* (1903) contained the famous scene in which a bandit pointed and fired a gun at the stunned audience. The success of the Selig Polyscope's *Dr. Jekyll and Mr. Hyde* (1908) and of Nordisk Company's *The Necklace of the Dead* (1910) and *Ghosts of the Vault* (1911) proved that horror could also be successfully exploited. In 1910 cinema made its first inroad into Shelley's story with the Edison Company production, *Frankenstein*.[4] Directed by J. Searle Dawley from his own screenplay, the film was registered for a copyright on 18 March 1910 and consisted of one reel of nine hundred and seventy-five feet.[5] The cast included Charles Ogle as the Creature, Augustus Phillips as Frankenstein, and Mary Fuller as the fiancee.

In reaction to adverse reviews of the film, of which perhaps no more than one hundred copies were struck, Edison removed it from Nickelodeons soon after its release. Since that time, cinema historians have pondered its disappearance; in 1980 the American Film Institute's archivists even placed it on a list of the ten most important "lost" films.[6] Over the last twenty years several historians have researched the disappearance of the film,[7] but it was not until 1979 when Al Bates discussed a purported copy that expectations peaked.[8] Recently a print was located in the collection of Alios F. Dettlaff, a Wisconsin film collector.[9] Unable to view the film, I base the present discussion on documents in the Museum of Modern Art in New York, on cinema archives at the Lincoln Center branch of the New York Public Library, on other published critical discussions, and on a telephone interview with Mr. Dettlaff.

In many ways, the Edison *Frankenstein* resembles the tawdry melodramatizations of the novel undertaken in the 1820s in that, as in so many early silent films, it is dominated by nineteenth-century staging and acting. For example, every piece of music from the film's score derives from popular stage pieces of the preceding century. Twice Lady John Scott's "Annie Laurie" (1838) accompanies the action, and at the beginning of the film the tender music of "Then You'll Remember Me" from William Balfe's *The*

Bohemian Girl (1843) is played as Frankenstein leaves behind his loving family in pursuit of higher goals. Balfe's music fades in the next scene when Frankenstein enters his laboratory (figure 19). The music then changes to a moderato, followed by an agitato that resonates throughout the creation scene as the Creature assumes his form in a frothy vat of chemicals. The main selection, one played at every entrance of the Creature, derives from Weber's *Der Freischutz,* the opera that perhaps influenced the music of gothic melodrama more than any other.

Like the early dramatizations, every character in the film has been cast as a melodramatic stereotype. Elizabeth is the victimized heroine; Frankenstein plays the mad alchemist whose evil ambition is conquered by love; the Creature appears as the antagonistic opposite of Elizabeth. The film even presents a laboratory assistant, although the script fails to delineate the servant's character beyond the cryptic remark "Servant appears—monster disappears"—almost as if the Creature is subsumed by the servant. Mirroring the early melodramas, the demonic Creature bursts through the laboratory door immediately after his creation. Interestingly enough, the synopsis forecasts quite remarkably the treatment of this scene by later cinematographers:

> *Frankenstein realizes that he has created a monster and tears himself away from the door and stands watching in terror. The iron bars are broken from the doors. Door slowly opens and the hand of the monster appears as Frankenstein dashes off.*

And finally, just as all previous dramatizations gave a terrestrial name and visage to what Judeth Wilt has called the featureless face of dread,[10] so the Edison *Frankenstein* quickly seizes upon the Creature as a powerful image of horror. Charles Ogle as the Creature appears as a hideous wretch—more terrifying than any previous stage creature (figure 20). His Kabuki-like expression, deformed visage, and protruding bulbous eyes instill fright, and his misshapen body, malformed—or unformed—hands, patches of mangy hair sprouting from cadaverous arms, and tattered clothing all suggest a Creature from beyond the grave. Once again, Shelley's intentions are sacrificed to the exigencies of mass appeal.

Eighteen of the film's twenty-five scenes are tinted yellow and orange, and the penultimate scene blue. Although prints of early-century silent films were commonly tinted—blue tint, for example, to represent a night scene—Dawley utilizes tinted scenes to suggest Frankenstein's altered states of consciousness. The tinting achieves its most powerful effect in the creation scene where it is coupled with close-up shots of Frankenstein and medium shots of a fluid-filled vat in which the Creature transubstantiates from primeval elements into a sentient being. The "fluid" obviously al-

The *March 15th* KINETOGRAM 3

EDISON FILMS

Released between March 16th *and* 31st

Edison Film No. 6604 **Copyrighted, Mar., 1910** **Released, Mar. 18, 1910**

Code, VESTIGLO **Approx. Length, 975 feet**

Frankenstein

(DRAMATIC)

A liberal adaptation of Mrs. Shelley's famous story

"FRANKENSTEIN" is considered by nearly all readers of fiction the most harrowing tale that has ever been placed in the field of literature, but strange to say it was created in the spirit of amusement. Lord Byron, Mr. and Mrs. Shelley and one other author, whose name we do not know, were stopping at Geneva, and in order to pass away the time each in turn agreed to write a story of some gruesome, ghastly subject. Of the four that were written Mrs. Shelley's alone remains to be handed down as a work of art. The creation of the Frankenstein monster slowly grew in Mrs. Shelley's mind, possibly much the same as it developed in the character of Frankenstein himself. As a story that reaches the climax of horror and awful suggestion this work stands alone.

In making the film the Edison Company has carefully tried to eliminate all the actually repulsive situations and to concentrate its endeavors upon the mystic and psychological problems that are to be found in this weird tale. Wherever, therefore, the film differs from the original story it is purely with the idea of eliminating what would be repulsive to a moving picture audience.

The Story of Frankenstein as depicted in the film runs as follows:

Frankenstein, a young student, is seen bidding his sweetheart and father good-bye, as he is leaving home to enter a college in order to study the sciences. Shortly after his arrival at college he becomes absorbed in the mysteries of life and death to the extent of forgetting practically everything else. His great ambition is to create a human being, and finally one night his dream is realized. He is convinced that he has found a way to create the most perfect human

Figure 19. Augustus Phillips (right) as Frankenstein in his laboratory and Charles Ogle (left) as the Creature in Edison's *Frankenstein, The Edison Kinetogram* (15 March 1910) (New York Public Library, Billy Rose Theatre Collection).

Figure 20. Charles Ogle as the Creature in Edison's *Frankenstein, The Edison Kinetogram* (15 March 1910) (New York Public Library, Billy Rose Theatre Collection).

ludes to an alchemical elixir vitae, but the juxtaposition of scenes is surely meant to symbolize the formation of an evil subconsciousness. The script reads:

SCENE 7—*Room-In[terior]—Showing the Doors of the Vat—Frankenstein Looks In—Orange & Yellow*

SCENE 8—*Vat—Monster Forming—Orange & Yellow*

SCENE 9—*Room-In—Vat—Frankenstein Looks In—Orange & Yellow*

SCENE 10—*Vat—Monster Forming—Orange & Yellow*

SCENE 11—*Room-In—Vat—Frankenstein Looks In—Orange & Yellow*

SCENE 12—*Vat—Monster Forming—Orange & Yellow*

SCENE 13—*Room-In—Vat—Frankenstein Looks In—Orange & Yellow*

SCENE 14—*Vat—Monster Forming—Orange & Yellow*

SCENE 15—*Room-In—Vat—Frankenstein Looks In—Orange & Yellow*

SCENE 16—*Vat—Monster Forming—Orange & Yellow*

SCENE 17—*Room-In—Vat—Frankenstein Looks In—Orange & Yellow*

SCENE 18—*Vat—Monster Formed—Orange & Yellow*

This realm of narcissistic self-projection culminates in what the synopsis describes as a "closing scene which has probably never been surpassed in anything shown on the moving picture screen." This climax presents the Creature gazing into a mirror in a veiled reference both to the novel and to *Paradise Lost:*

> [W]e see the remarkable sight of the monster's image reflected instead of Frankenstein's own. Gradually, however, under the effect of love and his better nature, the monster's image fades and Frankenstein sees himself in his young manhood in the mirror. His bride joins him, and the film ends with their embrace, Frankenstein's mind now being clear of the awful horror and weight it has been laboring under for so long.[11]

By casting the Creature as Frankenstein's double, Dawley's film quite remarkably forecasts one of the central themes in twentieth-century interpretations of Shelley's novel. The doppelgänger theme has so preoccupied modern critics that the editors of the best collection of essays on the novel "assume rather than argue it."[12] But whereas the novel treads ambiguous ground in suggesting tragic analogues between every character—even between the Creature and Elizabeth—the film follows melodramatic precedent by reducing them to moral contrarieties.[13] Thus, the Creature and Elizabeth represent antipathetic and absolute divisions of good and evil in the solipsistic mind of Frankenstein. As beauty and the beast, they form diametric opposites locked in a spiritual battle for Frankenstein's soul.

Only through Elizabeth's virtuous intercession does Frankenstein survive. As the synopsis specifies:

> [T]he story of the film brings out the fact that the creation of the monster was only possible because Frankenstein had allowed his normal mind to be overcome by evil and unnatural thoughts . . . [W]ith the strength of Frankenstein's love for his bride and the effect of this upon his own mind, the monster cannot exist.

In retrospect, the gothic elements of Edison's *Frankenstein* seem almost to have been written to be filmed. Cinema's special qualities—double exposure, track shots, dissolves, long shots, and most especially, the close-up—adapted horror perfectly to celluloid.

* * *

Twentieth-century drama's first inroad to *Frankenstein* adaptations occurred in 1915 when on 29 July the Thirty Ninth Street Theatre presented a farce entitled *The Last Laugh*. Written by Paul Dickey and Charles Goddard and produced under the management of the Shuberts, *Last Laugh* ran only fifty-two performances, despite predictions by at least one reviewer that it would be a "smashing hit" that would "last a year."[14] The truncated run seems surprising because the play had enjoyed outstanding reviews upon its premier in New York and in both of its out-of-town previews, first in Atlantic City at the Apollo Theatre (29 April), and then in Boston at the Court Theatre (12 May).[15]

Dickey and Goddard's play ignores any philosophical and psychological interpretations and dismisses out of hand the possibility of animating dead tissue. The play's central plot, from which emerge two minor plots, culminates in a practical joke—the last laugh. This plot concerns Dr. McElry Bruce (Henry Harmon) who, fully realizing the impossibility of animating dead tissue, sets out to deceive his mean-spirited associates into thinking he has constructed and animated a creature. In actuality, Dr. Bruce has simply purchased a cadaver in order to teach anatomy to young Dr. David Francis (Everett Butterfield), the fiancé of Dr. Bruce's daughter. The curtain rises on the day Dr. Bruce plans to "animate" the creature. Prior to the curtain, however, Dr. Bruce has surreptitiously replaced the cadaver with his chauffeur, Mike, whom he has anesthetized. In one of the minor plots Dr. Francis replaces Mike, whom he believes to be a real cadaver, with a young jockey named Jim (Edward Abeles, the star of the show) in an effort to avert a failure in what he wrongly believes is Dr. Bruce's final effort to save his reputation. In the other plot, Jim attempts to secure from Dr. Francis his payment of one thousand dollars for posing as a cadaver, while trying to avoid his termagent wife, Marie (Louise Corbin). The replace-

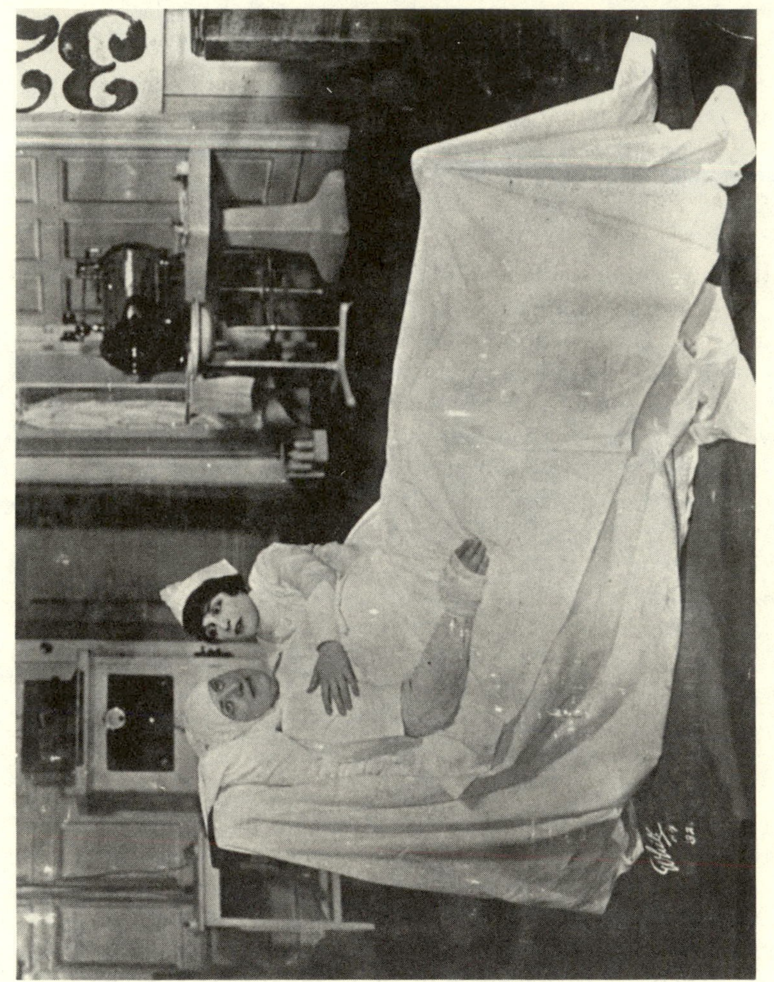

Figure 21. Edward Abeles as the Creature and Inez Plummer as the nurse in *The Last Laugh*, Thirty-Ninth Street Theatre, 1915. (White Studio Photograph, New York Public Library, Billy Rose Theatre Collection).

ment of Mike for Jim sets the stage for a farcical recognition scene between the two "corpses." Moreover, when Mike regains consciousness and pops out of a large crate into which he had been stuffed, only Dr. Bruce realizes the substitution—the rest of the cast assumes that Dr. Bruce has actually succeeded in imparting life to the cadaver. The play bristles with other farcical stage business. The most riotous scene in the play occurs when Jim, as new-born progeny, begs for attention from his gullible young nurse, Eugenia Bruce (figure 21). The *Herald Tribune* described the scene:

> If any audiences have laughed harder than did last night's when Edward Abeles lay back in his chair pretending that he was a full grown baby just brought to life, his head and body swathed in bandages, a pretty girl who believed that he really was a baby cuddling him, and his wife all the while hurling furious insults at him, those audiences will be hard to recall.

But farce is not the most interesting aspect of *Last Laugh*. It will be remembered that many nineteenth-century dramatizations employed farcical scenes. *Frank-in-Steam; or, The Modern Promise to Pay* (1824), for example, concludes when Frank-in-Steam shoves an irate bill collector (a "Spectre Bum") into the boiler of a ship, and *Model Man* (1849) ends with the Creature dancing on stage to the music of a magic flute in a parody of Congreve's observation on music's power over the savage breast. Rather, the most interesting aspect of *Last Laugh* is its abandonment of every popular conception of the myth that had developed through the nineteenth century. Not only does it douse skepticism over the very possibility of animating the dead, but its twentieth-century setting excludes all gothic trappings. Dr. Bruce's laboratory is that of a modern scientist. The policeman who enters with Jim's wife is dressed in an "up-to-date uniform." At one point a character refers to the Woolworth building across the street. And although its music occasionally strikes a melodramatic chord—the first act opens to "weird music"—all of the play's selections derive from popular music of the day. Most importantly, nowhere in the play is the name of Frankenstein mentioned; several reviews even confuse creator and created. For example, the *Sun* (30 July) noted that "the sufferings of the substitute Frankenstein [Edward Abeles] are more humorous to others than to himself." Another review remarked that "Edward Abeles appeared as funmaker extraordinary and Frankenstein pro-tem." And whereas all previous dramatizations present the act of creation as a solitary undertaking pursued by a "mad" young scientist in an alchemist's laboratory, the Frankenstein figure in *Last Laugh* is an aging anatomist whose act of creation is witnessed by three assistants: Dr. Francis, Dr. Dunlop, and Eugenia Bruce, Dr. Bruce's daughter (figure 22). And rather than a lonely and mysterious project, Dr. Bruce's undertaking is currently under discussion in leading medical journals. The first stage description reads: "Act I—Cur-

Figure 22. The Creation Scene from *The Last Laugh,* L to R: Everett Butterfield as Dr. Francis, Inez Plummer as Eugenia Bruce, Henry Harmon as Dr. McElroy Bruce, Albert Gran as Dr. Dunlop, and Edward Abeles as Jim (the Creature). (White Studio Photograph, New York Public Library, Billy Rose Theatre Collection).

tain goes up to reveal Dr. Bruce reading a medical journal article: 'Aged Surgeon's pitiful folly': 'McElroy Bruce, once America's leading Anatomist, tries again to create life.'"[16] And finally, in place of Frankenstein's desire to "penetrate into the recesses of nature," Dr. Bruce is driven by nothing more than the paternal desire to ensure that his daughter marry a successful surgeon.

In keeping with its modern setting, and marking its most important innovation, *Last Laugh* is also the first adaptation in which electricity rather than alchemy provides the primary means of animation. The script devotes three pages of description to the laboratory and its supplies and one and one-half pages to the electrical props. One early reviewer concluded his article: "The scenic effects of the play are impressively realistic; in fact, the operating room, with its electrical machines buzzing, [and] the oxygen and apparatus around to give the average layman the creeps." Actually, electricity figures as the final step in a five-stage process of rejuvenating the "Creature's" senses. But, as the process has nothing to do with animating dead tissue, it serves merely as a stage gimmick. In act two the characters gather around Dr. Bruce, who presides over the elaborate ruse:

Dr. B. Now, gentlemen, we have stimulated the various senses. The eyes with light, the nostrils with ammonia, the ears with sound, the lungs are filled with Oxygen. There remains but one thing more, the final stimulus. When you are ready, Doctor [Meaning Dr. D.] We will apply the current to the nervous system . . .

((lights to blue.))

(Then he goes to C, upstage, starts motor, and works lever reads dial as lights go on, this dial is worked by Electrician off.)

Dr. D. (Reads dial.) 66–85–90 . . .

(One bulb lights on each number called. Dial stops.) 110 doctor—110.

Dr. D. (Reads.) 110—*(dial moves notch on each number)* 105–110 . . .

(Stops dial. All six bulbs now on, stay on till later cue.)

Dr. B. Ready now, doctor?

Dr. D. How long a shock?

Dr. B. Until I stop you.

(Dr. D. turns on switch on control table, Dr. F. comes down with Electrode. Long glass tube, connected to Frequency machine and stands ready at L. end of case.)

Now!!

(Dr. F. puts electrode against the band of iron around Jim's feet. The purple flame shoots, thru glass tube, Jim arches his back in case. Jumps convulsively, at end of shock.)

Dr. B. (Raises his hand, speaks loud.) Stop!! Stop!! *(Dr. F. takes off electrode, hangs it up on bracket up stage. Current still shoots thru Electrode.)*

Dr. B. (Dr. D. shuts off Resonator, switches on control table.) ((Lights ready)) It moves, it moves . . . Do you see it? That's not electricity. The current is off the case. That's life, my creature lives!

Not until Peggy Webling's *Frankenstein: An Adventure in the Macabre* (1927) would Shelley's novel again be dramatized. Analogous to the stitched-together being that Frankenstein created in his "work-shop of filthy creation," the play itself underwent a series of radical transformations.[17] Originally composed as a companion piece for Hamilton Deane's *Dracula* (1925), Webling's play conveniently brings full circle the histories of Lord Ruthven and Victor Frankenstein, two fictional characters who enjoyed a symbiotic relationship throughout the nineteenth century dating back to the summer of 1816 when, at the Villa Diodati and Maison Chappuis respectively, John Polidori composed "The Vampire" and Mary Shelley began *Frankenstein*. In the present case, Deane's *Dracula* can be linked not only to the premier of *Adventure,* but to its revision in 1930 by John Balderston, and ultimately to its incorporation into Universal Studios' *Frankenstein* (1931). Hence, a brief overview of Deane's *Dracula* will help to illustrate the genesis of Webling's production.

Allardyce Nicoll speculates that Deane dramatized Bram Stoker's novel inspired by José Levy's Grand Guignol playlets presented during the early 1920s at the Little Theatre.[18] Another plausible source would be F. W. Murnau's *Nosferatu* (1922). In any case, as Arthur Lennig notes, to the disdain of sophisticated London audiences, Deane premiered *Dracula* in Wimbledon on 9 March 1925.[19] The play succeeded and toured the provinces for two years before finally opening in London at the Little Theatre on 14 February 1927. As Deane had suspected, some critics derided the production;[20] nevertheless, the play enjoyed a successful run of 391 performances.[21] The play crossed the Atlantic in 1927 after being purchased by publisher and theatrical producer Horace Liveright, who had traveled to London from New York "in search of best-sellers and dramatic hits."[22] Liveright most probably hoped to purchase a novel or the performance rights to a play that would allow him to achieve the kind of success he had experienced in 1925 when he published and then produced at the Fulton Theatre in New York Theodore Dreiser's *An American Tragedy.* Film contracts were also a possibility since, as Walter Gilmer indicates, the dramatization of *An American Tragedy* was undertaken specifically to entice a Hollywood studio (139). Liveright returned to the United States with several projects, although according to Gilmer, *Dracula* was the only play optioned in England that he ever produced (150). With the American performing rights in hand, Liveright commissioned John Lloyd Balderston, whose *Berkeley Square* had recently enjoyed success on both sides of the Atlantic, to modernize the dialogue and to tighten the plot (Lennig 66). Featuring Bela Lugosi as Count Dracula, the play premiered first at the

Shubert Theatre in New Haven on 19 September 1927 before opening officially on Broadway at the Fulton on 5 October. The "lousy little play," as Liveright later called it (Gilmer 180), ran 261 performances before closing on 19 May 1928 and going on tour for two years.

Back in London the tributes to *Dracula* were not lost on Peggy Webling, a friend of Hamilton Deane. On 16 November 1927 she submitted to the Office of the Lord Chamberlain a play in three acts and a prologue entitled *Frankenstein: An Adventure in the Macabre*. On 25 November the play received a license, and in Preston on 7 December it premiered alongside *Dracula* with Deane playing the role of the Creature. The two plays toured together for two years, during which time Webling continually revised it. Finally on 10 February 1930 *Adventure* opened at the Little Theatre in London.[23] Although it did not achieve the same success as *Dracula, Adventure* still enjoyed seventy-two matinee and evening performances.

At the very least, *Dracula* kept *Adventure* afloat until its discovery by Liveright. Certainly, Hamilton Deane played an important role, for, just as T. P. Cooke inaugurated both the role of the Vampire and the Creature in the first successful dramatizations of those stories, so Hamilton Deane inaugurated the most important roles in *Dracula* and *Adventure*. And as in 1823 when *Bell's Weekly Messenger* (3 August) noted that *Presumption* was "something in the style of the Vampire, which was so attractive last season," so critics in the twentieth century immediately linked *Dracula* and *Adventure*. An anonymous review states that during the run of *Dracula* "hospital nurses paraded the auditorium on the lookout for fainting subjects. They had better get their uniforms ready again for *Frankenstein*."[24] And while a reviewer for the *Sketch* labeled the play a "junior Dracula," another began his review: "It seems that we are in for another *Dracula*."[25] That *Dracula* preceded and, more importantly, succeeded on Broadway proved that the horror genre was welcome on American shores. Accordingly, on 7 September 1928 Webling submitted one of her final revisions for an American copyright. By the time *Adventure* closed at the Little Theatre on 12 April 1930, Universal was only a few months away from its first treatment of *Dracula*. And less than two months after the film debut of *Dracula,* Liveright had commissioned John Balderston to revise Webling's play for Broadway.

Utilizing the London script, Balderston undertook the revision with apparently little assistance from Webling; according to the *Catalog of Copyright Entries* for 1931 (1 : 3, no. 1614), however, the revision was undertaken with the stipulation that it would be copyrighted in the name of both playwrights.[26] Unfortunately, Balderston's revision was never performed. Less than one month after he filed for copyright, Universal purchased the rights to his dramatizations as well as that of Webling for $20,000 plus one percent of the world gross. Gregory William Mank specifies that the copyright contract "engaged Balderston to provide Universal with a screen adaptation of Miss Webling's play."[27] Nevertheless, so little of Balderston's dramatization appears in the final print that it seems highly possible Universal purchased the rights simply to forestall any unnecessary competition; that is, so that two adaptations of *Frankenstein* would not play simultaneously in New York in 1931, one at the Fulton and one at the Mayfair, where the film opened on 4 December. Perhaps also the script went through so many alterations that elements of Balderston's play became barely recognizable. This second option seems likely, especially since on its way to the Mayfair the film went through two directors (Robert Florey and James Whale), two conclusions (one in which Frankenstein died and one in which he lived), two Creatures (Bela Lugosi and Boris Karloff), one disastrous two-reel test film by Florey, and at least three screenplays: one by Garret Fort and Robert Florey; one by James Whale, who incorporated Florey's ideas, including the substitution of a criminal brain for the Creature (which removes culpability from Frankenstein), and the final conflagration at the windmill;[28] and one by Garret Fort, Francis Edwards Faragoh, and John Russell. German Expressionist cinema also figures as an important influence. Both Florey and Whale reviewed many Expressionist films in preparation for shooting Shelley's novel. A final important influence was Universal Studios' make-up artist Jack Pierce. Obviously influenced by the physical characteristics of the Creature in Paul Wegener's *Der Golem* (1920), of Cesare in *The Cabinet of Dr. Caligari* (1920), and of the Phantom in *The Phantom of the Opera* (1925), Pierce sculpted a cult image—the icon of what Mary Shelley's Creature had become in the one hundred years since he first appeared on the stage.[29]

These sources severely reduced the influence of Webling and Balderston on the final screenplay. As released, the film cast the Creature in the mold of a nineteenth-century dumb show character, added scenes of grave robbing and mountain pursuit, and transformed Frankenstein's home into a Gothic castle and the humble living room in which the creation scenes of Webling and Balderston had occurred into a cavernous laboratory located, as in the early melodramatizations, at the top of a flight of stairs. (In fact, Peake's *Presumption* may have been used as a source for the screenplay because in the Universal film the character of Fritz makes his first appearance since the 1820s.)

The genesis of Webling's play aside, it should be noted that the play's tone and content differ from any previous dramatization of the novel. To a large degree the play can be seen in the context of the theatrical ferment and general disillusion following World War I and preceding the Great Depression, events that validated some of the worst scenarios of the Frankenstein story. Indeed Webling's play may be viewed in terms of an age frightened by a spectre of its own creation. It thus presages the most popular modern theme associated with the novel: society's ability to destroy itself. For only in the twentieth century does the Frankenstein myth fully achieve its apocalyptic dimensions, and only in this century do the topoi of the myth climax in the image of the robots of Karel Capek's *R.U.R.* (1921). However, unlike a challenging piece like *R.U.R.,* which pursues with unrelenting fervor the ramifications of a society capable of destroying itself with its own technology, *Adventure* imbues its plot with a religious diatribe contrary to the novel. In a review of *Adventure, The Sketch* (19 February 1930) immediately noted the indebtedness of *R.U.R.* to Shelley's novel and the manner in which Webling had failed Shelley. As the reviewer observed:

> But the difference between the robot play and the Frankenstein "adventure in the macabre" . . . is that, in "R.U.R." the imagination of the authors created a semblance of reality, whereas this melo-drama is merely a pile of horrors with a gruesome central figure on top, and around him a group of "feeders" who utter bombastic language in order to lead up to terrorizing incidents.

At its best, *Adventure* is the first dramatization to revise completely several popular notions of the Frankenstein myth. But even though it was inspired in the spirit of Levy's Guignol pieces, *Adventure* contains a ponderous three-act format that belies the striking effects achieved in the Guignol playlets. In truth, it contains only an occasional horror and is a pretty dreary treatment of the novel.

Unlike the situation in Mary Shelley's novel, in which Frankenstein renounces alchemy in favor of "new science" only to animate the Creature with what seems to be a combination of both, Webling's Frankenstein never relinquishes his associations with alchemy. As Victor Moritz exclaims to Frankenstein in the first scene: "You wanted to be an alchemist in those days, studying how to turn base metals into gold, or discover the elixir of life." Later in the same scene Frankenstein pulls out a vial and exclaims: "The Elixir—the Elixir of life! I found some of the formula in those old black letter books—I worked out the rest for myself."[30] These alchemical influences recall many nineteenth-century Gothic melodramas, and, therefore, it seems a misnomer to label *Adventure* a "scientific thriller," as does a caption published with a photograph from the London premier (figure 23). Science first enters this dramatization in John Bal-

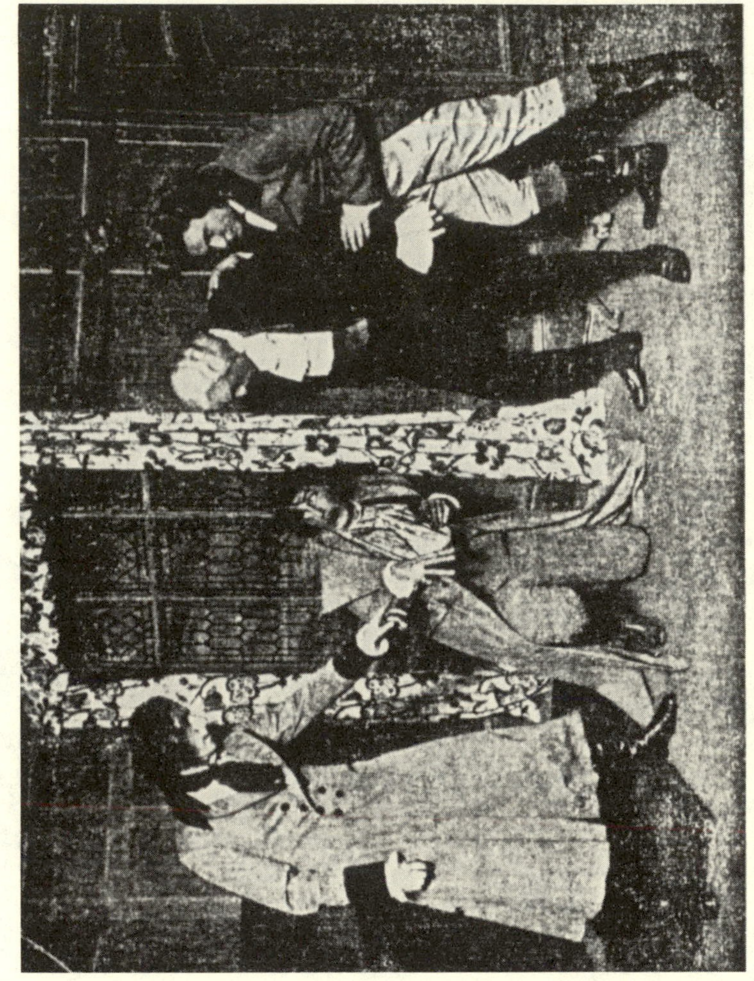

Figure 23. Scene from Act 2 of *Frankenstein: An Adventure in the Macabre* (1930) (London, Mander and Mitchenson Theatre Collection).

derston's revision, in which Frankenstein animates the Creature through a combination of alchemy *and* science. The first scene of Balderston's play presents a "large intricate machine—like a galvanic battery" that dominates the stage. The animation itself may have influenced the Universal production:

Henry. Now is the supreme moment, shall I triumph or shall I fail? *(Attaches wires of galvanic battery to arm, machine fizzes and gives off queer lights, and sends out sparks. Henry rushes to cupboard, brings out small bottle, and pours contents down throat of the body.)*

Victor. What is that?

Henry. The Elixir—the Elixir of life! I found some of the formula in those old black letter books—I worked out the rest for myself. Look—look—both of you.

(They approach fascinated)

Victor (Whispers hoarsely) In the name of religion, Dr.—no! But in the name of Science—do you want him to succeed?

Waldman (Enthusiastically) Yes! Yes—no! God forgive me, what am I saying?

(Silence) You have failed Henry, and I thank Heaven for it.

(Pause) (Thunder and lightning)

Henry (With a scream) I have succeeded.

(The body very slowly clenches and unclenches the right hand that has dropped to the side of the stretcher, makes a gutteral sound, half a groan, half a breath, lifts right arm stiffly, lifts head a few inches, stares at Henry, then drops back. They all stand motionless)

Henry (In wild exaltation) I have made life out of matter that was dead!

Waldman. You make yourself equal with God—that was the sin of the fallen angel!

(As Curtain falls—he drops on knees mumbling) God forgive him, (etc.)

CURTAIN on SCENE ONE

Balderston even offers a pseudo-scientific (albeit anachronistic) explanation for the process of animating dead tissue for the heretofore unexplained "light" that broke in upon Frankenstein as he probed into the causes and generation of life. In the first scene Frankenstein haughtily queries Waldman:

Henry. Dr. Waldman—what is the highest color in the spectrum?

Waldman. Violet.

Henry. Beyond that—we cannot see it—is another stronger violet—an ultra-violet—In the future its rays will be used for health. Beyond that is still another ray, hotter than ultra-violet—life-giving—even life-creating! In the beginning of the world—of all things—

Waldman. In the beginning was the word and the word was God—

Henry. Perhaps He is a ray—an unseen ray beyond the visible spectrum! . . . In this machine—all the rays of the spectrum—the ultra-violet, beyond that—and the *great ray* beyond that—which in the beginning brought Life into the world as the hot mass cooled—

(Gesture) But you would not understand.

Waldman. In the name of Religion, I forbid your experimenting.

Henry. In the name of Science—remain and verify it!

Dr. Waldman's prominent appearance in this scene may be traced to Webling's play, where he appears for the first time in any adaptation. In her play he figures as a moral cynosure, thereby attaining a prominence never accorded to him in the novel where he merely mediates between the scientific rationalism of Dr. Krempe and the romantic ideals of Frankenstein. Balderston imbues this role with some of the attributes of Van Helsig in *Dracula,* which, as I have noted, he had just rewritten for Hamilton Deane. Balderston also expands Waldman's role by polarizing the play between science and religion—Frankenstein rejecting the latter and Waldman, cast as both a scientist and a priest, resenting the perfect moral balance between the two. Hence, Webling and Balderston inject into their dramas an active arbiter of morality akin to the figures of divine intervention encountered in countless nineteenth-century melodramas.

A few of Webling's alterations proved significant. For example, no previous dramatization of Shelley's novel had employed the doppelgänger theme. Nonetheless, as in the Edison film, Webling employs the theme mainly to illustrate a Manichaean battle within the mind of Frankenstein. As Frankenstein observes to Waldman: "I think I was possessed by a devil to begin such a work. All that was dark and hidden and evil in my man's nature gave me power. I was driven on and on by the pride of Lucifer, and in the minute of my triumph I fell! As Frankenstein came to life, my heart died in my breast." Not only does the Creature assume the surname of his maker—"I call him by my own name," Henry Frankenstein says. "He *is* Frankenstein"—but he appears on stage clothed like him as well. Made in his creator's image, the Creature is nevertheless quite hideous. "I can't bear to look at him," remarks Victor Moritz to Frankenstein. "He is strangely like yourself in gesture and movements . . . but a sullen devil looks at me out of his eyes." On 19 February these similarities assumed their most outrageous form when *Punch* lampooned them as clown-like buffoons (figure 24).

Webling extends this doubling to include almost every character in the play. The Creature experiences an overwhelming attraction for Frankenstein's angelic sister, Katrina (figure 25). He also feels drawn to Frankenstein's fiancée, named Emily by Webling and Amelia by Balderston. The fiancée even experiences an attraction to the Creature and a temptation to respond to his advances. "There was some call from his body to mine that I could not deny," Amelia tells Frankenstein. "It was as if one heart, torn asunder, throbbed in his breast and in my own. Our blood ran in the same swift current. He is part of you and part of myself, and we are all one." Furthermore, Victor Frankenstein and Henry Clerval in the novel have

Figure 24. Henry Hallatt as Frankenstein and Hamilton Deane as the Creature, *Punch* (19 February 1930).

Figure 25. Dora Patrick as Katrina and Hamilton Deane as the Creature in *Adventure in the Macabre* (London, Mander and Mitchenson Theatre Collection).

now become Henry Frankenstein and Victor Moritz, suggesting a doubling between the two male companions. Balderston's conclusion carries the doubling even further when after Henry Frankenstein's death Amelia seeks shelter in the arms of Victor Moritz, exclaiming "don't leave me, don't ever leave me." (Frankenstein in this version has after all stolen the heart of Amelia from Victor, to whom she was originally engaged.[31]) Perhaps we should also see sexual ambiguity in Justine Moritz's surname being applied to the Clerval of the novel.

Breaking with Mary Shelley, Webling and Balderston dismiss out of hand her Rousseauistic conception of the Creature as a Noble Savage; instead they cast their Creature as a loutish brute imbued with a child's longing for pleasure and acceptance. While his demeanor has been elevated one notch above the dumb show Creatures of the 1820s, his attraction for Frankenstein's sister and fiancée mirrors the Beauty and the Beast episodes of the earlier dramatists. And contrasted with the Parliamentary rhetoric of Shelley's Creature, who reads Volney and Goethe and who cogitates on the implications of Milton's *Paradise Lost,* the Creature of Webling and Balderston mumbles inchoate syllables, becomes excited by pondering the word "kill," and prays to the sun.[32] "Sun worship—fire worship," scoffs Frankenstein to Waldman in Balderston's version, "he is going through all the instinctive processes of primitive man—both in religion and behavior. Growing children do it too." In this context, "primitive man" has a closer relationship to Hobbes than to Rousseau.

The most important revision made by Balderston to Webling's play concerns the third and last act. Act 2 of Webling's two versions concludes with the Creature's accidental drowning of Katrina. Act 3 then opens the following dawn in the Jura mountains, where the Creature has fled for seclusion. Balderston rewrites Webling's play so that Act 2 closes with the Creature's demand for a mate. Act 3 opens six months later in a hut in the Jura mountains on the day in which Frankenstein finally plans to bring the mate to life. Dr. Waldman arrives in time to persuade Frankenstein to abandon his operation and to destroy the being. When the Creature discovers the mutilated body of his mate, he kills Frankenstein by breaking his back. Waldman then approaches the Creature to enlighten him with Christian repentance and forgiveness:

Frankenstein. Soul—what is soul?

Waldman. It is the part of God He gives to every man who lives. It is the part of man God calls back to himself after man dies. *(FRANKENSTEIN murmurs: "not man.")* That's why I'm not afraid to die. You can kill the body, but not the soul . . .

Frankenstein. Where is God? I thought he — *(Points to Henry)*. God—my God.

Waldman. (Holds crucifix up) No—God is there. Here—everywhere. . . .

Frankenstein. Show—way to Him. Not want . . . kill . . . more.

Waldman. (Holds crucifix up) No—God is there. Here—everywhere. . . .

Frankenstein. Show—way to Him. Not want . . . kill . . . more.

LIGHTNING

Waldman. I cannot do that. I can only tell you—that you must ask him yourself. Ask His forgiveness for your murders.

Frankenstein. (Flash of old ferocity) Men hate me.

(LOUDER THUNDER)

Waldman. Katrina did not hate you. You killed Katrina.

Frankenstein. (Suddenly sobs loudly, backs towards window, holds up hands) Katrina . . . Friend . . . God! *(Stretches up arms)* God help me.

(Lightning strikes hut—some of which crumbles. Lamp goes out—darkness but for brazier. Frankenstein falls, dead, face near brazier, look of peace. . . .)

By borrowing from the novel the demand and partial creation of a mate, Balderston introduces for the first time in any adaptation the theme of self-propagating evil.[33] In terms of the doppelgänger, however, this conclusion has broader implications. For whereas Frankenstein is capable of engendering the male image in the Creature, he cannot project that of the female, the anima, the image that the Creature also lacks. Frankenstein's effort cannot succeed: in terms of Shelley, his failure embodies a renouncement of the Romantic quest; in terms of Balderston, only God can project both the male and the female image. The self can only engender the self in a parthenogenetic and even homoerotic form of creation.

In conclusion, the melodramas of Balderston and Webling culminate over one hundred years of dramatizations of *Frankenstein;* after 1931 the influence of the first Universal film revitalized the myth and echoed through every sphere—dramatic, cinematic, and literary. Given the continued vitality of the Frankenstein legend, it is interesting to remember William Beckford's contumelious remark: "This is, perhaps, the foulest Toadstool that has yet sprung up from the reeking dunghill of the present time."[34] Foul toadstool it may at times be, but it has proven to be a rather resilient toadstool nonetheless.

NOTES

1. Between 28 July 1823, when Richard Brinsley Peake's *Presumption: or, The Fate of Frankenstein* opened at the English Opera House, and 24 December 1887, when *Vampire's Victim* opened at the Gaiety, Mary Shelley's novel was staged seventeen times. Several studios have concerned themselves with these early dramatizations. For a brief bibliography see Steven Earl Forry's "The Hideous Progenies

of Richard Brinsley Peake: *Frankenstein* on the Stage, 1823–1826," *Theatre Research International* 11 (1985) and "Dramatizations of *Frankenstein*, 1821–1986: A Comprehensive List," *English Language Notes* (1988). Excluded from this estimate is the anonymous *Frankenstein; ou, Le Prométhée moderne* (1821), which was never performed and is extant today in a fragmentary manuscript. For a brief discussion of this play see "The Hideous Progenies of Richard Brinsley Peake." Douglas William Hoehn's "The First Season of *Presumption!; or, the Fate of Frankenstein,*" in *Theatre Studies* 26–27 (1978–81): 79–88, concludes with the rather shortsighted observation: "The significance of *Presumption!* from an historical standpoint lies in its relative importance in certain theatrical careers and in its relation to a trend toward melodramas of the preternatural in the London popular theatre of the 1820s" (87). The theatrical careers of the major actors—T. P. Cooke, Robert and Mary Ann Keeley, and James Wallack—were all established before *Presumption,* whose significance lies in its impact on popular conceptions of the Frankenstein myth rather than its impact on melodramas of the preternatural.

2. George Odell notes that at the Olympic Theatre "Professor Tobin's illusion of Frankenstein was shown on February 3rd" (Odell, *Annals of the New York Stage* (New York: Columbia University Press, 1927) 9:274). The *New York Times* (3 February) merely lists Tobin's "wonderful Optical Illusion" (7) among a series of nine other performances comprising a variety show entitled *Alhambra,* which ran eight performances during a one-week engagement beginning 3 February. No mention of Frankenstein appears either in the *Times* or the *New York Post* during this week, but the words "Optical Illusion" must indicate some sort of projected image.

3. Two minor cinematic versions will not be dealt with here: Joseph W. Smiley's Ocean Film Corporation production entitled *Life Without a Soul* (1915) and Eugenio Testa's Albertini Film production entitled *Il Mostro di Frankenstein* (1920). No prints of these two films are believed to exist. *Il Mostro di Frankenstein,* directed by Eugenio Testa from a scenario by Giovanni Drovetti, starred Luciano Albertini as Frankenstein and Umberto Guarracino as the Creature. In *Mary Shelley: An Annotated Bibliography* (New York: Garland, 1975) 224, W. H. Lyles indicates that his correspondence with the Cineteca Nazionale in Rome and the Museo Nazionale del Cinema in Torno verified the existence of the film but failed to locate a synopsis or even photographic stills. A rather troglodytic beast is presented in an early advertisement for this film, which Donald Glut reproduces in *The Frankenstein Catalog* (Jefferson, N.C.: McFarland, 1984) 178. In his *Reference Guide to Fantastic Films: Science Fiction, Fantasy and Horror* (Los Angeles: Chelsea-Lee, 1973) 2:316, Walt Lee notes that in the film Frankenstein "pieces together a creature out of parts of dead bodies and brings it to life." His comment is not documented, however, and probably reflects an assumption on the nature of any story of Frankenstein. *Life Without a Soul* (1915) appears never to have been copyrighted, although the procedure was uniformly adopted for motion pictures in 1912. Directed by Smiley from a screenplay by Jessie J. Goldberg, the film featured William Cohill as Frankenstein and Percy Darrell Standing as the Creature. The five-reel, fifty-five minute melodrama was filmed on location in parts of Georgia, Florida, and Arizona. Smiley even filmed on a steamship in the Atlantic, which must have served as a backdrop

for Walton's ship. The film compromises the novel, however, by including a postscript that explains that the story was simply an horrific dream-vision.

4. In *Motion Pictures 1894–1912* (Washington, D.C.: U.S. Library of Congress, 1953) 21, Howard Lamarr Walls lists a film entitled *Frankenstein's Trestle,* produced in 1902 by the American Mutoscope and Biograph Company (copyright 21 May 1902, H 17964). In *Motion Pictures from the Library of Congress Paper Print Collection, 1894–1912* (Berkeley: University of California Press, 1967) 289, Kemp Niver specifies, however, that *Frankenstein's Trestle* is a 16mm newsreel named after the city in which it was filmed:

> The camera was placed at a distance from a trestle to photograph the full span. The trestle is of a unique design. A steam locamotive, which does not appear to be of American manufacture, pulls four cars toward the camera position and crosses the trestle. The film was photographed in Frankenstein, New Hampshire, in the White Mountains.

5. *The Edison Kinetogram* 2.4 (1910): 3 and *The Bioscope* (5 May 1910): 40. A working scenario dated 14 January 1910 indicates a pre-production estimate of seven hundred feet. See also Walt Lee's *Reference Guide to Fantastic Films* (1:148) and Einar Lauritzen and Gunnar Lundquist's *American Film Index, 1908–1915* (Stockholm: Film-Index, 1976) 204, both of which record the second figure.

6. *Boxoffice Magazine* 5 May 1980. For years it was believed that the only extant documents relating to the film were held in the archives of the Museum of Modern Art in New York, which preserves typescripts of the shooting script, musical score, and press releases, and in the Edison Archives in North Orange, New Jersey, which preserves a copyright file that contains four bromide paper prints of scenes from the film and a letter from the Library of Congress indicating the receipt of material for copyright. In their *Focus on the Horror Film* (Englewood Cliffs, N.J.: Prentice-Hall, 1972), Roy Huss and T. J. Ross reproduce the Museum of Modern Art scenario. Moreover copies exist of *The Biograph* (5 May 1910), which prints a description of the film and of both the 1910 American and English editions of *The Edison Kinetogram,* the cover of which bears a photograph of the Creature (figure 20). All quotations from material held in the Modern Art Museum are used with permission. The *Kinetogram* also contains a detailed plot synopsis and two small stills from the film: one of Frankenstein in his laboratory and one of the Creature in Frankenstein's sitting room (figure 19).

7. See Edward Connor, "The Saga of *Frankenstein,*" *Screen Facts* 1 (1963): 15–30; "*Frankenstein*—1910," *Famous Monsters of Filmland* 23 (1963): 44–45; "The First Frankenstein," *The Monster Times* 21 (1973): 15; and Robert Quackenbush, *Movie Monsters and Their Masters: The Birth of the Horror Film* (Chicago: Whitman, 1980).

8. Bates, "Thomas Edison Created a Monster: Edison's *Frankenstein* is Found" *Clouds* 21 (1979): 8. The existence of the film was confirmed to me in 1980 when Mr. Ted Newsom wrote in private correspondence that late in the 1970s Mr. Dettlaff, who presented himself as an anonymous entrepreneur, had traveled to Los Angeles where he held a private screening for several associates of Mr. Newsom, including

Forrest J. Ackerman. Both Mr. Newsom and Mr. Ackerman provided timely encouragement and invaluable assistance in my search for the Edison film.

9. Acquired thirty years ago from the grandmother of Dettlaff's wife, the film has a running length of 16 1/2 minutes at silent film speed. In a telephone interview conducted on 10 June 1986, Mr. Dettlaff indicated that when he purchased the film stock it has already undergone an 8% shrinkage. To preserve the delicate nitrate, he struck prints on 35, 16, 8, and super 8mm. film and on video cassette. The Museum of Science and Industry in Chicago, The Modern Art Museum in New York, and the Ford Foundation have offered to buy the film, but their low offers have continually been rejected. At some future date Mr. Dettlaff plans to donate the film to the American Academy of Motion Picture Arts and Sciences. In 1985 the Academy planned to use a portion of the film on its Academy Awards show, but producers could not find time for a three-minute excerpt. Therefore, the only circulating footage of Edison's *Frankenstein* exists in a British documentary produced in late 1970 by Polydore, which paid $2,000 for a three-minute excerpt. For other sources of information on Dettlaff and his Frankenstein film see the *Milwaukee Sentinel* (17 December 1976 and 18 March 1985), and *The Milwaukee Journal* (18 March 1985).

10. Wilt, *Ghosts of the Gothic: Austen, Eliot, and Lawrence* (Princeton, N.J.: Princeton University Press, 1980) 6.

11. *The Biograph* shortened the text and published it on 5 May 1910 as a review of films released for that week. "The Return of Frankenstein," in *Famous Monsters of Filmland* 10 (1974): 61, reprints the synopsis of the 15 March *Kinetogram.*

12. George Levine and U. C. Knoepflmacher, *The Endurance of Frankenstein: Essays on Mary Shelley's Novel* (Berkeley: University of California Press, 1979) 15.

13. In "Thoughts on the Aggression of Daughters," Knoepflmacher observes: "yet the beautiful and passive Elizabeth and the repulsive, aggressive monster who will be her murderer are also doubles—doubles who are in conflict only because of Victor's rejection of the femininity that was so essential to the happiness of his 'domestic circle' and to the balance of his own psyche" (Levine, *Endurance* 109).

14. Unless otherwise indicated, all references to and quotations from reviews of *Last Laugh* derive from clippings in the Billy Rose Theatre Collection of the New York Public Library, which has also given permission to quote from the play.

15. For Atlantic City reviews see *The Dramatic Mirror* (5 May), *The Press* (30 April), and *The Morning Telegraph* (30 April). For reviews of the premiere in New York see the *New York Herald, Evening Sun, Globe and Commercial Advertiser, Evening Telegram, New York Tribune, New York Press* and *Sun* for 30 July. See also *Billboard* (5 August), and the *New York American* (9 August).

16. Regarding community and creation in *Frankenstein,* see Wilt's perceptive comments in *Ghosts of the Gothic.* At one point she observes: "it makes *all* the difference in the . . . story of Victor Frankenstein that there is no community present at his Mass—not even an altar boy and certainly not the 'Igor' of popular fancy" (62).

17. Webling's two versions will be distinguished by the city of their debut; thus, the 1927 play will be called the "Preston version," and that presented at the Little Theatre in 1930 will be called the "London version." Where no version is indicated, it is to be assumed that both versions are intended, as is true for the versions of

Webling and Balderston. The Preston and London versions may be read in typescripts located respectively in the British Museum (LCP 1927 B) and in the Library of Congress (D86282). Balderston's revision may also be read in a typescript in the Library of Congress (DU 9603). Quotations from these plays are made with permission of their respective libraries.

18. Nicoll, *A History of English Drama: 1660–1900* (Cambridge: Cambridge University Press, 1955) 6:205–06.

19. Lennig, *The Count: The Life and Films of Bela "Dracula" Lugosi* (New York: Putnam's 1974) 65. Lennig's account also contains an excellent discussion of the filming of *Dracula*.

20. A critic for the *Times* (15 February) attacked the "dreadfully stilted style of speech" that "was so obtrusive that it almost seemed to be an intentional device to assist in making the flesh creep" (10). The critic also noted Hamilton Deane's "moderately efficient performance," while pointing out that the other performances "were not very satisfactory."

21. This figure derives from Alice Katharine Boyd's *The Interchange of Plays Between London and New York, 1911–1939* (New York: King's Crown, 1948) 90. *The Stage Year Book* of 1928 indicates that the performances were spread over four theatres: the Little (from 14 February), the Duke of York's (from 25 July), the Prince of Wales's (from 29 August), and the Garrick (from 10 October).

22. Walter Gilmer, *Horace Liveright: Publisher of the Twenties* (New York: David Lewis, 1970) 150.

23. The conclusion of this play can be contrasted with that of the first registered version as a good example of the type of revision Webling undertook. In the Preston version, the Creature commits suicide by leaping from a rock and Frankenstein is forgiven for his transgressions. When the play opened in London it concluded with the Creature moaning over Frankenstein, whom he has just killed. The Creature then rises, cries out to God, and is quickly struck dead by a lightning bolt from Heaven.

24. Clipping (11 February), Enthoven Collection, Victoria and Albert Museum. The process of introducing nurses into the theatre was obviously for publicity. It was also tried in New York where publicity proved especially important due to heavy competition from other plays on Broadway. As Gilmer notes:

> Worried by the competition of a Theatre Guild production scheduled to premiere on the same night, Liveright and his theatrical manager, Louis Cline, hired a seventy-five man claque to appear at their opening applauding and shouting vociferously. The critics fell for the trick, and the next morning, while they had some reservations about the play, they duly reported that it had elicited cheers and an ovation from the audience. (148)

25. Anonymous clipping (11 February), Enthoven Collection, Victoria and Albert Museum.

26. The copyright contract between Universal and the two playwrights clarifies the fact that Balderston alone was responsible for the revision. Undertaken by Universal in preparation for rewriting *Frankenstein* into a screenplay, the contract was

executed on 8 April 1931. In it the playwrights assigned to Universal "the sole exclusive, free and unencumbered motion picture rights . . . throughout the entire world" to the following:

> (1) The dramatic composition entitled "Frankenstein" based upon the novel by Mary Wollstonecraft (Mrs. Percy B. Shelley) which said dramatic composition was registered for copyright in the United States of America by and in the name of PEGGY WEBLING, September 7th, 1928 under entry NO. D86282.
>
> (b) The dramatic composition as adapted by . . . JOHN L. BALDERSTON based upon the aforesaid dramatic composition, written by PEGGY WEBLING, which said composition was copyrighted as follows: by and in the name of JOHN LLOYD BALDERSTON and PEGGY WEBLING under date of March 11th, 1931 under Entry NO. D89603. . . .

27. Mank, *It's Alive! The Classic Cinema Saga of Frankenstein* (San Diego: Barnes, 1981) 13.

28. The idea for the windmill conflagration came to Florey as he gazed out the window of his apartment on Ivor Street in Hollywood. Below his window stood the windmill trademark of Van de Kamp bakery. As Florey later commented on his alterations:

> Je dissimulais, dans mon histoire, le laboratoire du chimiste Frankenstein dans une ruine de moulin à moitié détruite depuis plus d'un siècle. Je batis ensuite l'épisode de la substitution des cerveaux et de la création du monstre; mille details des films macabres des vieux films muets allemands, des situations grand guignoles du Théâtre de l'Epouvante française, tous les récits d'horreur que nous absorbions en cachette, autrefois, au collège me revenait en tête, mais j'évitais de me laisser aller à ces reminiscences trop faciles en tachant de créer du nouveau, d'écrire dans le domaine du fantastique quelque chose d'un peu différent. Florey, *Hollywood d'hier et d'aujourd'hui* (Paris: Editions Prisma, 1948) 164.

29. For an interesting discussion of these influences see Albert J. LaValley's "The Stage and Film Children of *Frankenstein:* A Survey," in Levine, *Endurance* 243–89. See also Mank's excellent *It's Alive!* and John Stoker's *The Illustrated Frankenstein* (New York: Sterling, 1980).

30. In Preston and in London, Frankenstein, whose given name Webling altered to Henry, administers the elixir before wheeling the Creature on stage where he comes to life. The Preston version of the creation scene (in which "F." in the stage directions refers to the Creature) reads:

> *Henry.* No! I have succeeded. Look!
>
> *(Henry slowly draws drapery off F. After a slight pause, F. very slowly clenches and unclenches his hand hanging down at side of lounge. Then stretches his arms over his head and raises himself on one elbow. Henry utters a wordless exclamation, or groan, but the other men remain speechlessly gazing. F. stands up, thrusts both hands in front of him, as if groping in the dark, his head sunk on his chest. After a few seconds he lifts his head, in the full light of the lamp, his mouth a little open, eyelids quivering. At last he opens his eyes and stares blankly in front of him.)*

When it reached London, the scene for some reason had been rewritten into a remarkable anticlimax in which the Creature clenches and unclenches his hand, groans slightly, lifts his head—and faints.

31. Universal very clumsily retains a hint of this attraction when Victor informs Elizabeth: "You know I'd go to the ends of the earth for you." To which Elizabeth replies: "But I shouldn't like that. I'm far too fond of you." Victor then muses: "I wish you were here." The only hint of the doppelgänger that Universal retains occurs when the Creature and Frankenstein gaze at each other across the spinning cogs of a wheat grinder in the burning mill.

32. As versions of the play evolved from Preston to Balderston, the Creature gradually became fiercer. For example, in Preston, upon hearing the word "kill," the Creature reacts by *"interrupting quickly"* and reciting "Kill? Kill!" In London the text becomes: "*(loudly and fiercely, springing to his feet)* Kill! Kill! Kill?" Finally, in Balderston's revision we read: "*(Fiercely questioning, but questioning triumphantly)* Kill? KILL! *KILL!*"

33. It must be noted that *Vampire's Victim* (1887) includes a vampire-mate for the Creature. In that play, however, the situation is employed simply to burlesque the frustration of the mate, who cannot suck blood from the veins of her terra cotta husband. Therefore, procreation is not really an issue.

34. Howard B. Gotlieb, *William Beckford of Fonthill* (New Haven, Conn.: Yale University Press, 1960) 61.

4

Afterword and List of Plays, 1821–1986

"Betty, we haven't created puppy dogs; we've
created Frankenstones!"
Wilma Flintstone

THE CARTOON-WORLD of the Flintstones draws its vitality from anachronism.[1] Their world extends beyond the too-cuddly and diminutive Pebbles, beyond the rambunctious, club-wielding Bambam, and beyond the huge brontosaurus burgers ordered by Fred at late-night drive-ins. "Frankenstone" in Wilma's mouth evokes an immediate image in the minds of twentieth-century viewing audiences. But her evaluation of Fred and his neighbor Barney Rubble, both hypnotized into following their wives' every command, derives its comedy not from the anachronistic juxtaposition of stone-age somnambulists and a fictional character from a nineteenth-century novel so much as it does from the unexpected yoking of the avuncular Fred and Barney with the frightening image of Boris Karloff and his modern prototypes. And just as her pusillanimous exclamation derives comedy from referentiality, so every post-Karloff adaptation of *Frankenstein*—consciously or unconsciously—cannot be viewed outside the context of the prototypes that descend from Karloff.

The influence of these prototypes has echoed through every genre—dramatic, cinematic, literary . . . and cartoon. In fact, comic books and strips have regularly feasted on the Frankenstein story, playing an important role in the formation of modern perceptions of the myth.[2] To cite but one example from Glut's excellent *The Frankenstein Catalog,* the first Frankenstein comic book series "began as a straight and grisly horror strip and continued in that style for many continued episodes. Gradually, however, the Monster (or "Frankenstein" as he came to be called) lost much of his size and menace, becoming a patriotic hero during World War II. By the end of the series the strip had evolved into an outright humorous feature with no resemblance at all to the earlier tales."[3] Obviously 1931 stands as the watershed in terms of Frankenstein adaptations. Since that date over one hundred films and, as I have noted, over seventy dramatizations have been completed.[4] And whereas before 1931 *Frankenstein* had been translated into only three languages—French, Italian, and German—after this date it appeared in at least nineteen, including Hindi and Sanskrit. Finally, where only twenty-two editions of the novel were published prior to 1931, since that date over eighty English and foreign-language editions have been printed.[5]

Like the fanzines, post-War dramatizations gleefully set on the story of Frankenstein. As I conceive the whole, the plays of this period may be divided into at least four groups, although several plays overlap and many other small variations exist. Significantly, and not surprisingly, each trend develops in reaction to the impact of cinema, first to the eight movies that comprise the Universal cycle (1931–1948), and then to the enormous number of B-rate productions spawned by "The Curse of Frankenstein" (1957), the first of the Hammer cycle.

The first group includes comic dramas in the tradition of Universal's "Abbott and Costello Meet Frankenstein" (1948). These dramatizations achieve their comic effect simply through parody and allusion. For example, Tom Eyen's *Frankenstein's Wife* (1969), one of four plays in the program *Four "No" Plays,* mocked the pretentiousness of the then popular Living Theatre *Frankenstein.* In the stage directions to *The Frankensteins are Back in Town* (1981), Tim Kelley, the most prolific adaptor of Shelley's tale, specifically indicates that the Creature's mate wear a "hairstyle in the classic 'Bride of Frankenstein' film." The cover drawing of his *The Bride of Frankenstein* (1976) presents a flower-bearing Boris Karloff and an angry-looking Elsa Lanchester. And on the cover of his *Frankenstein Slept Here* (1974), a Karloff-like Creature sits erect upon an operating table connected to a transformer that showers the laboratory with electrical sparks.

The true beginnings of this type of comic adaptation may be dated from 1970 when Sheldon Allman and Bob Pickett mercilessly spoofed *Frankenstein* in their *I'm Sorry the Bridge is Out, You'll Have to Spend the Night,* which featured not only Frankenstein and his Creature, but Igor, Count and Countess Dracula, the Mummy, and Prince Rex Talbot. Following suit, the dramatis personae of Steven Otfinoski's delightful *Love of Frankenstein* (1979) includes Ygor, Bela Lugosi, a transvestite Ludovic Praetorius, the Creature's bride; and a lycanthropic Lawrence Talbot in the role of a timid Reverend. A playbill for the production portrays the Karloff-Creature delivering a box of Valentine chocolates to his mate (figure 26). The opening stage directions clearly state a desire to mirror the Universal cycle:

The curtain rises on a large room in the Castle Frankenstein. Or to be more accurate, the Castle Frankenstein as it would appear in a grade B horror movie of the forties, a poor man's version of Kenneth Strickfadden's famous laboratory set for Universal's classic Bride of Frankenstein.

In a wonderful gibe at the horror tradition, the climax of the play presents Reverend Talbot who, while joining in matrimony the Creature and his mate, begins to transform into a werewolf:

Talbot. Marriage not only curbs our appetite for the flesh . . .

(Talbot's hairy hand, like Dr. Strangelove's, is taking on a life of its own. It is scratching his chest.)

But also exalts it to a higher spiritual plane.

(He suddenly sights the hairy hand, stares at it and grabs it with his other and forces it down to his side.)

Indeed, without marriage, what would become of our society?

(He begins to scratch one leg with the other, as a dog would) . . .

Therefore, as we proceed with the sacred ritual, let each and every one of us pray . . .

(He manages to get back to an upright position and slip the garlic necklace over his neck. He turns back to face audience with more confidence.)

. . . that these two (*looking at couple*) somethings, will find the strength . . .

(His "bad" hand is trying to tear off the garlic. He grabs it again with other hand and forces it behind his back clasping both hands there as if it were a natural pose.)

. . . and fortitude to live up to the full challenge of their vows today and for the rest of their natural . . . lives . . .

(He throws back his head and lets out a blood-curdling howl. In mid-howl he clamps his "bad" hand over mouth, looking from side to side for the reaction of the others, who stare in disbelief, too shocked to take any action . . . He picks up the pistol and prepares to shoot himself in the head with the silver bullet; he recites the following very fast.)

Do you, whatever-you-are, take this woman to be your wife, to have and to hold, for richer or poorer, in sickness and in health, for better or worse, til DEATH DO YOU PART?!

(He fires, but his hand is fighting against him and the bullet goes astray, striking the Monster in the stomach.)

Monster. ARRGGGGHHHHHH!

Talbot. (Dropping his pistol, the noise bringing him back to himself). I'm sorry, come again?

Ygor. (Holding back Monster from attacking Talbot, nodding head wildly). He said YES!

Talbot. (Reaching for stake and mallet). Good! Then by the power invested in meeeEEEE!

(He puts the stake up to his heart and draws back the mallet with the other hand.)

I . . . now . . . pronounce . . . you . . . MAN AND WIFE!

(He drives the mallet into the stake. Blood pours forth, he goes rigid and falls back across the altar, dead. The others start to move in toward him. Before they get too close, he suddenly lifts his head and speaks in his normal voice.)

You may now kiss the bride.

Figure 26. Playbill from Steven Otfinoski's *Love of Frankenstein* (1979).

The majority of musical adaptations of *Frankenstein* fall into this first category. Richard O'Brien's *The Rocky Horror Show* (1973), which now also circulates as *The Rocky Horror Picture Show* (1975) and *The Rocky Horror Picture Show Book* (1979), must be regarded as the most successful modern musical adaptation of Frankenstein themes. Four other musical comedies can also be noted. Greg Sandow and Thomas Disch's *Frankenstein* (1981), Peter Walker and Katherine Jean Leslie's *Frankenstein Follies* (1977), Tony Connor's *Dr. Crankenheim's Mixed-Up Monster* (1974), and Roger David Lewis and Lloyd Lockwood's *Frankenstein Crankenstein; or, Body Building for Beginners* (1981).

Written for teenagers, *Frankenstein Follies* is a juvenile comedy that utilizes the familiar plot of lost vacationers who inadvertently come across a haunted castle. The story concludes with the moral that behind an ugly (and probably bepimpled) face lies a beautiful person. As one character observes: "When Mike and Judy take off their [monster] make-up, they'll probably find that the outer appearance didn't matter that much. There must have been something more to it than mere appearance." Tony Connor intends his *Dr. Crankenheim's Mixed-Up Monster* for an even younger audience, but there exist in his play a joy and frivolity absent from *Frankenstein Follies*. Connor knows his audience well and never loses touch with its expectations. His play concerns mad Dr. Crankenheim who, with the aid of a Psychophysical Resuscitator, hopes to animate the perfect being. Unfortunately his laboratory assistant, Joey, alters the machine's dials, resulting in a botched job and a hideous parti-colored Creature with a huge nose and ears. Recruited to star in "Godzilla Meets Son of the Loch Ness Monster," Dr. Crankenheim and his Creature soon learn that their devious director, Ulysses X. Zonk, is nothing more than a criminal. Crankenheim and the Creature flee to the laboratory, where the Creature is placed back in the Psychophysical Resuscitator and transformed into a handsome rock star.

Not much needs to be added concerning Lewis and Lockwood's *Frankenstein Crankenstein,* set in the Black Forest health institute of Dr. Frank Norman Stein. The institute functions as a ruse to entice health-conscious people who, upon arrival, are dissected and stored in a refrigerator by Igor, the laboratory assistant. The play concludes when Frankenstein, struck and supposedly killed by a bolt of lightning, returns from the grave in the midst of a revelling chorus that sings:

> Frankenstein, Crankenstein
> Never to be released.
> Frankenstein, Crankenstein
> Surely by now deceased.

You would think by now they would know better.

Dramatizations of the second group reject distortions wrought on the myth by popular media and return to the novel as a source of inspiration. For example, many playwrights now quote directly from the novel. Fred Fondren's *Frankenstein* (1981) concludes with the Creature paraphrasing the last words of the novel. Victor Gialanella's much maligned *Frankenstein* (1981), which lost two million dollars when it closed on Broadway the day after its premier, begins with a voice-over in which Walton narrates his letters to his sister. Similarly, Alden Nowlan and Walter Learning's *Frankenstein: The Man Who Became God* (1974) opens aboard Walton's ice-bound ship with Walton reading from his diary-like letters. Several playwrights even state their outright opposition to the cinematic dominance of the myth. Tim Kelley remarks in the preface to his *Frankenstein* (1971) that it is "Perhaps the truest adaptation of Mary Shelley's classic yet." In the preface to *Frankenstein: The Man Who Became God* (1974), Nowlan and Learning announce: "Our play . . . is . . . the first dramatic version faithful in design and spirit to the book." John Edwards has a similar goal when in the program notes to *Frankenstein; or the Modern Prometheus* (1958) he writes: "Our production is the novel—just as Mary Shelley wrote it—without a line changed or rewritten." Most importantly, these dramas debunk any presentation of the Creature as a ferocious beast bent on man's destruction. Kelley forthrightly observes in the preface to his 1971 drama: "The Creature of Mary Shelley is not the monster of the film versions." Libby Jacobs echoes this concern in the preface to her absorbing *Sparks* (1984): "The Creature who confronts Victor is not the clenched monster of the Hollywood versions of the novel, but is instead the flawed, articulate innocent conceived by Mary Shelley." In plays like Fred Fondren's *Frankenstein* (1981) and especially Laurence Maslon's recent *Mary Shelley's Frankenstein* (1985) the Creature expresses enormous sensitivity and intelligence. In fact, Guy Paul's brilliant performance as the Creature in the latter production saves a rather lackluster dramatization. In the case of Fondren's play, the Creature exhibits more humanity than any other character. And as in the novel, the play concludes with the Creature's promise to destroy himself in a funeral pyre.[6] At the play's conclusion, Frankenstein dies in the Creature's lap after having accidentally shot himself with a bullet meant for the Creature. Elizabeth, her gypsy maid Eitsirhc Ahtaga, who, like her name (an anagram for Agatha Christie), speaks backwards, and the butler Noryb Drol (Lord Byron) gather around him:

> *The Creature. (Realizing that VICTOR has been wounded, he gently holds him as if trying to defend the breath of life. Then pleading desperately.)* Maker, do but live. I must tell you something!
>
> *Elizabeth.* So you are the murderer he sought . . .
>
> *The Creature.* Do not fear. I mean you no harm.

Eitsirhc. (With great fright.) Mistress, Nomedyfonam, Nomedyfonam. [Man of demon, Man of demon.]

The Creature. (Still cradling VICTOR's now lifeless body, he screams back.) NO!

(Then more normally as if confessing.)

Nomedyfonam atonmai. [I am not a man of demon.]

(. . . quoting from Paradise Lost).

"Did I request thee, Maker, from my clay to mould me man?
Did I solicit thee from darkness to promote me?"

(Then as if to defend himself to the others.)

I did intend him now no harm. His death was not my revenge . . . I have no God! My creator is here, lifeless, destroyed by my hands. No guilt, no misery can be found comparable to mine . . .

(Elizabeth reaches The Creature who passes to her the burden of his Maker which she accepts, holding Victor to her.)

You were created in God's image, but I was created in man's image and learned my sins from him. But fear not that I shall be the instrument of future crime. No death but mine is needed to consummate the series of my being.

Elizabeth. You would try to exonerate your sin by the sin of suicide?

The Creature. (As he descends the stairs and moves to the front door.) I have no law and no soul to be saved by following the law. Even the Fallen Angel has associates in his desolation.

(Pause. Then with the quiet finality but great passion of a Prometheus on the mountain.)

I am alone . . . If thou canst hear my prayer, Frankenstein, know that I shall seek the northern-most extremity of the globe and consume in flame this miserable frame that its remains may afford no temptation for another as I have been. My ashes will be swept into the sea by the winds. I and your misery shall be extinct forever. Farewell, Frankenstein!

(He springs out the door and after one beat too fast)
BLACKOUT
CURTAIN

The third group contains the widest number of plays because it embraces both Shelley and her adaptors, especially the Universal cycle. Although Ken Eulo's *The Frankenstein Affair* (1979) presents a provocative biographical reading of Shelley, its playbill still presents a full-length profile of a growling, Karloff-like Creature (figure 27). Nowlan and Learning include in their play a laboratory assistant named Fritz (figure 28), and Christopher O'Neil, in *Frankenstein: The Monster Play* (1980), presents an extremely sensitive Creature and yet also includes a laboratory assistant named Igor and concludes the piece with a conflagration. And despite his prefatory remarks to the contrary, Tim Kelley's melodrama contains a somewhat Karloff-like Creature. As the production notes indicate:

> . . . his makeup should reveal many stitches. Corners of the mouth, neck, eyes, forehead, as well as the wrist. Perhaps a bolt or two here and there. . . . Some clumsy boots help to enhance the effect. . . . and his costume should be dark and threadbare and homespun in appearance. The jacket should be too short in the sleeves to give a "gangling" effect.

Figure 27. Playbill from Ken Eulo's *The Frankenstein Affair* (1979).

Figure 28. Bill Cole as Victor Frankenstein, Claude Rae as Fritz, and Larry Aubrey as Clerval in Alden Nowlan and Walter Learning's *Frankenstein—The Man Who Became God* (1974).

In plays of this group the Creation scene represents the best example of the influence of Universal Studios, for electrical apparatus reminiscent of Kenneth Strickfadden still figures as the most popular means of animating the Creature. The creation scene of Dan Duling's exciting *A Dream of Frankenstein* deliberately alludes to James Whale's film when at its pyrotechnic conclusion the exhausted Frankenstein cries: "It lives! It lives!" The most outstanding creation scene ever presented on stage occurred in Victor Gialanella's *Frankenstein*. Modeled on Strickfadden's set (figure 29), Brian Ferren's laboratory contained an electric coil capable of producing two million volts and called for 32,000 watts (as compared to 800 to 1,500 watts for a typical Broadway musical).

Playwrights of the fourth and smallest play grouping politicize the novel in terms of apocalyptic observations of life in the modern age. Megan Terry and Dan Newmark's *Frankenstein,* a musical produced at the Scorpio Rising Theatre in Los Angeles on 26 July 1974, serves as an excellent example. Glut summarizes the play in his *Catalog:*

> Set in "Amerika . . . a little bit in the future." Handsome "Frankenstein" is cloned from the cells of the most brilliant and physically perfect man of all time, to save the world from oppression. He becomes, instead, corrupted by young revolutionaries. When his maker lets his newly created Mate live and then die, "Frankenstein" kills the doctor and prepares to launch himself into the sun, reducing himself to primal matter to be reborn in the future.

The first post-1931 dramatist to employ the story in this fashion was Gladys Hastings-Walton, whose *Frankenstein: A New Version of an Old "Thriller"* (1933) borrowed its plot and dialogue from Peake's *Presumption* while prefacing the action with the caveat that the Depression was a Frankenstein-like creation. Two years later Alfred Kreymborg employed the same theme in his poem "Frank and Mr. Frankenstein: A Play Upon the Dollar," which criticized the Capitalistic ventures of Mr. Frankenstein, a banker, at the expense of Frank, the working man.

The Living Theatre *Frankenstein* (1965) is probably the best-known representative of the "activist" school, although Clive Barker's *Frankenstein in Love; or, The Love of Death (A Grand Guignol Romance)* (1982) is arguably the most challenging adaptation ever written. The play, set in a banana republic undergoing a state of siege, captures the plight of humankind caught in a dystopic, godless universe. Frankenstein appears as a sadomasochistic vivisectionist who at one point orders that the Creature, like St. Bartholomew, be flayed alive (figure 30). Driven by such diverse forces as the Grand Guignol, the theatre of Artaud and of the Absurd, Jacobean masques, and Wells's *The Island of Dr. Moreau,* Barker's play is unrelenting in its pessimistic view of the sordid acts to which humans somehow aspire.

Figure 29. Keith Jochim as the Creature in Victor Gialanella's *Frankenstein* (1981). Photo: Martha Swope.

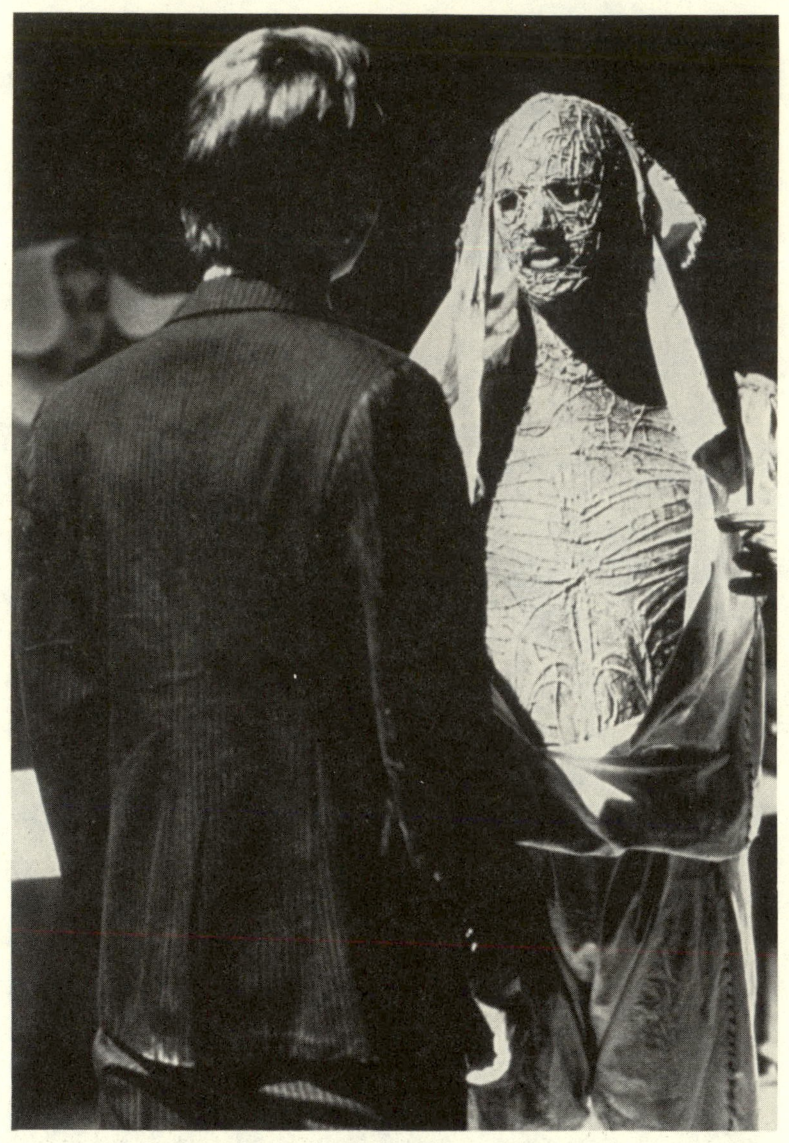

Figure 30. Oliver Parker as the Creature and Douglas Bradley as Dr. Joseph Frankenstein in Clive Barker's *Frankenstein in Love* (1982). Photo: John Greenwood.

The play is haunted by the figure of Maria Reina Duran, a palm-reader and fan-dancer who, like a zombie, returns nightly to relive the scenes of her death and to retell the tale of Frankenstein. Many excellent scenes could be quoted at length to illustrate the fervor of Barker's prose and the intensity of the play. One of the most moving occurs when Maria attempts to read the Creature's palms. Called El Coco in the play, the Creature has two lifelines because he has been constructed from two different corpses: he represents a living conundrum, the embodiment of the contradictions of existence (figure 31):

Maria. Your hands, they're odd. They don't match. Why don't your hands match?
El Coco. Poor workmanship. Read!
Maria. It frightens me; I don't want it. There's something wrong.
El Coco. Read!
Maria. I can't make sense of two futures: they're different.
El Coco. Tell what's there. Please . . .
Maria. *(She looks at the left hand)* Gentle. *(right hand)* Murderer. *(left hand)* No children. *(right hand)* No father. *(left hand)* Long life. *(right hand)* Short life: dead: already over. It makes no sense. *(left hand)* Old. *(right hand)* Young. It's all contradictions. It's nonsense.
El Coco. Read. The future.
Maria. There's no future for dead men. Wait. The life line stops and starts again. *(left hand)* Success. *(right hand)* Violent death. *(left hand)* and yet success. *(right hand)* Horrors: pain: murder. You commit murder. Many murders. *(left hand)* Joy: marriage: love forever.
El Coco. Love?
Maria. Content?
El Coco. You wouldn't lie?
Maria. There's no pattern to it: just chaos.
El Coco. I'll make sense of it . . . I can tell you who my hands are. This *(the left)* is a writer's hand; he died old, and blind. He wants nothing better than to hold a pen and write fictions. He obeys me, sometimes.
Maria. And the other one?
El Coco. A dice-player: he shot his children, then himself.
Maria. A young man?
El Coco. Twenty-three. Impulsive; proud; angry. He wants freedom. He wants to be away, off like a spider to find a grave. Sometimes I see him smiling at me with his creases and his tucks. They hate each other, the writer and the dice-player. And you know what's worst about that? I can't pray—*(He brings his hands together: they fight)*—because they hate each other so much. *(He pulls them apart)* Is there salvation for a man whose hands won't pray?

* * *

To this brief overview I now append a comprehensive list of dramatizations of Shelley's novel. In this list the plays are cited by year, playwright, title, and (when known) theatre and date of first production. Unless otherwise specified, all productions occurred in London. For pre-1931 adaptations I include in brackets the locations of manuscripts and typescripts; when a play has been published, I include the publisher's name and the year of publication. I

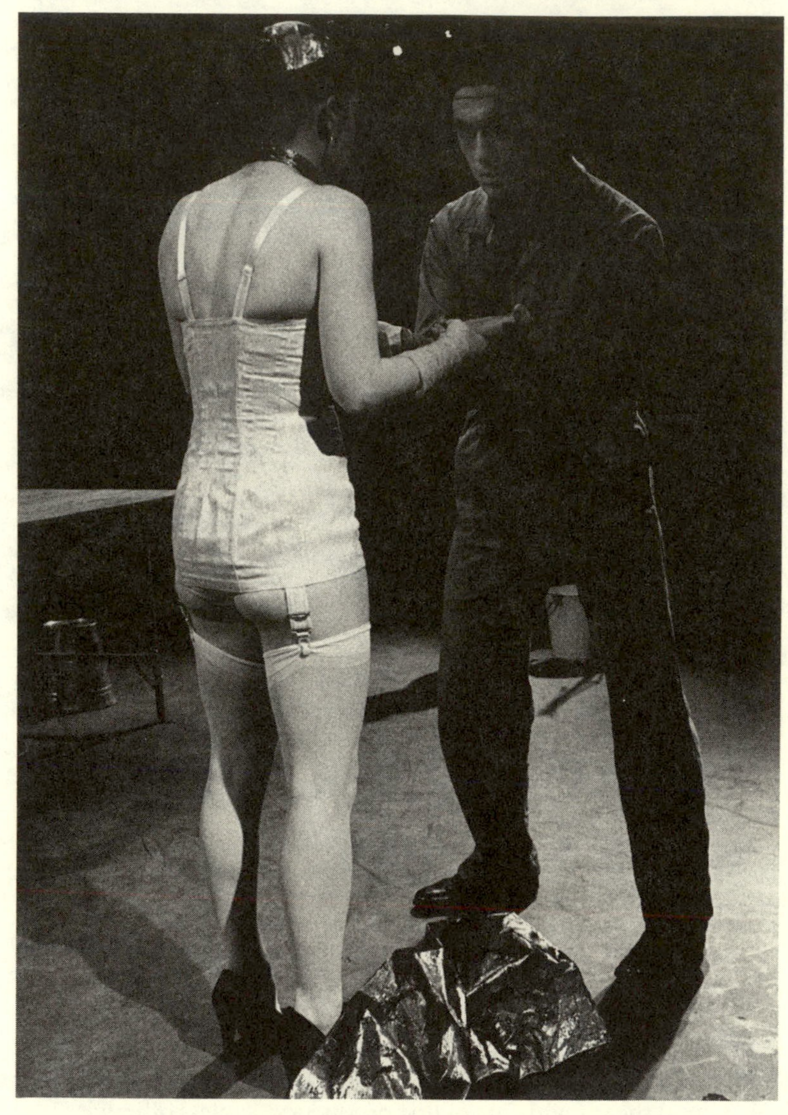

Figure 31. Oliver Parker as the Creature and Lynne Darnell as Maria Reina Duran in Clive Barker's *Frankenstein in Love* (1982). Photo: John Greenwood.

list only plays written to be performed as dramatic pieces, a decision that eliminates such obviously unperformed titles as *Presumption; or, The Fate of the Episcopals,* the monster-filled sixth act of *Hamlet* as published in *The Man in the Moon* in 1847, and Alfred Kreymborg's poem "Frank and Mr. Frankenstein." Parenthetical numbers following pre-1931 productions indicate the approximate number of performances achieved by each play upon its debut. Citations followed by the word "Glut" and a page reference refer to plays listed in Glut's *Catalog* that I have been unable to verify. Any additions or corrections to this list will be gratefully acknowledged.[7]

LIST OF DRAMATIZATIONS

1. 1821—*Frankenstein; ou, Le Prométhée moderne* (No record of performances). [Bibliothèque de l'Arsenal MS. p. fol°, aoust 1821./A.T. sc Ms carton 8]. [Note: This play consists of a fragmentary manuscript of one act (six leaves) and a single leaf of act two.] (Never performed)

2. 1823—Richard Brinsley Peake, *Presumption; or, The Fate of Frankenstein* (English Opera House, 28 July 1823). [Huntington Library MS., LA 2359; *Dicks* (no. 431). c. 1865] (37) (Subsequently produced at the Royalty Theatre for twelve nights under the title *Frankenstein; or, The Danger of Presumption.*)

3. 1823—Henry M. Milner, *Frankenstein; or, The Demon of Switzerland* (Royal Coburg Theatre, 18 August 1823). (8)

4. 1823—*Humgumption; or, Dr. Frankenstein and the Hobgoblin of Hoxton* (New Surrey Theatre, 1 September 1823). (6)

5. 1823—*Presumption and the Blue Demon* (Davis's Royal Amphitheatre, 1 September 1823). (2)

6. 1823—Richard Brinsley Peake, *Another Piece of Presumption* (Adelphi Theatre, 20 October 1823). [Huntington Library MS, LA 2374] (9)

7. 1824—*Frank-in-Steam; or, The Modern Promise to Pay* (Olympic Theatre, 13 December 1824). [British Library MS, Add. MSS 42869] (4)

8. 1826—Jean Toussaint Merle and Antoine Nicolas Béraud [pseud. Béraud Antony] *Le Monstre et le magicien* (Paris: Théâtre de la Porte Saint-Martin, 10 June 1826). [Paris: *Bézou,* 1826] (94)

9. 1826—Henry M. Milner, *The Man and the Monster; or, The Fate of Frankenstein* (Royal Coburg Theatre, 3 July 1826). [*Duncombe* (vol. 2), c. 1828; *Lacy* (vol. 75), 1867. Stephen Wischhusen reprinted the Duncombe edition in *The Hour of One* (London: Fraser, 1975)] (8)

10. 1826—Nicolas Brazier, Guillaume Dumersan and Gabriel-Jules-Joseph de Lurien, *Les Filets du Vulcain; ou, Le Vénus de Neuilly* (Paris: Théâtre des Variétés, 5 July 1826). [Paris, Duvernois, 1826] (23)

11. 1826—Jules-Henri Vernoy de Saint-Georges and Antoine-Jean-Baptiste Simonnin, *Le Petit monstre et l'escamoteur* (Paris: Théâtre de la Gaîeté, 7 July 1826). [Paris: Boquin de la Souche, 1826] (37)

12. 1826—Claude-Louis-Marie de Rochefort-Luçay [pseud. Edmond Rochefort], Esperance-Hippolyte Lassagne, and Mathurin-Joseph Brisset, *La Pêche de Vulcain; ou, l'île des fleuves* (Paris: Théâtre du Vaudeville, 10 July 1826). [Paris: Brunet, 1826]. [Note: The title page of the printed play incorrectly dates the premiere as 5 June.] (1?)

13. 1826—*Le Présomteueux* (Paris: Théâtre de M. Comte, 11 July 1826). (5)

14. 1826—P. Carmouche, *Les Filets de Vulcain; ou, le lendemain d'un succès* (Paris: Théâtre de la Porte Saint-Martin, 15 July 1826). (?) [Note: *Le Journal des Débats* (18 July) indicates that "Carmouche," is a pseudonym for "a well-known triumvirate."]

15. 1826—*Le Monstre et le physicien* (Paris: Théâtre de M. Comte, 3 August 1826). (29)

16. 1826—John Kerr, *The Monster and Magician; or, The Fate of Frankenstein* (New Royal West London Theatre, 9 October 1826). [London: Kerr, c. 1826] (4?)

17. 1849—William and Robert Brough, *Frankenstein; or, The Model Man* (Adelphi Theatre, 26 December 1849). [British Museum MS, Add. MSS. 43023] (54)

18. 1861—Ferdinand Dugué, *Le Monstre et le magicien* (Paris: Théâtre de l'Ambigu Comique, 22 June 1861). [Paris: Libraire Théâtrale, 1861] (60)

19. 1887—Richard Henry [pseud. Richard Butler and Henry Chance Newton], *Frankenstein; or, The Vampire's Victim* (Gaiety Theatre, 24 December 1887). [British Museum TS, L.C. 53392B] (106)

20. 1915—Paul Dickey and Charles Goddard, *The Last Laugh* (New York: Thirty-Ninth Street Theatre, 29 July 1915). [NYPL, TS., NCOF p.v. 303; deposited with Library of Congress on 19 May 1915, TS, D40698] (52)

21. 1927—Peggy Webling, *Frankenstein: An Adventure in the Macabre* (Preston, England: Empire Theatre, 7 December 1927). [British Museum, TS, L.C.P. 1927 B] (4)

22. 1928—Peggy Webling, *Frankenstein: An Adventure in the Macabre* (Little Theatre, 10 February 1930). (72) [Note: This play is a revision of the 1927 typescript. It was deposited with the Library of Congress on 7 September 1928, TS., D86282. In April of 1964 Webling's play was revived by the Little Theatre Club. See *The Stage Year Book* (London: Carson and Comerford, 1965) 54; see also a review in *The Stage* (9 April 1964) 15. In the Little Theatre Club production an extra character named Hanz was added. Perhaps he played the part of the laboratory assistant.]

23. 1930—John Balderston, *Frankenstein* (No record of performances). [A complete revision of Webling's *Adventure in the Macabre;* carbon typescript registered and deposited in the Copyright Office of the Library of Congress on 11 March 1931, DU 9603] (Never performed).

24. 1933—Gladys Hastings-Walton, *Frankenstein: A New Version of an Old "Thriller"* (Glasgow, Scotland). [Typescript in the British Library]

25. 1939—*Frankenstein.* [Note: The only reference to this production derives from the *New York Post* (17 June 1939), which notes under shows scheduled to open on Thursday 22 June: "HARTFORD, Conn.—Foot-guard Hill's Capitol Players will give "Frankenstein" as their second bill of the summer."] (9)

26. 1940—*Goon With the Wind* (Manion, Indiana: Fairmont Public School; Glut 146).

27. 1950—Kenneth Monk, *Frankenstein* (Brighton: Brighton Play-house, 14 March 1950).

28. 1958—John Edwards, *Frankenstein, or The Modern Prometheus* (Dayton, Ohio: Wright College Theatre, 20 November 1958).

29. 1959—David Campton, *Frankenstein: The Gift of Fire* (Scar-borough: Library Theatre, 16 July 1959). [London: J. Garnet Miller, 1973 as *Frankenstein: A Gothic Thriller in Two Acts;* also printed in 1973 by Miller in *Three Gothic Plays: Frankenstein, Usher, Carmilla*]

30. 1955–59—*Frankenstein and His Bride* (Los Angeles: Strip City; Glut 145: "Late 1950s").

31. 1965—The Living Theatre, *Frankenstein* (Venice: Teatro La Perla, 26 September 1965). [New York: Bobbs-Merrill, 1970; City Lights Journal, no. 3, 1966]

32. 1965—Carroll Borland, *My Fair Zombie* (Los Angeles, Presented by the Count Dracula Society, 31 October 1965; Glut, 138).

33. 1963–69—*Get the Picture* (Chicago: LeShow; Glut 146: "Middle 1960s?").

34. 1966—Hugh Whitmore, *Frankenstein* (BBC 2 production, 13 Oc-tober 1966).

35. 1966—Joseph Singer, *Frankenstein!* [Library of Congress, TS, Du 67116; registered on 14 November 1966].

36. 1967—San Francisco Mime Troupe, *Frankenstein* (San Francisco, 1967).

37. 1968—Paul Guay, *The Battle of the Monsters* (San Mateo, Ca.: St. Matthew's Episcopal Day School, n.d.; Glut 146: "Early 1968").

38. 1968—Edward Field, *Frankenstein* (A Play for Children). [Depos-ited with Library of Congress on 12 November 1968; TS, Du 72884]

39. 1969—Tom Eyen, *Frankenstein's Wife* (One of four plays in the pro-gram entitled *Four No Plays*) (New York: Cafe La Mama, 5 February 1969).

40. 1969—Michael Sarne, *Frankenstein* (Musical) (N.p.: 9 April 1969).

41. 1970—Peter Fernandez, Claire G. Miller and Selma R. Brody, *Fran-*

kenstein. [Deposited with Library of Congress on 6 November 1970; TS, Du 78537]

42. 1970—Sheldon Allman and Bob Pickett, *I'm Sorry the Bridge is Out, You'll Have to Spend the Night* (Hollywood, Coronet Theatre, 28 April 1970).

43. 1971—Tim Kelly, *Frankenstein* (Stagebrush Theatre, Scottsdale, Arizona, 28 February 1972). [New York: Samuel French, 1974]

44. 1972—Sally Netzel, *Frankenstein's Monster* (Dallas: Dallas Theatre, Summer 1972).

45. 1972—Gilbert Garcia, *Frankenstein's Godfather*. [American copyright DU 85584; filed 18 December 1972]

46. 1972—*H. R. Puffnstuff* (Glut 147: "Toured the United States" in 1972).

47. 1973—Richard O'Brien, *The Rocky Horror Show* (Royal Court Theatre Upstairs, 19 June 1973 [previews]; King's Road Theatre, 3 November 1973 [premiere]).

48. 1973—John Stevenson, *Frankenstein* (ITV Production for series "Once Upon a Lifetime," 2 September 1973).

49. 1973—*The World Festival of Magic & Occult* (New York: Madison Square Garden, Spring 1973; Glut 155).

50. 1973—Off-Center Theatre Group, *Frankenstein* (New York: Society for Ethical Culture, 1 December 1973).

51. 1973—Stewart M. Aldowitz, *Frankenstein's Nephew on His Father's Side*. [American copyright filed in 1973]

52. 1974—Wolfgang Deichsel, *Frankenstein Aus Dem Leben Der Angestellten (Frankenstein: From the Life of Employees)* (Zurich: Theatre am Neumarkt, 25 September 1982).

53. 1974—Lemuel E. Harris, *Frankenstein is a Soul Brother* [American copyright C 29917; filed 30 January 1974]

54. 1974—Del Tenney, *Frankenstein Meets Dracula* [American copyright DU 89520; filed 22 February 1974]

55. 1974—Samuel A. Rulon (book) and John L. Chamness (music), *Frankenstein*. [American copyright DU 90867; filed 8 July 1974]

56. 1974—Alden Nowlan and Walter Learning *Frankenstein: The Man Who Became God* (Fredericton, New Brunswick, 17 July 1974). [Toronto: Clark, Irwin, 1976]

57. 1974—Willard Simms, *Thursday Meets the Wolfman*. [Denver: Pioneer Drama, 1974]

58. 1974—Megan Terry (book and lyrics) and Dan Newmark (music), *Frankenstein* (Los Angeles: Scorpio Rising Theatre, 26 July 1974).

59. 1974—Tony Connor, *Dr. Crankenheim's Mixed-Up Monster* (Oxford Playhouse, 12 December 1974).

60. 1974—Tim Kelly, *Frankenstein Slept Here.* [Denver: Pioneer Drama, 1974]

61. 1975—Theodore Roszak, *The Crime of Dr. Frankenstein: A Pop Myth and Monster Show* (Vancouver, 9 April 1975; Glut 153).

62. 1975—Buddy Stern, *Frankenstein* (Brooklyn: St. John-St. Matthew Emmanuel Lutheran Church, 5 December 1975).

63. 1975—Alan Ormsby, *The Monster Frankenstein!* [New York: Scholastic Book Services, 1975; Glut 152]

64. 1975—*Frankenstein* (New York: Henry Street Settlement, 8 February 1975).

65. 1976—Stephen C. Wathen, *Frankenstein* [American copyright DU 97679; filed 5 February 1976]

66. 1976—*Frankenstein* (New York: Off-Center Theatre, July 1976).

67. 1976—Tim Kelly, *Bride of Frankenstein.* [Denver: Pioneer Drama, 1976]

68. 1977—Stephen C. Wathen, *Frankenstein* (Santa Clara, Ca.: Saratoga Civic Theatre, 5 March 1977; Glut 154).

69. 1977—Dallas Murphy, *Frankenstein* (San Francisco: American Conservatory Theatre, 11 May 1977).

70. 1977—Peter Walker and Katherine Jean Leslie, *Frankenstein Follies* [Elgin, Ill.: Performance Publishing, 1977]

71. 1978—Georgina Tolson, *Frankenstein's Rib* (New York: 18th Street Playhouse, 21 January 1979).

72. 1978—*A Taste of Rocky Horror* (San Diego: San Diego Comic Convention, El Cortez Hotel, July 1978; Glut 154).

73. 1979—Paul Guay, *End of the Line for Frankenstein* (Claremont, Ca.: Mudd Theatre, 5 April 1979; Glut 146).

74. 1979—Steven Otfinoski, *Love of Frankenstein* (New York: Actors' Playhouse, 21 January 1979).

75. 1975–79—James Gillhouley, *Frankenstein* (Hammersmith; Glut 146: "Late 1970s?").

76. 1975–79—*Frankenstein* (New York: Academy Arts Theatre; Glut 145: "Late 1970s?").

77. 1979—Ken Eulo, *The Frankenstein Affair* (New York: Courtyard Playhouse, 13 November 1979).

78. 1980—E. Burns Elliston, Jr. *Frankenstein; or, The Doctor Made Me Do It* (St. Louis: Golden Showboat Nostalgia Theatre, 19 August 1980).

79. 1980—Tim Kelly, *The Frankensteins Are Back in Town.* [Schulenburg, Tx.: I. E. Clark, 1980]

80. 1980—Christopher O'Neal, *Frankenstein: The Monster Play.* [Schulenburg, Tx.: I. E. Clark, 1980].

81. 1981—Victor Gialanella, *Frankenstein* (St. Louis: Loretto-Hilton

Repertory Theatre, 1979; New York: Palace Theatre, 1 January 1981).

82. 1981—R. N. Sandberg, *Frankenstein* (Seattle: Skid Road Theatre, 22 January 1981).

83. 1981—Dan Duling, *A Dream of Frankenstein: A Black Comedy of Maternal Darkness* (Los Angeles: Fifth Street Theatre, 9 May 1981).

84. 1981—Fred Fondren, *Frankenstein* (New York: National Arts Theatre, 27 February 1981).

85. 1981—Roger David Lewis (book and lyrics) and Lloyd Lockwood (music), *Frankenstein Crankenstein; or, Body Building for Beginners* (Hereford, England: Nell Gwynne, May 1981).

86. 1981—Greg Sandow and Thomas Disch, *Frankenstein* (Opera) (C. W. Post, Long Island University, 26 June 1981).

87. 1981—Marjorie Bicknell, *Frankenstein* (Chicago: The Theatre Building, 3 December 1981).

88. 1981—Echo Theatre Ensemble, *Frankenstein* (Echo Theatre, 23 December 1981).

89. 1982—Clive Barker, *Frankenstein In Love; or, The Love of Death (A Grand Guignol Romance*) (Cockpit Theatre, 13 April 1982).

90. 1984—Jim Diaz, *Frankenstein/The Broadway Version* (a revised and shortened version of Gialanella's *Frankenstein*) (New York: Jim Diaz Gallery, 29 March 1984).

91. 1984—Libby Jacobs, *Sparks* (Akron, Ohio: Coach House Theatre, 15 November 1984).

92. 1985—Laurence Maslow, *Frankenstein* (adapted from a treatment by Bob Hall and David Richmond) (New York: City Stage Company, 21 April 1985 [previews]; 24 November 1985 [premiere]).

93. 1985—Phillis Craig, *Frankenstein's Wife* (New York: Court Theatre, December 1985).

94. 1986—L. K. Aubrey, Mark Oates, and Stephen Pell, *Frankenstein: A Modern Prometheus* (New Hope, Pa.: Tweed Ensemble, Solebury School Theatre, 6 August 1986).

95. 1986—Fred Fondren, *Frankenstein's Folly* (New York: Prometheus Theatre, 25 October 1986).

96. 1986—Penny Rockwell and Joel Greenhouse (book), Dick Gallagher (music), *Have I Got a Girl for You: The Frankenstein Musical* (New York: Inroads Theatre, Spring 1986 [previews]; Second Avenue Theatre, 29 October 1986 [premiere]).

NOTES

1. On several occasions *Flintstone* episodes are devoted to "Frankenstone." See Donald F. Glut, *The Frankenstein Catalog* (Jefferson, N.C.: McFarland, 1984)

296–97, 318. Glut cites the following episodes: "The Flintstones' New Neighbors," televised 26 September 1980, "The Flintstones Meet Rocula and Frankenstone" (3 October 1980), and "The Frankenstones" (22 November 1980). See also "The Flintstones Meet Frankenstein and Dracula," in *The Flintstones* published by Gold Key Comics as number 33 in April of 1966. Glut also cites an untitled episode televised in 1966 in which "Dr. Len Frankenstone, a mad doctor (patterned after television's 'Ben Casey') uses Fred as a guinea pig to test his personality-transfer machine and switches his mind with that of Dino, his pet dinosaur" (297).

2. Glut lists in his *Catalog* over two hundred sixty comic books and fourteen comic book series, including *The Spirit of Frankenstein, The Monster of Frankenstein,* and *The Spawn of Frankenstein* (306–400). But perhaps the most popular publication was *Castle of Frankenstein,* a magazine that went through twenty-five numbers between January of 1962 and June of 1975. (See Glut, *Catalog,* 68–72) Other magazines included *Journal of Frankenstein, Famous Monsters of Filmland, House of Hammer, Mad Monsters, Monster World,* and *World Famous Creatures.*

3. Glut, *Catalog* 341. Except for issues 10 and 55, the series, written and illustrated by Dick Briefer, appeared in issues 7 through 68 of *Prize Comics* between December of 1940 and March of 1948.

4. Figures for dramatizations derive from my own research; however, figures for films derive from Glut's *Catalog* 156–241. When independent or non-professional films are added, the figure rises to over one hundred ninety films. See also the following filmographies: Michel Boujut, "Preface and Filmography," *Frankenstein* (Levallois-Perret: Cercle du Bibliophile, 1969); Carlos Clarens, *An Illustrated History of the Horror Films* (New York: Putnam's, 1967); Dennis Gifford, *Movie Monsters* (London: Dutton, 1969); and Gregory William Mank, *It's Alive! The Classic Cinema Saga of Frankenstein* (New York: Barnes, 1981).

5. These figures derive from my own research, informed by that of W. H. Lyles's *Mary Shelley: An Annotated Bibliography* (New York: Garland, 1975) 6–20, Frederick S. Frank's "Mary Shelley's *Frankenstein:* A Register of Research," *Bulletin of Bibliography* 40 (1983): 163–87, and Glut's *Catalog* 1–15.

6. Nonetheless, it must be noted that despite this re-evaluation of the Creature's nature, the majority of playwrights destroy their Creatures on the stage, usually by shooting the Creature numerous times. Sally Netzel's *Frankenstein's Monster* (1972) stands out because it contains the most gruesome death scene of all. In her play the Creature shoves a burning stake down his throat and, as he writhes on the ground, is shot three times by Dr. Waldman.

7. Glut could not locate information on the following plays: "a 1940s stage show performed by 'Tony Karloff, the Son of Frankenstein'; a 1950s Frankenstein play by Lee Richards, performed in Bangor, Pennsylvania; *The Maniac,* possibly performed during the 1950s, an existing photo showing the Frankenstein Monster playing cards with a skeleton and a magician; *The Monster Show,* performed in Brazil; [and] the French puppet show *Les Poupées de Paris,* featuring a marionette Frankenstein Monster" (133). I have been equally unsuccessful in locating information on these pieces. On page 153 Glut also lists *Prometeo Moderno* as a play that was performed in London and the United States in the "1800s." I have located information on no such title.

PART II

The Plays

Textual Note

This study presents unmodernized critical texts of the seven dramatizations: four melodramas and three burlesques. The texts of French plays are not represented, except for quotations that appear in the historical introduction. Among the major nineteenth-century British dramatizations, only Richard Butler and Henry Chance Newton's *Frankenstein; or, The Vampire's Victim* (1887) remains unrepresented in this edition partly because of its length—over 150 manuscript pages—but mainly because the play illustrates more the development of musical burlesque than the transformation of the Frankenstein myth on stage. Most importantly, by the late nineteenth century, the themes of Frankenstein had run their course on stage, having been usurped in the public's eye by the political cartoon. Nevertheless, three songs from the libretto of *Vampire's Victim* are reproduced in an appendix.

The original texts are followed in both substantives and accidentals, and the edition makes no attempt to impose a consistent style or to modernize any of the idiosyncrasies of a particular text or author. Substantives are emended when judged to be compositorial or scribal errors. For instance, in *The Man and the Monster* "think" is incorrectly printed for "thing" (199.29), and "to" for "too" (201.27); in *Presumption* "ground" is incorrectly printed for "groaned" (138.3), "takes" for "tastes" (146.19), and "County" for "Country" (157.2); and in *Another Piece of Presumption* "Were" is written in place of "They" (172.15). Alterations judged to be authorial have also been incorporated into the present edition. For example, in the second impression of *The Man and the Monster* "that" replaces "hat" (201.27) and "sleeves" replaces "stripes" (190.8).

This edition preserves all of the accidentals (i.e., italicization, capitalization, spelling and punctuation) found in the copy-text. Accidentals have, however, been emended when the text is obviously in error, as in omitted end-line punctuation and spellings that do not conform to contemporary standards. Thus this edition adds end-line punctuation to *The Monster and Magician* after "heaven" (209.21), "attained" (211.14) and "invade" (211.44), and in *The Model Man* alters the spelling of "hymenial" to "hymeneal" (228.36), "pestal" to "pestle" (233.11), and "Tassaud" to "Tussaud" (233.41). In the printed plays typographical errors are also corrected, such as "misfortnnes" (208.48) and "proceediugs" (209.1) in *The Monster and Magician,* "gesturess" (194.44), "Aud" (203.19), "uature" (196.1), and "humun" (202.16) in *The Man and the Monster,* and "thiis" (153.38) and "fram" (157.4) in *Presumption.*

In the only other instance of emendations to accidentals, copy-text punctuation is altered when it interferes with the textual meaning. For example, the three manuscripts at times lack even the most rudimentary punctuation. Although an unemended transcription of each manuscript might tell us something of the scribal habits of its author or scribe, such a transcription would not be of primary interest or the most practical use to the general student of literature or to the theatre historian, the main audience for this edition. Punctuation has therefore been supplied throughout the manuscripts in cases where some form of punctuation is clearly absent or when a lack of punctuation obscures meaning. The text of *The Model Man* proves exceptionally replete with troublesome readings. For example at 235.28–29 the manuscript reads: "All wax mind for expence I wont be nice/No composition I dont care for Price." The line has been emended to read: "All wax, mind, for expence I won't be nice./No composition, I don't care for Price." Periods and commas are the most frequent additions in the manuscripts, although question marks have also been added to sentences where a character poses an obvious question. When a stated question is followed by a dash (such as at 165.32, 170.30, and 170.36 of *Another Piece of Presumption*), the dash is replaced by a question mark. Other instances are not so clear. For example, sometimes a dash functions as a period or as some other form of punctuation. To replace a dash in these instances would not only impose a particular editorial style on the manuscript, but might distort the original meaning. Therefore, the dash has been replaced only when it stands for a question mark.

Several plays, John Kerr's for example, provide many examples of apparently aberrant punctuation that cannot in the final analysis be emended. Many times in *The Monster and Magician* a word is printed in several different forms. For example the contraction of "it is" appears as "Tis" (207.28, 213.23), "tis" (208.31, 220.12, 222.14), and "Tis" (214.3). Like the Broughs in *The Model Man,* Kerr contracts "should not" as "should'nt" (209.44), "is not" as "is'nt" (210.13), "did not" as "did'nt" (216.36), and so forth. In one sentence (218.35) "do not" is contracted once as "Don't" and twice as "do'nt." We also find such spellings as "cant" (217.19), "lets" (218.28), and "its" for "it's" (214.8). Frequently possessives are not indicated, as when we read "fashion minions" (211.39), "A peasants simple lot" (211.41), "my very hearts blood" (218.6), and "my sisters love" (222.43). No firmly established grammatical rules governed the contraction of words in the nineteenth century, and thus our approach must accept and encompass a variety of forms. Variant forms of contractions can be distinguished from misprints such as "plaiuly" (214.17) and "Misfortnnes" (208.48), and from outright misspellings. For example, the printing of "do not" as "do'nt" cannot be called a misspelling since its use was common in the nineteenth century. Quite different effects result, however, from the printing of "whose" for "who's" (208.32), "fashions" for "fashion's," and "its" for "it's." The present edition admits the contractions "do'nt," "did'nt," and is'nt," while it emends outright misspellings. Thus emendations are made to correct such readings in *The Model Man* as "too" for "to" (240.45), "lets" for "let's" (237.33), "your" for "you're" (240.34) and the possessives, "fashions," "peasants," "hearts," and "sisters."

The copy-texts of *Presumption, The Man and the Monster* and *The Monster and Magician* derive from manuscripts held in two libraries: the British Library (for *Presumption*) and the Beinecke Library of Yale University (for *The Man and the Monster* and *The Monster and the Magician*). The copy-text of *Another Piece of Presumption* derives from a manuscript held in the Huntington Library, and the texts of *Frank-in-Steam* and *The Model Man* from manuscripts held in the British Museum. John Balderston's *Frankenstein* exists in a carbon of a typescript located in the Library of Congress. This carbon forms the copy-text of the present edition.

No other form of the text is known to exist for five of the seven plays in this edition: *Another Piece of Presumption* (manuscript), *Frank-in-Steam* (manuscript), *The Model Man* (manuscript), *Monster and Magician* (printed edition), and *Frankenstein* (carbon of a typescript). Obviously, for these five plays no debate exists about copy-text selection. And even though *The Man and the Monster*, the sixth play, went through two editions, the first of five impressions, the choice of copy-text is relatively uncomplicated: the first impression is emended with substantive variants deriving from impressions two through five. Only Peake's *Presumption* exists in both a manuscript and a printed form, one of which must be chosen as a copy-text. The rationale for selecting a copy-text for Peake's melodrama deserves special attention.

Editors of drama encounter a situation not usually faced by editors of other literary works in regard to copy-text selection since the texts of many plays may be said to have reached their final form only in performance. Dougald MacMillan broaches the issue of copy-text selection of nineteenth-century plays when he comments on the Lord Chamberlain licensing manuscripts and their relationship to the published version. As he observes:

> The fact that these [manuscripts] are official copies sent by the managers of the theatres, not the authors, to the Office of the Examiner, places them in a different category from that of most literary texts. Their relation on the one hand to the acted version and on the other to the published work raises complicated problems that can be solved only individually.[2]

MacMillan's statement calls attention to the fact that authorial intention did not always dictate what was presented on the stage. Therefore the development of these plays was determined to a large degree by external forces—be it audience reaction, a theatre manager's dictates, or, in the case of *Presumption,* a performance by T. P. Cooke as the Creature that transformed the playwright's original conception. For example, less than two months after the debut of *Presumption,* the *Examiner* (10 August) announced: "*Frankenstein* is much improved by condensation." Specifically, the published text of *Presumption* embodies the play as it was performed on stage and that this "performance version" rather than the scribal copy takes precedence in copy-text selection. Thus although the manuscript of *Presumption* may contain more of Peake's accidentals, I have chosen as copy-text the published text of the play because it contains additions incorporated into the play during performance as well as many stylistic clarifications such as fuller stage directions, more complete dialogue, and the addition of the full texts of songs. Clearly, no pre-performance licensing manuscript, copied by scribes and submitted to the Office of the Examiner of Plays to fulfill legislative guidelines, could ever hope to reflect the text as it was finally performed. Thus, *Presumption* as published by John Dicks becomes the copy-text for this edition.[3]

NOTES

1. Nine melodramas and thirteen burlesques appeared between 1821 and 1930, of which eight melodramas and nine burlesques are extant.

2. MacMillan, *Catalogue of the Larpent Plays in the Huntington Library* (San Marino, Ca.: San Pasqual Press, 1939) vii.

3. For a more detailed discussion of the text of each play and a complete list of adopted readings, emendations, and list of substantive variants, see my dissertation on this subject: "The 'Hideous Progenies' of Richard Brinsley Peake: Dramatizations of *Frankenstein,* 1821–1986," Columbia University, 1987.

Richard Brinsley Peake

Presumption; or, The Fate of Frankenstein

(1823)

FRANKENSTEIN.
A ROMANTIC DRAMA, IN THREE ACTS.
BY RICHARD BRINSLEY PEAKE.

DRAMATIS PERSONÆ

Frankenstein	Mr. Wallack.
Clerval (his friend, in love with Elizabeth)	Mr. Bland.
William (brother of Frankenstein)	Master Boden.
Fritz (servant of Frankenstein)	Mr. Keeley.
De Lacey (a banished gentleman—blind)	Mr. Rowbotham.
Felix De Lacey (his son)	Mr. Pearman.
Tanskin (a gipsy)	Mr. Shield.
Hammerpan (a tinker)	Mr. Salter.
A Guide (an old man)	Mr. R. Phillips.
* * *	Mr. T. P. Cooke.
Elizabeth (sister of Frankenstein)	Mrs. Austin.
Agatha (daughter of De Lacey)	Miss L. Dance.
Safie (an Arabian girl, betrothed to Felix)	Miss Povey.
Madame Ninon (wife of Fritz)	Mrs. T. Weippert.

Gipsies, Peasants, Choristers, and Dancers (Male and Female).

Scene.—*Geneva and its vicinity.*

COSTUME

The Monster's Appearance and Dress.–Dark black flowing hair—*à la Octavian*—his face, hands, arms, and legs all bare, being one colour, the same as his body, which is a light blue or French gray cotton dress, fitting quite close, as if it were his flesh, with a slate colour scarf round his middle, passing over one shoulder.

Frankenstein.–Black velvet vest and trunk breeches—gray tunic, open, the sleeves open in front, slashed with black—black silk pantaloons and black velvet shoes—black velvet hat.

Clerval.–Blue-coloured tunic, trimmed with velvet, and silk puffs at arms—braided pantaloons—boots—drab hat and white feather.

William.–Fawn-coloured tunic, trimmed with light blue—white silk pantaloons—scarlet bottmes—white satin Italian cap.

Fritz.–Buff jacket and trunks, trimmed with orange—blue stockings—russet shoes—small three-cornered drab hat.

De Lacey.–Dark green doublet—vest trunk breeches to match—brown stockings—russet shoes—and cloth hat.

Felix.–Green hunting tunic, trimmed with black braid—russet boots—black hat and feather.

Tanskin.–A tight goatskin jacket, leaving the throat and arms bare—a coarse canvas shirt seen through it, with ragged sleeves, extending nearly down to the elbow, and hanging loose there—goatskin breeches, extending half way down the thighs, with ragged under-dress or trousers of canvas, reaching within an inch of the knees—legs bare, sandaled with leather thongs, the hair confined in a long Italian net—the dress confined at the waist by a belt, in which a knife is stuck—slouched hat.

Hammerpan.–Same as Tanskin, with the addition of a leather apron—wallet—bald wig—and one eye blind.

Guide.–Peasant's tunic—red pantaloons—russet boots.

Elizabeth.–Gray silk dress—trimmed with white fur—hat to correspond.

Agatha.–Short pelisse of a dark brown, over a slate-coloured petticoat—dark brown Italian cap.

Safie.–Short frock of crimson cloth, trimmed with silk—turban head-dress—red shoes—and full silk trousers—large silk shawl or scarf to give an Oriental appearance.

Ninon.–A showy Italian peasant's dress, with apron—head-dress hair confined by long gold pins.

STAGE DIRECTIONS

Exits and Entrances.–R. means *Right;* L. *Left;* D. F. *Door in Flat;* R. D. *Right Door;* L. D. *Left Door;* S. E. *Second Entrance;* U.E. *Upper Entrance;* M. D. *Middle Door;* L. U. E. *Left Upper Entrance;* R. U. E. *Right Upper Entrance;* L. S. E. *Left Second Entrance;* P. S. *Prompt Side;* O. P. *Opposite Prompt.*

Relative Positions.–R. means *Right;* L. *Left;* C. *Centre;* R. C. *Right of Centre;* L. C. *Left of Centre.*

R. RC. C. LC. L.

*** *The Reader is supposed to be on the Stage, facing the Audience.*

Act I. Scene I.—*A Gothic Chamber in the House of Frankenstein.*

Fritz discovered in a Gothic arm-chair, nodding asleep. During the symphony of the song, he starts, rubs his eyes, and comes forward.

Air—Fritz

Oh, dear me! what's the matter?
How I shake at each clatter.
My marrow
They harrow.
Oh, dear me! what's the matter?

If mouse squeaks, or cat sneezes,
Cricket chirps, or cock wheezes,
  Then I fret,
  In cold sweat.
Ev'ry noise my nerves teazes;
Bless my heart—heaven preserve us!
I declare I'm so nervous.
  Ev'ry knock
  Is a shock.
I declare I'm so nervous!
I'm so nervous.

Fritz. Oh, Fritz, Fritz, Fritz! what is it come to! you are frightened out of your wits. Why did you ever leave your native village! why couldn't you be happy in the country with an innocent cow for your companion (bless its sweet breath!) instead of coming here to the city of Geneva to be hired as a servant! *(Starts.)* What's that?—nothing. And then how complimentary! Master only hired me because he thought I looked so stupid! Stupid! ha, ha, ha! but am I stupid though? To be sure Mr. Frankenstein is a kind man, and I should respect him, but that I thinks as how he holds converse with somebody below with a long tail, horns, and hoofs, who shall be nameless. *(Starts again.)* What's that! Oh, a gnat on my nose! Oh, anything frightens me now—I'm so very nervous! I spill all my bread and milk when I feed myself at breakfast! Lauk, Lauk! In the country, if a dog brayed or a donkey barked ever so loud, it had no effect upon me. *(Two distinct loud knocks, L. H.—Fritz jumps.)* Oh, mercy! I jump like a maggot out of a cheese! How my heart beats!

Cler. *(Without, L. H.)* Fritz, Fritz! open the door, Fritz!

Fritz. Yes, It's only Mr. Clerval, master's friend, who is going to marry Miss Elizabeth, master's sister. *(Opens side door, L. H.)*

Enter Clerval.

How d'ye do, sir!

Cler. Good morning, Fritz! Is Mr. Frankenstein to be seen?

Fritz. I fear not, sir, he has as usual been fumi—fumi—fumi——

Cler. Fumigating.

Fritz. Yes, sir—fumigating; thank'ee, sir—fumigating all night at his chemistry. I have not dared disturb him.

Cler. Mr. Frankenstein pursues his study with too much ardour.

Fritz. And what can be the use of it, Mr. Clerval? Work, work, work—always at it. Now, putting a case to you. Now, when I was in the country, with my late cow (she's no more, poor thing!) if I had set to and milked her for a fortnight together, day and night, without stopping, do you think I should have been any the better for it? I ask you as a gentleman and a scholar.

Cler. Ha, ha, ha! Certainly not!

Fritz. Nor my cow neither, poor cretur. *(Wipes his eyes.)* Excuse my crying—she's defunct, and I always whimper a little when I think on her; and my wife lives away from me, but I don't care so much for that. Oh! Mr. Clerval, between ourselves—hush! didn't you hear a noise!—between ourselves, I want to unbosom my confidence.

Cler. Well!

Fritz. Between ourselves—there's nobody at the door, is there?—*(Crosses to L. H. door.)*—No! well, between ourselves, Mr. Clerval, I have been so very nervous since I came to this place.

Cler. Pshaw!

Fritz. Nay, don't "Pshaw!" till you've heard me out. Oh, Mr. Clerval! I'll tell you. One night Mr. Frankenstein did indulge himself by going to bed. He was worn with fatigue and study. I had occasion to go into his chamber. He was asleep, but frightfully troubled; he groaned and ground his teeth setting mine on edge. "It is accomplished!" said he. *Accomplished!* I knew that had nothing to do with me, but I listened. He started up in his sleep, though his eyes were opened and dead as oysters, he cried, "It is animated—it rises—walks!" Now my shrewd guess, sir, is that, like Dr. Faustus, my master is raising the Devil.

Cler. Fritz, you are simple; drive such impressions from your mind. You must not misconstrue your master's words in a dream. Do you never dream?

Fritz. *(Mournfully.)* I dream about my cow sometimes.

Cler. Your master is a studious chemist—nay, as I sometimes suspect, an alchemist.

Fritz. Eh! Ah, I think he is. What is an alchemist, Mr. Clerval?

Cler. Does he not sometimes speak of the art of making gold?

Fritz. Lauk, sir! do you take Mr. Frankenstein for a coiner?

Cler. Did you never hear him make mention of the grand elixir which can prolong life to immortality?

Fritz. Never in all my life.

Cler. Well, go—find out if it is possible I can see him. I will not detain him.

(Clerval crosses to L. H.)

Fritz. Yes, sir. Oh, that laboratory! I've got two loose teeth, and I am afraid I shall lose them, for whenever I go up towards that infernal place my head shakes like a dice-box! *(Goes to R. H.)* Oh, mercy! what's that? Two shining eyes—how they glisten! Dear, dear, why I declare it's only the cat on the stairs. Puss, puss, pussy! How you frightened me, you young *dog,* when you know I am so very nervous!

[Exit Fritz, R. H.

Cler. Frankenstein, friend of my youth, how extraordinary and secret are thy pursuits!—how art thou altered by study! Strange, what a hold has philosophy taken of thy mind—but thou wert always enthusiastic and of boundless ambition. But Elizabeth—the fair Elizabeth, his sister—what a difference in disposition! Everyone adores her. Happy Clerval, to be now the possessor of Elizabeth, who, unconscious of her beauty, stole thy heart away!

Song—Clerval

Ere witching love my heart possest,
   And bade my sighs the nymph pursue,
Calm as the infant's smiling rest,
   No anxious hope nor fear it knew.

But doom'd—ah! doom'd at last to mourn,
   What tumults in that heart arose!
An ocean tumbling, wild, and torn
   By tempests from its deep repose.

Yet let me not the virgin blame,
   As tho' she wish'd my heart despair,
How could the maid suspect a flame,
   Who never knew that she was fair.

—But Frankenstein approaches.
Enter Frankenstein, thoughtfully, R. H., shown in by Fritz, who exits, L. H.

My dear friend!

Frank. Clerval!

Cler. Frankenstein, how ill you appear—so pale! You look as if your night-watchings had been long and uninterrupted.

Frank. I have lately been so deeply engaged in one occupation that I have not allowed myself sufficient rest. But how left you my sister, Elizabeth?

Cler. Well, and very happy, only a little uneasy that she sees you so seldom.

Frank. Aye; I am engaged heart and soul in the pursuit of a discovery—a grand, unheard-of wonder! None but those who have experienced can conceive the enticements of science; he who looks into the book of nature, finds an inexhaustible source of novelty, of wonder, and delight. What hidden treasures are contained in her mighty volume—what strange, un-dreamed-of mysteries!

Cler. But some little respite—your health should be considered.

Frank. (Abstracted.) After so much time spent in painful labour, to arrive at last at the summit of my desires, would be indeed a glorious consummation of my toils!

(Frankenstein crosses to L. H.)

Cler. How wild and mysterious his abstractions—he heeds me not!

Frank. This discovery will be so vast, so overwhelming, that all the steps by which I have been progressively led will be obliterated, and I shall behold only the astounding result.

Cler. Frankenstein!

Frank. Ha! (*To Clerval.)* I see by your eagerness that you expect to be informed of the secret with which I am acquainted. That cannot be.

Cler. I do not wish to pry into your secrets, Frankenstein. I am no natural philosopher; my imagination is too vivid for the details of science. If I contemplate, let it be the charms of your fair sister, Elizabeth. My message hither now—I wish to fix the day for our nuptials. But we must be certain, on so important and happy an event, that we shall enjoy the society of our Frankenstein.

Frank. Pardon me, Clerval! My first thoughts should recur to those dear friends whom I most love, and who are so deserving of my love—name the day?

Cler. On the morn after to-morrow, may I lead the charming Elizabeth to the altar?

Frank. E'en as you will—e'en as you will! *(Aside.)* The morn after to-morrow—ere that—my wonderful task will be completed. It will be animated! It will live—will think!

(Crosses in deep reflection—afterwards turns up the stage.)

Cler. (Apart.) Again in reverie! this becomes alarming—surely his head is affected. I am bound in duty to counteract this madness, and discover the secret of his deep reflections.

(Frankenstein sits down—musing.)

Farewell, Frankenstein! He heeds me not—'tis in vain to claim his notice—but I will seek the cause, and, if possible, effect his cure. No time must be lost. Fritz must assist me, and this way he went.

[Exit Clerval.

Frank. Every moment lost, fevers me. What time have I devoted? (*Rises.)* Had I not been heated by an almost supernatural enthusiasm, my application to this study would have been irksome, disgusting, and almost intolerable. To examine the causes of life—I have had recourse to death—I have seen how the fine form of man has been wasted and degraded—have beheld the corruption of death succeed to the blooming cheek of life! I have seen how the worm inherited the wonders of the eye and brain—I paused—analysing all the minutiæ of causation as exemplified in the change of life from death—until from the midst of this darkness, the sudden light broke in upon me! A light, so brilliant and dazzling, some miracle must have produced the flash! The vital principle! The cause of life!—Like Prometheus of old, have I daringly attempted the formation—the animation of a Being! To my task—away with reflection, to my task—to my task!

[Exit Frankenstein.
Enter Fritz and Clerval.

Fritz. Yes, there he goes again, amongst otamies, and phials, and crucibles, and retorts, and charcoal, and fire, and the Devil—for I'm sure he's at the bottom of it, and that makes me so nervous.

Cler. Fritz, you love your master, and are, I know, a discreet servant—but his friends and relations are all unhappy on his account. His health is rapidly sinking under the fatigue of his present labours—will you not assist to call him back to life and to his family?

Fritz. La! I'd call out all day long, if that would do any good.

Cler. I know his mind has been devoted to abstruse and occult sciences—that his brain has been bewildered with the wild fancies of Cornelius Agrippa, Paracelsus, Albertus Magnus, and—

Fritz. Oh! Mr. Clerval! how can you mention such crazy tooth-breaking names? There sounds something wicked in them.

Cler. Wicked! Psha, man! they are the renowned names of the earliest experimental philosophers. The sages who promised to the hopes of the laborious alchymist the transmutation of metals and the elixir of life.

Fritz. O! Ah! indeed! Lack a daisy me!

Cler. *(Aside.)* I suspect this fellow is more knave than fool—he wants a bribe. Now, sirrah! answer me with candour. What is it you like best in the world?

Fritz. Milk!

Cler. Simpleton! I mean what station of life would you covet?

Fritz. Station?

Cler. Yes. Would you like to be master of a cottage?

Fritz. What, and keep a cow?—the very thing. Why, Mr. Clerval, you're a conjuror, and know my thoughts by heart.

Cler. Fritz, I want to discover—but you must be prudent. *(Takes out purse and gives a florin to Fritz.)* Here's an earnest of my future intentions touching the cow and cottage.

Fritz. Bodikins! a florin! *(Examining money.)*

Cler. Friend Fritz, you must some time, when Mr. Frankenstein is absent from home, admit me into his study.

Fritz. Oh, dear, I can't!—don't take your florin back again—*(puts up money)*—for he always locks the door. To be sure, there's a little window a-top of the staircase, where I can see when he puffs up his fire.

Cler. Well, they say the end justifies the means; and in this case I admit the maxim. You can peep through that window, and inform me minutely of what you see.

Fritz. But what is to become of my nerves?

Cler. Remember your cottage—

Fritz. And the cow!

Cler. Put me in possession of the secret, and both shall be secured to you. Some one approaches.

Fritz. Mr. Clerval, I'm your man. I'm nervous, and the devil sticks in my gizzard; but the cow will drive it out again. *(Starts.)* What's that? Oh, nothing—oh, dear, I'm so nervous.

[Exeunt Fritz and Clerval.

Scene II.

Part of the Villa Residence of Elizabeth, at Belrive.—Garden Terrace from 2 E. R. H.—Entrance into the House, 2 E. L. H.—William discovered sleeping on a garden bench near R. H.—During symphony enter Elizabeth from house, 2 E. L. H.

Song—Elizabeth

The summer sun shining on tree and on tower,
And gilding the landscape with radiance divine,

May give to the heart o'er which pleasure has power,
But eve's pensive beauties are dearer to mine.

Through trees gently sighing, the cool breeze of even
Seems sympathy's voice to the ear of despair;
And the dew-drops (like tears shed by angels of heaven),
Revive the frail hopes in the bosom of care.

(During this scene the stage becomes progressively dark.)

Mad. Ninon. (Within, L. H. 2 E.) William! little William!

Eliza. Where can our little favourite have secreted himself?

Enter Madame Ninon, from the house, L. H. 2 E.

Ninon. Heaven bless Mont Blanc and all the neighbouring hills! Why, where is the boy? How angry shall I be with him for staying out so late.

Eliza. Why, Ninon, assuage your friendly wrath—yonder is William.

Ninon. (Goes to the child.) Fast asleep, I declare, the pretty boy—how like his poor mother, who is gone. La, la, I daresay my Fritz was just such another, only his hair was red. Pretty William—he was the pin basket. Bless the thirteen cantons, I nursed him. William—*(kisses him)*—a pair of gloves, sir! *(William waking.)* Fie, you little urchin, sleeping so early this beautiful evening.

(William rises. All come forward.)

Will. Indeed, dear Ninon, I know not how I fell asleep; but I rose with the sun, and thinking I would lie down with it, I closed my eyes, and—

Ninon. Slumbered like a young dormouse?

Eliza. But, William, you have not neglected your books?

Will. Oh, no; for then I should not be such a scholar as my elder brother, Victor Frankenstein.

(Runs to the end of terrace, R. H. 2 E.

Eliza. Alas, poor Frankenstein! he studies indeed too deeply; but love—blighted love, drove him to solitude and abstruse research.

Ninon. Ah, madame, may love make you happy! Mr. Clerval was here this morning, and looked as handsome—

Eliza. Peace, Ninon! And yet, why should I check your cheerfulness? Ninon, I have given orders to my milliner to make you a handsome new cap. When your husband, Fritz, comes from Geneva, he may call and bring it.

Ninon. Thank you, dear madam; but see—

Re-enter William from terrace, R. H. 2 E., and runs, crossing behind to L. H.

Will. Oh, sister—oh, Madame Ninon! two travellers are coming up the hill—such a beautiful lady—but her guide, I think, has fallen from his horse. See—here's the lady, helping the poor man.

(Melo-music.)

Enter Safie, supporting the Guide, from terrace, 2 E. R. H.

Eliza. Madame, allow me to offer you assistance.

Safie. Thanks—thanks, fair lady; it is not for myself I require rest or help, for I am young. But this aged man, my faithful follower, is completely worn with fatigue.

Eliza. Ninon, see him conveyed into the house. Give him your support, and assist to welcome our guests.

Ninon. (Crossing to Guide.) Lean on me, old sir—aye, as heavy as you like; bless you, my arm is strong. Come, gently—gently—there—there—

(Ninon leads the guide into house, L. H. 2 E., William following them. By this time the wing lights are turned off.)

Safie. I can only weep my thanks, of late I have been unused to kindness.

Eliza. Your garb and manner denote you a stranger here—yet you are acquainted with our language, and you appear to have travelled a great distance.

Safie. From Leghorn, a wearisome journey. How far am I distant from the Valley of the Lake?

Eliza. But a few leagues.

Safie. Then to-night I probably could reach it?

(Animated.)

Eliza. I would not advise the attempt till the morning—the sun is down now; you are distant from any inn; your horses are fatigued; permit me to offer in my house refreshment and repose.

Safie. No, no; no repose until my purpose is accomplished. Yet my poor follower needs rest; generous stranger, I gratefully accept your hospitality.

Eliza. And be assured such comfort as Eliza Frankenstein can offer shall be freely yours.

Safie. You—you mention the name of Frankenstein!

Eliza. I bear that appellation.

Safie. How fortunate! happy chance that brought me to your hospitable door. Know you the family of De Lacey?

Eliza. I knew it well, but years have elapsed since I have heard of them.

Safie. I seek their retreat. Exiled from France, they now exist in the Valley of the Lake.

Eliza. So near, and I not acquainted with their residence! Does the gentle Agatha de Lacey yet live?

Safie. To-morrow's noon I trust I shall discover her.

Eliza. What rapturous news for my dear brother, Frankenstein. Let us in and converse further on this subject, which is of deep interest to me. Night approaches.

Safie. On such a night was I torn from Agatha's brother. Felix, Felix! sad was the moment when you last enfolded poor Safie in your affectionate embrace.

Song—Safie

Each mountain was tinged with the sun's latest beam,
Sinking red in the fathomless deep;
The pale watch lights of heaven shed their rays o'er the stream;
And nature seem'd lulled into sleep.
All was silent and hush'd over lake, lawn, and fell,
Save the whisper that breathed in the lover's farewell;
When at Fate's stern command two fond hearts doom'd to sever,
And poor Felix and Safie were parted for ever.

[Exeunt into house, L. H. 2E.

Scene III.

The Sleeping Apartment of Frankenstein. Dark. The Bed is within a recess between the wings R. H. U. E., enclosed by dark green curtains. A Sword (to break) hanging on 3 E. R. H. A Large French Window on L. H. U. E.; between the wings a staircase leading from L. H. 2 E. to a Gallery across the stage, on which is the Door of the Laboratory above, near to R. H. A small high Lattice in centre of scene, next the Laboratory Door. A Gothic Table on stage near R. H. 3 E., screwed. A Gothic Chair in centre, and Footstool. Music expressive of the rising of a storm. Enter Frankenstein, L. H., with a Lighted Lamp, which he places on the table. Distant thunder heard.

Frank. This evening—this lowering evening, will, in all probability, complete my task. Years have I laboured, and at length discovered that to which so many men of genius have in vain directed their inquiries. After days and nights of incredible labour and fatigue, I have become master of the secret of bestowing animation upon lifeless matter. With so astonishing a power in my hands, long, long did I hesitate how to employ it. The object of my experiment lies there *(Pointing up to the Laboratory)*—a huge automaton in human form. Should I succeed in animating it, Life and Death would appear to me as ideal bounds, which I shall break through and pour a torrent of light into our dark world. I have lost all soul or sensation but for this one pursuit. I have clothed the inanimate mass, lest the chilly air should quench the spark of life newly infused. *(Thunder and heavy rain heard.)* 'Tis a dreary night, the rain patters dismally against the panes; 'tis a night for such a task. I'll in and complete the wondrous effort.

[Music.—Frankenstein takes up lamp, cautiously looks around him, ascends the stairs, crosses the gallery above, and exits into door of laboratory.

Enter Fritz, with a candle, L. H.

Fritz. Master isn't here—dare I peep. Only think of the reward Mr. Clerval promised me, a cow and a cottage, milk and a mansion. Master is certainly not come up yet. My candle burns all manner of colours, and spits like a roasted apple. *(Runs against the chair and drops his light, which goes out.)* There, now, I'm in the dark. Oh my nerves. *(A blue flame appears at the small lattice window above, as from the laboratory.)* What's that? Oh, lauk; there he is, kicking up the devil's own flame! Oh my cow! I'll venture up—oh my cottage! I'll climb to the window—it will be only one peep to make my fortune.

(Music.—Fritz takes up footstool, he ascends the stairs, when on the gallery landing place, he stands on the footstool tiptoe to look through the small high lattice window of the laboratory, a sudden combustion is heard within. The blue flame changes to one of a reddish hue.)

Frank. *(Within.)* It lives! it lives!

Fritz. *(Speaks through music.)* Oh, dear! oh, dear! oh, dear!

(Fritz, greatly alarmed, jumps down hastily, totters tremblingly down the stairs in vast hurry; when in front on stage, having fallen flat in fright, with difficulty speaks.)

Fritz. There's a hob—hob-goblin, seven-and-twenty feet high! Oh, my nerves; I feel as if I had just come out of strong fits, and nobody to throw cold water in my face—if my legs won't lap under me, I'll just make my escape. *(Crosses to L. H.)* Oh, my poor nerves!

Exit Fritz, crawling off L. H.

(Music.—Frankenstein rushes from the laboratory, without lamp, fastens the door in apparent dread, and hastens down the stairs, watching the entrance of the laboratory.)

Frank. It lives! I saw the dull yellow eye of the creature open, it breathed hard, and a convulsive motion agitated its limbs. What a wretch have I formed, his legs are in proportion and I had selected his features as beautiful—beautiful! Ah, horror! his cadaverous skin scarcely covers the work of muscles and arteries beneath, his hair lustrous, black, and flowing—his teeth of pearly whiteness—but these luxuriances only form more horrible contrasts with the deformities of the monster. *(He listens at the foot of the staircase.)* What have I accomplished? the beauty of my dream has vanished! and breathless horror and disgust now fill my heart. For this I have deprived myself of rest and health, have worked my brain to madness; and when I looked to reap my great reward, a flash breaks in upon my darkened soul, and tells me my attempt was impious, and that the fruition will be fatal to my peace for ever. *(He again listens.)* All is still! The dreadful spectre of a human form—no mortal could withstand the horror of that countenance—a mummy embued with animation could not be so hideous as the wretch I have endowed with life!—miserable and impious being that I am! Elizabeth!

brother! Agatha!—fairest Agatha! never more dare I look upon your virtuous faces. Lost! lost! lost!

(Music.—Frankenstein sinks on a chair; sudden combustion heard, and smoke issues, the door of laboratory breaks to pieces with a loud crash—red fire within.—The Monster discovered at door entrance in smoke, which evaporates—the red flame continues visible. The Monster advances forward, breaks through the balustrade or railing of gallery immediately facing the door of laboratory, jumps on the table beneath, and from thence leaps on the stage, stands in attitude before Frankenstein, who had started up in terror; they gaze for a moment at each other.)

Frank. The horrid corpse to which I have given life!

(Music.—The Monster looks at Frankenstein most intently, approaches him with gestures of conciliation. Frankenstein retreats round to R. H., the Monster pursuing him.)

Frank. Fiend! dare not to approach me—avaunt, or dread the fierce vengeance of my arm.

(Music.—Frankenstein takes the sword from off nail 3 E., points with it at Monster, who snatches the sword, snaps it in two and throws it on stage. The Monster then seizes Frankenstein—loud thunder heard—throws him violently on the floor, ascends the staircase, opens the large window on L. H. 3 E., and disappears through the casement. Frankenstein remains motionless on the ground.—Thunder and lightning until the drop falls.

END OF ACT I.

Act II. Scene I.

An Apartment in the House of Elizabeth, at Belrive.—Table and chairs. The hurried music from the close of the First Act to play in continuance until this scene is discovered, and Frankenstein enters L. H., hastily, to centre of stage. Music ceases.

Frank. At length in my sister's house!—and safe! I have paced with quick step, but at every turn feared to meet the wretch—my heart palpitates with the sickness of fear! What have I cast on the world? a creature powerful in form, of supernatural and gigantic strength, but with the mind of an infant. Oh, that I could recall my impious labour, or suddenly extinguish the spark which I have so presumptuously bestowed.—Yet that were murder—murder in its worst and most horrid form—for he is mine—my own formation. Ha! who approaches?

Enter Elizabeth, R. H., they embrace.

Eliza. My dear Victor! my dear brother!

Frank. Elizabeth!

Eliza. You come to stay, I hope, till our wedding is over. Clerval will be here presently. Alas! Frankenstein! your cheek is pallid—your eye has lost its wonted lustre. Oh, Victor, what are the secrets that prey upon your mind and form?—The pernicious air of your laboratory will be fatal to you.

Frank. *(Apart.)* Fatal indeed!

Eliza. I pray you, for my sake, cease—I understand upon one subject you have laboured incessantly.

Frank. One subject! *(Aside.)* Am I discovered?

Eliza. You change colour, my dear brother. I will not mention it—I—there is a wildness in your eyes for which I cannot account.

Frank. *(Starts.)* See—see—he is there!

Eliza. Dearest Frankenstein—what is the cause of this?

Frank. Do not ask me. I—I thought I saw the dreaded spectre glide into the room.

Eliza. Calm your mind, Victor.

Frank. Pardon me, Elizabeth. I know not what you will think of me.

Eliza. I have intelligence of one dear to you, and for whom, prior to your close attention to study, you had the tenderest regard.—Say, Victor, will you not be glad to hear that I have a clue to lead you to your lost love, Agatha de Lacey!

Frank. Agatha! dearest Agatha! her name recalls my sinking spirits—where—where is she to be found? Oh, would that I ne'er had been robbed of her! 'Twas her loss that drove me to deep and fatal experiments!

Eliza. A traveller! a beautiful Arabian girl, was here but last night; she was seeking Felix de Lacey, the brother of Agatha, to whom she had been betrothed—she gave me the information that the family are but a short distance from hence—the Valley of the Lake.

Frank. And Agatha there?—Agatha! there is yet life and hope for me—Ah, no. *(Aside.)* The dreadful monster I have formed!—away with thought! Elizabeth, I will instantly seek her. Agatha's smiles shall move this heavy pressure—to the Valley of the Lake.—Farewell, sister, farewell!

(They embrace, and exeunt Elizabeth R. H., Frankenstein, L. H.)

Scene II.

A wood in the neighbourhood of Geneva. On L. H., a Bush—a Gipsy's fire flaming near 3 E. R. H., over which hangs a cauldron. A group of Gipsies discovered surrounding the fire in various positions. All laugh as the scene discovers them. When Tanskin, Hammerpan, with others, (male and female) advance to sing the following.

Chorus.
Urge the slow rising smoke,
Give the faggot a poke,
For unroofed rovers are we;
Whilst our rags flutt'ring fly,
We the brown skin espy,
Our vellum of pedigree.
Behold each tawny face
Of our hard-faring race,
Which the cold blast ne'er can feel;
See our glossy hair wave,
Hear us, loud, as we crave
But dumb only when we steal!

Tan. I tell you it was even so, friend Hammerpan—a giant creature, with something of a human shape; but ugly and terrible to behold as you would paint the Devil.

Ham. And does this monster any mischief, or is he a pacific monster?

Tan. I never heard of any being harmed by him.

Ham. Then why are you so frightened, Master Tanskin? For my part, should he come across my path, let who will fly, I'll stand my ground like an anvil!

Tan. And get well beat for once for your pains. *(Flute heard.)* What sounds are those?

Ham. (Returning to the fire, 3 E. R. H.) Why, 'tis Felix, the son of old De Lacey. The young fellow is much famed for his excellence upon the flute, as the father for his piety, charities, and twanging on the harp, which, together with the beauty of his daughter, seems to have turned the heads and won the hearts of all the surrounding country. But come, my merry wanderers, our meal is smoking. I'faith, I'm in a rare relishing humour for it, so, prithee, dame, ladle us out our porridge. Fegs, it scents rarely! *(Sniffs.)* Leeks, mutton, porridge, with a whole dead sheep in it.

(The gipsies crowd round the fire with their bowls.)

Tan. *(Pointing off, L. H.)* See there! that's he! that's the tall bully. He looks like the steeple of Ingoldstadt taking a walk. See yonder, comrades!

Ham. See what?

Tan. *(Trembling.)* As I'm a living rogue, 'tis he!

Ham. One of the Devil's grenadiers, mayhap! Pooh! Pooh! old Tanskin, we all know you are a living rogue, but you won't frighten us with your ten feet. Come, give me my drink, I say. *(One of the gipsies gives him a wooden bowl.)* Gentlemen gipsies, here's all your good—ha! ha! ha!—

(Music.—The Monster appears on an eminence of the bush, L. H. 2 E., or a projecting rock.)

Ham. Help! murder! wouns! 'tis the Devil himself! Away with the porridge!

[Music.—Hammerpan and all the Gipsies shriek and run off, R. H. U. E. The Monster descends, pourtrays by action his sensitiveness of light and air, perceives the gipsies' fire, which excites his admiration—thrusts his hand into the flame, withdraws it hastily in pain. Takes out a lighted piece of stick, compares it with another faggot which has not been ignited. Tastes the food expressive of surprise and pleasure. Footsteps heard, and the Monster retreats behind the bush, L. H.

Enter Agatha, followed by Felix, his flute slung at his back, L. H.

Aga. Yes, my dear Felix, our father is anxious for your return. He bade me seek you, and conducted by the mellifluous sounds of your flute, the task was not one of great difficulty. Oh, Felix! how delightful is the reflection that both you and my father possess the skill of banishing for a few moments the horrors of our present misery. In the midst of poverty, how consoling it is to possess such a brother as you are. Dear, thoughtful Felix, the first little white flower that peeped out from beneath the snowy ground you brought, because you thought it would give pleasure to your poor Agatha.

Felix. We are the children of misfortune—poverty's chilling grasp nearly annihilates us. Our poor blind father, now the inmate of our cottage—he who has been blessed with prosperity to be thus reduced—the noble-minded old De Lacey. Wretched man that I am, to have been the cause of ruin to both father and sister.

Aga. Nay, Felix, we suffered in a virtuous cause! Poor Safie, thy beloved—

Felix. Is, I fear, lost to me for ever. The treacherous Mahometan, her father, whose escape I aided from a dungeon in Paris (where he was confined as a State prisoner), that false father has doubtless arrived at Constantinople, and is triumphing at the fate of his wretched dupes.

Aga. Nay, Felix—

Felix. Alas, Agatha! for aiding that escape, my family—my beloved family—are suffering exile and total confiscation of fortune.

Aga. But Safie still loves you?

Felix. That thought is the more maddening! Safie! fairest Safie!—and she was my promised reward for liberating her faithless father—dragged away with him and forced to comply with his obdurate wishes. Oh, she is lost—lost to me for ever! *(Crosses to L. H.)* The early passion of each of us has been blighted, our rigorous imprisonment and sudden banishment have driven all trace of thee from thy admirer, young Frankenstein.

Aga. Dear Felix, press not more wretched recollections on my mind. I consider Frankenstein lost to me for ever. In abject poverty, dare I hope that the brilliant and animated student could e'er think of the unfortunate Agatha. *(Weeps.)* Let me dry these unworthy tears and exert a woman's firmest fortitude. My soul is henceforth devoted exclusively to the service of my poor dark father. Felix, you shall behold me no longer unhappy.

Duett—Felix and Agatha
Of all the knots which Nature ties,
The secret, sacred sympathies,
That, as with viewless chains of gold,
The heart a happy prisoner hold,
None is more chaste—more bright—more pure,
Stronger, stern trials to endure;
None is more pure of earthly leaven,
More like the love of highest heaven,
Than that which binds in bonds how blest
A daughter to a father's breast.

[Exeunt Agatha and Felix, R. H.

(Music.—The Monster cautiously ventures out—his mantle having been caught by the bush, he disrobes himself, leaving the mantle attached to the rock, on L. 2 E.; he watches Felix and Agatha with wonder and rapture, appears irresolute whether he dares to follow them; he hears the flute of Felix, R. H. 2 E., stands amazed and pleased, looks around him, snatches at the empty air, and with clenched hands puts them to each ear—appears vexed at his disappointment in not possessing the sound; rushes forward afterwards, again listens, and, delighted with the sound, steals off, catching at it with his hands, 2 E. R. H.)

SCENE III.

Exterior of the Cottage of Old De Lacey. On R. H. U. E. a hovel, with a low door, near which are two or three large logs of wood and a hatchet; a small basket with violets on a stool at the R. H. side of the cottage door, and a stool also on the L. H. side of the cottage, whereon De Lacey is discovered seated, leaning on his cane, a common harp at his side.—Music.

De L. Another day is added to the life of banished De Lacey. *(Rises and comes forward.)* But how will it be passed—like the preceding days—in wretched poverty, hopeless grief, and miserable darkness! *(Calls.)* Agatha! Felix! Alas! I am alone. Hark! 'tis the flute of Felix!—my children come. They must not suppose me cheerless—my harp is here—'tis a fair deceit on them—my harp which has so oft been damped with the tears from my sightless eyes—the sound of it is the only indication I can give that I am contented with my lot!

(Music.—De Lacey returns to his seat L. H. of cottage, and plays the harp. The Monster enters, L. H. 2 E., attracted by the harp, suddenly perceives De Lacey, and approaches towards him—expresses surprise by action that De Lacey does not avoid him—discovers his loss of sight, which the Monster appears to understand by placing his hand over his own eyes, and feeling his way. At the conclusion of the music on the harp—occasioned, as it were, by the Monster having placed his hand on the instrument—a short pause, and during which the Monster, having lost the sound, appears to be looking for it, when the harp music is again resumed. In the midst of the music (without ceasing) a voice is heard.)

Felix. (Within, R. H.) This way, Agatha.

(The Monster, alarmed, observes the little door of hovel, which he pushes open, signifies that he wishes for shelter, and retreats into this hovel or wood-house by the ending of the harp music by De Lacey, when

Enter Felix and Agatha, R. H.

Felix. (Apart to Agatha.) Observe his countenance, beaming with benevolence and love—behold those silver hairs—and, Agatha, I—I have reduced him to this pitiable state of poverty!

Aga. Cease, Felix, this self-reproach. *(Goes to her father.)* We have returned, dear father. Have you wanted us?

(Agatha leads her father forward.)

De L. *(C.)* No, no, Agatha! You anticipate all my wants, and perform every little office of affection with gentleness.

Aga. *(R.)* Is it not my duty, and am I not rewarded by your kind smiles?

De L. Amiable girl, let thy poor father kiss thee. *(They embrace.)* Felix, my son, where are you? *(Felix comes forward, L. H., and takes his hand.)* Now I am cheerful—I am happy!—indeed I am, my children! Let me encourage you to cast off your gloom. What—a tear, Agatha!

Aga. Nay, dear sir!

De L. 'Tis on my hand.

(Pressing her hand to his lips, which he had held in his while speaking to Felix.)

Felix. *(Assuming gaiety.)* Now must I to labour again. Our fuel is nearly exhausted. My time has been so lately occupied I have omitted my task in the forest.

(Music.—Felix takes up a hatchet and chops a log of wood at U. E. R. H.)

Safie. *(At a distance, U. E. L. H.)* Felix!

Aga. What voice was that?

Felix. It cannot be—no—it was but fancy!

(Music resumed.—Felix chops the log in continuance—at a similar break in the tune the same voice heard again, nearer.)

Safie. *(Without, U. E. L. H.)* Felix!

(No music.)

Felix. That magic sound! Alas! no—there is no such happiness in store for me!

Safie. *(Without, at 1 E. L. H., louder.)* Felix! Felix!

(Music.—Felix drops the hatchet, rushes forward.—At the same instant Safie enters, L. H., and falls into the arms of Felix.)

Felix. 'Tis she!—Safie! Beloved of my soul!—Ah! revive!

De L. *(On R. H.)* Safie, the traitor's daughter? Impossible!

Aga. *(On L. H.)* 'Tis, indeed, our sweet Safie!

Felix. *(2nd on R. H.)* We never will part more! Father! father! would that you could behold her! It is my dear, lost Safie.

(Music.—Safie revives, crosses to old De Lacey, kneels, and kisses his hand, during which the Monster appears at the little hovel, watching them, and then retires within again.)

De L. Bless you, my child! where is your father—where the treacherous friend who devoted us to ignominy?

(Safie rises.)

Safie. I have fled from him; he would have sacrificed his daughter, loathing the idea that I should be united to one of Christian faith. I—I have sought the love and protection of my Felix!

Felix. Faithful girl! Your constancy shall be crowned by my eternal love and gratitude.

Aga. *(L. H.)* But, Safie, you are fatigued. Come, dear girl, and on my lowly couch seek repose.

(Music.—Safie affectionately kisses and presses De Lacey's hand, embraces Felix, crosses back to Agatha, and is led into the cottage by Agatha and Felix.)

Felix. (Who returns with a gun from cottage-door.) Father, I am wild with joy!—no longer the sad, pining Felix. The sun of prosperity again gleams on us—Safie has returned! I am rich!—happy! But hold! I must procure refreshment for our guest. Our larder is not too much encumbered with provision. I'll to the village—I'll cross the forest—I'll hunt, shoot—and all in ecstasy! Farewell, father! I'll soon be back. Farewell!

[Exit Felix, R. H.

(Music.—De Lacey turns up the stage, and again seats himself on his cottage stool, L. H. side of door.—Re-enter Monster, examines log of wood, takes up hatchet, intimating he understands the use of it, and rushes off with the hatchet, L. H.—Music ceases.

De L. (Calls.) Agatha!

Enter Agatha from cottage.

Aga. Did you call, father?

De L. Sleeps your sweet guest?

Aga. Fatigue will soon lull her to repose. I should not have left her had not I thought I heard you call me.

(Exit Agatha into cottage again.—De Lacey rises and takes up the basket of flowers from stool on the R. H. side of the cottage door.)

De L. (Smelling the violets.) How delightful is the perfume!—more exquisite because I am debarred the pleasure of beholding these sweet emblems of spring! The touch and scent elevate my spirits! How ungrateful am I to complain! In the contemplation of thee, oh, Nature, the past will be blotted from my memory!—the present is tranquil, and the future gilded by bright rays of hope and anticipations of joy!

(Music.—De Lacey replaces the basket of flowers, and returns to his seat, leaning pensively on his cane.—The Monster, L. H., enters with a pile of green faggots with foliage on his shoulders.—Crosses to U. E. R. H., and throws them loosely on the stage—Smiles with gratulation at that which he has accomplished.—Approaches De Lacey, falls flat at his feet, then kneels to him, and is about to press his hand.—De Lacey feels around him with his cane and hand, without the knowledge of anyone being near him, and seated all the time—then calls.)

De L. Agatha! Agatha!

(Music.—The Monster instantly retreats into hovel, and Agatha enters from cottage door.)

—Agatha, child, I pray you lead me in.

(Rises from his seat, and comes forward.)

Aga. Yes, father. Good heavens! why, Felix could not have returned from the forest so quickly? What a quantity of wood!

De L. How?

Aga. Here is fuel to last us for a long time. How could we have been so bountifully supplied? Come, father, to the cottage—come!

(Music.—Agatha leads De Lacey into cottage, afterwards comes forward.)

—Frankenstein! vain is the endeavour to drive you from my recollection. Each bird that sings, each note of music that I hear, reminds me of the sweet moments of my former love!

Song—Agatha

(Flute accompaniment, L. H., behind the scenes.)

In vain I view the landscapes round,
  Or climb the highest hill;
In vain, in vain, I listen to the sound
  Of ev'ry murmuring rill.
For vain is all I hear or see,
When Victor dear is far from me. *(Thrice.)*
But hark, hark, hark,
My love, my love is near,
His well-known dulcet notes I hear. *(Thrice.)*

Oh, yes, my love is near,
  I hear him in the grove;
Soon will he be here,
  And breathe soft vows of love.
Oh, fly not yet, ye blissful hours,
  Oh, fly not yet away;
While love its soft enchanting pours,
  Prolong, prolong your stay! *(Thrice.)*
Oh, yes, my love is near,
  I hear him in the grove,
Soon will he be here,
  And breathe soft vows of love!

[Exit Agatha into cottage.—(The cottage door in centre of flat.)

SCENE IV.

A Wild Forest.—1st Grooves.

Enter Felix, L. H., with his gun.

Felix. Not a shot yet—and, egad, joy has made my hand so unsteady, that were a fine pheasant to get up, I could not bring it down again. Thy return, sweet Safie, has restored me to existence. When I thought I had lost thee for ever, I was occupied by gloomy thoughts, and neither heeded the descent of the evening star nor the golden sunrise reflected on the lake; but now my love fills my imagination, and all is enjoyment!

Song—Felix

Thy youthful charms, bright maid, inspire,
  And grace my fav'rite theme,
Whose person kindles soft desire,
  Whose mind secures esteem.
Oh, hear me then my flame avow,
  And fill my breast with joy—
A flame which taught by time to grow,
  No time can e'er destroy.
My tender suit with smiles approve,
And share the sweets of mutual love.

When autumn yields her ripen'd corn,
  Or winter, darkening, lowers,
With tenderest care I'll soothe thy morn,
And cheer thy evening hours.
Again, when smiling spring returns,
  We'll breathe the vernal air;

And still when summer sultry burns,
  To woodland walks repair—
There seek retirement's sheltered grove,
  And share the sweets of mutual love.

(Felix retires up stage, R. H.)
Enter Frankenstein, L. H.

Frank. In vain do I seek a respite from these dreadful thoughts—where'er I turn my eyes I expect to behold the supernatural Being!—to see him spring from each woody recess—but on, on to Agatha, and repose.

Felix. A traveller! and surely I know his air and manner. *(Comes forward on R. H.)*

Frank. Good stranger, can you direct me to the habitation of old De Lacey?

Felix. Better than most persons, I trust.

Frank. How! Felix De Lacey!

Felix. The same! the same! Frankenstein! your hand, my friend—'tis long since we have met.

Frank. Your strange and sudden disappearance from Paris—

Felix. Makes as strange a story, with which I shall not now detain you. Come to our humble cottage. Egad! I'm overjoyed to see you!

Frank. And Agatha?

Felix. Has still a warm corner of her heart for you. Come, we have only to cross the wood.

Hammerpan. *(Without, R. H.)* Any good Christians in the neighbourhood?

Felix. What have we here!

Enter Hammerpan, 2 E. R. H., with a long pole, tinker's utensils, fire kettle, &c.

Ham. Real Christians! human beings! Oh, good gentlemen, have you seen it?

Felix. It!—what? *(Crosses to him.)*

Ham. Ah! that's it! As I live, an hour ago, I saw it in the forest!

Felix. What do you mean by *it?*

Ham. My hair stood on end like mustard and cress, and so will yours when you see it!

Felix. Get you gone! you are tipsy!

Ham. I wish I was. As I take it, you are Master Felix, of the Valley of the Lake; we've done business together before now.

Felix. I know you not!

Ham. I mended your kettle t'other day. You did me a good turn—one good turn deserves another—I'll put you on your guard—the very devil is abroad.

Frank. *(Aside.)* How!

Felix. *(Laughs.)* Ha! ha! ha! You romancing tinker!

Ham. You may laugh, but the other gentleman don't laugh. You may perceive *he* believes it. *(To Frankenstein.)* I saw it—I saw it with *this one eye.*

Felix. One eye!

Ham. Yes, I've lost the other—a little boy threw a pebble at it, and I've been *stone* blind ever since, gentlemen. He was ten feet six long, *(holds his pole high up.)* with a head of black lanky locks down to his very elbows.

Frank. 'Tis the demon! *(Apart to himself.)* What did this strange object! *(To Hammerpan.)*

Ham. It didn't speak to me, nor I to *it.* I saw it at first in the forest picking acorns and berries—and then, after it had dispersed our tribe, like a ferret among the rats—it took a drink of our broth, and burnt its fingers in our fire.

Frank. And what became of this creature?

Ham. I wasn't curious enough to inquire. My wife was in fits at the sight of the devil—so I was obliged to keep my one eye upon her.

Felix. Your one eye has been pretty well employed. Come, come, gipsy, we'll cross the wood, and see if this man mountain is to be met.

Ham. The good genius of wandering tinkers forbid!

Felix. *(To Frankenstein.)* And now, my friend, we'll on to the cottage.

Frank. So, so! *(Apart.)* I will follow ye!

[Exeunt Hammerpan and Felix, R. H.

Frank. So! the peasants have already been terrified by the ungainly form! Ambitious experimentalist! The consciousness of the crime I have committed eternally haunts me! I have indeed drawn a horrible curse on my head! He may be malignant, and delight in murder and wretchedness! a whole country may execrate me as its pest! Every thought that bears towards my baneful project causes my lips to quiver and heart to palpitate. I must now to the cottage of Felix. Agatha, fairest Agatha, instead of smiles, your lover will meet you with dark and hopeless despondency.

[Exit Frankenstein, R. H.

Scene v.

Evening.—Interior of the cottage of De Lacey.—The thatched roof in sight. On R. H. U. E. a wood fire.—Through an open rustic porch, C., are visible a rivulet, and small wooden bridge—a wooden couch on L. H.—Music.—De Lacey discovered seated thereon, with Agatha next him in attendance. The Monster appears through the portico, C., watching them, and regards Agatha with rapture.—Agatha kisses her father's hand, crosses to R. H., takes a small pail or hand bucket, and trips through the portico on to the bridge to procure water. The Monster having retreated on Agatha's approach, pursues her on the bridge. Agatha, turning suddenly, perceives the Monster, screams loudly, and swoons, falling into the rivulet. The Monster leaps from the bridge, and rescues her.

De L. *(Speaks during the melo music.)* Gracious Heaven! *(Starting forward from the couch.)* That cry of horror! Agatha!—Despair!—My sweet child where art thou? Agatha! Agatha!

(The Monster appears at the portico entrance, with Agatha insensible in his arms.—The Monster comes forward to L. H., gently places Agatha in her fathers arms, tenderly guiding the hand of old De Lacey to support his daughter.—Agatha recovers, and perceiving the Monster, with a shriek, again faints—the Monster hovering over them with fondness.—Felix, with his gun (loaded), suddenly enters through the open portico from U. E. L. H., and speaks whilst entering—walks on to R. H.)

Felix. Agatha! Victor Frankenstein is here! What horrid monster is this! Agatha!—my father in danger!

(Music.—The Monster retreats from L. H., and walks round to R. H., Felix following him—discharges his gun—wounds the Monster in the shoulder—who writhes under the agony of the wound from which the blood flows—would rush on Felix, who keeps the gun presented—he is deterred by fear of a repetition of the wound. Felix remaining on the defensive.—Safie, alarmed at the firing of the gun by Felix, rushes on to Agatha and De Lacey.—Enter Frankenstein through the portico, from L. H. U. E. The Monster rushes up to Frankenstein, and casts himself at his feet, imploring protection.)

Frank. Misery! the Fiend! *(Crosses to R. H.)* Hence, avoid me! do not approach me—thy horrid contact would spread a pestilence throughout my veins!—hence—no, no! You shall not quit this spot—but thus—thus I destroy the wretch I have created!

(Music.—Frankenstein endeavours to stab him with his dagger, which the Monster strikes from his

hand—and expresses that his kindly feeling towards the human race, have been met by abhorrence and violence; that they are all now converted into hate and vengeance.—In desperation, the Monster pulls a flaming brand from the fire, R. H. U. E., and in agony of feeling, dashes through the portico, setting fire to the whole of the portico, and the entire back of the cottage—the thatched roof and rafters.)

Felix. Ha! Frankenstein! 'tis no time to parley—the cottage is on fire! that fierce gigantic figure of terrific aspect waves aloft his torch, as if in triumph of the deed.

(The large doors in the centre are suddenly closed from without, as if to prevent escape. A coarse yelling laugh is heard.)

Frank. Ha! 'tis that hideous voice! Quick, quick, let us fly! his hellish malice pursues me, and but with his death or with mine, will this persecution cease. Could I but place you beyond his power.

(Felix and Frankenstein (as soon as the Monster disappears, having climbed outside of the portico) force open the doors, when flaming faggots are thrown down at the portico entrance, and falling trees on fire block up the entrance. Felix and Frankenstein place the couch longways over the fallen trees, and fiery pile of faggots at the portico entrance, and Felix forces his way through the flames with old De Lacey, and then Safie—and, lastly, Frankenstein rushes out, bearing Agatha in his arms over the couch, in the midst of which parts of the building fall. The Monster brandishing the burning brand on the bridge, laughs exultingly, on which the drop falls.—Continue the "Presto music" until

END OF ACT II

Act III. Scene I.

The Garden of Elizabeth, at Belrive.—Morning. (Same as Act I, Scene II.)

Enter Clerval from terrace entrance R. H.

Cler. What a delightful morning! It is an auspicious commencement of the day which is to make me happy in the possession of my love! Elizabeth yet sleeps, peaceful be her slumbers, soft, she approaches.

Enter Elizabeth from the house on L. H.

Cler. Elizabeth, my love, why that look of anxiety?

Eliza. Oh, Clerval! we have had strange occurrences since you quitted me yesterday, our house is full of guests, my brother has brought here the family of De Lacey of whom you have heard me so often speak—

Cler. The family of De Lacey, the relatives of Agatha.

Eliza. By some extraordinary mystery, which is yet unexplained to me, the cottage in which Frankenstein discovered his mistress and her family was destroyed by fire; they arrived late last night, and all appear overcome with fatigue and terror; some dreadful calamity hangs about my dear brother.

Cler. How astonishing is his conduct. Alas! my sweet Elizabeth, in the midst of all this misery I am selfish—I trust these singular occurrences will not postpone our marriage. Consider, our friends are invited, the church is prepared.

Eliza. A few hours may explain these mysterious transactions. See now *(Looks towards house L. H.)* Frankenstein approaches—observe his agitated countenance and restless step; he has not slept since his return—he has armed himself with pistols and appears continually watching.

Cler. We will retire and avoid him for the present. This way, love.

[Exeunt Elizabeth and Clerval R. H., and enter Frankenstein from house.

Frank. Oh! how to avoid the powerful vengeance of the monster formed by my cursed ambition. I gave him energy and strength, to crush my own guilty head! My hours pass in dread, and soon the bolt may fall which will deprive me of existence! Yet *he* preserved the life of Agatha—he had some feeling of affection—how were those feelings requited!—by detestation, scorn, and wounds!—his look of everlasting malice! He will watch with the wiliness of a serpent, that he may sting with its venom! There is no hope but in his destruction. *(Takes out pistol.)* I dare not cease to guard and protect my friends. *(going to the door.)* Agatha has arisen. *(Conceals pistol.)*

Enter Agatha, a locket round her neck, from the house L. H.

Aga. Frankenstein, I behold you unhappy—flying to solitude—and I cannot help supposing that you might regret the renewal of our intercourse. Dear Frankenstein, I still love you, and confess that in my airy dreams of futurity you have been my constant friend and companion.

Frank. Agatha, you shall be mine! I will then divulge to you the secret which disturbs—nay, distracts me. *(Music, the Harmonica.—Distant bells.)* Those cheerful chimes announce the wedding day of Elizabeth and Clerval. My care-worn looks will but damp their merriment.

[Music.—Exeunt Frankenstein and Agatha, R. H.
Enter Felix and Safie from house, L. H.

Felix. Listen, Safie, to those merry village bells; they ring a rare contrast to our last night's misery. Soon, my Eastern rose, will they chime for us; and then away with care. This kiss—*(Embracing her.)*

Safie. Fie, Felix! in open daylight. You will deepen the blush of your Eastern rose.

Duet—Safie and Felix
Come with me, dear, to my mountain home,
And Hymen shall hallow the peaceful dome.
Leave all the world for love and for me,
And I will be all the world to thee.
Our life shall be all holiday—
Shall be all holiday.
Come o'er the dew-bespangled vale,
Where the violet blue and primrose pale
Peep from the verdant shade.
Come o'er the dew-bespangled vale,
Where the violet blue and primrose pale,
Where the violet blue and primrose pale
Peep from the verdant shade.
Come o'er the dew, &c, &c.

We'll fly to the shady grove,
And sigh and whisper, love
Till day begins to fade,
Till day begins, &c., &c.
We'll roam, and I will woo thee, love,
Where birds sing sweetly through the grove—
Where birds sing sweetly thro' the grove

Till day begins to fade.
We'll roam, and I will woo thee, love,
Where birds sing sweetly thro' the grove—
While birds sing, &c., &c., &c.

(Music, with the Bells.—Enter Madame Ninon, leading a group of Dancing Villagers, from the terrace entrance, R. H., and Elizabeth, with Clerval, re-enter, R. H. 1 E., the dancers having all ranged themselves on L. H.)

Ninon. Now, Madame Elizabeth—now, Mr. Clerval—we are all ready, and the priest is in waiting.

(Music resumed.—Elizabeth and Clerval, as also Safie and Felix, join the procession, and all the villagers dance off to music along the terrace, R. H., except Madame Ninon.

Ninon. There they go to be coupled, pretty dears! *(Calls towards, R. H.)* Fritz! Fritz! where is my stupid husband? I've stretched my neck out of joint looking for him. I expect him from the market at Geneva with a cargo of eatables and my new-fashioned beehive cap—all for our wedding festival of Mr. Frankenstein, who has brought his bride and her family here in consequence, as I am told, of their cottage being accidentally destroyed by fire last night. Oh! here the fellow comes, with his basket at his back, creeping like a snail.

Enter Fritz, from terrace entrance, R. H., with hamper at his back containing various articles, a lady's cap, and a live duck.

Fritz. Here I am, spousy. I've brought your list of articles. *(Ninon assists him in putting down the basket.)* Here's the trout, and the sugar-loaf, and the melons, and the nutmegs.

Ninon. But dear Fritz, where's my new beehive you were to bring from the milliner's at Geneva?

Fritz. Somewhere, I know. *(Looking and examining the contents of the hamper, cautiously opening the top.)* The three live ducks are lying a top of the maccaroni, squeezed up under the large Gruyere cheese.

Ninon. I hope to goodness my cap is not squeezed up!

Fritz. It's quite safe, I tell you. I put it at the very bottom of the basket.

Ninon. It will be in a nice state for my head, then!

Fritz. Lord, here's a rummaging fuss for the cap. I'm so nervous about it—you cautioned me so, you know. *(Still kneeling and searching the hamper.)* Oh, dear, where is it now? Oh, la, to be sure, spousy—here it is at last; la, I knew it was safe.

(He pulls the cap out, with a live duck in it.)

Ninon. *(Takes her cap from him.)* Oh, Fritz, it's spoiled! That duck has been laying in it!

Fritz. Not an egg, I hope, Ninon!

Ninon. Alas! see how it is rumpled.

(She takes from the cap two or three of the duck's small feathers, which fall on the stage.)

Fritz. *(Aside.)* Ha!—he! he! Cap and feathers!

Ninon. You careless, good-for-nothing fellow! take the basket in, you sinner!

(Having first replaced her cap in the hamper.)

Fritz. Oh! *(To the Duck.)* You look very jolly, my fine fellow, considering you are going to be killed for dinner. Wait till the peas are ready! I never saw such a piece of *quackery* as that cap in all my life!

(Draws the basket after him into the house, and comes forward on the L. H. during the duet.)

Ninon. My finery destroyed by that varlet! But even *that* shall not disconcert me. My sweet mistress is united to-day to the man of her heart, and in spite of my loss I will be merry, and dance till I can dance no longer.

Duet—Ninon and Fritz

(Welsh air.)

Ninon. Oh! I'll hail the wedding day,
And be the gayest of the gay,
Till age has tripp'd my steps away.

Fritz. (Re-entering from house, L. H.) Away!

Ninon. Your manners were not taught in France.

Fritz. La, wife! you never learnt to dance,
A horse at fifty—(Aside)—cannot prance—
Ah, nay!

Ninon. While pipes and tabors playing sweetly,
With all my soul I'll foot it featly,

Fritz. Yes, I guess you'll hobble neatly.
Wife!

Ninon. Don't wife me, you saucy fellow!
Sure you're tipsy—

Fritz. Only mellow.
We'll all be so, for that is fun and life!

Ninon. } *Together* Don't wife me, you saucy fellow.
Fritz. } I won't wife you, I'm only mellow.

Ninon. I ne'er was tipsy.

Fritz. You ne'er were tipsy, only mellow.
Wife!

[Fritz dances her up to the house, L. H. Ninon turns, boxes his ear, and they exeunt into house, L. H. Music.—The Monster appears from terrace entrance, watching about, and retreats R. H., as Fritz re-enters from house, L. H.

Fritz. Oh! *(Rubbing his cheek.)* What's the use of a fine cap to her? she's so short, unless she stood on a chair, in a crowd—no one would see her, or her new-fashioned bee-hive either.

(During the above speech William comes from the house, L. H., behind Fritz on tiptoe, and gives Fritz a smark smack on the back, who being fearfully alarmed, cries out lustily.)

Fritz. Oh, dear! who's that? There now, that's the way just to make me nervous again. What do you want, Master William?

Will. (On L. H.) I can't get a soul to speak to me in the house—some are busy—some are gone to be married—will you play with me, Fritz?

Fritz. I like a game of play—it's so relaxing. When work was over I used to play with my cow's calf.

Will. Do play with me, Fritz.

(Music.—Dances backwards towards the balustrade of terrace, when the Monster, during the foregoing speeches had been watching the child, then disappearing by falling flat on his face between the balustrades of the terrace, waits the opportunity as William is tripping backwards, and suddenly seizes the child, throws him across his shoulder (à la Rolla), and rushes off, R. H. terrace entrance, to hurried music. Fritz, turning round, sees them, utters a cry of horror, and speaks through the music.)

Fritz. Help, help, murder! Wife! the devil! Oh, my nerves!

[Exit Fritz, frightened, into house, L. H.

Scene ii.

A Country View. Rustic Church in the distance. On R. H. 3 E. a large Yew Tree, spread plentifully with boughs. Music.—A Foreground on L. H. 3 E., with pathway behind it. The procession, as before, returning from the marriage ceremony. The corps de ballet, Villagers, preceding, dancing, followed by Felix, Safie, Clerval, and Elizabeth, all L. H.

Ninon. *(Heard without, R. H.)* Oh, mistress! Oh!

Fritz. I couldn't help it—murder!

Enter Ninon and Fritz, R. H.

Ninon. But where did you leave him?

Fritz. I didn't leave him, he left me. Oh, dear. *(Cries.)* Murder! My nerves!

Ninon. Oh, wicked Fritz!

Eliza. What is the matter, good Ninon?

Fritz. She says her husband's wicked.

Ninon. *(To Elizabeth.)* William, your brother William is the matter; the boy is lost, no one can find him. I sent him to that Fritz, that he might be out of the way.

Fritz. Yes; and now he's out of everybody's way.

Eliza. This is most extraordinary—a frolic of the little rogue.

Fritz. No, no, it isn't; I saw—my nerves! Oh, dear! I saw—a great something snatch him up. *(Cries.)* I—oh!—oh—dear! Oh, oh, oh! Murder!

Cler. There's Frankenstein.

Enter Frankenstein, L. H., with a pistol.

Eliza. My dear Victor, know you aught of William? The child has been missed in a most unaccountable manner.

Frank. My brother missing!

Ninon. Fritz was with him.

Fritz. Oh, master! a great creature—oh! oh! oh!

Frank. Oh, horror!—the demon!

Cler. Hasten, my friends, one and all—all search. Our pastime is marr'd till the boy is found.

[Music.—All exeunt in consternation at different entrances, excepting Frankenstein, who appears lost in desponding reverie.—He turns; the boughs of the yew tree, R. H., are pulled apart, and the Monster is discovered behind it, with William in his grasp.—Frankenstein draws a pistol, and points it—the Monster holds forth the child, when Frankenstein lowers his pistol, and kneels.—The Monster again shoulders the child, and rushes off within the path, L. H. 3 E.—Frankenstein rises, and pursues them in despair. L. H. 3 E.

Scene iii.

An Apartment in the Villa at Belrive.—In C. of F. a wide folding window opening to the Garden, closed.—A side door, U. E. L. H.—Another, U. E. R. H.—A table in C. of stage, with red baize covering.

Agatha and Ninon enter, R. H.

Ninon. The most unaccountable disappearance of my dear little boy, at such a moment—on such a day—when we should have been so merry!

Aga. It is indeed strange and fearful; let us hope that William will soon be discovered, and brought home. *(Aside.)* The wild phantom that fired our cottage, surely, is not concerned.

Ninon. I can do nothing but think of William—that is your room, ma'm—*(points, L. H. U. E.)*—you will find it well furnished—with such sweet blue eyes—everything is comfortable—unhappy little boy! There's a fine grate in the room—with two little dimples on each cheek! There's a cabinet in the corner—curly locks! Forgive me, ma'am; I fostered the pretty child, and I cannot get him out of my head.

Aga. Pray leave me, Ninon, and give me the earliest intelligence of Mr. Frankenstein's return.

Ninon. All the festivities of the wedding-day destroyed, till the dear unlucky urchin is found. *(Sobbing.)* The sweet little, naughty, rosy-cheek'd rogue! how I will whip him when he comes home.

[Exit Ninon, R. H.

(During the above the Monster is seen at the window watching, and disappears.)

Aga. Frankenstein! what a singular fatality is attached to you—with wealth and friends, doomed to be miserable!—This mystery!—I feel a heavy foreboding of mischance! a presentiment of evil pervades my mind. I may regret the day that I have given my affection to Frankenstein—I may rue the hour that I left our homely hut.

[Exit Agatha into door, U. E. L. H., afterwards enter Frankenstein, R. H., reflecting—two pistols in his belt.)

Frank. One sudden and desolating change has taken place—the fangs of remorse tear my bosom and will not forego their hold!—pursue the wretch! One might as well attempt to overtake the winds, or confine a mountain torrent. My poor brother—I—I am thy murderer—the author of unalterable evils. There is scope for fear, so long as anything I love remains. *(Goes to door U. E. L. H.)* Agatha! she reclines sleeping on yon sofa.

(The Monster during the above soliloquy reappears on the balcony of the window—and while Frankenstein is looking in at the door, U. E. L. H., the Monster creeps in at the window, crouching beneath the table, unseen.)

Frank. Sleep on, sweet innocence! I dare not leave you; I will stay and guard your slumber, or the remorseless fiend will snatch your breath away.

(Music.—Frankenstein takes out a pistol and primes it—holding it in his hand.)

Frank. The wretch e'en now may be haunting the room—let me search around.

(Music.—Frankenstein fearfully examines each avenue, advancing on L. H., to the front, and crossing to R. H.—The Monster, unperceived by him, follows his footsteps, making an ineffectual attempt occasionally to gain his loaded pistol. Frankenstein leads on, looking in at door, U. E. R. H., passes behind table, when the Monster falls flat before table, still unseen by Frankenstein, who then places the loaded pistol on table, and turns to close the folding large window. While Frankenstein has his back turned, the Monster snatches up the pistol, hugs it, and escapes into door U. E. L. H. Frankenstein having closed the window comes forward.)

Frank. Oh, Agatha! would that I had banished myself for ever from my native country, and wandered a friendless outcast over the earth, rather than I had again met you—perhaps to bring you in the grasp of my fiendish adversary—perhaps to—

(Pistol shot heard, U. E. L. H., and a piercing shriek.)

—My blood curdles! *(Goes to door, L. H. U. E.)* Ah! what do I behold? My last, last hope!

Music.—He rushes off into door, U. E. L. H.

Scene iv.

An Ante-chamber in Belrive.

Enter Elizabeth, R. H., hastily, meeting Ninon, L. H.—Music ceases.

Eliza. Whence is this fresh alarm?

Ninon. I know not, madam. Oh, wretched day for poor Ninon! Mr. Frankenstein is stark mad; he ran out but this instant, jumped into his boat, and rowed off rapidly.

Enter Fritz, L. H., alarmed.

Fritz. Oh, oh, oh!—I've seen it—I've seen it again! The great creature, it got out of one of our windows and scudded off in a boat, and there's Mr. Frankenstein got another boat, and is going after the great creature like lightning.

Eliza. Where—where are our friends?

Fritz. Oh, I don't know; there's Mr. Frankenstein gone after the great creature, Mr. Clerval and Mr. Felix have gone after Mr. Frankenstein, and I'm going after them all.

[Crosses, and runs off, R. H.

Safie. *(Without.)* Help! ah, help!

Enter Safie, L. H.—Crosses to Elizabeth, and throws herself into her arms.

Safie. Ah, Madame! Agatha, my sister—the gentle Agatha—I fear, is no more.

Omnes. Agatha!

Eliza. Gracious Heaven! what horrible destiny hangs over us?

Safie. Stretched on the ground she lies. Ah! Elizabeth, the spark of life may yet not be extinct.

Eliza. Hasten—hasten to the apartment.

[Hurried music.—Exeunt hastily, L. H., Elizabeth, Safie, and Madame Ninon.

Scene V.

Wild Border of the Lake. At the extremity of the stage, on U. E. R. H. (into flies), a lofty overhanging mountain of snow.

Music.—All the Gipsies discovered in various groups.

(A pistol shot is heard, R. H. The Gipsies start up alarmed. A second pistol is fired nearer. The Monster rushes on with the locket worn by Agatha during the piece, from R. H. 1 E. The Gipsies scream out and fly in all directions. Hammerpan is on the point of escaping, L. H., when the Monster seizes him, and Hammerpan falls down on being dragged back near R. H. The Monster points off to R. H., to intimate that Frankenstein is approaching, throws down the locket, commands the gipsy, Hammerpan, to show it to Frankenstein—the Monster threatens him, and rushing up the mountain, R. H. U. E., climbs, and disappears.)

Enter Frankenstein, 2 E. R. H., with two loaded pistols and a musket unloaded. At the same time Hammerpan rises and gets near 1st wing, L. H.

Frank. In vain do I pursue the wretch, in vain have I fired on him. *(Throws his gun from him, R. H.)* He eludes the bullet. Say, fellow, have you seen aught pass here?

Ham. The giant creature, who aroused us in the forest, rushed upon me but this instant, and pointing to the path by which you came, intimated that I should give you this.

(Presents locket to Frankenstein.)

Frank. 'Tis Agatha's—the murdered Agatha! Malicious fiend! it will joy you to know that my lacerated heart bleeds afresh. Revenge shall henceforth be the devouring and only passion of my soul. I have but one resource—I devote myself either in my life or death to the destruction of the Demon! Agatha! William! you shall be avenged.

Ham. See yonder *(points U. E. R. H.)*, the monster climbs the snow.

Frank. Then this rencontre shall terminate his detested life or mine!

(Music.—Frankenstein draws his pistol—rushes off at back of stage—leading to R. H. U. E.—The gipsies return at various entrances—both from L. H. and R. H.—At the same time, enter R.

H., Felix and Clerval with pistols, and Safie, Elizabeth, and Ninon following.—The Monster appears at the base of the mountain, Frankenstein pursuing R. H. U. E.)

Cler. Behold our friend and his mysterious enemy.

Felix. See—Frankenstein overtakes him—let us follow and assist him.

(Is going up stage with Clerval towards U. E. R. H.)

Ham. Hold, master! if the gun is fired, it will bring down a mountain of snow. Many an avalanche has fallen there.

(Music.—Frankenstein discharges his pistol.—The Monster and Frankenstein meet at the very extremity of the stage.—Frankenstein fires his second pistol—the avalanche falls and annihilates the Monster and Frankenstein.—A heavy fall of snow succeeds.—Loud thunder heard, and all the characters form a picture as the curtain falls.)

END

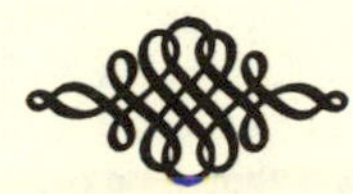

Richard Brinsley Peake

Another Piece of Presumption

(1823)

DRAMATIS PERSONAE

Devildum
Lee
Deputy Manager
Hobgoblin
Frankinstitch
Shovelhat
Ashpicker
Phoenix
Frizzy
Cleaver
Peacock
Jack in the Green
D. Lazy
Mrs. Frankinstitch
Cinderella
Mob—Journey Tailors—Drum & Fife—Dancers &c. &c.

Act 1st Scene 1st

Stage of the Adelphi Theatre.

Act Drop—Enter Mr. Lee & Under Prompter.

U. Prom. Mr. Lee, Sir you are wanted.

Lee. A person enquiring for me—Who is it?

U. Prom. I don't know, Sir—an odd looking fellow—from his impatience, and the papers in his pockets, I think he is an Author—

Lee. Damn those Authors—the Public do so now and then, or we should be over-run with them—What does this odd looking fellow want with me?

U. Prom. He says that while you were out of Town the Managers of the Adelphi Theatre accepted a Piece of *particularly peculiar* interest.

Lee. Well, I know there is a strange sort of thing come into the house—a Drama with a Spirit or Devil in it, or some such nonsense.

U. Prom. The Piece has been ordered for rehearsal Mr. Lee; and all the Performers have got their parts.

Lee. Not into their heads yet I'll be bound.

U. Prom. I can't say as to that, Sir—but there has been sad grumbling behind.

Lee. Grumbling behind?—Let me see my position—What do you mean?

U. Prom. Why the Ladies and Gentlemen are not pleased with their parts.

Lee. The performers are such funny folks, they don't know whether they are before or behind—but if the proprietors have directed this Piece to be rehearsed—It must be done you know—Send the Author up here on the stage—What's his name?

U. Prom. Here's his Card, Sir—written on a piece of paper.

Lee. Whitey-brown-paper—some poor Devil! Who can't afford fools-cap. *(reads)* Mr. Dramiticus Devildum. Devildum—What a name—Devil—he's below, is he?

U. Prom. Yes, Sir—standing by the fire—below—*(Exit U. Prom)*

Lee. Very singular that I should not have heard something of this Drama before—to be sure I have been out of Town, and it is within these two hours that I have had the pleasure of appearing before my friends in London.

Devild (without). Hollo!—call boy!—plague take you—Hollo!—you are making me a *call boy—(Enters)* Eh! here's the first Entrance, and gad, 'tis my first entrance here—*(bows)* Sir, I presume that you are denominated Mr. Lee the Stage Manager of the Adelphi—I have the honor to be to the most profound depths and innermost pits of respect your most obedient, obsequious, and much obliged Servant.

Lee. Sir—I—

Devil. You got my Card—hem!

Lee. Sir I—

Devild. I know what you are going to say, my fine fellow!—Your ineffable complacency & managerial urbanity would prompt you to speak thus—"My dear Devildum you are an aspiring and successful young man—depend upon my patronage and hearty concurrence to all your meritorious exertions."

Lee. I was precisely going to say all that, Mr. What's your name?

Devild. Devildum—Dramaticus Devil-*dum!*—If you were not going to say all that Mr. Lee—I think I see by a sparkle in your intelligent Eye, that you were about to add—my dear Devil-dum—*I,* that is *you* you know, am stage manager here, and anything you require in the shape of superb scenery, complicated machinery, costly properties, splendid decorations, you can immediately command—I am quite aware of your kind attentions.

Lee. Again, Sir—I have not nor cannot say so much to a perfect stranger.

Devild. Perfect—I am—stranger is a name I wish to avoid.

Lee. To business.

Devild. Business—mine's *a play—*

Lee. A play upon words, Sir—I think—favour me with the name of your Piece.

Devild. The Piece is here—Sir—here—no—not that—I have so many—I write for all the Theatres—

Lee. That must bring you a vast deal of money.

Devild. I don't know much about money—but I have a great many *pocket pieces*—here it is—no this is not that—that is the "*Mysterious Rat-Catcher*" and I flatter myself that's a very taking title—that is if you understand trap—if you bring out the *Mysterious Rat-Catcher* I shall want every trap on the stage—here it is—no that's the *Gloom Grand-father; or, The Sorrows of Three Generations,* in five acts.

Lee. Let me see your position, and be kind enough to confine yourself to the particular peculiar Drama.

Devild. Lawk Sir—I'm not confin'd at all—tho' sometimes Mrs. Devildum is—I've four or five little devildums at home—want anything of that sort, at a short notice, I am your man.

Lee. The production, Sir—the production—!

Devild. Here it is at last—here—bless you—*(kisses it)* you darling—here it is—"*Another Piece of Presumption.*"

Lee. Why, Sir—a Drama of that Title has already been many nights before the Town.

Devild. Talk of my Drama—but mine?—fie—psha! psha!

Enter John Shaw.

Shaw. Did you call, Sir?

Devild. No—not by any means!

Lee. My name is Shaw, Sir.

Devild. Your name Shaw. Well, the next time I want to express contempt, I won't call out your name—I'll say "Pish!" There's nobody of the name of "*Pish!*" in the House is there—? *(Shaw smiles)* You look unutterable nothings! there go about your business *(Exit Shaw)* Mr. Lee allow me to inform you that piece of *Presumption* can no more compare with this piece of presumption than I could hold a rushlight to be Billy Shakespear.

Lee (looking at MS.) Founded on *Frankenstein!*

Devild. Yes that is the principal gentleman in it, excepting another gentleman who is a nameless nothing—

Lee. But Mr. Devildum—have not I heard that there is something of an immoral tendency in this story?

Devild. So much the better—every body will come and see it—The moment I told my wife of its being improper she went and laid out her last 2 shillings in the gallery—the children cried in bed all the evening, & I went without my supper!

Lee. That piece, Sir—had a great deal of detraction—

Devild. And a great deal of *attraction*—Bring my *Presumption* out, Sir—and you'll probably set the zealous friends of morality to work—

Lee. Well, Sir.

Devild. That will make your fortune!—an abortive attempt to ruin the interests of a Theatre, or a performance is sure to add to its popularity—it sets all the world talking—it sets the Ladies all talking and when the Ladies begin to talk, Mr. Lee, Heaven knows when or where it will end—

(Enter Under Prompter)

U. Prom. All is ready, Sir, for rehearsal!

Devild. What, and are the performers dress'd, as I requested?

U. Prom. Yes, Sir, excepting the Gentleman that is not yet made—the piece is quite up—dresses—scenes—properties—

Devild. Well then I hope it will turn a little property into my pocket.

Lee. Come Mr. Devil-dum I must get you out of the way—suppose you let me put you in this Box here, over the Stage Door to see the rehearsal.

Devild. Bless my soul—What care they take of me—They are going to put me in a *Box!* I'm a very valuable piece of Mechanism, and they must have directions to keep this *side uppermost*. Come along Mr. Lee.

(Exeunt)

Overture continued.

They Enter & seat themselves in a Box.

Scene 2nd

Antechamber in the House of Frankinstitch.

Frizzy discovered in a chair.

Frizzy. Oh Frizzy! Frizzy! Why did you ever leave Whitechapel? What a situation for a Tailor!—Whitechapel—Where all the Needles come from!—there where your Mother—sold roasted apples—savoury & spitting—sauce for goose!—you must come here you spooney, and hire, and hire yourself as light porter to a first rate clothier! Where for your labour, you get your bed and vegetables, your couch & cabbage!—Mr. Frankinstitch is my Master, and a good sort of body, but that he is always wrapt up in his thoughts like a pair of breeches in brown paper. (*a knock*) What's that? every knock reminds me of those I get on my head with the sleeve board when my Master is in one of his *pillow*-fossical humours.

Cleaver (knocks) Frizzy!—Frizzy!

Friz. I declare it is Mr. Cleaver, Master's friend.

Enter Cleaver

Cleaver. How are you Frizzy? Can I see Mr. Frankinstitch?

Friz. I don't know Mr. Cleaver—he has as usual been pondering all night over a bason of water-gruel!

Cleaver. Why what the devil is come to Mr. Frankinstitch?

Friz. That's what I want to know!

Devild (in Box) Now you'll hear some of the story.

Lee. I'm glad of that—hush!

Devild. I will—it is interesting!

Friz. Mr. Frankinstitch sits all day ruminating & unconsciously snapping his sheers—oh, Sir!

Devild. Now you see he is leaning on Cleaver.

Lee. If I was Cleaver I'd cut him.

Devild. Why—he is going to be confidential.

Lee. Do be quiet—

Friz. I know you take your friendly pipe & toasted cheese together at Offleys & he respects you—but Mr. Cleaver I must unbutton my confidence—I fear that Mr. Frankinstitch has for some time past had dealings—

Cleaver. Large ones, I know, with the old clothesmen!

Friz. No—somebody deeper than them—Oh, I'll tell you—

Devild. Now it's coming.

Lee. Pray be still, Sir.

Friz. I have something wonderful to communicate; the other night he went to bed—

Cleav. Wonderful!

Friz. And something more astonishing, he got up again!

Cleav. Astonishing!

Friz. Hush!

Devild. I didn't speak.

Lee. Silence Mr. Devildum—keep your position.

Friz. Mr. Frankinstitch was fast asleep—but with his Eyes open like the front windows of a hackney chariot—"I shall manufacture it" he exclaim'd—"It will be all alive oh."—"If there is no baulk it will walk, stalk, talk!" Lauk, thought I, Master's like Dr. Faustus, he is raising the Devil!

Cleaver. You tedious fine drawn fool—your Master had been supping at the Goat and Boots, and the Welsh rabbits were hard of digestion—Go up to his cutting room—& see if he will *see* me.

Friz. I got to *see* double!—I know I shall get my nose snapt off either by Frankinstitch's ill temper, or by his sheers. What a heavy life for a light porter! *(Exit Fritz)*

Clea. 'Pon my life friend Frank-in-stitch! You are running your rigs prettily—What the plague have you got in your head? there was always room for something in it, for it was generally as empty as the poor Debtors' Box in Fleet Market—

Solo & Chorus of Tailors. Air, "Chough & Crow"

Cleav. My friend, the *Sneider's* wits are gone
From I can't say what loop—
With Ev'ning sigh, and morning moan,
Oh he's a nincompoop—!
With sheers and yard neglected then
His shopboard would be clear—
If 'twas not for his merry men—

Tailors (without). And we've all come from beer!

(They Enter)

Uprouse ye then my merry men—
For we've all come from beer!
But if his spirit does get low,
His trade gives up the Ghost.
Expect at length short commons then—
They will be short I fear—
Uprouse him then my merry men
Or you'll get no more beer—

Chos. Uprouse him &c.

1st Tai. Christopher Cabbage is my name
I'm known by my one Eye.
2nd Do. I'm Patrick Longmeasure the lame.
3d Do. And Bob Blue-thread am I.—
4th Do. My name is Baste—they call me Ben.
Clea. Your Master's spirits cheer—
Uprouse him then my merry men
Or you'll get no more Beer.
Chorus. Uprouse him &c.

(Exeunt Tailors into Workshop)

Cleav. Nine as civil *bodies* as I ever met with and good *hands* too, I'll be bound.

Enter Frankinstitch

Devild. There—that's the Hero of my piece—you see he's absorb'd—look at him—did you ever behold such a penitentiary figure? he's going to speak—he'll say something to the purpose—

Frank (starts). Ha!—Mr. Jemmy Cleaver!—

Clea. Good lauks—Frankinstitch! how ill you look! Your Eyes and Eyelashes look like red hairy gooseberrys!

Frank (starts again). Likely!—I have done a damn'd deal of thinking lately.

Cleav. No sure—

Frank. I am engaged heart, liver and lights in the pursuit of a wonderful object—I have it all in my head—

Cleav. What heart, liver, and all—you must be *light*headed.

Frank. Do not be too curious in your enquiries—you want to come for to go, for to find out what this curiosity is—but it is of no use your coming, for it's *no go*—my Master—

Clea. I don't want to pump you—Mr. Frankinstitch!

Frank. Pardon, pardon, Cleaver, my fine fellow—I'm hasty—hasty, as—hasty pudding!—over a segar to-night I perhaps may whiff out the grand, the wonderful secret, which makes my Eyes red—my sky blue nose draw up in nervous puckers, and liquid peas run down this manly brow—Leave me, my friend—I have something astonishing & damnable to do.

Devild. Now he's absorb'd again—he ceases to speak.

Lee. I wish you would—

Cleav. He's mad as an *April Rabbit.*

Devild. Now that is a little novelty of expression!—I think the words "Mad as an April Rabbit" more original than "Mad as a March Hare"—!

Frank (to Dev. & Lee) How long am I to be kept absorbed?—Go on and be hang'd to you.

Clea. Farewell—Mr. Frankinstitch—Bon Soir—Mute as second day's fish—I'll go and see if I can take out a *speaker's* warrant against him. *(Exit Cleav)*

Frank. Every moment lost sticks in my gizzard! Good gracious how I have been *cogibundating* since I read that wonderful peculiar romance—I have cut out many a gentleman's coat, waistcoat and breeches, but now my ambition is to manufacture a gentleman itself.

Song—Frankinstitch
Air: Cookery Song in Bee Hive
Some say—what can a man do?
But I'll show 'em soon what I can do.
Oh give me the Limbs and you'll see
A Being so quick stitch'd up by me.
Give me material
He won't appear ill
Legs for his walking
Tongue for his talking
Bosom to throb in
Brains for his nob in
On each toe a nail
And a long pig tail
His nose fat—a ridge on
To keep the bridge on
Eyebrows so arch'd
Neck stiffly starch'd
And line his belly
With vermicelli
Clean, plump, and portly
Air spruce and courtly
Eyes wink
And blink
The Ladies say
Ah well-a-day
Upon the whole
A charming soul
Look all who can
At this made man—
Legs Coat
Pegs Throat
Eyes Wrists
Thighs Fists

Hair Hips
Stare Lips
Ears Face
Tears Grace
Wig Arms
Jig Charms
Nose Knees
Toes Ease
Joints Points
Nail Tail
Busy at cookery
Scarecrow for Rookery!
Prometheus of old
Wasn't half so bold
I'll do all I can
To make this made man—

But for the materials—give me but the arms & legs and appurtenances, and I'll stitch up a notable chap—if I don't Jemmy Johnson squeeze me. And now to accomplish this matter—this packet—this is Nun Vourica, vulgarly call'd Rat's bane! this will effectually put an end to the lives of my nine men—*(they sing)* "Rule Britannia." Poor devils! little do they think that like Swans, they will sing over their own *Geese*—but damn me, I'll stop their loyalty—This Henry Meux—*(tastes)* No it's Barkley & Perkins, and dev'lish good too—Now, here goes the *pisen*—*(Empties the contents of paper into it)*

Music—Enters the Room & places the can on the work-board—he watches—The Tailors come out one by one & drink—he counts them—At a pause in the Music, they all groan—(a voice) "Oh! Oh! the beer!"

Frank. Ah, they will each want a *Bier* now! for they are all gone to pot.

He turns the bodies of the Tailors from one side of the Room to the other.

Now for the grand secret—now for the tip top of my ambition! My nine journeymen, by drinking the poison'd porter, lie dead as small Beer!—Nine!—nine!—I have somewhere read that nine Tailors make a man—these—these are my materials—to my task—away with reflection—to my task. *(Exit into Room)*

Lee. But what is he going to do now?

Devild. Do you suppose I shall be such a fool as to tell you all?—He's murder'd his nine Journeymen. Well—with their giblets &c. he is to make a new man.

Lee. The Devil!

Devild. Aye, and pretty Devil it will be—hush—be quiet now—he's done the Job—

Lee. He hasn't been long about it—

Devild. Oh they never are on the Stage—be quiet—he comes—Now this is the most interesting bit in the whole piece—

Music Enter Frankinstitch

Frank. I have lock'd the workshop up—What a wretch have I form'd—There's Jemmy Wilson's hair—Billy Boroughs's head—Bobby Bluethread's arms—Old Nicholas's neck—Christopher Cabbage's back—Ben Baste's one leg, and Patrick Longmeasure's tother—Dreadful incorporation of nine Tailors—but my man *is* made! I have animated him with the parlour bellows, and heard him whistle and all is hush'd. *(listens)* I hear him wheeze & learning to cough—the beauty of my dream has vanish'd! and melodramatic horrors assail me—Mrs. F—My Wife—Mary—Betty—Cook—Frizzy!—never more shall I have the assurance or pleasure to look again into your countenances—I'm faint—no—I ain't—I'm better—Now for the object of my solicitude. *(Goes to the Window)*

Song "Rest Thee Babe."
Oh slumber my darling
For Daddy you've none,
Unless in the making
I'm consider'd as one—
Then rest thee babe, rest thee babe
Rest while you can,
For the parts of nine Tailors
Have made you a man—

Music—(sinks into a chair)

Shop Window is smashed—The Hobgoblin jumps out—& sits upon a Table cross-leg'd.

Hob. How are you?

Frank. Thou thing of threads & patches—avaunt!

Hob. But where am I to go?—

Frank. Go to the Devil—anywhere!

Hob (Getting off the Table)

Frank. Approach not—you Tom Tawdry!—Would that I had never put you together—

Hob. Then you are the Gentleman that I have to thank—It is quite a new sensation!

Lee. I beg pardon for interrupting—but the Demon or Hobgoblin appears to speak English very well for a new made man!

Devild. Why he has got Billy Burrows's head on—that's the reason.

Lee. Oh.

Hob. You should have an affection for me. *(fondly)* Love your little a little—

Frank. Never!—This poor unletter'd creature will be quite at a loss for want of words. I'll give him an Enticks' Dictionary—here—*(gives a Book)*

Hob. What's this?

Frank. A Volume of words which will find you meat, drink, washing, and lodging—let me put it in your pocket—there—!

Hob. Pocket—thank you. *(snuff box upset—Hob sneezes)* that is a new sensation—how nice—I'll do it again—No—I can't—tell me, why am I manufactured?

Frank. Do not grumble—you are a *made* man!—How wildly he looks—he has never yet been out of the room—and knows not how to conduct himself—he moves.

Hob (Walks—runs his head against Wall) Oh, damn it!

Frank. What's the matter?

Hob (rubbing his head). That's a new sensation! What was that I knock'd my forehead against?

Frank. The Wall.

Hob. I shall have a *Wall* Eye?

Frank. Now he is rolling his Billy Burrows's twinklers at me—Don't come near me—Dreadful Monster in a human form—keep off—*(Strikes Hob with a pair of sheers.)*

Hob. There's another new sensation!

Frank. Go—quit my presence—or these sheers!—

Hob (Seizing & pulling them in two) I'm a cut above them—and now my old cock—for a bit of fun with you. *(takes hold of him)*

Frank. Hold—hold—wretched professional man that I am!

Music—they are in an attitude.

Devild. Stop—Stop—here's the place for a little thunder—have you no thunder in the House?

Hob. How long am I to hold this heavy back'd Christian in this position, Mr. Author?

Devild. Now thunder—thund away & bundle old Frankinstitch by his waistband out of the window—bravo—bravo—

Violent Music—the Hobgoblin struggles with Frankinstitch & succeeds in putting him out of the broken window.

(ACT DROP FALLS)

ACT 2ND SCENE 1ST

A Room in Frankinstitch's House
Mrs. Frankinstitch Discovered

Mrs. F. It is in vain—What's the use of *tatting*—it is no relief to the mind *(throws her work down)* How lonely—Oh Mr. Frankinstitch—for the matter of a Husband I might as well be without one—plague take his philosophy and his experiments—I have no family—it is very tiresome, and yet I love you my dear little man.

Song—Air "Beautiful Maid."
When absent from him my soul holds most dear
Stop my fidgets, my fidgets who can.
In my bosom what thrilling what hope and what fear
I endure for my dear little man.
In vain I sip sherry to lighten my grief
In vain cool myself with my fan.
Nor sherry nor fanning will yield me relief
When away from my dear little man—

Enter Frankinstitch

Ah my dear Husband—you have come to me at last.

Frank. Yes, and I've come to *myself* at *last!*

Mrs. F. How?

Frank. I've been in fits for the last hour—& I've just come to *myself—*

Mrs. F. Come, come, you are joking!

Frank. Upon my soul and body!

Mrs. F. And no one to help you?

Frank. The Housemaid burnt a bit of buckram under my nose or I might have laid nodding & wagging my fins like a live turtle at the Piazza!

Mrs. F. But what is the cause?

Frank. *(starts)* Ah!

Mrs. F. Have you seen a Ghost—or did a mad bull run after you?

Frank. Oh, it is a mixture of a Ghost & a mad bull! Such a drab of a devil!—see—see—he is there—no—I'm a story teller!—he isn't—

Mrs. F. He—who is *he?*

Frank. Why—*it.*

Mrs. F. And what is *it?*

Frank. Ah—that's the thing!

Mrs. F. My dear you look as pale as a lump of Hog's lard. I must insist upon your taking a little beef tea—or Hunt's breakfast powder.

Frank. No—no—

Mrs. F. Some chocolate!

Frank. Wife I've had a *shock-o-late!*

Mrs. F. You may have been shock'd, but you shouldn't make such bad puns—Let your gentle Duck, as you sometimes call me, cheer you—come perk up a bit.

Duett—Air "Out of my sight, or I'll box &c."

Mrs. F. Perk up a bit my husband dear.

Frank. Lovey you often my spirits cheer.

Mrs. F. With spirits alive who is afraid?

Frank. *(aside)* I am when I think of the chap that I've made.

Mrs. F. Come let's be funny.

Frank. I'm dull and dummy.

Mrs. F. Cheer up.

Frank. I'm as the back Kitchen-low.

Mrs. F. Let's dance and sing & kick up a row.

Frank. I'm not in the humour to do it now.

(Exeunt)

SCENE 2ND

Battle Bridge

De Lazy discovered sitting on a stool against the poling, and playing a Barrel Organ, a dog by the side of him—he ceases.

D. Lazy. Pity the poor blind!—not a penny have, a penny have I taken the whole of this blessed morning!—*(whistles)* Pincher, Pincher!—the dog is here—tho' all the rest of the family have left me—and my comfort too is here. *(taking a bottle from under his stool)*—My boy Phoenix is gone to be married—I call him Phoenix because he was brought up among the cinders here—I have never seen his wife, because why, my blinkers are out of repair—I hope my boy will treat his Missus well & not *(feeling for the dog)* Pincher—Pincher—Phoenix will be back soon—*(feeling)* where's the young dog—now for one more turn—& if I don't get a halfpenny I'll shift my quarters—*(he plays the organ)*

(Enter Hob, who dances to it)

Hob. How melodious!—quite a new sensation!—it has stopp'd—What sweet sounding entrails has that box!—pray, Sir, will you be so obliging as to inform me? Why he don't look at me!

D. Lazy. I'm blind as a Bat, Sir.

Hob. How comes that about?

D. Lazy. I was born so—or my friends would have sent me to *sea*—pray, Sir, give me a halfpenny—

Hob. A halfpenny—what is that? Oh my book—H—Hal—Half—Oh—here?—"Halfpenny a Copper Coin of which 2 make a penny"—I haven't got one—pray if I may be so bold, what do you call that square grinding box of music?

D. Lazy. A *H*organ to be sure—

Hob. Thank ye—now I don't know what an organ is. Again, my Dictionary—"natural Instrument as the tongue is the organ of speech."

D. Lazy. Come, you are jesting with me, Master—I must on to earn my day's living—good morning Master. *(goes off playing—Hobgoblin takes his bottle)*

Hob. It's uncommon nice—quite a new sensation. It delights all my senses. *(Empties the bottle & goes)*

Enter Shovelhat & Ashpicker

Ash. What lark's that they're up to yender, Master Shovelhat?

Shov. Vy don't you know—it's a vedding!

Ash. Vot?

Shov. A vedding!

Ash. Who's got a Vife?

Shov. Vhy he vot's married to be sure—but Master Ashpicker, I got summut pertickler to tell you—at day break this morning, I volks up to the cinder heap—vat do you think I see?

Ash. See—vy the vomen sifters—the donkies—the chickens and the sows.

Shov. That warn't all—I see—but I'll tell you—

Song—Air "Gile's Scraggin's Ghost."
This morn as I volk'd up the heap
Ri tol di &c.
For van awake I never can sleep
Ri tol &c.
The time it vas half ater three
Ri tol &c.
Up jumps something & frightens me
Ri tol &c.
The greatest guy I never did see
Ri tol &c.
He had two *hies* vot star'd like pigs
Ri tol &c.
His hair resembled bird lime twigs
Ri tol &c.
Tho' frightful he vos a figure of fun—
Ri tol &c.
And he got a ear like a hot cross bun
Ri tol &c.
A shilling leg & a fourteen penny one
Ri tol &c.
Ven I vos satisfied with my peep
Ri tol &c.
Vot can he vant on our dust heap?
Ri tol &c.
Vot brings you here you guy I said?
Ri tol &c.
So I throws a pickaxe at his head.
Ri tol &c.

Shov. Now vot d'ye think of that there?

Ash. Gammon—you vas vandering in your mind.

Shov. I saw him as plain as I now twigs you. *(Drum and Fife without)* huzza!

Ash. Hark the marriage percussion.

Shov. Vere's your English and be damn'd to you? marriage percussion!—marriage percession if you please.

Ash. Vy they've got a Jack in the Green vith them.

Shov. Vot's a vedding vithout a Jack in Green.

Enter Drum & Fife Jack in the Green &c.

Pea. Hollo boys—Hollo!

Mob. Huzza!

Phoe. Silence—silence you noisy old crow—Gemmen and Ladies, allow me to return my sincere thanks for as far as ve've gone—I hopes you all likes Coat and Vaistcoat.

Cin. My dear Billy I—

Phoe. Hush Chucky—this is my vedding day, and I vill have my vay for vonce.

Pea. We have right to speke, Massa Phoenix!

Phoe. Hush you ungrateful black pudding!—haven't I treated you at every house hintertainment from that there place vere I vas married to this here place vere ve are now jawing—the Cloves and Anniseed at the Crown and Cushion—a fallow of Double X at the Lord Nelson—didn't ve Jack?

Jack. Aye—aye—

Pea. And a flash o' lightning each at the World's End—

Mob. Hurra— *(rolls of Drum)*

1st Mob. Master, I made myself werry *ot* pulling the bells for you.

Phoe. Ah—They were *wringing* wet—give him some Gingerbread Nuts Mr. Peacock—

Pea. No—Massa Phoenix—

Phoe. Silence old surly gills—I don't care for your looking black Mr. Peacock—I vill have my own vay on my vedding day!

Ash. As the Gemman seems a Gemman, and they are going to spend the arternoon here—tell 'em of the guy of a ghostess vot you see this morning—to *spile* your vedding—but—

Phoe. But what?

Shov. There's a rum cove of a ghostess a *aunting* the cinder heap—

Cind. A Ghostess—I declare I should *perspire* if I seed a Ghostess.

Phoe. Damn the Ghostess—pluck up a sperrit, wife—only let him come near me—he'd have to look out for a volloping—come, my Lads, let's have another jig. How are you Jack?

Jack. Plaguy dry!

Phoe. Come my Chucky—a double shuffle—& then to the Cat and Bagpipes for a pint of peppermint—strike up Band—and those what are Bawdy don't dance.

A Regular 1st of May pas de trois
the Hobgoblin dances in among them—
general confusion—the escape.

Hob. Well, this is quite a new sensation—Is there any thing so infernally ugly in me? I suppose I'm a queer one—my joints don't fit comfortably together—my left hip keeps creaking and grating against my back bone like a Coffee Mill—my nose is loose, and my elbows dangle like flails—but what have we here? A Bush—I saw a Tree before this morning—and heard the sweet notes of a Bird in it—I wonder if there is a bird in that bush—and whether it will sing? hark!

Jack (putting his head out). I say—my rum ones—what are you arter? All gone!—Dash my Tom cat! *(sees Hob)* Oh! help—help—murder—the! Devil!

(scampers off with the green hastily.)

Hob. Now what the plague has made that bush bumble in that way? how very ignorant I am—it is quite astonishing!—I'll study my Dictionary.

Cin. (peeps in) The ugly wretch who made us so timbersome is gone!—Where's my husband? Where is my dear Billy?—Billy, my love, where are you?

Hob. (seizes her, she screams). Hush—stop your *squacking*—that is a new and unpleasant sensation!

Cin. Oh dear!—dearee me—Oh Monster!—pity a poor *Gal.*

Hob. A what?

Cin. A *Gal.*

Hob. Stop a moment—*(reads)* "G. Girl—a young woman—a female"—What an indescribable emotion does the touch of her hand give me—Stand still you little frightened fool—I won't hurt you—how she trembles, and I'm no great shakes—

Cin. What a hojus creter!—but I know what female charms will do—If I'm civil to him—he won't bite me—Who, and what are you, Sir?

Hob. Why, I am rather in doubt—as to who I am and what I am—*(she struggles)* No—no, my lady you are not a going to give me the slip—

Cin (aside). I'll try to employ his mind if he has any—how old are you, Mr. Monster?

Hob. About an hour and a half—

Cin. You are a fine boy of your age—

Hob. 'Pon my life I think I am—

Song—Tune "I'm a Yorkshireman."
I'm a gentleman just born and bred
  And my coming to life is a gay thing
Life in London is now very dead
  So I am come out as a *play* thing.
Mr. Frankinstitch put me together
  And blew up my lungs with his bellows.
So I'll leave to the world to say whether
  I'm the rummiest of comical fellows.
  Rum ti iddity &c.

Cin. And who taught you to sing?

Hob. It came naturally—as I have Billy Burrows's head on, I suppose I have Billy Burrows's voice—you are a sweet dainty creature tho' you live on a dust heap—and by the honor of a Demon my new sensations quite overpower my prudence—one—one—what is it—*(reads)* One "K—Kiss—salute given by joining the lips."

Cin. And do you suppose I will let such a fright as you kiss me?

Hob. Fright! *(reads)* "F—fright—a sudden terror." She call me a sudden terror—Oh pretty Chuckaberry I am all in a ferment—I'm hot and cold in the same moment—My Eye balls twinkle—I pant—sigh—I—*(reads)* "am in—" L—love "the passion between the sexes."

Cind. Psha!

Enter Phoenix, Peacock &c arm'd with sticks—all are alarmed.

Hob. I feel a all *overishness*—I suppose 'tis Love—how my heart is beating—What a thumping is here—*(they bang him)* Hollo! hollo!—more sensations!—be quiet—for shame you hard hearted scoundrels—I'll have you all up under Mr. Martin's act—it is cruelty to a poor *h*animal—*(a hurry, he escapes.)*

Enter Mr. Lee, and Devildum

Devil. But Mr. Lee—

Lee. Sir I cannot longer withold my opinion—the scene being over, I must make a few remarks on your piece.

Devil. The fewer the better!

Lee. Your Drama has not an atom of nature in it.

Devil. Nature!—Mr. Lee you are a *natteral*—I really took you for a man who knew something of the Theatrical world—What has nature to do with the Drama of the present day? Will Nature bring you a hundred pound house?—No it is not in its nature to do it—

Lee. But in your piece there are such abominable inaccuracies—Who taught that damn'd Demon to read?

Devil. As I said before—he had a tailor's head on—and that Tailor subscribed to a Circulating Library!

Lee. Yes, but are the Ladies and Gentlemen in the front to know it?

Devil. How—why by instinct, to be sure—but I have depended a little too much on that Billy Burrows's head—it is hazardous—but now my next scene—The house on fire—Carpenters!

Lee. Hush—the House on fire is cut out—

Devil. Cut out by the Carpenters—I'm aware—

Lee. No, Sir—the County Fire Office won't stand it—that is doubly hazardous!

Devil. Cut out my house on Fire—you've cut out the principal Engine in my piece—it is a burning shame—it would have drawn all the sparks in Town—

Lee. Be cool, Sir—

Devil. How can I be cool, Sir, when you won't permit the whole place to be burnt down. Where's the child, and the gentleman and Lady the Demon kills by giving them a Nip?

Lee. Giving them a *Nip*—Do you suppose yourself at the Burton Alehouse Sir?

Devil. You may make your jokes, Mr. Lee with your Nip—but allow me to say it is no *go*—Mr. Lee—you've ruined me—but I know the cause! It is jealousy because you are not in my piece—I'd write a part in it for you—but that you are only fit to play a river.

Lee. The River *Lea,* Sir—or as it would be my appearance in some such part—perhaps the *new River* would be more appropriate—Well, Sir, I should still have *a run,* & float on the stream of public favour—but I beg to *waive* it—See, Sir—your last scene is ready—

Devil. The last Scene already—Why, Sir, there was two hours more stuff in my piece—

Lee. Depend upon it—Sir—there is quite stuff enough.

Scene changes

A Market Gardener's Ground—a board with "a Spring Gun is set here"—Cabbages, Carrots &c. Enter Devildum and Lee.

Devil. Now you observe Mr. Lee, your cutting out the Scenes put me to the necessity of explaining that this Garden belongs to the father of Mrs. Frankinstitch—She has come here to spend a few days with her husband, to try to get rid of his melancholy among the melon beds.

Lee. Oh—a single line will do your business with the audience.

Devil (aside). A *single line* will do *your* business some of these odd mornings and be *hang'd* to you—in the *ordinary* way of business—no matter Sir—it will be all the same a hundred years hence.

Lee. Silence—here's Mr. Frankinstitch!

Enter Frankinstitch with a Sun Flower

Frank. How the gentle perfume exhilirates my spirits—a sun flower—Where's my son now?—the whole neighbourhood of Pentonville has been disturbed by the freaks of my Infant! he's been *Tom* and *Jerrying* it—frighten'd the Watchman—upset the oyster tubs and swallowed shells and all—I wish he would go *off* but I can't *discharge* him—this is my father-in-law Mr. Vegitable Marrow's garden—if that scamp of a devil finds his way into it he'll play old gooseberry among the currant bushes—But soft—I feel pensive—I'll retire and watch the Lizards amorous in the hot beds—*(Exit to Music)*

Enter Hobgoblin eating a bunch of Trick Carrots.

Hob. How good—*(swallows one)*—quite a new sensation—*(eats another)*—they are uncommonly crisp and nice—*(eats several others)*—this makes 13—a Baker dozen—I must look in my book and find out what they are—if I had not found these savory red cowhorn things I should have satisfied my appetite by swallowing my Dictionary and so have eaten my words at once.

Devil. What an excellent way of digesting knowledge—Now the Demon's going to do something with that notice about the Spring Gun—which will hasten the catastrophe of the Drama.

Lee. I hope it will for I want my supper.

Hob. *(runs up against the post)* Oh!—that knock is as cruel as those brutes of scavengers—I'm spiteful—I'll pull it up by the roots—"Spring gun" Oh—to guard the Summer Cabbages—*(tears the board down & throws it away)*

Enter Frankinstitch

Frank. There is not an amorous Lizard!—or lovesick frog to be seen, ha!—my infernal protégé!

Hob. What, my jolly old cock! Do we meet again—now I'll act a Tragedy with you—

Frank. Come on—damn the bottle holders, I'll have it out with you and scuttle your unnatural nob. *(they tussle.)*

Enter Mrs. Frankinstitch

Mrs. F. Oh—my dear husband—he's fighting with all his men combin'd in one—hold—hold—

Frank. No I'll fix him—damn him—

Enter Phoenix &c.

Shov. Two to one on the ghostess—

Phoe. Three to nothing on the Tailor!

Frank. Oh Monster—what strike your father!—I'm down—*(trips)* Oh you bastard!

Mrs. F. (screams). Ah! my husband—take care of the Spring Gun.

All. The spring gun!

Shov. Yes—if that goes off it will cause an avalanche of cabbages and cauliflowers—see they fight—

Music—Hob. treads on spring gun—it goes off and shoots Frank and Hob—the cabbages are brought down from waggon by the report.

Hob (getting up). Stop where's my Dictionary—I want to know what an avalanche is—great A, little A, bouncing B—

Frank. Lie down my unnatural son—you know you've got a bullet through your gullet. *(they expire)*

Frank. Brat!

Hob. Father!

Finale—Black Spirits &c. Macbeth
Good friends and true,
Low spirits and gay,
Mingle, mingle, you mingle,
Mingle tears you may.

Enter Ghosts

Pat. I'm come for my leg.

Cab. O give me my arms I beg.

Ben. I want my lips.

Nich. And I want my hips.

Enter ghost of Frizzy leading the Ghost of Billy Burrows with a head.

Friz. Here's poor Billy Burrows—long since quite dead, For you see—he's lost his white head!

All the Ghosts. Give us all these and make us men, Hold and divide us into nine again!

The Tailors seize their individual parts—& the body of the Hobgoblin disappears "a la Vampire."

Full Chorus
Round about—round about—
Set our piece running,
Sure there's some fun in,
Round about—round about—

Curtain falls—Devildum comes forward

Ladies and Gentlemen, tho' I am willing to allow that my Drama is a farrago of perfect nonsense—Yet as you have done me the honor to laugh—with your permission we'll rehearse it again to-morrow.

FINIS

Frank-in-Steam; or, The Modern Promise to Pay (1824)

DRAM PERS.

FRANK-IN-STEAM.—*The Modern Promise to Pay—a natural and experimental Philosopher—in love and debt.*
FRITZ.—*His Servant—nervous and subject to fits.*
PONTIE—*Friend to Frank-in-Steam.*
XXXXXX—*No relation to the great Unknown.*
DE LACY—*A retired Staymaker.*
DUNSTAN
BEETLE } *Guardians of the Night.*
CHARLEY
Servants &c.
PENELOPE—*Daughter to De Lacy.*
DOLLY—*her Maid.*

Scene—London and Suburbs
Time—That of Representation

SCENE 1ST ACT 1ST

A Hall in the House of Frankinsteam—Fritz—asleep in an armchair.

Fitz (dreaming). I tell you there's no use in waiting, for my Master's gone out and won't return home until midnight—*(waking)* ya!—ya!—What a hard thing that I cannot get a wink of Sleep—day or night—owing to my Master's duns whom I am obliged to answer every hour—Besides I'm so nervous—What's that? Sure I heard something knock—no!—'twas only the cat jumping about to divert her hunger. Why did I ever leave the Country where I sold asses milk to all the neighbours around me? Why did I ever come up to town to live with a wild young medical Student who I believe deals with somebody with horns? he's over head-and-ears in debt and has tired out all of his friends and relations. He expects the Bailiffs to nab him every hour—Those Bailiffs always frighten me—I'm so nervous—He must cross the water and live within rules or it will be soon all over with him—oh dear—oh dear—What between my Master's troubles and my own I am grown as thin as that Skeleton of rattling bones in his Study—I'm so nervous.

Song—Fitz—Air
"Good old days Adam & Eve"

I

I sing oh dear what is not funny,
My Master's always dunned for money.
His creditors each hour are rapping,
Just like the woodpecker a tapping.
In vain he promises and cozens,
I tell them whoppers too by dozens.
They come again with cat tat tooings,
And soon there will be ugly doings.
  Sing hey—sing ho—a dismal tale,
  My Master sure must go to Jail.

2

I'm grown besides so mighty nervous,
My limbs can scarce perform their service.
Such throbbings and such palpitations,
But not produced by strong potations.
For nine months I've been on board wages,
I only eat by lengthened Stages.
I'll give my weeping eyes a kind wipe,
My Stomach thinks I've cut my wind-pipe.
  Sing hey—sing ho—for want of bail,
  My Master sure must go to Jail.

(end of Song—a knock heard)

My goodness—how nervous I am—*(another knock)* more of the dun family—I'm a coming—don't be so impatient.

(Opens doors. Enter Pontie).

Oh Mr. Pontie is it you—I didn't know it was or I would have came before—I'm so nervous—So many people come to enquire after the health of Mr. Frank that to be frank with you—

Pon. That you are obliged to answer them eh Fitz.

Fitz. Exactly so—

Pon. Well but where is he—how is he—what is he about?

Fitz. Why, Sir, he has been locked up in his study for the last three hours poring over the big books with the Skeleton figures. He's certainly going to raise the devil or Doctor Foster.

Pon. Pshaw!

Fitz. You may Pshaw!—but do you know that between ourselves—hush—it's a secret—which I'll tell you—I'm so nervous.

Pon. Ridiculous Blockhead—is that your secret? Why don't you cure yourself and take some anti-nervous drops.

Fitz. Drops—bless you—I never tastes a drop of nothing, but that's not the secret—Oh Mr. Pontie—between ourselves—do you know that I think Mr. Frank-in-Steam intends to blow his brains out?

Pon. Impossible.

Fitz. Maybe so—but blow me if I don't think he will commit Shoe aside—or fellow d'ye see—I popped my ear to the key hole and heard him exclaim—"Yes—the grave is my last resource—it shall be accomplished!"

Pon. Fitz, your fears magnify trifles into horrors—Your Master was only philosophizing—did you never philosophize?

Fitz. Anon!—Oh yes—I was in a brown study when I lost my poor Donkey Nimrod—

Pon. Go tell your Master I am here.

Fitz. I will Mr. P.—I'm so nervous.

Exits

There must be some mistake in this—Surely Frankinsteam could never think of shooting himself on the Eve of Matrimony—What other cause—I have it!—The want of Cash—to buy a licence or carry her off in a Post Chase—Well Cash—must be raised for without it there is no such thing as following the fashions or joining in the revelries of London.

Re-Enter Fitz.

Here he comes Mr. Pontie—how rumpled his Brutus is—his arms are folded and he's talking to himself; that's his constant custom—it makes me quite nervous.

(they retire up a little)

Enter Frank-in-Steam—(abstracted)

Every moment that passes is frought with the success or failure of my future fortune—Should I succeed in my projected undertaking a lovely girl and plenty of Cash will enable me to bid defiance to John Doe and Richard Roe—Yet—what other way to raise the wind? None but that of raising a Body to supply the Surgeons—Aye—this night—the Grave—I am resolved—*(turns round)* Ah Dick—how goes it—leave us Fitz—

Exit F.

How do you carry on the war—eh Dick?

Pon. It lingers my dear Frank—for I want Cash—imperatively.

Frank. Don't mention it—so do I—but I've such news.

Pon. What?

Frank. Why Snatch the Bailiff—You knew Snatch.

Pon. Yes—a little or so—but proceed.

Frank. Well then Snatch—my chief Creditor—who was always fond of a tap, is at length floored by a drunken frolic, in other words, he drank himself to death in despair of catching me and was buried last night.

Pon. My dear fellow—let's embrace—I want cash amazingly.

Frank. So do I—but I shan't want it long—This night—it shall be done—"I've set my life upon a Stake and will stand the hazard of the die!"

Pon. What? Seven's the mean?

Frank. No—I mean—the grave—This night shall end my cares.

Pon. Die—tonight—pooh—nonsense—commit suicide so near your marriage with *Penelope*.

Frank. The *Web* of my existence cannot be more intricate—'Tis a revolting act but I will accomplish it. *(goes over, sits down—lost in reflection)*

Pon. He takes no more notice of me than if I was the Statue of King Charles at Charing Cross—He must be sent to Hoxton immediately—I'll seek Fitz—This way he went.

Exit Pontie

Frank (recovering from thought). Gone—So much the better—it will afford me time to make the necessary preparations for my task—Let me see, five or six guineas will do the job—Should I be found out tho'—Ha!—discovered like a Vampyre preying on the loathsome tenants of the Grave—Body snatching—clear case—tried—found guilty and sentenced to the Tread Mill—Agonizing anticipation—but away with fear—to my task—to my task.

I must raise Cash by break of day
The *Subject brooks*—no more delay.

Exit

Scene 2nd Act 1st

Outside of Cottage Ornée—Enter Dolly with various flowers which she places on a Stand.

Dolly. Heigho—what do I sigh for? There, I think that will do—I have arranged them all in Apple Pie order—That will please Old Mr De Lacy and young Miss Penelope. Tho' he's so short sighted that he can't almost see the flowers he always likes to smell their perfume—Poor old man—His only enjoyment now is to play upon the finger organ—pad about the garden—smoke his Cigar and talk about the different measures that were pursued in his time when he was a Stay-maker and before he retired from business. Aye—aye—Miss Penny can do with him just what she likes—but—mum—here she comes.

Enter Penelope—from door in front

There—that will do—very well—now Dolly go in and prepare breakfast for Papa—I'll follow directly.

Dolly. Yes—Miss Penny.

Pen. And be sure to make the tea strong—I like it strong.

Dolly. Yes—Miss—

Pen. Now mind it's all gunpowder or you'll get a blowing up.

Dolly. Very well, Miss Penny.

Exit

I wonder what keeps my dear Frank-in-Steam? I suppose he is so taken up with Scientific Study that he scarcely allows himself time for domestic enjoyment—Well, after we are married I'll soon cure him of that. Well for my part I cannot imagine what pleasure man can derive from poring over ponderous volumes of musty learning full of dust and cobwebs when the fair page of woman is open to their gaze—Now, I am uncommonly fond of reading—but then it is of the most agreeable kind—viz charming novels and delightful Romances!

Exit into House

Scene 3rd Act 1st

A Street with Church and Burial grounds in perspective—Charley discovered asleep in his box—the Clock strikes five as he awakes.

Charley. So that's all right and snug—'tis time for me to leave my beat. Thanks to the Magistrates and the Tread Mills we may now sleep in some comfort without being upset by either a Tom, Jerry or Logic. Tom has bolted to fight the battles of the Greeks—Jerry instead of running after larks in London is shooting woodcocks in the Country—while Logic has forsook his studies in the Fleet to study Colonization in Van Diemans land—

Enter Beetle & Dunstan

Come my hearties—let us toddle to the watchhouse peel there and all of us go home—What say ye?

Beetle. Aye—after all there's no place like Home.

Air—and Chorus—Watchmen

I

Midst streets lanes and allies altho' we may roam,
Be it summer or winter there's no place like Home.

A Glass of blue rum we tipple off there,
Which, seek where we will, an't so potent elsewhere.
  Home—home—sweet sweet Home!
  There's no place like Home!
  There's no place like Home!

2

A Charley on beat by the gas-light's pure gleam,
May snore in his Box—till a Box wakes his dream.
The Birds that are dicky soon move at our call,
It's all dicky with them if they can't tip at all.
  Home, home—sweet, sweet, Home!
  There's no place like Home!
  There's no place like Home!

Exeunt

Enter Fitz—trembling

Oh dear how I shiver and shake all over with cold and fright. I'm so nervous!—What can Mr. Frank mean by ordering me to meet him (when the watch went off their beat) at the Gate of yonder churchyard? Oh! dear what's that? I'm so nervous—If I am catched hereabouts they'll take me up and give me a milling at Brixton—I don't like milling—I'm so nervous—I wish I had a glass of ass's milk or Cherry Bounce or even Brandy and Water—hot—strong and—Oh! dear—what's that?

(Frank enters softly behind & taps him on the shoulder)

Frank. Hush!

Fitz. I'm a dead man—Oh is it you Mr. Frank? Why would you frighten me when you know I am so nervous?

Frank. Make no noise—be silent as the Grave—look out and see if anyone approaches—be cautious or we may be discovered—look out—

Duett—Air "My Pretty Page"

Frank. My trusty Fitz look out afar &c.
  Spy you the Cart from Holborn Hill,
  Or watch from Temple Bar?
  My trusty Fitz—look out afar &c.

Fitz. I've strain'd my eyes but cannot see
  A Cart or Charley near.
  Oh what do you want to do with me,
  And why have you brought me here?
    Oh Mr. Frank—&c.

Frank. My trusty Fitz look again &c.
  Spy you the Cart from Grays Inn Lane?
  The Cart from Grays Inn Lane,
    My trusty Fitz look out again &c.

Fitz. Oh yes a Cart I plainly see
  And Driver—driving quick this way.

Frank. Be off then I say.

Fitz. Don't send me away
  I shall weep if you do,
  For I fear you will go to I know who.

Frank. To you know who?

Fitz. Yes you know who.
Frank. Be off Fitz I say.
Fitz. Must I go?—well a day!

Exeunt—Severally
End of the First Act

Scene 1st Act 2nd

Exterior of the Study of Frankinsteam—flight of stairs leading to Corridor—
Enter Frank—cautiously

Yonder is the closet where the subject of my enterprise lies stretched in all the horrors of grisly death. How shall I convey it to its proper destination? I have it—I'll box it to prevent discovery—send Fitz for a coach and then a fig for detection. Yet stay—Should I be found out I shall be pummelled by the Populace and receive a body blow that may do one bodily harm. Banish such thoughts. I can fight as well as the best of them—I am resolved—fate cries out—I hear its voice—I obey.

(Music—Frank enters the Study)
Enter Fitz.

There he goes into that terrible room—I am sure he was about nothing good in the churchyard which was the reason he sent me away this morning. He's nothing better than a vampyre!—Then Mr. Pontie says he is out of his senses and he has *promised* me the price of a Donkey if I find out what my Master is about—Here goes then—Oh dear—I'm so nervous—the rushlight burns all manner of colours—

(Approaches door—looks thru key hole & rushes down)

Frank (within). It lives—it snores—it cries!

Fitz. Oh dear—I wish I was able to stand upright. What a horrible Hobgoblin—What will become of me? I'm not able to run away I'm so nervous—I shall never get the better of this shock and that horrid sight ah—he's a coming—I'll be going—

(Staggers off while Frank comes down)

Confusion. What have I done? Instead of raising a dead body to raise the wind I've raised a live Bailiff to arrest me. The figure's features—nose—lynx eye—all—all—proclaim the well known Bum—Plague on all Body Snatching say I—It militates against the liberty of the Subject. Snatch the Bailiff whom I have snatched from death must have been buried in a trance and the Monster, to reward me for saving his life, will pursue me from post to pillar till I'm nibbled. I shall be blown—exposed—locked up—Ha—he comes—the shoulder tapping Demon approaches.

(Music—Snatch comes forward in grave habiliments—follows Frank round the Stage to solemn music and then drops)

Oh dear what can the matter be?
Dear dear what can the matter be?
Oh dear what can the matter be,
I shall die of a cold I'm afraid.
I've dreamt of all manner of things you could mention,
Allow me to say that if good's your intention,
I'd think it a very great mark of attention,
To send for some medical aid.

Snatch. Where am I? it's very cold—I must have slept a long time—Why did you wrap this sheet about me and above all what the devil did you lock me up for?

Frank (aside). Because you wanted to lock up me.

Snatch. 'Tis him! I have him at last—Mr. Frank-in-Steam, The Modern Promise to Pay—who always kept out of the way—Ha now I recollect—A new light breaks in upon me.

Frank (aside). I wish he had broken his neck over the banister. I'll not give in tho'—yes—I'll shew fight—Besides he cannot have any writs about him at present—now for it—hem!—How dare you fellow burglariously enter a Gentleman's house—Steal down to his cellar, guzzle up some of his primest black strap, and then frighten the whole of his family by powdering that ugly mug of yours and rolling a sheet about you—Be off—I say or I will send for an Officer and have you taken up—*(aside)* I wish I had not taken him up.

Snatch. Hark ye my young son—I'm not to be done. I see it all—got drunk last night—somebody has been playing off a lark on me—I know you as well as the Bench—long watched you—never to be had—I have you now safe enough and taddle off you must.

Frank. Keep off you blue devil—You mixture of Indigo and Whiting—I hate your touch—It's worse than that of a Torpedo—I laugh to scorn your boasted power—You have no writ about you—So I don't care this pinch of 3% for you—What do you say to that my Regular?

Snatch. Say—why that you have baffled me so often that I gave positive directions even if I died to have my writ buried along with me and here it is—Now what do you say to that my Regular?

Frank. Zounds—here's a go—nabbed at last—I must fight it out and escape the best way I can—Here Snatch come to the Scratch. Here's at you my Pippen!

Music

(They fight—Frank floors Snatch and escapes out of the Window and the Bailiff jumps after him)

Scene 2nd Act 2nd

The Inside of Whalebone Cottage—the residence of De Lacy who enters followed by Penelope.

De L. Well, well. Say no more you coaxing rogue. I give you leave to fix the nuptials with your lover—but what prevents him from calling as frequently as he used?

Pen. Ah 'tis he is so fond of Study.

De L. That's right—whatever is a Man's business or profession he ought to stick to it as close as possible—That's the way I always got on and I would not be so well off now if I did not stay at my trade as long as I could.

Pen. Yes, Papa! You were long celebrated as a Stay-maker.

De L. So I was—but now I think on it—write a letter to him from me—send it by Dolly and I warrant he'll come immediately—There's Pen and Ink on the table—you can write while I take a turn in the Garden—good-bye you little wheedling beggar.

Exit

Pen. Write a letter—My dear Papa, I have anticipated your wishes in that respect—Dolly went long since and I wonder what detains her—Oh here she is—

Enter Dolly

Well Dolly, did you see him—will he come?

Dolly. Come, lord Miss—he's gone.

Pen. Gone!

Dolly. Yes and what is worse—nobody knows where—When Mr. Fitz opened the door he was crying his Eyes out for the loss of his Master and told me such a strange Story of Mr. Frank's sudden disappearance—I declare it quite shocked me—it did indeed Miss—

Pen. Keep me not on the rack—explain—quick.

Dolly. Why that Mr. Frankinsteam was locked up with a Spectre, no—an orrible

Hobgoblin—(that was the word Fitz said) and when he went to tell his master Dinner was ready he found the room empty and the window open through which the Hobgoblin must have ran away with poor dear Mr. Frank—

Pen. Pshaw!—nonsense—this is more like a fairy tale.

Dolly. It's the tale of Mr. Fitz I assure you Miss—and I think it true enough for I smelt the brimstone in the very room myself.

Pen. Fitz is out of his senses and you are no better. I am sure if Frank is gone that he is on his way here.

Dolly (looking out) Well—I declare if you an't a witch—here he comes through the garden—lawks how he runs and how pale he is—

Enter Frank

Pen rushing to Frank (embracing). My Frank!

Frank. My Penny!

Pen. What is the cause of this perturbation and the strange Story that Fitz tells?

Frank. Fitz—has he been here—what did he say?

Pen. Why that—ha! ha! I cannot help laughing—it's so very ridiculous—that some horrible hobgoblin had ran away with you—

Frank (forcing a laugh). Why this is a capital story—ha! ha! It certainly was a Spectre—*(aside)* Bum!

(Snatch appears & hides behind the chimney board)

Pen. What's the matter Frank you look quite pale?

Frank. No wonder when by Fitz's account I have seen a Ghost. But I see you and my happiness is complete.

Pen. Come, Sit—Dolly open the window and remove the fire screen—the room is so warm.

Dolly. Yes, Miss—

(Dolly removes the board—Snatch darts out—the women scream and run off)

Frank. Horror! here's Monsieur Tonson come again!

Snatch. It's no use to keep this game up longer come let's toddle to the Bench—

Frank. I will—

(Runs round room pursued by Snatch—makes a feint at the window—but steps aside—while the Bailiff jumps out of it. Frank laughs & Exits by the House door)

Scene 3rd Act 2nd

Outside of Frank-in-steam's House
Enter Fitz—disconsolately

Oh dear—oh dear what will become of me? At last that hideous hobgoblin has carried off my Master and I shall never more see either him or my wages. I am afraid to look round for fear I shall encounter another Spectre—I'm so nervous—I'm very hungry—I'll go inside—There's some bread and cheese in the Cupboard that was left since last Wednesday fortnight if the mice haven't nibbled it—Oh dear—I don't think I'll survive my Master long—I'm so nervous—I seem only to be born for misfortune.

Song—Fitz—Air "Billy Lack-a-Day"

I

Since I was born but for disaster,
I've lost my wages and my master.
There never was a youth such trouble in,

Caus'd by an orrible Hobgoblin—
His face the stoutest heart would frighten,
'Tis wash'd with Indigo and whiting.
He comes to scare us all good gracious,
Just like a Vampyre that's Voracious.
Oh Lack-a-Day &c.

2

To go to bed I dare not venture,
For through a key hole ghosts can enter.
I shake and quake so (Heaven preserve us!)
And every day become more nervous.
What shall I do—where shall I turn me?
The Ghost has given the heart burn me.
My Donkey pleasures past I sigh at,
For never shall I more know quiet.
Oh Lack-a-day &c.

Exit into House
Enter Frank—(out of breath)

Pooh—this confounded bailiff has almost ran me off my legs—I'm completely winded—How unlucky that I should have bolted by accident to Whalebone Cottage—But, they'll never imagine him a *Bum*—they'll swear he was a *Spectre*—Let me reconnoitre if the caitiff is in view—Yes—I think I am safe—that tumble on the summer house cut him up a little—Sure of all the evils that man is subject to there's none so harassing as being in debt beyond the power of payment with all the touching et ceteras.

Song—Frank
When a man is in debt over head and ears,
The devil's to pay when a bailiff appears.
Like a thief in the night time he—stealing—stealing,
Touches your shoulder and there you are.
When a man is in debt &c.

Writs and Detainers the office shews,
But the lack of house is worse than those.
Cash flies like winking
For eating and drinking,
Cleans you out like a sponge and completes your woes.
Writs & Detainers &c.

End of Song—he raps loudly at the door—

What delays Fitz? *(rings the bell)* Why Fitz I say—Open the door—directly—rascal.

Fitz (from Window). That must be either my master or his apparition—Oh Mr. Frank is it really you? how did you escape from the Spectre?

Frank. That Spectre was a Bum!

Fitz. A Bum!—a Spectre Bum—now you're going it.

Frank. Don't stand chattering there but come down you tortoise and immediately let me in—immediately.

Fitz. I will—directly.

Frank. The laziness of that fellow will ruin me—by all that's unlucky, here's the Demon of the Bench again—Where shall I fly to? here goes neck or nothing. *(rushes off)*

Fitz opens door & comes out

I came as quick as I could—Oh Mr. Frank—Where is he gone? the Spectre Bum has got him again.

(As he speaks Snatch enters—shoves him down and pursues the direction Frank took)
Enter De Lacy—Pontie, Pen and Dolly

Pon. Why Fitz—what's the matter? Who knocked you down and what's become of your master?

Fitz. Oh is it you—Why the tall Hobgoblin came here again just now—Master fled and I fell into a fit—I'm so nervous.

De Lacy. That Hobgoblin must be the very devil that escaped from the man trap—let us after him—Which way did he go?

Fitz. That way—I'm so nervous.

Pon. Come along Fitz and assist to find your master.

Fitz. I'm not able—but first let me lock the door—this way Mr. De Lacy—Mr. Pontie—Miss Penelope—Oh Dolly I'm so nervous.

Exeunt

Scene Last

(The Tower Stairs—Margate Steam boat lying close to distant view of shipping along the river—Music—Frank enters pursued by Snatch & Exeunt by opposite wing. Fitz, Pontie, De Lacy, Penelope & Dolly appear at the top of the Stage)

Fitz. Stand aside—here they come again in full chace. That's Master and that's the Spectre Bum—I'm so nervous. Now Mr. Frank makes for the Stairs. Now he jumps on board the Steam Boat. Now—there the Spectre Bum jumps after him—there they struggle—Now Mr. Frank shoves him down through the boat—There he goes—huzza—huzza I'm not nervous now—success to Frank-in-steam.

Frank. Victoria—Victoria—*(Explosion heard)* the Spectre Bum has upset the Boiler and the Bailiff is blown up!

Omnes. Success to Frank-in-Steam.

Finale

Now from every danger free,
  My best congratulation
Is when my friends around I see,
  Smiling approbation.
Bailiffs now avaunt, I say,
  Pen—no more we'll sever.
I've *here* a willing *debt* to *pay*,
  My *Gratitude* for Ever.

Chorus Now from Every danger &c.

Fitz

May poor Fitz now speak a bit,
  Oh keep me in your service.
For if you don't I'll have a fit,
  I'm so exceeding nervous.
Spectre Bums no more shall fright,
  While you all protect me.
Your applause is my delight,
  Do not, pray—reject me.

Chorus Now from every danger free &c.

Henry M. Milner

Frankenstein; or, The Man and the Monster (1826)

John Duncombe's Edition.

FRANKENSTEIN;

OR,

THE MAN AND THE MONSTER!

A PECULIAR ROMANTIC, MELO-DRAMATIC

PANTOMIMIC SPECTACLE,

IN TWO ACTS.

Founded principally on Mrs. Shelly's singular Work, entitled,
"Frankenstein; or, The Modern Prometheus;"
and partly on the French Piece,
"Le Magicien et le Monstre."

BY H. M. MILNER.

THE ONLY EDITION CORRECTLY MARKED FROM THE PROMPTER'S BOOK, WITH THE STAGE BUSINESS, SITUATIONS AND DIRECTIONS.

As it is Performed at

The London Theatres

London:
PRINTED AND PUBLISHED BY JOHN DUNCOMBE,
19, LITTLE QUEEN STREET, HOLBORN.

DRAMATIS PERSONÆ.

PRINCE DEL PIOMBINO .... Mr. Hemmings.
FRANKENSTEIN ...... Mr. Rowbotham.
RITZBERG .... Mr. Meredith.
QUADRO .... Mr. Goldsmith.
STRUTT .... Mr. E. L. Lewis
JULIO .... Miss Burnett.
(* * * * * *) .... Mr. O. Smith.
ROSAURA .... Mrs. Lewis.
EMMELINE .... Mrs. Young.
LISETTA .... Mrs. Rowbotham.

Nobles, Guards, and Attendants on the Prince, Peasants, &c. First performed at the Coburg Theatre, July 3, 1826.

Scene—The Estate of the Prince del Piombino, near the foot of Mount Etna.
Time—From Sunset on one day, till Midnight the next.

COSTUME;

PRINCE DEL PIOMBINO.–Green Italian tunic, richly embroidered with silver, crimson sash, white pantaloons, yellow boots, Italian cap and feathers.

FRANKENSTEIN.–Black velvet vest and trunk breeches, grey tunic open, the sleeves open in front, slashed with white, black stockings and shoes.

QUADRO.–Blue doublet, vest, trunk breeches, and stockings.

RITZBERG.–Dark brown doublet, mantle, trunk breeches, stockings, and cloth hat.

STRUTT.–Blue doublet with long tabs, dark brown vest and light pantaloons, boots, small three-cornered cloth hat.

JULIO.–White satin embroidered tunic, white silk pantaloons, scarlet bottines, white satin Italian cap.

(* * * * * *).–Close vest and leggings of a very pale yellowish brown, heightened with blue, as if to show the muscles, &c. Greek shirt of very dark brown, broad black leather belt.

ROSAURA.–Embroidered dress of pink satin.

EMMELINE.–Short German pelisse of a dark brown, over a slate colored petticoat, dark brown Polish cap.

LISETTA.–Italian peasant.

ACT I. SCENE 1.

The Gardens of the Prince del Piombino's Villa.—At the back a River, beyond which, Picturesque Country. On the P.S. side, the Entrance to the Villa. On the O.P. side, a small Pavilion.

Enter Quadro, Strutt, and Lisetta, from the Villa, meeting male and female Villagers.

Lis. And you think yourself a vastly great man, Mr. Strutt, I suppose.

Strutt. Philosophers are not content with thinking, I know it. My master's a great man, and I'm like the moon to the sun, I shine with a reflected brightness.

Quad. Great man, indeed! I should like to know what there is great about either of you. A couple of adventurers, whom my poor silly dupe of a master, (Heaven help him!) has brought from that beggarly place, Germany; and I suppose you'll never leave him whilst he has got a ducat.

Strutt. Pooh! for his ducats! we want his ducats, indeed! when we could make gold out of any rubbish; your worthless head, for instance, Signor Quadro. My master is the most profound philosopher, and consequently the greatest man that ever lived; to tell you what he can do is impossible; but what he cannot do, it would be still more difficult to mention.

Quad. Yes, his way of making gold, I fancy, is by convoying it out of other people's pockets. He may make gold, but he'd much rather have it made to his hand, I've a notion.

Strutt. Signor Quadro, it is fortunate for you that my master does not hear you, and that (considering the choice bottles of Catanian wine, that you have from time to time been pleased to open for me) I'm too discreet to tell him;—for, oh! signor Quadro, his power is terrible;—he could prevent you from ever passing a quiet night again!

Quad. When I've got three quarts of good Rhenish in my skin, I'll give him leave, if he can. Your master is a water-drinker, sir, he keeps no butler; I never knew any good of a man that drank water and kept no butler.

Strutt. At all events, master Quadro, that's an offence which you cannot lay to my charge; I have the most philosophical principles upon the subject;—I drink water, Signor Quadro, only when I can't get any thing better.

Quad. And that's generally the case, I fancy, when you can't find some good-natured simpleton, like the Prince del Piombino, to keep you and your master together. Instead of board-wages, he billets you upon the kitchen of any body that's fool enough to take you into it.

Strutt. Be assured of this, Signor Quadro, I am not ungrateful; when any kind friend has the goodness to take me in, I do the best in my power to return the compliment.

Quad. The devil doubt you.

Strutt. But for my master, signor Quadro, don't think that all the wine in Sicily is any object to him; he could turn that river into wine if he thought proper,—I've seen him do it, sir, and convert a quart of simple water into a bottle of prime Burgundy.

Quad. Can he? can he do that? Then he has an easy way of making me his sworn friend for life. Only let him turn—I won't be unreasonable; I won't say a word about the river—only let him turn the pump in our stable-yard into a fountain of claret, and I'll never purloin another bottle of my master's, so long as I'm a butler.

Lis. And pray, Mr. Strutt, has all this philosophy and learning quite driven the thoughts of love out of your head? I suppose you fancy yourself now quite above us poor weak women?

Strutt. Not at all, my dear creature; for the man who has the Impudence to fancy himself above the fairest half of human nature has sunk immeasurably below it.

Quad. Egad! philosophy has not made quite a fool of the fellow. But pray now, my good Mr. Strutt, amongst all this transmuting of metal, and converting of water, can you inform us what it is that this wonderful master of yours is doing in that pavilion, where he remains constantly shut up, day and night, and into which no mortal but himself is ever permitted to penetrate?

Strutt. You would like to know, would you?

Quad. Yes I should, very much indeed,

Lis. Oh yes, I'd give the world to know, I should so like to find out the secret.

Strutt. *(after a pause)* And so should I.

Quad. What then, you can't tell us?

Lis. Or perhaps you won't.

Strutt. Why you see—I'm not exactly certain—but I partly guess—*(they cling to him with eager curiosity)*—that is, I suspect—that it is—something that will astonish your weak nerves, one day or another.

Quad. Pshaw!

Lis. A nasty, ill-natured fellow—see how I'll serve you, the next time you try to kiss me. *(Music without.)*

Quad. But hark! his highness approaches with his lovely sister, the lady Rosaura. Back! back! all of you, show him proper respect.

(They are joined by other domestics, male and female, who form in order. A Gondola approaches the shore, from which the Prince, Rosaura, and Attendants land. As the Prince advances, all salute him.)

Prince. Enough, enough, my friends, hasten to the villa, and busy yourselves in preparations for the festival I wish to give in honour of the illustrious genius, who honours my house with his presence.

Quad. *(aside)* A festival, too! for a man who drinks no wine. Well, there's one consolation; there'll be more for those who do—and I'll do my best to make up for his deficiencies, he may depend on't.

Strutt. *(to Lis.)* If there's dancing, may I claim the honour—?

Lis. Will you try to find out your master's secret for me?—

Strutt. It is positively against his orders, to pry into his concerns; and do you know, there is but one person in the world whose commands could induce me to disobey those of my master.

Lis. And who may that be, pray?

Strutt. My mistress, you jade. *(takes her under his arm, and exeunt with Quadro, Domestics, &c. into the Palace.)*

Prince. I feel most deeply that rank and opulence can never do themselves greater honour, than by protecting and assisting talent and genius.

Ros. And never, surely, did genius clothe itself in a more enviable guise, than in the person of Frankenstein. How different is the unassuming modesty of his demeanour, his winning gentleness, from the harsh pedantry and formal solemnity of schoolmen in general.

Prince. Theirs is the solemn mockery of mere pretension, which genius, such as Frankenstein's, despises.—The Universities of Germany have all bent to his prodigious talent, and acknowledged his superiority:—the prince who, conscious of his merit, rewards, assists, and forwards it, not only reaps the fruit of his sublime discoveries, but becomes the sharer of his immortality.

Ros. Oh! may virtues and talents such as Frankenstein's, ever receive the patronage and protection of such men as the Prince del Piombino.

Prince. I rejoice that my dear Rosaura's admiration of this illustrious foreigner almost equals the enthusiasm of her brother's. Has her penetration ever hinted to her that last, that best, inestimable reward with which I meditate to crown my favours towards this Frankenstein?—

Ros. *(Turning away)* Ah, my brother!—

Prince. That blush, that downcast look, assure me, that should my admiration of his merit induce me to confer on him a gift so precious as my sister's hand, I should not in her heart find an opposer of my generosity:—I will not tax your delicacy for a frank avowal, but in your silence read your acquiescence. This night, amidst the joyous mirth that fills our halls, will I hint to our philosopher, the dearer pleasure that I have in store for him.

Ros. My dear, dear brother!—A heart like yours will ever find the secret of making all around it happy.

Exeunt into Palace.

Scene II.

A Nearer View of the Outside of the Pavilion, appropriated as Frankenstein's study; practicable door, and transparent window above. (dark.)

Enter Frankenstein, from the Pavilion.

Fran. It comes—it comes!—'tis nigh—the moment that shall crown my patient labours, that shall gild my toilsome studies with the brightest joy that e'er was yet attained by mortal man.—What monarch's power, what general's valour, or what hero's fame, can rank with that of Frankenstein? What can their choicest efforts accomplish, but to destroy? 'Tis mine, mine only to create, to breathe the breath of life into a mass of putrifying mortality; 'tis mine to call into existence a form conceived in my own notions of perfection! How vain, how worthless is the noblest fame compared to mine!—Frankenstein shall be the first of men!—And this triumph is at hand; but a few moments and it is accomplished! Burst not, high swelling heart, with this o'erwhelming tide of joy!

Enter Julio. O. P.

Ju. Ah! my dear sir, I have not seen you before, today; I am so glad to meet with you.

Fran. *(Abstractedly)* 'Tis well, boy.—Good even to you.

Ju. There are such doings in the palace; such feastings, and such merry-makings, and all, as they say, for you.

Fran. Why that is better; 'tis as it should be. Doubt not, I will be with ye. Let the full bowl high sparkle, let the joyous note swell loud; I will be there, exulting in my triumph.

Ju. Aye, but moreover than all that, I could—but I don't think I shall, because it was told to me as a very great secret—I could tell you of something that would make you so happy.

Fran. I shall, I must be happy; the secret is my own. Leave me, boy, leave me.

Ju. Nay, now, you do not love your poor Julio; I'm sure I know not how I have offended you; but you never spoke to me thus harshly before.

Fran. *(embraces him)* Nay, my pretty pupil, my affectionate Julio, I must love thee, ever. I am disturbed by intense study, and for a few moments I would be alone.

Ju. If you are sure you love me, I will leave you; but if I had offended you, I would not leave you till you had forgiven me, I would not, indeed; we shall see you anon. I shall know where to find you, by my pretty aunt Rosaura's side. Oh, if you did but know what I could tell you!

He runs off. O.P.

Fran. The time is come, the glorious moment is arriv'd. Now, Frankenstein, achieve the mighty work, gain that best of victories, a victory o'er the grave!

Exit into the Pavilion.

Enter Strutt, with a Ladder,—and Lisetta.

Strutt. Well now, do you know, Lisetta, I'm going to do a great deal more for you, than I dare to do for myself. I'm dying to know what my master is about yonder, but if he should catch me peeping, what a jolly thump o' the head I shall get, to be sure; and then, Lisetta, you have it in your power to break my heart, and that's a great deal worse.

Lis. Well, now, without any more ado, you put the ladder against the window, and hold it fast, whilst I mount up and see what he is about.

Strutt. Fie, for shame, Lisetta, what are you thinking about? I'll get up the ladder, and I'll report all that I see, to you below.

Lis. Well, just as you please, only I'd rather peep myself, because, you know, seeing is believing. *(Strutt places the Ladder against the window of the Pavilion, mounts it, and peeps in; a faint glimmering of light is seen through the window.)* Well, now, what can you see?

Strutt. Why, I can see a little fire, and a great deal of smoke.

Lis. And I suppose all your boasted discoveries will end in smoke.

Strutt. Oh! now I can see better;—and would you believe it, Lisetta, from all I can see, I really do think, at least it seems so to me, that my master is making a man.

Lis. Making a man!—What is not he alone?

Strutt. Yes, quite alone. *(A strong and sudden flash of light is now seen at the window; Strutt slides down the Ladder.)* Oh, Lord! that's too much for me!—he's raising the devil—he's blown off the top of the pavilion!—Run, run, Lisetta, or the old gentleman will have you!

Lis. Nay, then the devil take the hindmost, I say!

They run off. O.P.

Scene III.

The Interior of the Pavilion.—Folding Doors in the Back. On a long Table is discovered an indistinct Form, covered with a black cloth. A small side Table, with Bottles, and Chemical Apparatus,—and a brazier with fire.

Frankenstein is discovered, as if engaged in a Calculation.

Fran. Now that the final operation is accomplished, my panting heart dares scarcely gaze upon the object of its labours—dares scarcely contemplate the grand fulfilment of its wishes. Courage, Frankenstein! glut thy big soul with exultation!—enjoy a triumph never yet attained by mortal man! *(Music.—He eagerly lays his hand on the bosom of the figure, as if to discover whether it breathes.)* The breath of life now swells its bosom. *(Music.)* As the cool night breeze plays upon its brow, it will awake to sense and motion. *(Music.—He rolls back the black covering, which discovers a colossal human figure, of a cadaverous livid complexion; it slowly begins to rise, gradually attaining an erect posture, Frankenstein observing with intense anxiety. When it has attained a perpendicular position, and glares its eyes upon him, he starts back with horror)* Merciful Heaven! And has the fondest visions of my fancy awakened to this terrible reality; a form of horror, which I scarcely dare to look upon:—instead of the fresh colour of humanity, he wears the livid hue of the damp grave. Oh, horror! horror!—let me fly this dreadful monster of my own creation! *(He hides his face in his hands; the Monster, meantime, springs from the table, and gradually gains the use of his limbs; he is surprized at the appearance of Frankenstein,—advances towards him and touches him; the latter starts back in disgust and horror, draws his sword and rushes on the Monster, who with the utmost care takes the sword from him, snaps it in two, and throws it down. Frankenstein then attempts to seize it by the throat, but by a very slight exertion of its powers, it throws him off to a considerable distance; in shame, confusion, and despair, Frankenstein rushes out of the Apartment, locking the doors after him. The Monster gazes about it in wonder, traverses the Apartment; hearing the sound of Frankenstein's footsteps without, wishes to follow him; finds the opposition of the door, with one blow strikes it from its hinges, and rushes out.)*

Scene IV.

Outside of the Pavilion, as before.

Frankenstein, in great agitation, rushes from the Pavilion, locking the door after him.

Fran. *(After a pause of much terror.)* Have all my dreams of greatness ended here? Is this the boasted wonder of my science,—is this the offspring of long years of toilsome study and noisome labour? Is my fairest model of perfection come to this—a hideous monster, a loathsome mass of animated putrefaction, whom, but to gaze on chills with horror even me, his maker? How, how shall I secrete him, how destroy—? Heaven! to think that in the very moment of fruition, when all my toils were ended, and I should glory in their noble consummation, my first, my dearest, only wish, is to annihilate what I have made! Horrible object! wretched produce of my ill-directed efforts! never must thou meet another eye than mine—never must thou gaze upon a human being, whom thy fell aspect sure would kill with terror! *(A tremendous crash is heard, the Monster breaks through the door of the Pavilion)* Ah! he is here! I have endued him with a giant's strength, and he will use it to pluck down ruin on his maker's head. *(Music.—The Monster approaches him with gestures of conciliation.)*—Hence! avoid me! do not approach me, wretch! thy horrid contact would spread a pestilence throughout my veins; touch me, and I will straightway strike thee back to nothingness!

The Monster still approaches him with friendly gestures—Frankenstein endeavours to stab him with his dagger, which the Monster strikes from his hand;—whilst the Monster is taking up the dag-

ger, and admiring its form, Frankenstein steals off.—The Monster, perceiving him gone, rushes off, as if in pursuit, but in an opposite direction.

Scene V.

The heart of a gloomy and intricate Forest.—Tremendous Storm, Thunder, Lightning, Rain, &c. Enter Ritzberg,—and Emmeline, bearing the Child.

Em. The thunder's awful voice, and the fierce tumult of the wildly raging storm, have drowned thy plaintive wailings, my poor babe, and thou art hushed to silence. Sleep on, my babe, let thy mother's throbbing bosom shelter thee. We shall find him soon,—yes, I am sure we shall.—And when he sees thy ruddy smiling cheek, and marks his Emmeline's wan and haggard features, his heart will turn to us, he will again be all our own.

Ritz. I don't believe a word of it. Talk of his heart, indeed! he has no heart: if ever he had any, it has evaporated in the fumes of his diabolical preparations. He love and protect you!—all his affections are in the bottom of a crucible; and in the wild chimeras of his science, and the dreams of his mad ambition, all his human feelings are lost and annihilated.

Em. Oh, no! my father; the enthusiasm of knowledge, the applauses of the powerful, may for a time, have weaned him from us, but my own kind, gentle, Frankenstein, can never be inhuman.

Ritz. Can't he? Well, I don't know what you may call it; but to deceive and trepan a young, innocent, confiding creature, as you were, and to leave you and your child to poverty and want, whilst he went rambling in the train of a prince, after his own devilish devices;—if that is not inhuman, I don't know what is.

Em. Ah, my father; I have heard that the Prince del Piombino has an estate in this beautiful island; that he has, attached to his household, a wonderful philosopher—I am confident 'tis he—and oh! my heart tells me, that he will shortly bless us with his returning love.

Ritz. Yes, and with this fine tale; and because I could not bear to see you pining away in hopeless sorrow, have you lured me to quit my quiet, peaceful abode in Germany, and come wandering over here to Sicily. And today you must march out on a pretty wild-goose chase, to endeavour to trace him in the household of this prince; till we have lost our way in the mazes of this forest, and can't trace a path back again to the hovel I have hired. And it's my belief, that if you found him in the Prince's palace, you would be driven away from the gate like a common beggar.

Em. Oh, say not so, my father; do not destroy my hope, for in that consists the little strength that now remains to me.

(Storm rages furiously.)

Ritz. And a pretty night this for a young, delicate creature like you, with your helpless infant, to be out in.—Curses, a thousand curses on the villain—!

Em. Oh, no, my father, no!—Do not curse him.—Curse not the husband of your Emmeline, the father of her child!

Ritz. Well, well, I won't—the damn'd good-for-nothing vagabond!—I daren't stir a step in this plaguy forest, for all the storm keeps such a beautiful hubbub about us, for fear of straying further out of the way; and I am sure you have no strength to waste.—But here, I have it. You stay here, exactly where I leave you; give me the child, for you must be tired of carrying it, and I'll endeavour to find the path.—When I have traced it, I'll return for you.—There, stay here, just under this tree; it will afford a partial shelter. I warrant me, that with the assistance of the lightning, which keeps flashing so merrily, I shall soon discover the path.—I think I've got an inkling of it now. *(Takes the Child from Emmeline, and goes out as if endeavouring to trace the path. U. E. P. S.)*

Em. My spirits fail me, and my strength is exhausted. Whilst I bore the child, nature gave me powers, and I could not sink beneath the grateful burthen.—Ah, what a peal was there!—Heaven itself joins in the persecution of the hapless Emmeline.—Father, father! come to me!—I sink—I die—oh, Frankenstein! Frankenstein! *(She falls on the ground—the storm still continues to rage. The Monster enters in alarm and wonder, stares wildly about him; at length perceives Emmeline extended on the ground—is struck with wonder, approaches and raises her; is filled with admiration; expresses that the rain occasions inconvenience, and that the lightning is dreadful, his pity for Emmeline being exposed to it, his wish to procure her shelter; at length takes her up in his arms, and bears her off.)*

Re-enter Ritzberg, with the Child.

Ritz. Come, Emmeline, I think I have found it at last, and we shall be snug at home before the thunder can give another growl at us.—*(Perceives that she is gone.)* Merciful Heaven! not here! Where can she be gone? Surely no danger can have approached her.—She has wandered on, endeavouring to overtake me, and has mistaken the path, and so increased our troubles. Imprudent girl!—Emmeline, my child, my girl, my Emmeline!

Exit with the Child, calling aloud.

Scene VI.

The Inside of Ritzberg's Cottage.—Entrance Door in Flat; in some part of the Scene, a Fire-place.

(The Monster dashes open the door, and enters, bearing Emmeline; he places her in a chair, and looks round for some means of assisting her; perceives the fire, discovers by touching it, that it yields heat; removes the chair with Emmeline, to the fire, and remains watching her. The Child enters, on perceiving the Monster utters a shriek of terror, and runs across the stage, exclaiming, 'Mother!—mother!' Ritzberg then enters, is likewise alarmed at the appearance of the Monster. The Monster observes the Child with admiration and beckons it to approach him, which the Child refuses to do; he then softly approaches the Child with gestures of conciliation, the Child endeavouring to escape from him. Emmeline utters a piercing shriek. Ritzberg snatches up his gun, fires at the Monster, wounds it in the shoulder. The Monster puts down the Child, who rushes to his mother's embrace; expresses the agony occasioned by the wound; the rage inspired by the pain! would rush on Ritzberg, who keeps the gun presented; it is deterred by fear of a repetition of the wound; rushes out of the hut; Ritzberg remaining on the defensive; whilst Emmeline thanks Heaven for the preservation of her child.

Scene VII.

A Landscape.

Enter Julio.

Ju. I can't conceive what has happened to Mr. Frankenstein; when I spoke to him this evening, he was so cross, and so abstracted, and so mysterious; and now here my father, the Prince, has given a grand festival, expressly to do him honour, and he is no where to be found. I wish I could meet with him. I think he loves me, and I would coax him out of his gloomy humour, and lead him smiling and good-natured to my aunt Rosaura, or I'd know the reason why, I am determined. *(Music.—The Monster furiously rushes on.)* Ah! what dreadful gigantic creature is this? *(The Monster approaches and seizes him.)* Oh!—help,—mercy,—spare me,—spare me!—

(The Monster expresses that his kindly feelings towards the human race have been met by scorn, abhorrence, and violence, that they are all now converted into hate and vengeance; that Julio shall be his first victim; he snatches him up and bears him off; Julio crying 'Mercy!—help, help!'

Scene VIII.

Splendid Banqueting Hall in the Palace, open in the back upon the Garden, and giving a View of the Lake, Banqueting Tables, &c.

The Prince and Rosaura discovered, on a Throne under the centre Arch. Company of both sexes, Attendants, &c. A BALLET is performed, after which the Prince and Rosaura advance.

Prince. I know not why it is, that he in whose honour this entertainment was expressly given, should so long absent himself from our revels. Surely, for one night he might have relaxed from his deep studies.

Ros. I think he scarce will tarry longer, for I have sent Julio in search of him.—Ah! he is here.

Enter Frankenstein, in great agitation.

Prince. At length you are arrived. Be assured, my friend, your absence has been both felt and regretted.

Fran. Accept my humble and sincere apology. I was engaged, most intently engaged, in the solution of a Problem, on the result of which I had much at stake. *(aside)* My every hope depended on it, and the solution has stamped me a wretch for ever!

Prince. A truce to study, now, and moody thoughts.—Let the grape's sparkling juice chace from your brain all dark chimeras; partake the joy that smiles around you:—anon, I have a proposal to make to you, that will not damp your mirth, I trust.

Fran. Aye, let me be joyous; let me seek joy even at the bottom of the maddening bowl; I cannot find it in my own heart.—Give me wine;—quick, let me drain a flowing goblet, perchance it may chace—oh! oh, no, it can never drive from my remembrance that form of horror that exceeds conception.

Ros. From my hand will the cup bring less of joy?—Dear Frankenstein—I would say, learned sir, what means the dreadful wildness that gleams on your countenance?

Fran. Dear and most lovely lady, 'tis the intoxication of high swelling mirth, of gratitude, of animating hilarity. Fair lady, permit the humblest of your slaves to pledge you. *(He is raising the cup to his lips, when Quadro hastily rushes in.)*

Quad. Oh, my lord, my lord!—such intelligence of horror!—the young prince, Julio, has been murdered!

Fran. *(Dashing the cup from him.)* Eternal Heaven!—that fiend has perpetrated it!

Ros. Julio murdered!

Prince. My boy! my pretty, innocent, affectionate boy! say where, how, by whom?

Quad. He was found in the pavilion where Mr. Frankenstein pursues his studies, the door thrown from its hinges: from the mark on his neck, he appears to have been strangled.

Fran. *(aside.)* Then my worst fears have proved too true!

Prince. How could that lovely child provoke his fate? Robbery was not the object. Who could have the heart to harm that unoffending, darling child!

Quad. Can your highness doubt?

Prince. Speak, what mean you? On whom do your suspicions fall?

Quad. Who should it be, but this foreign adventurer, this Frankenstein?

Prince. Frankenstein!

Ros. Oh, Heavens!

Quad. Has any one else access to the pavilion, or ever presumes to enter it, or would have done now, except in eager search for the young prince?

Prince. I scarcely can believe it possible; but yet his lengthened absence from the festival at the very hour, his palpable agitation when he entered.—Frankenstein, what say you to this dreadful accusation?

Fran. I say that I am guilty, guilty a thousand times!

All. Ha!

Fran. Not of the crime of murder. I could not lay a finger in the way of violence on that lovely Child. Mine is a guilt a thousand times more black, more horrible. I am the father of a thousand murders. Oh! presumption, and is this thy punishment? has my promised triumph brought me but to this?

Prince. Frankenstein! for mercy's sake explain. What horrid mystery lurks beneath thy words?

(Shots and noise of pursuit heard without—the Monster rushes in through the archway in the back, pursued by Peasants variously armed—all shriek with horror—he rushes up to Frankenstein, and casts himself at his feet, imploring protection.)

Fran. Hated, detested fiend! now reeking with the blood of innocence—fiend of malice and destruction—here on thy hated head, I now invoke a father's and a prince's vengeance. Die, monster, die! and quit the life thou hast disgraced by blood and slaughter.

He seizes on the Monster—the guards close round—the Monster dashes Frankenstein to the earth, and by an exertion of his immense strength breaks through the opposing line—the Prince gives the word to fire—the Monster, snatching up the Officer holds him as a target before him—he receives the shots and falls dead—the Monster rushes up the steps of the throne and laughs exultingly—a general picture is formed, on which the Drop falls.)

Act II. Scene I.

A Cellar belonging to the Villa, entered only by a ladder from a small Trap-door above.

Strutt. (discovered) Well, my master has done a nice job for himself, it should seem, with all his machinery and magic; the making of a man has rendered him a made man for life, and I seem destined to share all his advantages. Because his hopeful bantling chose to amuse itself with strangling a child, much in the same way, I suppose, that our ordinary brats do kittens, out of pure kindness, they have seized hold of me and popped me into this underground apartment, to keep me out of mischief; as if they thought I shared my master's propensities, and had a *penchant* for making of men and strangling of children.—And so, after having taught me philosophy, my master has left me here to practise it. Now, if this were a wine cellar, there would be some kind of consolation; I might, by the magic of a butt of good liquor, convert this dungeon into a fairy palace, and when I could stand no longer, fancy these hard stones were silken cushions. But every thing now has the appearance of a cursed uncomfortable reality. Ha! I think I hear some one coming. I suppose it's old Quadro, who is about to set me at liberty, or at least to afford me the consolation of a flaggon of his best. *(The trap-door above opens, a ladder is put down, and Quadro descends, followed by Lisetta.)* Ah! how d'ye do; I'm so glad to see you. I hope you are come to bring me comfort in one shape or the other.

Quad. Oh, yes! the best of all possible comfort, the news of a speedy termination to all your miscries; you will very shortly be exalted, my fine fellow, elevated, tucked up, dance upon nothing.

Strutt. Don't mention it. I assure you such allusions are altogether unpleasant to my feelings; for though you may consider my master a bit of a mountebank, I assure you that I have never been accustomed to dance on a tight rope; and as to hanging—*(to Lisetta)* oh! you dear little creature, I have dreamt of nothing but hanging round your neck—whilst for tucking up, I had hoped we should have been both tucked up together in the bridal bed, before this.

Lis. Oh! for shame, sir!

Quad. Oh! you did, did you? I can tell you that there is a very narrow bed in preparation for you, where you will find it most convenient to lie alone, and where you will be tucked up with the sexton's shovel.

Strutt. I am surprised at your mentioning such indelicacies before a young lady.

Quad. In the confusion occasioned by the appearance of his delectable companion, your pretty master effected his escape; but I took care to grapple you. I considered the nabbing of such a fellow as you to be in my department, and so I popped you into this cellar.

Strutt. It would have been much more handsome of you to pop me in the cellar where you keep the liquor.

Quad. And you will be hanged for having aided, abetted, and assisted your master in the formation of a monster, and as an accessary in the young Prince's murder.

Strutt. Signor Quadro, you shock me. Me accused of assisting to make a man! Let me tell you I was never before suspected of such an offence; not even by the beadle of our parish, and he was a sharp chap at nosing out such matters, I warrant ye.

Quad. But now, sir, you are in my clutches, you won't get off so easy you may depend on it.

Strutt. Oh, Mr. Frankenstein! Mr. Frankenstein! this is a pretty mess you have got me into, to stand god-father to your monster.—*(he sits down in the back.)*

Lis. Now, my dear father, how can you be so harsh to this poor young man? I don't really believe he had any hand in it; in my opinion, he would not be concerned in the making of any thing half so ugly.

Quad. Did not I say it from the beginning; did not I always insist that they were a brace of vagabonds, and that no good would come of harbouring them?

Lis. But now my own good, kind, dear father, seeing that what is done cannot be undone, and that hanging this young man would only make bad worse, could not you contrive to let him go?

Quad. Let him go, indeed! and what for?

Lis. Why just to oblige me, father; for really he is a tolerably well-behaved young man enough, and not so much amiss to look at.

Quad. Oh! you think so? And then, I suppose, the next thing is that you must go with him, eh, you minx? Go and see him hanged if you like.

Lis. Now my dear, beautiful father, you don't know, though you are rather old, how well you look when you are doing a good-natured action. *(She makes signs behind his back to Strutt, to take advantage of the opportunity and run up the ladder.)*

Quad. You coaxing Jezebel! But don't think to wheedle me out of my duty.

Lis. Now look in my face. *(places one hand on each side of his face, as if to turn it towards her; Strutt watches his opportunity and silently ascends the ladder)* Look in my face, and frown a refusal if you can. Will you let him go?

Quad. No, I won't.

Lis. You are sure you won't?

Quad. No, I'll be damned if I do. *(Strutt has now gained the top of the ladder.)*

Lis. Then I'd advise him to do as I shall, to be off without asking your leave, and let you enjoy the comforts of this place by yourself. *(She runs to the ladder, and with Strutt's assistance hastily ascends it, after which they quickly draw up the ladder.)*

Quad. Why, you jade, you vixen, you undutiful hussey, what do you mean?

Lis. Only to let you stay there, father, till the young man is out of your reach; for I could not bear that you should have his death upon your conscience, father, I could not, indeed.

Quad. Go, both of you, and people the world with monsters, if you will; you can produce none worse than an unnatural daughter.

Strutt. Good bye, old gentleman!

(Strutt and Lisetta disappear with the ladder, Quadro rushes out in a rage on the opposite side.)

Scene II.

The inside of Ritzberg's Cottage, as before.
Frankenstein rushes in, in great agitation.

Fran. Where am I? Let me a moment pause—collect my distracted thoughts—compose, if possible, this tumult of the brain. I have fled! and wherefore fled? Had not death been welcome? But then to perish on a scaffold—loaded with infamy—branded with a crime my very soul abhors—the murder of an innocent I would have died to save. No, no, it must not be—not yet. My life has been devoted to the fulfilment of one object, another now claims the exertion of its short remainder, to destroy the wretch that I have formed—to purge the world of that infuriated monster—to free mankind from the fell persecution of that demon. This, this is now my bounden duty, and to this awful task I solemnly devote myself.

Enter Emmeline and Child.

Em. A stranger here! Ah! can I believe my senses—am I indeed so blest, does he come to seek his Emmeline? My lord, my life, my Frankenstein!

Fran. What do I behold? Emmeline Ritzberg! Lost, guilty, cursed wretch! thy cup of crime and misery is full. Hell yawns for thee, and all thy victims now surround thee, calling down Heaven's vengeance on thy head.

Em. And is it thus? Is Emmeline's presence, then, a curse? Farewell, then, hope.—But we'll not persecute thee, Frankenstein, for with my child I'll wander where thou shalt never more be punished with remembrance of us, and where death will soon end our sorrow.

Fran. Emmeline! Emmeline! tear not my heart with words like those. What to a guilty wretch can be a greater curse than the presence of those he has injured? Now at thy feet behold me, Emmeline, in humble agony of heart, I plead for thy forgiveness. Oh! that I ne'er had quitted thy peaceful blest abode—ne'er let into my bosom those demons of ambition and fell pride, that now, with ceaseless gnawing, prey upon my soul.

Em. Not at my feet, but in my arms, dear Frankenstein, lose all the memory of sorrows past. Oh! if thy heart still owns thy Emmeline, all shall be well, be happy.—One fond embrace of thine repays an age of sorrow; in thy smiles and those of this sweet cherub, I shall again awake to joy.

Fran. Oh, Emmeline, since we parted, all has been crime; crime of so black a dye, that even to thy gentle forgiving spirit, I dare not confess it. Crime, whose punishment will be unceasing, will be eternal.

Em. Oh, no, my Frankenstein, guilt, to be absolved needs but to be abjured. Returned to virtue and domestic peace, thy Emmeline shall soothe thy every woe, and on her bosom thou'lt forget thy griefs.

Fran. I dare not hope it. But in this land I cannot hope a moment's ease. Quick, let us fly—far, far from this accursed spot, the bane of all my peace. These, to that calm retreat, where first thy angel charms awoke my soul to love, there let us quick repair. Oh, that in former and in happier scenes, I could forget the guilt, the misery that I have since been slave to.

Enter hastily Ritzberg, Door in Flat.

Ritz. Ha! Frankenstein here! but 'tis no time to parley; the cottage is on fire! That fierce gigantic figure of terrific aspect, waves aloft his torch, as if in triumph at the deed. *(a coarse yelling laugh is heard.)*

Fran. Ha! 'tis that hideous voice! Quick, quick, let us fly! His hellish malice still pursues me; and but with his death or with mine, will this fierce persecution cease. Could I but place you beyond his power—!

(With Ritzberg he attempts to open the door, they find it barricaded from without; the laugh is

repeated—the conflagration has enveloped the whole building—Frankenstein rushes off as if in search of some other outlet—Part of the building breaks—the Monster enters at the chasm, seizes on Emmeline and the Child, and bears them through the burning ruins, followed by Ritzberg. Frankenstein returns, perceives that Emmeline and her Child are gone, and in despair rushes after them.)

Scene III.

A Landscape.

Enter Strutt and Lisetta. (P.S.)

Strutt. Well, Lisetta, and now having by your assistance, escaped from the clutches of that cantankerous old father of yours. What is next to be done?

Lis. Why as I have got out of his clutches at the same time, and so lost my natural protector, what do you think you ought to do next?

Strutt. Why, I suppose you think I ought to marry you?

Lis. Whilst you, perhaps, are of a very different opinion.

Strutt. Not in the least, my angel; but then my poor master, he perhaps is in trouble, and requires my assistance; and to desert him in the hour of need, I could not do it, Lisetta, no, not to possess such a treasure as yourself.

Lis. And if you could I should despise you for it. But suppose, Mr. Strutt, we were both to go and assist him. Two heads, they say, are better than one, and so are two pair of hands; and instead of having one faithful follower he would have a couple, that's all.

Strutt. What, no, you don't mean it, do you? Will you really take me for better, for worse, and go with me in search of my poor dear master? Well, I always thought you were a good creature, but now you're a perfect divinity, and I'll adore you.

Lis. Who knows, perhaps Mr. Frankenstein may get married too, and then he'll have better employment than making monsters.

Strutt. Oh, that monster! don't mention him, Lisetta. If he should be with my master now, do you think you would have the courage to face him? I'm not quite sure that I should.

Lis. Oh! never doubt me; if I take him in hand, I'll bring him to his senses, I warrant me; for if a spirited woman can't tame him, he must be a very fierce ungovernable devil indeed.—*(a scream is heard without.)*

Strutt. Ah! what means that shriek? See, yonder, where the demon comes, he bears with him both a woman and a child. She does not seem to have made much of a hand of him, at any rate. Here, back, back, conceal yourself, Lisetta, I would not have him come within arm's length of you, for the world. *(he pulls her behind a tree.)*

(The Monster enters, exultingly bearing Emmeline and her Child, crosses and exits. Frankenstein follows him with a staggering step, almost overcome with fatigue and terror. (P.S.) to (O.P.)

Strutt. (coming from his concealment.) What, ho! Sir! master! Mr. Frankenstein! 'Tis Strutt, your faithful servant! He hears me not, but madly still pursues the fiend he cannot hope to master.

Lis. And will you, too, Strutt, be mad enough to follow him?

Strutt. Why not singly, because I think it would be to little purpose; but I'll tell you what I'll do—I'll first bestow you in a place of safety, and then I'll summon together a few stout-hearted fellows, and we'll see if we can't settle his monstership; for sooner than he should harm that poor woman and her infant, damme, he shall kill and eat me—but I'll endeavour to give him a bellyfull.

[Exeunt. (O.P.)

Scene IV.

A tremendous range of craggy precipices, near the summit of Mount Etna. On the P.S. a conspicuous pillar of rock stands on a lofty elevation. The only approach is from the depths below.

(The Monster, with gigantic strides, ascends from below with Emmeline and the Child—she is so overcome with fatigue and terror as to be unable to speak—The Monster gains the elevation, and with a cord that is round his waist, binds Emmeline to the pillar of rock—He returns to the Child—Emmeline sinks on her knees in supplication—Frankenstein with great difficulty ascends from below—he perceives his Child in the Monster's power—he is about to rush on him; the Monster defies him—and Frankenstein, recollecting his former defeats, abandons his threatening gestures and assumes one of entreaty.)

Fran. Demon of cruelty, art thou still insatiate with the blood of innocence? how many victims does it require to content thy rage? I do implore thee, I, thy creator, who gave thee life, who endued thee with that matchless strength I cannot hope to master, I, on my knees, entreat thee but to spare that innocent. If fury and the thirst of blood be in thy hellish nature, on me, on me glut thy fell appetite—but, oh! if in thy human frame there dwells one spark of human sympathy or feeling, spare, spare that unoffending child!

(The Monster points to his wound—expresses that he would willingly have served Frankenstein and befriended him, but that all his overtures were repelled with scorn and abhorrence—then, with malignant exultation seizes on the Child, and whirls it aloft, as if about to dash it down the rock—Emmeline screams, Frankenstein, with a cry of horror, covers his eyes—at this moment a thought occurs to Emmeline—she pulls from under her dress a small flageolet, and begins to play an air—its effect on the Monster is instantaneous—he is at once astonished and delighted—he places the Child on the ground—his feelings become more powerfully affected by the music, and his attention absorbed by it—the Child escapes to its father—Emmeline continues to play, and Frankenstein intently to watch its effect on the Monster. As the air proceeds his feelings become more powerfully excited—he is moved to tears: afterwards, on the music assuming a lively character, he is worked up to a paroxysm of delight—and on its again becoming mournful, is quite subdued, till he lays down exhausted at the foot of the rock to which Emmeline is attached.)

(Strutt now rushes on with Ritzberg, and a number of Peasants variously armed, and furnished with strong cords.)

Strutt. There he is! that's him! that's my gentleman! and luckily for us, he seems in a bit of a snooze—now's our time or never. On him, my lads, and bind him fast, and then we shall be all right.

(With Ritzberg and others, he immediately falls on the Monster, and they bind him stoutly with cords—Frankenstein has meantime released Emmeline—the Monster makes prodigious exertions of strength to burst his bonds, but he is overpowered by the number of his adversaries.)

Strutt. Away, away, sir, and place the lady and child in safety. I'll take care and accommodate this gentleman with snug quarters, and return immediately to attend your commands.

Fran. Faithful creature! Eternal Providence, receive my thanks; and if it be thy pleasure to inflict on me an added punishment, oh! on this guilty head alone direct thy wrath; spare those who are most dear to me, those whose innocence may challenge thy compassion! *(With Emmeline and the Child he commences the descent, and disappears.)*

Strutt. Now I think the best thing we can do is to fasten my gentleman to this pinnacle of rock; the cool air of this exalted region may give him an appetite; but he will stand very little chance of getting it gratified, unless the lava should flow from the volcano, and that may be a kind of cordial for him. *(They are binding him to the rock, the Monster making a furious resistance, in the course of which he hurls one of the Peasants to the depths below.)*—That's right, make a tight job of it, whilst you are about it; for if he once gets loose, he'll play the devil with you all; he'd crack you like so many walnuts. There, I think he'll do now; there's not much fear of his troubling us again for one while. If he gets away from here, and finds his way down to terra firma again, I'll give him leave to drink hob-and-nob with me, in the cup I have filled to celebrate his overthrow.

(They descend the precipice by means of ropes and ladders, leaving the Monster attached to the pinnacle of rock—when they are gone, he redoubles his efforts to escape from his bonds, and at length succeeds—he surveys the chasm, and is afraid to venture down it—he firmly attaches to the pinnacle one end of the cord by which he was bound—and by means of this lowers himself down the chasm.)

Scene V.

A Subterranean Passage hollowed in the Mountain.
Enter Strutt and Peasants. (P.S.)

Strutt. Faith, my lads, it's cold work this, climbing so near the summit of Etna, in a chill evening breeze—yes, and fatiguing work too—catching such game as we've been after is no boy's play. Lord, what a chap my master must be, to be sure, when he was making a man—he thought he might as well have a wapper at once, I suppose. Now I say, a little and good for my money. But, however, we have quieted my gentleman, and I think we have done a much better job than my master did in making him. And now I can tell you a secret. This passage leads to the hermitage of father Antonio; that you all know, so that's no secret; but what you perhaps do not know is, that old Quadro, the Prince's butler, whenever he visits the holy father to confess, always brings a bottle or two of prime old wine, which is received by the hermit in lieu of penance; and so he makes his master pay for all his sins, and purchases absolution for one by committing another. Now do you know, I really think, that we better deserve this wine than the reverend father, and my proposal is, that we adjourn to his cave and drink to the future prosperity of the heroes who subdued the monster.

Shout, and exeunt, (O.P.)

Scene VI.

Interior of the Hermit's Cave.
Strutt and Peasants discovered seated round a table.

Strutt. Well, upon my soul, it's a monstrous pleasant retreat. And now for the little store of choice Falernian.

Peas. (who has been hunting about the cave) Here it is, master Strutt; here's his reverence's holy water.

Strutt. Out with it, then, and in with it. If his reverence should miss it when he comes home, he knows where to get more. Old Quadro's sins will always keep his cellar well stocked. So now my lads, charge your cups—*(Peasants have meanwhile placed on the table several flaggons of wine, horns, &c.)* Now for it, fill all, and mind it's a bumper. *(all fill)* Here's confusion to any creature that would harm a defenceless woman and a helpless child; for be their shape what it may, they must be monsters indeed.

Peas. Bravo! with all my heart! *(all drink.)*

Strutt. And now I'll give you another. Here's our noble selves, and may all our future enterprizes be crowned with as complete success, as that which we have now so gloriously achieved.

(They have their cups raised to their lips, when the Monster, still lowering himself by his rope, descends from an aperture in the roof of the cavern, and stands on the table in the midst of them—they all

shrink back in terror with loud cries—the Monster, with one blow, dashes the table in pieces—all fly in extreme fear—the Monster in rage dashes about the seats—Strutt takes an opportunity to stab him in the back, and flies leaving the dagger in the wound—the Monster extracts it, and roaring with pain rushes off.)

Scene VII.

A narrow rocky Path-way, leading to the summit of Etna.

Enter Strutt and Peasants rapidly retreating from the Monster—the Monster follows in pursuit.—Frankenstein enters with Emmeline—they are followed by a party of Soldiers, whom Frankenstein encourages to the attack of the Monster.

They all go off in pursuit, from P.S. to O.P.

Scene VIII.

The Summit of Mount Etna—the Crater occupies the middle of the stage—near it is the Path-way from below—in very distant perspective are seen the sea and towns at the foot of Etna—the Volcano during the scene throws out torrents of fire, sparks, smoke, &c. as at the commencement of an eruption.

(The Monster ascends from below, faint from loss of blood and overcome by fatigue—he is followed by Frankenstein, whom he immediately attacks and stabs with the dagger he had taken from his wound—as Frankenstein falls, Emmeline rushes in shrieking and catches his lifeless body—the Monster, attempting to escape, is met at every outlet by armed Peasantry—in despair he rushes up to the apex of the mountain—the Soldiery rush in and fire on him—he immediately leaps into the Crater, now vomiting burning lava, and the Curtain falls.)

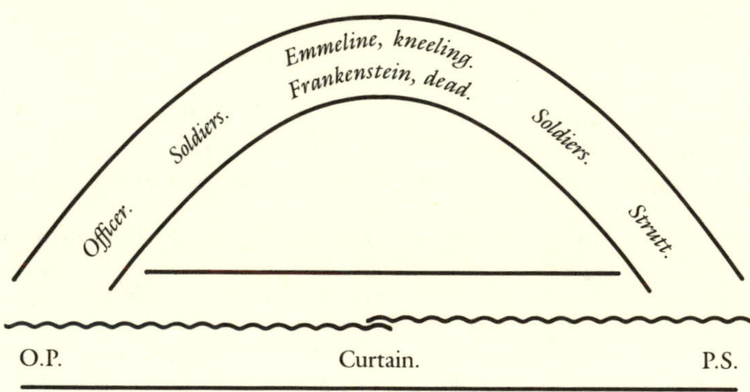

John Atkinson Kerr

The Monster and Magician;
or, The Fate of Frankenstein

(1826)

Original Translation from the French:

THE

MONSTER AND MAGICIAN:

OR THE

FATE OF FRANKENSTEIN.

A Melo-dramatic Romance, in three Acts

AS PERFORMED AT

THE ROYAL WEST LONDON THEATRE,

With unbounded applause, October 2nd. 1826.

Freely translated from the celebrated Drama of Messrs. Merle and Authory, entitled "Le Monstre et le Magicien," represented at the Theatre Port St. Martin, Paris:

By John Kerr,

Author of the BRAZEN CAVERN; MAN OF THE BLACK FOREST, &c

Printed & Published by J. & H. Kerr, 16, Henry Street Hampstead Road, and may be had at the Box office of the Theatre, and of all the Booksellers in Town and Country.

Price One Shilling.

CHARACTERS

MEN

Frankenstein	Mr. Harding.	Jansken	Mr. Brewer.
Antonio (his Son)	Miss E. Santer.	Petrusco.............	Mr. Atkins.
Holbien	Mr. Santer.	Zomar	Mr. Owlet.
Pietro	Mr. H. Beverly.	Swendor.............	Mr. Bosworth.
Litolf	Mr. Marquis.	Malfino (the Genie) ...	Mr. Addis.
Gontram.............	Mr. Fisher.	* * * (the Monster)	Mr. H. Beverly.

WOMEN

Cecilia	Miss Eldred.	Marana...............	Mrs. Fisher.
Mazzena	Mrs. J. Santer.	Freda	Mrs. T. Santer.
Offa..................	Miss Grosette.	Monica...............	Mrs. Owlet.

The Music Composed by Mr. Brown.
The Scenery by Master W. Beverly.
And the whole produced under the Superintendance of
Mr. H. Beverly.

Act I. Scene the First.

A dark Forest, in the centre of which is a Gothic Tomb, on the left a Rock.

A Storm—Petrusco, Zomar, & Swendor, followed by the band, consisting of Bohemians enter apparently much fatigued.

Chorus.
Tho' murkey the path, yet the light'ning illumes,
The blast of the gale with loud thunder attunes,
The beasts of the forest to shelter retire,
But we, the bold Outlaws, must brave all its ire:
Tho' drench'd with rain we like Tritons appear,
A bumper of liquor our spirits shall cheer.

Petru. 'Tis a fearful storm!

Zomar. Egad you may say that.

Petru. It has surprised us rather awkwardly—but why should we, poor Bohemian outcasts, complain of the elements, accustomed, as we are, to brave its fury.

Swen. We have worse enemies than the elements to dread! friend Petrusco, those curst Venetians, who are now on the hunt for us.

Zomar. There would be nothing to dread were our force but half equal to theirs—but reduced as we are:—

Petru. Resolution must supply the deficency—but see, our leader, Jansken, comes—*(Enter Jansken.)*—Welcome noble Captain—know you in what part of the forest we now are?

Jan. We shall learn anon. *(seeing the Tomb.)* 'Tis the Tomb of the Forest!—withdraw from it quickly!

Petru. Why so?

Jan. 'Tis an unhallowed spot! *(they advance from it)*

Petru. Is it here then we are to halt?

Jan. No: you will continue your route—I alone must remain; you will tarry for me on the summit of the black mountain, near the cottage of Holbien.

Zomar. But why do you not accompany us? Captain.

Jan. No more interrogations—Some of you must be in attendance here—away, be cautious of a surprise from the Venetian soldiers—they are not amongst the number of our friends.

Petru. We have given little cause for their being so—lead on. *(Exit Bohemians, &c. Jansken remaining alone.)*

Jan. What a perplexed destiny is mine—son of one of the richest inhabitants of the Tyrol,—now, leader of a wretched band of Bohemians—such is the result of misconduct—after reducing a parent to misery, I traversed the world, the sport of man and fortune—I was their prey—they were mine, nor did tranquillity partially dawn upon my blighted fate 'till quitting the society of knaves and sharpers I became the associate of brigands—but weary of my situation, I pant for a reconciliation with my aged parent.—Returning to my native country, I find, that aided by Frankenstein, my father and sister had taken up their residence near this spot—Frankenstein loves my sister, Cecilia, and their union will aid my projects, amidst the general joy will I present myself to my father, nor will he, I am assured, refuse forgiveness, and then farewell, an eternal farewell to the minions whom I command—to become an honest man is the warmest desire of my heart—yet, am I not without alarm, for Frankenstein is devoted to study; and the abstruse compositions of Albert and Faustus, have inflamed him with guilty pretensions—anon he is to repair to this forest—alas! for what a frightful purpose! but I must arrest him ere he plunges into the abyss—some one approaches. *(he retires to the back.)*

Music. Enter Pietro, with a Casket under his arm, much affrighted, followed by Frankenstein.

Pie. Plaguy forest! How cursed dark and frightful it is—there ayn't a single drop of blood flowing in my veins—Oh! my worthy master! now what the deuce could tempt you to quit the Castle?

Fran. *(in a reverie)* Peace.

Pie. Some sad misfortune will befal us—the ravens do so croak, and the owls play such a concert:—

Fran. Silence, I command you—Deposit yonder that Casket.

Pie. Yes, yes, my Lord. *(trembling)*

Jan. Yes! 'tis Frankenstein.

Fran. Some one approaches—Who's there? speak.

Jan. *(advancing)* A friend!

Fran. Jansken!—What brings thee here?

Jan. To converse with thee.

Fran. You have selected an improper moment, withdraw.

Jan. No! here will I remain.

Fran. On what intent?—

Jan. You shall know. *(motions Pietro to retire)*

Pie. *(not understanding him)* What's your pleasure, Sir.

Jan. Leave us.—

Pie. O law! you need'nt bawl so, I'm not deaf—where do you wish me to go? *(Jansken points to the back.)*

Jan. To a respectable distance.

Pie. *(aside)* O dear! a very respectable character it is who gives this command—well suited to the spot—I am going Sir—Yes! I'm gone. *(retires to the back.)*

Fran. What would you with me?

Jan. On our last meeting I had not sufficient time to inform you of my past misfortunes and my future prospects—even then your agitated looks escaped not my observation—I have watched thy proceedings and know all—but beware, Frankenstein! seek not to perfect the frightful deed!

Fran. What is it you require?

Jan. Your safety—my happiness—that of my sister & of my father.

Fran. To recede were vain—I have already embarked too deeply:—

Jan. You are then resolved on your own destruction!

Fran. After so many painful exertions:—

Jan. Be content with thy superior knowledge, nor seek to become the most culpable of mortals—Oh! my friend, on you depends the fate of Cecilia.

Fran. Cecilia!

Jan. You love her!—your son, fruit of your first marriage already repeats the endearing name of mother. Why then be discontented with your lot? Why seek to penetrate a mystery which heaven wisely conceals from the weakness of man?

Fran. My undertaking must be accomplished—nor can I now pause—the Genie of this spot is about to resign to me a slave who henceforth shall be submitted to my will, and soon perhaps I can assure to thee and to Cecilia ages of glory and felicity:—

Jan. Frankenstein I conjure thee, abandon thy frightful purpose—ere too late.

Fran. Leave me—

Jan. In pity ere you attempt its execution—wait but till you are united to my sister—

Fran. From what motive?

Jan. The virtue of Cecilia will then protect thee from the wrath of heaven.

Fran. Well—yes—it may be so.

Jan. Swear to return to the castle instantly!

Fran. Instantly!

Jan. Aye instantly—a moment must not be lost—

Fran. What would you exact?

Jan. Exact!—I exact not—I entreat—I supplicate it in the name of friendship, and of our general safety:—

(Enter Pietro.)

Pie. Oh Sir—my Lord—a man comes this way—

Fran. Who can it be? *(Petrusco enters.)*

Petru. The Venetians are in pursuit of us, and my comrades require thy immediate attendance—You are acquainted with the intricacies of the forest, hasten then to direct our retreat—

Jan. Cursed interruption—

Petru. Prithee delay not!—

Jan. However dangerous the duty, it shall be faithfully performed—my poor comrades have in me confided their safety, nor shall their confidence be deceived, I leave thee Frankenstein, but first swear instantly to quit this spot—

Fran. To quit this spot—well be it so—

Jan. We meet again this evening, when I hope to convince you. *(Jansken presses the hand of Frankenstein and exits with Petrusco.)*

Pie. That chap, spite of his strange appearance, seems a very good sort of a fellow and I should'nt have been sorry if he remained—faith I'm always afraid when alone with my master of beholding on a sudden some horrible apparition—

Fran. *(from his reverie)* Can Jansken be right? and ought I, in reality to dread least Cecilia—Cecilia beloved maid! 'tis to insure thy eternal happiness, that I am anxious to possess this secret—the terrors of Jansken, however may have some just origin—to some other period shall be deferred my final attempt—come Pietro we will return to the castle. *(Pietro takes up the casket.)*

Pie. With all my heart and soul. *(They are proceeding off when Frankenstein suddenly stops—.)*

Fran. No I cannot! a secret wish commands my proceedings and fortifies my heart against the throes of terror—about to gain the object of my desire—almost within my grasp shall I madly resign it perhaps for ever—no—no—it cannot must not be—

Pie. O lud! O dear! what is the matter now!

Fran. The favour I would solicit may entail on me my destruction; but should I retain it to myself, what will be the crime?—What shall I have to dread?—Nothing! mysterious treasure! I will attain it, and at least my labours will not be unrecompenced.—Yes, 'tis decided—

(He seizes the casket from Pietro.)

Pie. For the mercy of heaven, my lord, what are your intentions? I hope your mind is'nt changed—

Fran. Begone!

Pie. No, no, my dear master—no—I cannot. Of a certain you have some wicked intention—for heaven's sake drop it, and let us return together.

Fran. *(Withdrawing from the casket several cabalistical instruments)* Withdraw, Pietro!

Pie. For some days past the state in which I have seen you has really alarmed me—your continued sighs, your agitated looks—

Fran. Depart I say—I command—

Pie. My dear master, in the name of that which you hold most dear—I—

Fran. Remain then, since you are so inclined.

(He extends his arms towards Pietro, who is tranfixed and at the same time bereft of speech. Frankenstein now commences his operations—thunder—lightning—he is surrounded by a circle of fire.)

Fran. Genie whom I have subjugated, obey the voice of thy master.

Storm encreases, the Monument crumbles to atoms, and the Genie appears surrounded by flames, holding a Vase in its hand.

Gen. What would you with me?

Fran. You already know—that Vase encloses the reward of my labours.

Gen. Madman! What do you require!

Fran. That it should be mine!

Gen. I know to what ambitious extent thy presumption soars—but tremble wretched mortal!

Fran. Heed not me—but give as I command!

Gen. 'Tis my duty to obey a power more potent than my own, your happiness is cancelled beyond recall, and only in death will you again behold me.

The Storm increases, the Genie becomes enveloped in a flame of fire, Pietro utters a shriek and runs off, Frankenstein stands exultingly, and is enclosed by

SCENE THE SECOND.—*Lodge in the Castle of Frankenstein.*

Enter Litolf, followed by Mazzena.

Lit. I guessed that as usual you were to be found at the Lodge, Mazzena—was ever father served so scurvily by a daughter.

Maz. My dear father, if you will but listen to reason—

Lit. 'Tis you that should listen to reason, but you are deaf to every proposal for your advantage.—Does not Pietro enjoy the most intimate confidence of our worthy master, Count Frankenstein? does he not hold a situation in the Castle almost equal in authority to the one I fill—

Maz. Truly, father, the situation which Pietro holds weighs but little in my estimation—

Lit. The girl's a perfect natural.—Our master is liberality itself, and he is as careless of his ducats, as a prudent servant, who looks to his own interest would desire; now Pietro has so many favourable opportunities:—

Maz. Of plundering his benefactor—I trust father you have not to accuse yourself of this ingratitude?—

Lit. What me, child—I wonder how you could ever hint such a thing—not but what my nerves are tolerably strong—

Maz. 'Tis true, report speaks unfavourable of the means by which Frankenstein's wealth has been attained.

Lit. But that's no business of ours, and if it does come roguishly, we share it honestly, and if Pietro will but take care of himself—

Maz. I promise he shall never have me to take care of him—but why thus continually recommending Pietro, when I have told you over and over again that if ever I do marry it shall be to Gontram—

Lit. Gontram, a pretty bargain you would make forsooth—a sorry knave, the emoluments of whose pitiful place of gamekeeper but barely afford him a yearly jerkin—he's a keen shot, and faith Mazzena he knew where to scent when he took aim at you—but he shall find the game too distant to make sure of his aim, and talking of game is another proof of Gontram's neglect.

Maz. How father?

Lit. Is there not a profusion required for the entertainments that are to take place tomorrow?—the varlet instead of scouring the forest for his master, has been poaching in the preserves for himself—but I'll spoil his sport, be assured the larder shall be inspected, and should there still lack the requisite quantity, I'll see, though no sportsman, if I can't make him take wing from these premises—so think of him no longer—*(exit.)*

Maz. Ah father advice is easily given yet avails but little where the heart has made its election. *(Gontram steals on.)*

Gon. Those words spoke my own Mazzena—

Maz. Oh Gontram—you overheard then—

Gon. Yes, your father's partiality to Pietro, and the contempt which he entertains of me in consequence of my poverty, but assured of your love I fear not for the future since we have youth, health, and strength to aid our endeavours.

Chorus.

Maz. Let fashion's minions fondly shine
As high their lofty pennons wave,
A peasant's simple lot be mine
And health, the greatest boon I crave.
Gon. And pillow'd on the humble couch
No dreams our slumber shall invade,
Nor on our simple joys encroach
But sweetest thoughts our sleep prevade.
Both. Yes, dear the home—the hour how sweet
When labour o'er, the swain at eve,

Returns his constant swain to greet
And from her welcome kind receive.

(Enter Pietro alarmed.)

Pie. I've run myself out of breath, and thanks to heaven here are human faces at last—Oh! oh what a horrid sight—

Maz. A horrid sight—I hope, sir, you dont mean to say that my face is a horrid sight—

Pie. It's the most pleasant countenance I have seen since I left the Castle—Oh! Oh! Oh!

Gon. What then have you seen, Pietro?

Pie. What have I not seen Mr. Gontram?—had you witnessed the like your legs would never have served you so faithfully as mine did—

Maz. Pray what was it Pietro—

Pie. Oh such a Bogie.

Maz. A Bogie! what's a Bogie—

Gon. Oh a stray cat, that his idle fears have conjured into some unaccountable shape—

Pie. A stray cat—I tell you what, Gontram, had you beheld this cat you'd thought yourself lucky to get out of his claws, and however unaccountable it may appear, you'd give a very different account of the affair—

Maz. The coward—

Pie. Now you must know in the first place that no sooner had we gained the skirts of the forest, than it began to rain, thunder, and lighten—

Maz. Well!

Pie. No, it wasn't well, for I was speedily drenched through and through—and so—

Gon. Proceed.

Pie. I did proceed through brambles and quagmires, till we came to a dark, dreary glen in one of the most retired quarters of the black forest—the very thought of it makes me shudder still—"Pietro you may return to the castle" says my master—"what and leave you all alone in this place?"—says I in return—"No blow me if I do any thing of the kind"—cause I thought there would not be so much danger in remaining with him, as there would in returning alone—and so—

Gon. Now to scare the poltroon. *(who with Mazzena has stolen to the side)* Pietro.

Pie. Hey!

Gon. What's that behind you?—

Maz. A Ghost! A Ghost! *(runs off with Gontram laughing.)*

Pie. *(unable for some time to look round)* It's here again!—Oh ye saints! I'm a poor lost sinner—mercy—murder—mercy. *(he scampers off)*

Scene III.—*A Gallery in the Castle.*

At the back, a staircase, leading to the laboratory of Frankenstein. Antonio discovered sleeping in an arm chair.

Enter Cecilia.

Cec. I have seen my unfortunate brother, who informs me he possesses the means of restoring peace to the bosom of Frankenstein—Heaven grant him success and reinstate him in the tenderness of our parent! Antonio sleeps aware of my uneasiness at the absence of his father he endeavoured to offer consolation—dear child! soon will you call me by the name of mother! how sweet it will be to fulfil those duties—what can it be that thus alarms him! Antonio! Antonio!—

Ant. *(awaking)* Oh! is it you? my kind Cecilia!—I have been very much frightened:—

Cec. What has alarmed you?

Ant. Such a horrid dream!

Cec. A dream! what was it?

Ant. I thought we were in my father's laboratory, where you know, neither I, nor you, nor any one attempt to enter. I was seated on thy knees, and you kissed me tenderly, and my father also kissed me, when a tall man came in and threatened to kill me—you and my father hastened to my assistance, but he dashed you on the floor, and with my father was gone in a moment—was not this a sad dream?

Cec. Yes—yes—undoubtedly, but my dear Antonio it was but a dream.

Ant. I don't believe in dreams—for why should any one wish to harm me!

Cec. Why, indeed! my dearest Child?—but here is my father.

(Enter Holbien)

Ant. Ah, my kind good friend!

Hol. Every blessing attend you my sweetest boy—is not Frankenstein returned yet?

Cec. Not yet.

Hol. Night approaches—'tis time that we return to our cottage.

Cec. My dear father, let us tarry here some time longer.

Ant. Yes, pray don't go away so soon.

Hol. Frankenstein's stay alarms me—what can it be?—what can occasion it at this hour—Alas! for some time past how greatly is he changed by study; he seldom remains with us long, and when spoken to replies with difficulty.

Cec. He is constantly absorbed in study.

Hol. Would that he were less anxiously employed—if credit may be given to the reports, it arises from a guilty source, but 'tis not his riches that ensured my approbation and esteem, tis' his virtues alone induced me to consent to your union.

Cec. Nor doubt but he will prove the most tender of sons.

Hol. He will console me for the one I have lost, and whose memory I must ever hold in abhorrence.

Cec. My dear father—Jansken will love you with equal fervour.

Hol. Jansken! has he not been the cause of my ruin?

Cec. Was he to present himself, could you refuse to receive him to your arms?

Hol. Was he to present himself—but no—that is impossible. *(a knock is heard at the door.)* Hark!

Cec. Perhaps 'tis Frankenstein!

Ant. Yes, it is my father. *(Enter Jansken, the child utters a shriek and flies to Holbien.)*

Cec. Jansken:—

Jan. Heavens! my father!

Hol. Who is it?—Antonio appears alarmed.

Cec. Father, 'tis not a stranger, but a person attached to the castle. *(motions silence, Holbien sits down)*

Cec. *(aside)* What purpose brings you hither?

Jan. To calm and dissipate thy alarms—I have seen Frankenstein, who, thanks to my council and intreaties will not, I trust, execute a project which cannot be explained. Tomorrow he will conduct thee to the altar—another day would have been too late.

Cec. What, mystery!

Jan. More at present I cannot disclose—my followers await me, for dangers threaten, then tomorrow at daybreak seek the summit of the Black Mountain, there will I await thee, farewell—but ere my departure, might I not be permitted? *(pointing to his father.)*

Hol. Well Cecilia, brings he any comforting intelligence?

Cec. Father, you need not be uneasy:—

She holds the hand of her father, while her brother kisses it.

Hol. My dear child, you appear deeply affected: I even thought a tear dropt upon my hand! *(urged by his sister Jansken is withdrawing when he is run against by Pietro, he exits hastily.)*

Pie. Tis the devil—or rather the Chief of—

Cec. Hush!

Pie. Zounds! they're all of the same humour, not one of them will allow me to speak a single word.

Hol. Is that Pietro?

Pie. Yes, my Lord, it's I, Pietro.

Cec. Where have you left your master?

Pie. In the forest.

Cec. In the forest!

Pie. Yes, and i'faith was I to be bastionaded to death I'll relate the most fearful adventure which ever befel an honest man.—Only to suppose that after having travelled ever so many leagues in the forest, which is of a truth the abode of all the magicians and sorcerers of the country, we arrived at a spot where it was impossible to see your fingers before you even in broad day. *(Enter Frankenstein.)*

Pie. On a sudden I saw, as plainly as I see you—

Fran. Silence!—

Pie. Silence again—Oh Lord! Oh dear!—I'm silent sir—I'm dumb—

Cec. You are at length returned—

Hol. Dear Frankenstein—you have made us tarry late.

Fran. Pardon my dear sir, and yours Cecilia—important affairs detained me much longer than I expected—

Hol. You are here and all is forgotten; but pray be more careful of your health, nor thus alarm your friends: you know the reports that are spread of your mysterious proceedings, and on what condition I bestow the hand of my daughter—destroy the implements of a proscribed science, and I shall then be tranquil as to your future fate. It is tomorrow you are to call me father.

Fran. Yes, yes, tomorrow—tomorrow—I shall have that bliss.

Hol. At my abode your nuptials will take place—you will take Cecilia from a cottage, but forget not, that you loved her for herself—Your tenderness has afforded comfort to my declining days, and now you are about to add to my obligations by undertaking the happiness of my child—let the present night be dedicated to repose—my little Antonio will conduct me home, say will you not?

Ant. Most willingly.

Cec. Father I will follow you instantly *(exit Holb. &c.)* a word my friend, ere we part.

Fran. What would my dearest Cecilia?

Cec. You have seen my brother—but fear nothing—he has not made me the confident of your mysterious conduct—and this day I will still respect them—but tomorrow forget not that you ought no longer to have any mystery concealed from your wife.

Fran. Believe me, necessity alone:—

Cec. Nay— I ask nothing, nor will I this evening require the slightest explanation; but take the advice of my father, seek repose.—Your features are altered by so many painful exertions—Oh! Frankenstein let us live only for each other—'tis the choicest and sweetest study.

Fran. My dear Cecilia!

Cec. Rely on my tenderness—cannot I dissipate this sadness, this loathed melancholy, which even at this moment is depicted on thy visage, I shall then think you no longer love me, a reflection that will embitter my days, and soon—ah! soon deprive you of your Cecilia.

Fran. What say you! sooner would I die a thousand deaths than cause you a moments affliction—you exact that I should abandon my researches—You shall be obeyed—from to-morrow yon laboratory shall be closed for ever—and I will live but for my Cecilia—Happy possessor of an adored object, every thought, but her, shall be a stranger to my bosom.

Cec. You have given your promise—I ought and will believe it—now to join my father—farewell—till tomorrow.

Fran. Tomorrow I shall commence a new existence.

Cec. Think on your oath—farewell— *(exit)*

Fran. I have sworn—tomorrow,—tomorrow, but this night is still mine—I am alone—Why have they withdrawn—greatly did I need their presence!—Must my enterprise be left incomplete!—after so many years of anxious research—possessed of such an extraordinary power, must I behold it annhilated without attaining the slightest benefit. The object of my attempt is there—should I succeed—But those misfortunes with which I am threatened—Ha! a light breaks in upon me,—a power jealous of my potency, is perhaps desirous, by alarming, to oppose my triumph—Yes—that may be so. *(thunder)* Bugbears to frighten the irresolute.—'Tis a horrid night—the loud peals of thunder, and the broad glare of vivid lightning, accord well with the deed I am about to perpetrate.—Come,—for the last time—now fortitude assist. Yes?—it is resolved!

He goes up and enters the laboratory—Pietro enters with a lamp.

Pie. My master has not yet retired to his chamber; now would I wager that he is still in his laboratory, in the midst of his crucibles, alembecks, and devil's kitchen utensils. However he must be up betimes for Miss Cecilia has strictly cautioned me to—*(he tumbles against a chair and drops the lamp)* Oh lord! oh dear—here I am alone in the dark—what will become of me *(a blue flame issues from one of the laboratory windows)* good lord! what can that be? I'm burning to know—dont believe I ever felt such courage—hem hem, it's a good omen—here goes. *(He ascends the stairs.)*

Fran. (In the laboratory) What have I done? what have I accomplished? *(Pietro rushes down stairs, trembling in every limb, he falls on the floor.)*

Pie. What have I seen! wretch that I am, it's all over with me. *(hastens off)* I'm a dead man—help! help.

(Frankenstein rushes down.)

Fran. Horror! horror! back daemon, fiend, back to the cold and lifeless corpse you were before my folly gave you animation—what fearful monster has hell resigned, oh—I feel his cold and clammy hand upon me still—merciful Heavens what dreadful object have I created?—already is my punishment begun—already do I feel that I have merited the punishment of heaven,—all is tranquil—perhaps the monster has relapsed into oblivion—should it be so—But no—he lives to be my eternal curse—Antonio my son, dear Cecilia, you I dare no longer approach, I am lost—lost for ever!

He sinks exhausted in the chair, the door of the laboratory opens, the Monster springs over the balcony.

Fran. Heavens tis he!

Monster gazes at him attentively whilst he recoils with horror.

Fran. Monster approach me not—hence, or dread my vengeance!—No, no, you shall not quit this spot—but thus—thus I destroy the wretch I have created.

Frankenstein attempts to stab the Monster, who snatches the sword and breaks it, then disappears by breaking through the wall.—Frankenstein falls senseless, and the act finishes.

Act II. Scene the First.—*The Forest.*

The Bohemians discovered seated round a fire regaling.—

Air Zoma.
Tho' from man condemn'd to roam,
And like wolves to hunt for prey:—
Where we stray, we make our home,
Heedless of the coming day.

Chorus.
When danger threatens we're alert,
The call of joy we'll n'eer desert.:

Beneath the oak our tents we spread
The forest chase, provides our fare,
Luxurious meals we do not heed
Whilst we have generous wine to share.

Jan. It cannot be long 'ere Cecilia arrives—a few more hours and I dare entertain the hope that a father's malediction will no longer overwhelm me—Frankenstein has abandoned his fatal purpose, and this day he espouses my sister, an union which will wean him from his fatal purpose.

Enter Petrusco.

Pet. At length I have found my way back, *(giving a letter to Jansken)* here is a letter which an inhabitant of the neighbouring hamlet charged me to deliver.

Jan. 'Tis from Cecilia, *(reads)* "I cannot attend the prepared rendezvous, but have spoken to my father and every thing conduces to make me entertain the hope that he will pronounce thy forgiveness." This is the extreme of happiness! now then what have we to dread.

Pet. Nothing—the Venetians deceived by my stratagem have taken another route—and I have left two of our party at the entrance of the forest to apprize us should the enemy retrace their steps. Hark some one approaches.

Jan. I am not mistaken—'tis the valet of Frankenstein, he appears alarmed, what can it mean?

Pet. *(intercepting his passage)* Halt there!

Pie. Hillo, here's another stop gap, oh lord! oh lord! it's all over with me now, mercy—mercy sweet thieves.

(Bohemians enraged)

Thieves!

Pet. We are Bohemians my good fellow, do you comprehend.

Pie. Yes, yes, Bohemians not thieves, I did'nt mean to call you so, Bohemians, I mean good honest well meaning folks—who I am sure wont wish to do any harm to a poor devil—

Jan. Approach and fear nothing.

Pie. Why it's he again—it seems certain that I am to meet him in all parts.

Jan. Come hither I say!

Pie. Yes, Mr. Captain, I'm coming—here I am.

Jan. Answer me; where are you going.

Pie. To the Cottage of Holbein, an old blind man who lives—

Jan. From whence come you?

Pie. From my Master's Castle.

Jan. But why this haste—You appear agitated—say from what cause?

Pie. Oh precious serious cause I can assure you. Did you but know what took place last night at the Castle, and above all what I saw.—

Jan. Confusion! has Frankenstein forgotten his promise—friends you may withdraw.— *(exit Bohemians.)*

Pie. May'nt I withdraw as well, Mr. Captain?

Jan. No—stay where you are.

Pie. Stay where I am, here's a pretty go! But really my Lord I dont see you have any occasion for me—

Jan. Stay where you are, I say—I would speak with thee.

Pie. Speak to me—I would very gladly excuse the conversation—they seem all in the speaking way and wont allow me to wedge in a syllable.

Jan. Say, when I quitted Frankenstein last night near the old monument of the forest, did he retire forthwith.—

Pie. Not he, he remained, as worse luck would have it.

Jan. And how was he employed?

Pie. Faith I can't say precisely because my master do you see threw me into a sort of a—he did just so—and I was struck just so.—

Jan. What has passed at the Castle that has been so alarming—what did you behold?

Pie. Zooks I saw—I really cant tell you exactly what I saw—all that I can say is that I thought I beheld in master's laboratory something very unaccountable t'was a figure—a corpse—'pon my soul in all your gang in which they are, saving your presence a rascally set of ill-looking chaps that I don't believe you have one that's half so ugly.—

Jan. He is lost, and my sister my father—Oh may I at least protect them from the fatal influence which Frankenstein's compact has extended over them.

Pie. Is that all you wish to know?—may I now be permitted to—to—you know what I mean.

Jan. Yes, you may now withdraw, but beware of saying aught to any one of what you have witnessed—if you but prate:—

Pie. Prate! I guess then what I should have to expect, but I'll be mute as a stock fish since 'tis your pleasure—I beg pardon, Sir, but I think I perceive my master.—It's he sure enough, and a precious hurry he's in, one would suppose, that like me, fright had given a spur to his motion!

Jan. What a state of agitation—you may now withdraw.

Pie. Aye! and on a full trot—now to collect the wedding guests—what a mercy these chaps didn't put an end to my errand, for then there would be no chance of my dancing at the festivity. (*exit.*)

(Enter Frankenstein.)

Fran. Hence! hence! approach me not! living spectre, what would you with me? why arrest my progress? am I then the prey whom you would devour? yes 'twas I who gave you being, that crime is my work, and thine it is to avenge it—come then! engulph me in that hell from which I have dragged thee, but suffer me, at least, to be thy only victim.

Jan. Lost man! *(approaching him.)* Frankenstein—

Fran. Who calls?—

Jan. 'Tis I—Jansken,—thy friend.

Fran. Approach me not, you will become the associate of crime—like me the horror of the earth, accursed by heaven, the mark of all, the tortures hell has in store, the triumph of the damn'd!

Jan. Be thyself Frankenstein, despite thy crime, I pity thee:—

Fran. Pity—pity! have I entertained pity for my fellow creatures, when I cast upon the earth an execrable enemy—No, heaven is just, and since the moment I presumed to outrage humanity, its wrath has dwelt heavy on my devoted head.

Jan. Thy crime is frightful, but divine mercy is infinite—perhaps the monster to whom thy presumptive deed has given birth, has already yielded up his unhallowed existance.

Fran. No—no—this night—a night of horror, which curdles my very heart's blood—I beheld the monster appear—for some period he evanished, but his frightful image pursued me every where—frantic I quitted my abode and exhausted with fatigue sunk at the entrance of the forest, but scarcely had I sought a moment's repose—ere I again perceived the monster who seemed to triumph in my fears whilst the Genie of the Tomb stood smiling at my misery.

Jan. Perhaps your bewildered imagination gives birth to ideal horrors—all around us is in tranquility.

Fran. Aye, for the moment—but soon—hark! hear you not? I think that I perceive—

Jan. Nothing—come banish these vain terrors listen to the voice of reason and friendship.

Fran. 'Tis mine no longer; all is terminated—death! death! on which I call, can alone put a period to my torments—

Jan. Your son would you leave him without a protector, you may still hope for days of happiness—

Fran. Dear Jansken—with what consoling hope do you inspire me.

(Rustic music).

Jan. 'Tis my Bohemians, who are repairing to my father's cottage—come, I will conduct you to the frontiers of the forest.

They retire, the Monster now appears on the rocks—sees the fire and taking a piece of lighted wood, which burns his finger, he throws it from him, expressing the pain.—Hearing the Music he listens with ecstasy, endeavouring to catch it and exits following its modulations. Enter Pietro and Villagers.

Pie. Come, let's away to the wedding—I don't say who I'll dance with—but mind—no tearing caps about me.

Medley Song—Pietro
With shape and looks so killing
A handsomer youth you'll ne'er find
Then pretty girls if you are willing
Take a husband whilst I'm in mind—
Dont look shy—do'nt look shy—do'nt look shy
Well a day—On poor I
But come Young lasses and let us be gay
And merrily merrily dance away—
For a Waltz or Quadrille I'm in cue I must say
And willing as flowers in May
Come away
And we'll merrilly dance and play.

If there's a maid inclin'd to marry
I beg she'll not be o'er coy
And no doubt if hopes don't miscarry
We've at nine months a fine chopping boy
Pretty dear—pretty dear—pretty dear
Oh! dear—pretty dear—

And then with my mate I'll be happy and gay.
We'll laugh, dance and sing, and drive sorrow away
With the sweet little baby, lauks how he will play—
And teach him to dance like papa
Night and day
We'll merrilly dance and play.

Scene the Second—*Cottage of Holbien.*

Through an opening is seen a rustic bridge. On one side is a door, the other a stove. Village girls discovered with Cecilia.

Cec. Thanks, thanks, friends! I am now in readiness—but Frankenstein has not kept his promise; he should have been here ere now.—Antonio, where is my father!

Ant. He is gone to join my father.

Cec. Frankenstein is tardy in his arrival.—But why that noise?—Pietro comes, perhaps he can explain. *(Pietro enters.)* Pietro! what occasions this tumult?

Pie. Zooks! Miss Cecilia, 'tis these confounded Bohemians again.

Cec. Have they been pursued?

Pie. Quite the contrary, Miss—'tis they who are in pursuit. Why and wherefore I know not; but they are scampering here—coming to join the party.—Zooks, how they do stride!—I have a good pair of shanks of my own; but I couldn't gallop at such a rate.

Ant. As father is not come, I'll run and meet him—come along with me, friends. *(Exit, with villagers.)*

Pie. *(aside)* He's gone to fetch her a husband; but I have my doubts whether there will be any wedding.

Cec. Pietro, what are you talking about?

Pie. Nothing, Miss—absolutely nothing—and I beg it to be understood that I have said nothing—nothing at all.

Cec. Why so?

Pie. You'll recollect, Miss, that I said nothing, so that I may call you as a witness.

Cec. Since your arrival, Pietro, I have remarked that you have worn an air of mystery.

Pie. True, Miss; but then I have my reasons.

Cec. What are they?

Pie. Beg pardon—I have reasons for not telling you my reasons.

Cec. Well then, since there are secrets—

Pie. Yes, famous secrets!—and was I to tell you, why you'd be as wise as myself. Harkye, Miss—but I beg you won't make me babble—cause as how I'm much inclined to do so—and should that misfortune happen, I might get into a hobble.

Cec. I will not be indiscreet—but tell me, have you completed the preparations for the fete—is every thing in order in the garden?

Pie. Yes, yes, Miss—the tables, wine, orchestra, are all ready—we only want the dancers, the drinkers, and the musicians *(rustic music)* and, zooks! here they come in the nick of time. *(exit)*

The Monster enters and perceives Cecilia, at the moment she is retiring—he opens the door by which she has withdrawn, and regards her with rapture.—His eyes are now directed towards a mirror, and recoils on beholding his own resemblance,—he endeavours to catch his own reflection, and after some pantomime business, conceals himself upon the entrance of Jansken.

Jan. 'Twas impossible to overtake him. Heaven send that he may have fled far from this spot, nor bring amongst us terror and desolation. *(Enter Cecilia.)*

Jan. Dearest Cecilia—say is Frankenstein arrived.

Cec. Not yet—but his stay cannot be long.

Jan. *(aside)* He should have been here ere now—fatal delay!

Cec. What is it, Jansken?—you appear uneasy—you dread least my father should oppose your prayers. You received my letter—I wrote therein that every circumstance tended to promote our reunion.

Jan. Should you obtain my pardon, what other ties have I to form?—I shall then be reunited to those I love, and our father will then enjoy a life of tranquillity.

Cec. Heaven grant no obstacle may interpose to mar our felicity.

(Frank. and Holbien appear on Bridge.)

Cec. Frankenstein!

Jan. 'Tis he! anon we 'shall have nothing to dread.—My father too!—the anxiously-sought moment is at length arrived.

(Enter Holbien and Frankenstein.)

Hol. My children, I had but one prop—now I shall possess two.

Jan. You have not observed him—

Fran. No—and my hopes revive—

Cec. Father—here is a person enquiring for you!

Hol. What would he with me?

Cec. He brings information of one that is dear to us, and of whom I spoke to you but some moments since.

Hol. Who mean you?

Cec. Jansken, father—'tis of him he comes to speak.

Hol. Of my son!—does he still live?—But what would he inform me, Cecilia?—where is the person?—

Jan. *(approaching)* I am here, my lord!

Hol. Was it my son who sent you?

Jan. Yes, yes—it was.

Hol. What are his wishes?—Is then the pride of the haughty subdued?—You knew him—Frankenstein!—he became fascinated with a science which merited the wrath of heaven and the contempt of its creatures—he abandoned the pursuit of honour; and, deaf to my counsels and entreaties, entailed my ruin, dishonoured our name, and rendered me, like himself, the horror of our fellow-citizens; from whose society I have been compelled to withdraw.—Yes; to him I owe all the miseries of my existence; and, after a silence of six years, what motive can he now have for ever remembering his father?—

Jan. Oh, believe it not—never has he ceased to remember to bow with veneration at the name of father.

Hol. *(surprised)* What voice is that?

Jan. Great has been his guilt towards you—numerous his crimes—but did you know by how many sufferings he has expiated his faults—in pity shut not your heart against him—be not deaf to his prayer—and all his future days shall be dedicated to repair his misdeeds.

Hol. What?—can you be—

Jan. *(falling at his feet)* Yes, sire; yes—your son, your wretched son, who comes to implore pardon, and expire at your feet.

Hol. Powers of innocence;—away—approach me not.

Cec. Father!—can you be inexorable?

Fran. Will you accord no boon to the repenitent?—In the name of heaven, reject him not.

Hol. Cecilia, you have deceived me.—I had sworn to be inflexible—but he is there—nor have I sufficient fortitude to resist—I can no longer close my arms against him.

Jan. Father! *(embracing him.)*

(a shriek is heard) Enter Antonio and Villagers, in a state of alarm.

Hol. What means this alarm?

Jan. Why that fearful shriek?

(Pietro advancing) Hillo I say—what's all this?

Ant. Oh Cecilia—had you but seen—

Cec. Seen what?

Ant. You recollect, about the figure which I told you I saw in my dream—

Cec. Well!—

Ant. Just now—as I returned to the Cottage, I saw him.

Fran. Where?

Ant. There, yonder!

Jan. Could it be he?—come friends, let us endeavour to ascertain what has so greatly alarmed Antonio. *(exit villagers headed by Jansken.)*

Pie. Aye, aye, let them go and ascertain—As for me, I am not at all curious—I've already had my share.

Fran. *(aside)* My fortitude has abandoned me.—Heavens! are my fearful presentiments about to be accomplished?

Hol. *(aside)* Have you disregarded your oath? and am I to suspect, that far from abandoning your guilty labours—

Fran. No! no! believe it not:—

Hol. Yet your hand trembles, methinks in mine.

Enter Jansken with Villagers.

Jan. We have discovered no one—our little Antonio has been deceived:—

Fran. *(aside)* Can it be possible?

Cec. Yes, yes, 'tis probable—

Ant. Indeed I saw him plainly—*(The clock strikes four)*

Pie. Oh! Oh! at length there's the happy signal!

Hol. 'Tis the hour appointed for the ceremony, let us proceed—give the signal for departure, on friends?

Pie. Come along, I'll place myself at your head.

(Exit Holbien, Antonio, & Pietro.)

Cec. Ere we proceed to the Altar I would speak to you for an instant.

Jan. On what subject?

Fran. Dearest Cecilia, delay not a moment.

Cec. The interview is necessary—

Jan. Is it for thy happiness—

Cec. Yes 'tis in the name of that happiness that I entreat it—

Jan. Were you but to comprehend—

Cec. What then?

Fran. Nothing—nothing—dear Cecilia I will hear you—Jansken prithee retire, and like me, watch over her safety.

Cec. We are alone, and on this short interview will perhaps depend our future felicity, it is but justice I should possess your amplest confidence—would you disguise the trouble by which you are agitated—

Fran. Heavens! what would you say? *(aside)* I shudder with alarm.

Cec. You have not kept your promise.

Fran. I must avow to you that a dreadful secret presses on my soul—but I swear in the face of heaven which is about to receive our vows, you shall know it and you will then see far from breaking the bonds by which we are united, it ought to strengthen them still more. In conducting you to the altar, I do not alone recompence the virtues of Cecilia—my fate depends on her.

Cec. I ought to confide in your sincerity—yes to doubt that you love me it would be an outrage to us both—

Fran. Dearest Cecilia—you're mine—for ever mine.

The Monster approaches the lovers, expresses his admiration of Cecilia, becomes enraged at seeing her in the arms of Frankenstein.—He darts on Cecilia at the moment she quits her lover's embrace. She perceives the Monster, who extends his arms towards her—uttering a fearful shriek, she rushes off across the bridge.

Fran. Horror? 'tis he?

The Monster is about to pursue Cecilia. Frankenstein opposes his passage.—The Monster dashes him on the earth, and hastens across the bridge after Cecilia. He is about to follow, when at the moment several armed Villagers appear at the back, Frankenstein seizes a gun and exits. Cecilia appears on the bridge in the arms of the Monster. Holbien rushes on the bridge, to whose arms the Monster consigns her.

Hol. Dearest Cecilia! alas! she answers not.

Holbien enters supporting Cecilia, she revives, and perceiving the Monster, with a shriek again faints; at this moment Frankenstein enters, and firing, wounds the Monster, who utters a fearful cry, seizes a lighted brand from the hearth, fires the cottage. They all escape save Holbien, whom the Monster thrusts into the blazing ruins.

Act III. Scene the First.—*Chamber in the Castle.*

Cecilia discovered seated with Antonio—Jansken, Pietro, Mazzena, & Villagers.

Jan. Look up my dear Sister—alas! shall I have her death to deplore as well as that of my unhappy parent—oh Frankenstein—how much hast thou to answer for—

Maz. See, sir, my dear lady revives—

Cec. *(gradually reviving)* Where am I—what a frightful dream—But how is this?—these wedding garments—In the name of heaven dissipate my alarms, why am I here you answer not!—I perceive too clearly—'tis no dream, I have no longer a father—But tell me—has Frankenstein perished.

Jan. No—he lives for a life of protracted misery—an object of horror to all—but see he comes. *(Enter Frankenstein.)*

Vil. He is here let us away—

Fran. You have just cause to loath me; but you shall not much longer behold this hated form—Pietro conduct them to the castle hall, where I will make known my last resolve. *(Exit Pietro and Peasantry.)*

Fran. Jansken! Cecilia! too well I know my sight is hateful to you;—but in pity to my sufferings do not drive me to despair—

Jan. Frankenstein thy crimes have broken every tie by which we were united—regardless of my friendship and my sister's love, you have perpetrated a deed which entails our general ruin.

Fran. Oh reproach me not: Heaven has already amply avenged my crime—to expiate it there is no sacrifice, but what I am prepared to make—Cecilia, I am about to fly this spot as the only means of preserving those beings who are so dear to me—but ere I take my last farewell, may I not at least hope for thy forgiveness—

Cec. Oh Frankenstein thou hast blighted all my hopes of happiness—and the fondest dreams that mortal ever pictured have been destroyed by thy fatal presumption—

Fran. In the name of heaven upbraid me not—

Cec. Methought that when united, no cloud could disturb our tranquility—our only care would have been that of consoling the declining days of my aged parent—but even that sad consolation is denied me—and to you, to you alone all this is owing—

Fran. Heaven in pity terminate my wretched being.

Jan. Why would you appeal to the divinity, you have so much outraged to curtail your existence in the very moment of guilt—seek rather to live, that by prayer and penitence, you may attone to that power whose mercy is never utterly denied even to the most sinful of its creatures—do this Frankenstein and rank me still amongst the number of thy friends—

Cec. Nor can my affection be witheld, for despite thy crime—I find you are so entwined around my affections that to rend the bond is unavailing.

Fran. Oh Cecilia when I look on thee—on Jansken—on my darling boy, I can but marvel that I have sinned so greatly: *(Enter Pietro and Petrusco).*

Pet. All is lost—the Venetian Soldiers, whom we have twice escaped, have discovered our retreat.

Fran. Confusion!—

Pet. They are armed against you Frankenstein against you, to whom we owe all the dangers with which we are threatened—they grant but four hours ere you yield yourself up—and if this is not accorded, the Castle with all its inmates is to be given up to the flames—

Jan. Four hours—then there is still time left for escape—Frankenstein you shall yet be saved, there are certain outlets in the Castle leading to the sea, which shall be explored—in the interim to your charge I consign my Sister, Pietro, see that the child has some repose, nor suffer him for a moment from your presence. *(Exit with Petrusco.)*

Pie. You shall be obeyed Sir—come along my little darling. *(Exit with Child.)*

Cec. With what horrors are we environed—

Fran. Regardless of my own safety yours is now my only care. *(they retire)*

Monster enters, examines round—observing some one approach, he conceals himself.
(Enter Pietro with Antonio and Litolf.)

Pie. Now are you sure it's a bottle of good stuff?

Lit. That I'll warrant, for I've just partaken of a fellow bottle—but hearkye, Pietro! don't you make too free, for the liquor is potent, and may steal away your senses.

Pie. Don't be afraid of that, old gentleman.—You see what courage I must possess, or master would never trust me as he has done. So good night, old gentleman. I've got the key of the door; and, to make all safe, will lock myself in.—Come along, Antonio.

Lit. There's a man of courage.

Second Scene—*Dormitory.*

(Enter Pietro, with Antonio.)

Pie. There, now all's safe; and so, Antonio, you may go to sleep as soon as you please.

Ant. I'm not sleepy—I want to go to my father.

Pie. But, I tell you, you must'nt go to your father—I'm to father you now—I'm to protect you, for I'm a man of courage—

Ant. Which you always shew by running away—*(aside)* as I will do the first opportunity.

Pie. Well then, sit down; and, as you are not sleepy, we'll have something to eat and drink.

Ant. Aye, Pietro, and then you shall tell me one of your pretty stories.

Pie. That I will—I shall have somebody to listen to me at last. *(They sit down when a slight noise is heard.)*

Pie. There's that confounded tom cat scratching at the door—go along, puss!—Now I'll tell you my story; and, talking about tom cats, it's all about a cat, called Grimalkin. Now Grimalkin had a little kitten—its name was Colleywabble; and Colleywabble was such an expert mouser that nothing escaped it—mice, rats, aye, and even the dairy-maid's cream were all tasted by Colleywabble—it even made free with poor Grimalkin's allowance—plundered its own poor mother—now wan't that too bad—so says Grimalkin to Colleywabble—

During the above, the child takes the key, opens the door and is about to escape, when Pietro discovers his absence, brings him back, in the interim the Monster enters and conceals himself.

Pie. Oh, you little varlet! to serve me so. But I'll stop your games; for I'll lock the door, and put the key in my pocket.

Ant. You're a very ill-natured man, and I won't listen to your story; but I'll go to sleep to spite you. *(lies down.)*

Pie. Can't say I much like his going asleep and leaving me here to entertain myself—and I think a storm is brewing—nothing but storms of late. However, I've got a book, and so I'll seat myself at the foot of Antonio's couch, and read and watch him at the same time.

Monster advances from his concealment, but is unable to seize the child, fearful of alarming Pietro.

Pie. Now who could have thought that I should have brought a book with me all about ghosts and hobgoblins—but never mind, I'll read a little of it—I'm not much afraid—"The turret clock struck twelve; all was silent as the grave, at that instant, the light, which burned but dimly;"—*(the Monster extinguishes the light)* Hey! what's that?—Oh, I suppose it was only the wind—but I can soon relight it at the fire—

The Monster attempts to seize the child, but retreats on the lamp being relighted.

Pie. There it's all right—egad, I begin to feel sleepy myself—but that won't do—no, I must try something to amuse me—I'll drink a little drop and I'll sing a little bit—.

He eats, drinks, and hums a tune, and gradually falls asleep: Monster watches the moment, seizes the child who shrieks aloud.—Pietro awakes in alarm, and missing his charge, shouts for help, rushing off.— Frankenstein enters with a pistol.

Fran. What cries are those? *(perceiving the Monster)* Ha! the Evil One again!

Ant. *(shrieking as he is extended in the Monster's arms)* Father! father!

Fran. Horror! my son! *(presenting his pistol at the Monster)* bold, execrable wretch!

He is about to fire—the Monster places the child before him as a target—Frankenstein drops the pistol—exclaiming in agony.

No, no: you have nothing to fear—spare but my son—restore him to these arms—my son—

Frankenstein kneels and implores compassion, but the Monster uttering an inarticulate shout bears him off.

He bears him from me, regardless of my cries.—My child! my child! *(He sinks on the floor.)*

(Enter Cecilia.)

Cec. What means this clamour? have they reached this spot? Frankenstein! what has happened?

Fran. Cecilia, you here!—fly! this is the abode of demons—fly! or you will become their victim.

Cec. In the name of heaven, Frankenstein, what mean you?

Fran. That I am the most wretched of parents. The ear of inexorable fate is deaf to my cries, and yields us to the enemy my presumption has created.—Hark! hear you not the dying groans of my child?—

Cec. Of Antonio?—

Fran. There! there! see you not his last convulsive struggles? hear you not his last agonizing shriek! the shriek of death—it vibrates on my brain and drives me to madness!—My boy! my Antonio! 'tis I—I have been thy assassin!

Cec. Antonio murdered?—*(Enter Jansken hastily.)*

Jan. We are overpowered, the majority of my followers are either slain or prisoners—but we have still means of escape: a vessel manned by my Bohemians floats in the adjoining bay—hasten then to the sally-port with my sister, whilst I secure a boat. Frankenstein, delay not: 'tis for thy eternal salvation. *(rushes off.)*

Fran. I am reckless of my fate—

Cec. Reckless of thy fate!—not so thy Cecilia: tarry here for a moment, whilst I speed and procure thee a disguise. *(Hastens off.)*

Fran. Is Hell pacified?—have I not undergone sufficient punishment?—what would it more? Amply has its minister performed the horrible task—he has deprived me of all—my son, wife, friend!—and I am now an isolated wretch!—But I still live—still render this spot unhallowed by my presence! The Council of Ten demand my head—no, no! 'tis not on the scaffold that my days must terminate—my fate is inseparable from the execrable executioner whom I have madly called into existence.—Monster appear! thou seekest a last victim!—be it the wretched, heart-broken Frankenstein!

The Monster appears—watches Frankensteins movement seizes the pistol which the former has laid down.—Cecilia enters with a cloak, and perceiving the monster exclaims

Cec. Spare—oh spare—my Frankenstein!

The Monster fires and Cecilia advancing receives the ball and expires in the arms of Frankenstein—who places her on the couch.

Seizes a dagger and rushes at the Monster—who escapes his arm—hurls him round and dashing him on the ground retires exulting in his villany.—

Scene the Third.

Exterior of the Castle, Bohemians cross the stage pursued by the Venetians.
(Enter Litoff.)

Lit. Here's an upset to all my prospects of aggrandisement!—The Venetians are battering the walls about our ears, and missles are flying in every direction—ah! they'll batter me, and make my ducats fly too, if they pop on my secret board— *(Pietro runs on, alarmed.)*

Pie. Here's an end of the world!—Was ever poor mortal exposed to so many ups and downs.

Lit. I'm getting on in years and my limbs fail me—now I'd give half my wealth, if I could but light on one to get me out of this danger—Pietro!—

Pie. Hey! is that you, Litolff?—what! not cut up yet.

Lit. Cut up!—I'm done up for certain—now, if you could only help me out.

Pie. I wish to the lord I could help myself out—every one here is taking care of himself—and here comes Gontram who it appears has sufficient courage to take care of one besides himself. *(enter Gontram and Mazzena.)*

Lit. He appears to take it as if nothing was the matter—whilst the Castle too is tumbling about our ears—

Gon. Consent to my union with your daughter, and I promise to ensure your safety—

Lit. Pietro—can you make the same promise—ensure my safety—

Pie. Oh 'pon my soul I can promise nothing, it's as much as I can do to secure my own preservation.

Lit. Since that's the case, I'll make a virtue of necessity, as danger threatens.

Quartetto.
Gon. Danger threatens—let's away
A faithful friend protests thy flight—
Lit. And that in trouble I must say
Is comfort to a wretched wight—
Maz. Hasten then to scape the strife
And whilst time serves, let us begone.
Pie. Since it is thus—upon my life
I'll not stop here to be undone,

SCENE THE LAST.—*The Adriatic Sea.*

A vessel is seen in the midst of the waves exposed to a violent tempest—on the deck of which is seen Jansken, Petrusco, and Mariners.

Frankenstein appears in a small boat, which is tossed to and fro, by the billows; on beholding him, those in the ship utter an exclamation of joy.

Jan. He's escaped the Castle's flames but how to gain the vessel!—providence protect thou.

Fran. Yes, yes, if contrition is entitled to commiseration, it will—it will.—

Throwing a rope towards Frankenstein which he vainly attempts to seize, the boat from a sudden gust of wind being driven at a still greater distance from the vessel.

The boat is again compelled towards the ship and Jansken endavours a second time to convey the rope to Frankenstein, but is again disappointed—at this moment the Monster appears on the rock uttering a shout of demonic joy on beholding him, Frankenstein utters a shriek of despair.

The Monster darts from the rock into the boat, seizes Frankenstein—a moment after a thunderbolt descends and severs the bark, the waves vomit forth a mass of fire and the Magician and his unhallowed abortion are with the boat engulphed in the waves.

FINIS.

Richard and Barnabas Brough

Frankenstein; or, The Model Man

(1849)

DRAMATIS PERSONAE

FRANKENSTEIN	Mr. Wright.	TIDDLIWINCZ ...	Miss Ellen Chaplin.
THE WHAT IS IT	Mr. Paul Bedford.	RATZBAEN	Mr. Mitchenson.
ZAMIEL	Mr. O. Smith.	FRIGHTZ	Mr. J. Sanders.
BARON VON DONNERUND-BLITZEN, F.R.S., A.S.S., & C.	Mr. C. J. Smith.	MASTER OF CERE-MONIES	Mr. Freeborn.
		UNDINE	Miss E. Harding.
		AGATHA	Miss Harriet Coveney.
OTTO OF ROSEN-BERG	Mill Woolgar.	BOBINETTA	Miss Turner.

SCENE I

Exterior of the Jolly Student public house at the University of Crackenjausen. German Students drinking, smoking, playing skittles &c. all dressed in the most intensely German style with beards of every variety of cut. Caps, blouses, meerschaum short pipes &c. peasants, girls &c. some dancing and singing.

Chorus Bohemian Girl
In the Student's life you may read
A very jolly life indeed.
  Thro' the world we're renowned
  For our studies severe,
  For our science profound,
And attachment to beer.
At smoking or thinking deep to cope
  With the whole wide world we dare,

Or at anything else save a liking for soap
Or shaving, or cutting our hair.

(Enter Tiddliwincz with a newspaper)

Tid. Friends, gentlemen and college chums, draw near,
Suspend awhile your skittles, pipes and beer,
And listen to a puff that's got inserted
In to-day's post. I think you'll be diverted.
1 Stud. Go it old fellow!
2 Stud. Strike a light!
3 Stud. Commence!
Tid. *(reads)* Hem! "University Intelligence."
"We understand—" Do you believe them?
1 Stud. No!
Tid. "The famous Mr. Frankenstein,"
1 Stud. Oh! Oh!
Tid. "Who when examined last—"
Stud. Last what? assizes?
Tid. Last term, "passed with eclat and lots of prizes
And took—"
2 Stud. Pooh! Gammon!
1 Stud. Stuff!
3 Stud. He did'nt!
4 Stud. *I* did!
Tid. "The highest honours,"
Stud. Honours were divided.
Tid. "Has a new work in active progress which
It is expected—" Listen this is rich.
"Will make a great sensation" stop "and throw
New lights upon a branch of science—"
1 Stud. Oh!
Tid. "Hitherto very little understood."
We wish him all success, is'nt that good.
1 Stud. Capital!
Tid. Stop, there's something more to read.
"The gentleman 'tis said will shortly lead
To the hymeneal altar a divinity
Long toasted and admired in this vicinity.
We give no names, but when we've intimated
That a rich baron justly celebrated
For his endowment of a certain College
And patronage of Science, Art, and Knowledge,
About these parts is the young lady's father,
Our readers perhaps will understand us—"
1 Stud. Rather!
Tid. Well, do you call that nothing? Eh! my buck.
But stop a minute—*(Takes the beer out of a student's hand and drinks)* gentlemen here's luck.

(Enter Otto of Rosenberg melodramatically)

Otto. Who talks of luck within my wretched hearing?
Tid. Ha Otto boy what cheer?
Otto. Who talks of cheering?
The blighted heart with hopeless passion sore
Will ne'er be visited by one cheer more.
I love—
Tid. *(interrupting him)* Yes, yes *we* know.
Otto. Suppose you do,
They don't you stupid. *(indicating audience)*
Tid. Oh ah! very true.
Otto. *(to Audience)* You must excuse a trifling deviation
From Mrs. Shelley's marvellous narration.
You know a piece could never hope to go on
Without love, Rivals, tyrant pa's and so on.
Therefore to let you know our altered plan,
I'm here to represent the "nice young man,"
And in the hero's person you'll discover,
On this occasion the obnoxious lover.
So in my character I beg to say,
(tragically) Heigho, alas, ah me! & welladay,
And every interjection now in fashion
Indicative of wild and hopeless passion.
Tid. Otto my boy this really did'nt ought to
The college cock a state of sniv'lling brought to.
You who two months since at the Procton Gate
Wopp'd a big bargeman twice your size & weight.
Otto. Bother, my anguish grows each moment stronger,
'Tis really—"I can bear my fate no longer."

Scena
Oh I can bear my fate no longer,
All mirth is banished from my soul.
Blue devils quite depress my spirits,
And o'er me exert their dark control.

Air Mary Blane
Oh once I loved a lark & led a roaring college life;
'Mongst all my college chums, not one for mischief was more rife.
In town & gown rows then I always entered might & main
But now I'm sad as that dark child who lost his Mary Blane.
Oh fare ye well (this Mary Blane's
A famous tune for grief and woe)
Ye happy days it's very plain
We'll never meet again.

Tid. If I was you, instead of taking on
I'd take her off.
Otto. I fear it can't be done.
The invention of the Telegraph has been
A dreadful blow to poor old Gretna Green.
Now self-willed heiresses who quit their sires,

Ere they've got far are caught like hares by wires.
But pshaw! an end to sorrow and invective,
'Twas but to make my entrance more effective.
Why hang it boys do you imagine I—
Am for a moment likely to say die?
A man of striking merit such as *mine*
Knock under to a muff like Frankenstein?

Tid. Well I thought not.

Otto. Hah! of the old one talk. *(Enter Frank smoking)*

Frank. Gentlemen all, I'll trouble you to walk.

Otto. *(drawing sword)* Villian & so forth.

Frank. Yes of course, we know;
Nevertheless just now you'll please to go.

Otto. Go!

1 Stud. Go!

2. Go!

3. Go!

Frank. Yes all of you get out

Tid. Pray who are you to order us about?
Are you the College Dean?

1 Stud. Or Procter?

Fran. Cease
Blockheads, are'nt I the hero of the piece?
And have'nt I a right to clear the stage
When in soliloquy I would engage?

Otto. If on that footing you're inclined to put it,
There's no alternative but we must cut it.
(melodramatically to Frankenstein)
But villain we shall meet again! *(all going)*
Holloa—
Here, stop; the Student's Chorus first you know.

Chorus as before
In the student's life you may read
A very jolly life indeed.

(exeunt all, singing, but Frankenstein)

Frank. Having packed off each individual shaver
And a clear stage secured, I want the favor
Of your attention while I tell you something,
A secret—you'll acknowledge it's a rum thing.
I've, stop—*(looking off)* how far are they? for 'pon my word
I should'nt like it to be overheard.
All right, the fact I was about to mention
Is, I'm engaged upon a great invention
Which—stop though—it would take me rather long
In speech—so I'll describe it in a song.

Song Steam Arm
Oh wonders sure will never cease
While works of art do so increase.

No matter whether in war or peace
A man can do whatever he please.

Ritoo *(stops suddenly.)*
That verse perhaps won't throw you in ecstacies
Not being new, but stop, just hear the next as is.

Sings

I've managed to make, strange it may seem,
A mechanical man with skill supreme.
Each joint is as strong as an iron beam
And the springs are a compound of clock-work & steam.

Ritoo *(stops as before)*
Which I may say without presumption vaunting,
Is just the sort of thing that's long been wanting.
It's plain the present style of folks don't do
For half the things they're wanted to get through.
For instance folks in courts & alleys lying,
Without fresh air and light they will keep dying.
And seampstresses who ought to work away
For fourpence, halfpenny or so a day,
Somehow will let their strength & spirits fail
And shock their better s nerves by growing pale.
Can you conceive a state of matters worse?
But stop young man I'll try another verse.

(To Leader)

His lungs are as strong he might almost dwell
Near a London Churchyard & still keep well.
And a nose of such virtue I've given the swell
He may swim in the Thames & not die of the smell.

Ritoo *(stage gradually darkens)*
But my design, I'm long in getting through with,
Like certain house Barry has to do with.
It's now—since for ideas I'm at a loss,
"Fixed as the monument at Charing Cross."
I don't get on. *(stage dark)* Holloa it's getting dark
(Wind) and stormy. *(wind very loud)* Such a howl as that's no lark
It's coming down. *(lightning)* Phew! & that angry light
Threatens what one may call a red cross night. *(Wind)*

(Rain & Thunder. Ratzbaen rises from shooting trap. Frank starts frightened)

Come I say don't do that again young feller.

(Ratzbaen pantomimes extravagantly)

Oh who can understand those fits & starts?

(to Audience)

I see he's not engaged for talking parts.

(Pantomime repeated)

What do you mean you aggravating elf?

(Gong Music. The bush opens & Zamiel appears suddenly pushing Ratzbaen aside)

Zam. Here, never mind, I'll introduce myself.
It's very hard in spite of all my grumbling,
You will keep wasting half your time in tumbling.
If you don't mind I'll get another flunkey,
Get home you wriggling good for nothing monkey.

Kicks Ratzbaen who disappears—

I beg your pardon sir, I sent him up,
The bungling blockhead (but for such a pup
To lose one's temper is really too absurd),
With you to beg the favor of a word.
Allow me. *(presenting card)*

Frank. Zamiel eh; the deuce you are.
Zam. Just listen if you doubt it. Hah! Hah! Hah!
Frank. The old original if folks should doubt it,
Do that & there'll be no mistake about it.
How are you?
Zam. How! Just look at me & guess.
Frank. Well you look seedyish I must confess.
Zam. You can't conceive the dreadful spirit level
To which I've lately been reduced—
Frank. Poor devil!
Trade bad?
Zam. There ne'er was known such a depression;
Knowledge has played the deuce with our profession.
Magic completely burked by facts and figures,
Charmed bullets superseded by hair triggers.
My celebrated gun trick what's it worth
When ev'ry juggling wizard of the north
Will coolly take a supercilious view of it
And tell you he can do a trick worth two of it?
(Sobs) In fact, excuse these tears that wet my cheeks,
I have'nt had a job for several weeks
To keep my magic spells in occupation
And my poor suffering demons from starvation.
Frank. Lor, only think, a case of real distress.
Can I do anything to serve you?
Zam. Yes,
Employ me.
Frank. How?
Zam. Why your invention mighty
Is standing still for an Elixir Vitae
Which I can furnish you with at a price
To suit the Times. "Alarming Sacrifice."
Fran. You can!
Zam. I can!
Frank. Then book the order please.
Zam. I will & execute it too with ease.

(Waves his hand. Music. A large Mortar surrounded by flames rises)

Behold the mortar for it.

Frank. You're a brick!
But could'nt you a place less public pick
For going thro' your forms of incantation?
Zam. What can I do? I've no accommodation,
They've built a railway over the Wolf's Glen.
Frank. Oh! well! I only spoke.
Zam. Then don't again.

Stamps his foot. Ratzbaen appears with an oilskin basket & apron and sleeves à la Doctor's boy. Zam takes basket.

Come now, exert yourself & no demurring,

(Ratz takes pestle)

Those who serve me had always best be stirring.

Takes ingredients out of the basket speaking as he throws the various ones into the mortar.

Macassar oil of virtues rare,
Give a nobby head of hair.
Grimstone's eye snuff give him sight,
Odonto, teeth of pearly white.
Slolberg's lozenge! for the voice,
Make him speak a language choice.
Cockle's pills your warmth impart,
To the cockles of his heart.
Last & greater than the whole,
All the others to control,
Charm vitality to give,
Charm to bid the patient live,
Charm of every power rife,
Parr's life pills shall give him life.

As Zamiel throws Parr's pills in the mortar Thunder Crash, Noise &c. A flash of fire out of the mortar. Ratzbaen who has been stirring up the ingredients throws himself into the most grotesque attitudes.

Probatum est! *(pours liquid from the mortar into a labelled vial with a punch ladle.)*
You may with this Elixer
Make your Automaton both live & kick sir.
Frank. *(taking it impatiently)* I long to make a trial. What's to pay?
Zam. Oh make yourself quite easy. I dare say
We shan't fall out about the terms.
Frank. So then
My workmanship and I are both made men.
Already my imagination views
My portrait in the *Illustrated News.*
Madame Tussaud the glowing picture backs,
And seals my fame with her approving wax.
Good night old chap, a friend in need you are. *(going hastily)*
Zam. Good night, but stop a minute! Hah! Hah! Hah.

(Exit Frank L)

Bus'ness is looking up from this night's deed;
I foresee lots of mischief will proceed.

I'm not quite sure since things seem on the rise
That I shan't be compelled to advertize
For help. A notice thus attractive:
"Wanted a few smart Demons strong and active."
Already I feel jollier, blither, stronger;
A good time's coming, wait a little longer. *(Exit)*

SCENE 2

An apartment in the Baron's Castle—an open Window showing a water butt. Enter Tiddliwincz cautiously R. he whistles.

Tid. I fear my parents missed their calculation
In giving me a college education.
My tastes are rather low I'm sure afraid,
I come to court the Baron's servant maid.
But pr'aps it's quite correct that I should do so,
Seeing I play now Friday to the Crusoe
Of her fair mistress' adorer, Otto.
But where the deuce have all the servants got to?
I might, were I inclined to, bone the spoons.
Oh! I forgot, they're hanging up festoons
And making custards for the Baron's rout.
To-morrow night—yes—that's the case no doubt.
(Song) The mistletoe's hung in the castle hall,
The Holly bush stuck in the old oak wall.
The Baron's retainers are polishing plate,
And taking down beds at the deuce of a rate.
For to meet at a ball he has asked a few friends,
In honour it seems of a match he intends
His fair daughter to make as the newspapers say.
So to finish my song in the usual way,
Oh the mistletoe bough &c.
She comes. *(Enter Bobinetta)*
My "trim built" stop the thoughts of "wherry,"
Suggest a smack. *(kisses her.)*
Bob. This is imprudent very.
How could you of the Baron brave detection
Knowing so follows his strong objection?
Tid. Follows pooh, in following my suit
I'll play my cards too well for the old brute.
But what's the matter?
Bob. Oh my poor dear missis,
She weeps a glistening tear my rough palm kisses.
And on her beauteous glowing cheeks a few drops
Shine like those early pearls best known as dew drops.
Tid. If your place is'nt comfortable dear
Another situation offers—here *(thumping his breast)*,
A place where but one lady's maid is kept.
Bob. Were I that situation to accept
And leave my missis in her sorrow here,

My conduct would be *out of place* I fear.
But hush! oh gracious goodness.
Tid. What's the matter?
Bob. Don't speak.
Tid. Not speak, you force my teeth to chatter.
Bob. The Baron comes.
Tid. Lor if he finds me here—
Bob. He'll call the police.
Tid. Of that there's not much fear,
Knowing I'm come to court the maid of course,
He'll fancy I myself am of the force—
Bob. Come to the butler's pantry.
Tid. There's a duck.
Bob. Yes and a cold boil'd tongue.
Tid. Zounds I'm in luck.
But when it's gone fo*w*l play'll be hinted at.
Bob. Do you suppose we have'nt got a cat.

(Exeunt R)

Enter the Baron, Agatha & Servants.

Baron. Now all in search of some employment, hook it!
There's lots to do—be sharp—tho' you can't look it.
Take up the carpets, pile them in a heap,
And let the floors receive a "monster sweep."
Stir up the kitchen fire, put on coal
To roast about a dozen oxen whole.
Put up sufficient candles for a blaze
To 'clipse the famous light of other days.
All wax, mind, for expence I won't be nice.
No composition, I don't care for Price.

(Servants bustling about as he is speaking)

Baron. *(to Agatha)* Crying again, thus must I ever find it.
This instant, please to wipe your eye or mind it.
You will keep sniv'lling—looking black as thunder.
Aga. Have I not cause?
Baron. Cause, pray what next I wonder.
Aga. Compelled to wed a man I hate.
Baron. Pooh! Pooh!
May I enquire if you ever knew
A baron's daughter not so situated?
It's an old law and shan't be violated.
Is'nt the man I've picked for your alliance
As Capt. Cuttle says, "chock full of science,"
Likely to set the blue moiselle on fire?
Aga. Alas, it's *heart* not science I require.
He's to his works so wedded by the wig-o-me
That if he marries me as well, 'tis bigamy.
Baron. One thing's decided—namely, your papa;
So I'd advise you not to go too far.

For tho' I'm an enlightened F.R.S.,
Patron of art and so forth, I confess
There's something of the ancient baron in me
Which makes it dangerous to go *agin* me. *(Exit)*

Aga. For my unhappy fate I can't discover
A single precedent, a learned lover.
Why it's in flat defiance of all rules
Of ancient, modern or mediaeval schools.
Search Opera, Drama, tragedy or play,
Lovers are always careless, dashing, gay,
Studying nothing but to please the fair,
Dress well, make love and fight.
(Otto jumps in at window) Huh who goes there?

Otto. My love, my life, my soul, my fancy's Queen.

Aga. Yes that's more like the sort of thing I mean.

Otto. I've risked my neck, I've braved—no matter what.

Aga. Lor! how extremely nice!

Otto. To reach this spot
Dangers enough the boldest heart to scare,
I've dared to grapple with—no matter where,
And overcome them all, no matter how,
To ask you "Will you love me then as now?"

Aga. Momentous question, will I love you then.
By Juno's vow, she breathes no matter when
Whose echo, piercing the Olympian sky,
Incensed the mighty Jove no matter why.
I'd gladly swear—if ladies ever swore,
An oath that "Dearest, then I'll love thee more."

Otto. Then, now that's settled to our satisfaction,
Listen I'll let you hear my plan of action.
Your ball's tomorrow.

Aga. Yes.

Otto. I'm not invited.
But I'll be there.

Aga. You will. I'm so delighted.
But how?

Otto. I've got an order from the press,
I've been to Nathans to engage my dress.
So after a deux temps & some schottisches
We'll just dance off, slip the old Baron's leashes.
A cab shall be in waiting.

Aga. Lor! how good!
I knew he'd do it Hansom if he could.

Otto. Yes first our capers then our luckies cut.
Holloa there's something in the water butt!

A splash of Water heard. Undine rises in water butt.

Aga. Something indeed, d'ye call that nothing pray?

Otto. May I believe my eyes?

Und. Of course you may,

I am Undine the spirit of the Flood.
My home is in the Rhine.
Otto. Among the mud.
Und. No among coral caves and pearly gems.
Otto. Lor what a different river to the Thames.
Und. I've come to say that I've made up my mind
To be your guardian genius.
Otto. Lor how kind.
Und. It's not my line of business, I'm aware;
Still, as you two are a deserving pair
And no one offers for the situation,
I'll undertake the part on this occasion.
Otto. But play it half as sweetly as you look it
And we will bless the day you undertook it.
Und. You're too polite I must get home again
They're turning off the water at the main.
So when you want assistance call Undine.
Good bye—remember: *(sinks)*
"Keep my memory green."
Otto. Duett (La ci dareme la mano)
Law she's a gem; there are no
Dangers that now need be
Dreaded—we'll let your pa know
We're not afraid of he!
Aga. Though from cold water springing,
None on our hopes she'd throw;
Though from the Rhine wet wringing,
She's no wet blanket, no.
Otto. By her enchantments aided,
Aga. By no ill luck invaded.
Otto. Oh! won't the days seem shorter,
Aga. Thanks to the spirits & water.
Together. Then come & let's be jolly,
Away with melancholy,
We'll ne'er be sad anymore.

Exeunt

Scene 3

Frankenstein's laboratory. A gothic chamber strewn about with chemical apparatus, books &c. Frankenstein at work putting the finishing touches on to the monster with a paint brush. The monster, as yet inanimate, stands on a pedestal in a statuesque attitude. Frankenstein sings as he paints.

I've put him together with joint & screw
And to finish him off a touch or two
Of red just here—and a tinge of blue
And I don't mind saying I think he'll do.

Ritoo (stops as before) (points to the symphony)

I may say, with of vanity a particle,
He's a superior manufactured article.
He's rather large, you'll say, but then 'od rat it,
It's best to make a big un while one's at it.
And that he's rather in the rough is true,
But for a first attempt I think he'll do.
So without any further pains bestowing,
Here goes to wind him up & set him going.

Takes the phial and pours down the monster's throat. Music. The Monster opens his eyes & stretches himself as if just awakened, gradually looking about surprised.

Hurray he moves! he acts! my work's completed!
Although that he should act might be expected.
I'll get out bills at once, a cab I'll call
To hire a room at the Egyptian Hall.
Or pr'aps he'd make more powerful sensations
At the art exposition of all nations.
Stay! of his head I don't admire the sit,
I'll take it off and alter it a bit.

Approaches the Monster who suddenly turns round and sees him for the first time and makes a threatening movement towards him. Fran starts away frightened. Tableau. Music.

Ah would you! *(The Monster approaches him)*

(Frankenstein holds up a chair)

No you don't my friend to-day.
There's gratitude, it always was the way;
Lift a man up in life & then see if he
Does'nt turn round upon you in a jiffey.

(Monster darts towards him again)

His aspect of ferocity increases,
I really think I'd best take him to pieces.
But he's so big I fear the dangerous touch of him.
Lor! what a fool I was to make so much of him.

Music. The Gavotte—Monster following Frankenstein round the room keeping time to the Tune. Frank (frightened as he retreats)

Oh I fear I've made a trifling error,
Oh I can't control my fright.
His movements make me quake with terror,
Avaunt and quit my sight.
I've made, oh gracious goodness,
A mull despite my shrewdness.
Sorry to have recourse to rudeness.

At the last line Frank has approached the door which he suddenly disappears through, slamming it in the monster's face who looks in astonishment after him, standing still during the last bar of the music—Music changes to the hurried melodramatic style. The monster rubs his nose and goes through pantomime indicative of revenge to express a sense of insult & injury at Frank's treatment.

Mon. Well though I have'nt mixed much in society,
That seems to me an outrage on propriety.

Closing by such unceremonious plan,
The only opening for a nice young man
In life but just begun, as one might say,
To look around him and to see his way.
But stop. Where am I, aye & likewise who?
How did I get here? that's a poser too.
How is it too that in my situation,
With no advantages of education,
My thoughts in words an utterance are seeking,
Though unaccustomed quite to public speaking?
But pshaw! I dare say it's a common thing,
For folks from nothing all at once to spring.
And of their means of doing it the history
Remain for some an unfathomed mystery.

Song I'm a gent
I'm a gent, I'm a gent, I'm a gent ready made,
Sprung up in a moment, a parvenu blade.
I'm a regular swell from the top to the toe,
But how I became so, I'm hanged if I know.
I've got no connexions not even a ma,
And I've no recollection of having a pa.

Scene 4

Street scene in the neighbourhood of the Castle. Lamplights. Guests in dominoes, Masks, Fancy Dresses &c. cross from L to R with umbrellas, great coats &c. Sink boys, men and boys selling noses masks &c. as at Vauxhall besetting the guests.

Boy. Domino, mask or nose Sir.
1st. Guest. Don't want any.
Woman. House programme, here you are sir, only a penny.
Boy. Half mask or nose sir?
2 Guest. Bother.
3 Guest. Oh get out!
Woman. House programme.
4 Guest. Are there no police about?

Enter Frankenstein looking behind him frightened

Frank. Well I declare my brains & senses dance
In worse confusion than affairs in France.
I don't know where I'm going, what I'm at,
And all this way from home without my hat.
Boy. House programme Sir, a penny, just the same
As them inside.
Frank. Go to the what's his name. *(Kicks him)*
2 Boy. Half mask or nose Sir?
3 Boy. Domino.
Frank. *(Kicking & driving them out)* Get out—*(Exeunt Boys)*
But what does all this mean? The Baron's rout
Which I had quite forgotten. There's a blunder.
But in my state of mind it's no great wonder
To think that after all the work I've had

With that young man he should turn out so bad.
I thought with pride and pleasure to have shewn him
What I'm to bring him up to—Eh that row—

(Looking off frightened)

Monster. (without) Holloa.
Frank. Oh! law! he's up to something now.
The wild young dog, I thought 'twas little use
Locking him up, he's out upon the loose.
He's coming and with looks so far from pleasant
That I'm in point of fact, no more at present.

(Runs off alarmed)

Music. The Cork Leg. Enter the Monster with the top of a lamp & a couple of knockers in his hand.

Mon. Already in my brief perambulations
I've seen some life & made a few sensations.
Though I must own it scarcely can be said
That I've a favorable impression made.
All folks I meet kick up a frightened bother,
Or cried "Good Gracious" and "Police" the other,
Though by Police I know not what they mean.
Doubtless some rarity that's seldom seen.
Some daring boys alone refused to fly,
Who whispered hints of "smugging for a guy."
From which I drew the inference distressing,
That my appearance is'nt prepossessing.
As yet but few adventures I have had,
These to begin with perhaps are not so bad.
They took my fancy, I took them in turn,
But I for deeds of more ambition burn. *(looking off R)*
Hah! Lights & Company! unless I'm wrong
Here seems a chance to come out pretty strong. *(Exit R)*

Scene 5

Ball Room at the Baron's. Masquers, Dominoes & Guests, Servants &c. A sideboard with refreshments L. Scene opens to the Drum Polka, a general dance by the whole of the Characters.

Baron. That's right my friends, you're welcome, make as free.
Ourself will mingle with society
As a spectator, dancing would fatigue us.
Here Sophia the pleasure of a glass of negus.

(Takes wine with a guest. Music)

Our son-in-law that is to be is late,
Detained most likely by affairs of weight.
Besides your studious men are always absent.
Aga. (listening) That's Otto's voice, he's just away a cab sent.

(Enter Otto as a red knight, his vizor down, & Tiddliwincz as a debardeur.)

Otto. Queen of my soul &c. here we are. *(seizes her hand)*
Aga. Not too affectionate for fear of pa.
Otto. The Cab's engaged & all prepared, are you?

Aga. Quite.
Otto. There's a duck, just a dance or two.
Aga. And then I understand as we intended.
Otto. But I say how d'ye like our costumes?
Aga. Splendid.
Though I this evening hoped for great delight,
I ne'er expected such a charming knight.
Tid. But is'nt mine a stunner?
Bob. Well I'm sure.
What does it mean though?
Tid. I'm a debardeur,
A French cross breed twixt bargeman & coal whipper.
Therefore silk sashes, velvet wigs and slippers
Are most appropriate. But let's be hopping.
Since the Casino's license they've been stopping,
Of dancing one can never get one's fill.
MC. Gentlemen, places for the next quadrille.
Frank. (to Otto) Face us old chap.
Otto. Of course man don't you see,
My helmet suits me for a Vizor vee.
But stay I'm rather dry. *(helps himself to a glass of wine; drinks and spits it out.)*
Bah! worst of washes!
Cape and not waterproof like Mackintoshes.
But nowadays folks drink no matter what,
Since a pure glass of water can't be got.

(Enter Frankenstein running frightened.

Fran. Here stop the ball.
Aga. Lor how he made me jump.
Otto. I spoke of water and here comes a pump.
Fran. A chair—some brandy—British I'd prefer,
That I may die at once.
Baron. What means this stir?
What has gone wrong?
Fran. (changing his manner) What! stop, they'll spoil my fun,
If I inform them what I've been and done.
Wrong! Nothing! gads I'm in a state of jollity,
At least a hundred sandboy pow'r in quality.
How are you governor? *(Hits Baron in the waist)*
What time d'ye sup?
My variegated tulips keep it up.
Baron. My son your conduct at the least is queer.
Study methinks has turned your head.
Otto. (severely) Or beer!
Fran. That beer was bitter, pray sir who are you?
Doing the sweet to my young woman too!
It's seldom I'm inclined to fight but now
I don't mind saying I should like a row.

Duett "The Cavalier"
You're a beautiful knight
And your spurs shine bright,
And you'll do for a masquerade.
But my gay cavalier,
With a flea in your ear,
I'll send you away dismayed
If you don't put a stop
To your blarney and drop
That lady's five fingers, for she
Is engaged and more-o-
ver I'd have you to know,
Sweet maid she loves but me.
Sweet maid &c.

Otto. *(to Aud)* Now of course you'd have thought
I to fight didn't ought,
As this is a peaceable age.
But such language you'll own
Would have certainly thrown
Mister Cobden himself in a rage.
Less mild by far
My propensities are,
And so my reply shall be
To this insolent muff
Give me none of your stuff,
You may go to Hong Kong for me.

Fran. To fight it scare can be against the law,
'Twas surely meant that Frankenstein should draw.

(Draws)

Ster-ike!

Otto. I will my boy & rather hard
So gardez-vous.

Baron. *(interrupting)* Who's talking about guard?
I'll call a vanguard; that is, a police one.
Put up your swords, that Congress is a "peace" one.

Otto. *(sheathing his sword)* Sir I.

Fra. He knows I could have beat him hollow.

Otto. *(aside to Tid, Aga & Bobi)*
We'd better cut at once; be off, I'll follow.

Exeunt Tid, Bob & Aga cautiously

As Hamlet says, I feel I've shot my arrow
Over the house and hurt.

Fran. You young cocksparrow.

(Zamiel rises suddenly & claps him on the shoulder)

Zam. Come draw it mild old chap.

Fran. The Devil.

Zam. True.
But quite invisible to all but you.
Hah! Hah! Hah!

Fran. Now don't do that in charity.
Zam. It's my distinguishing peculiarity.
Fran. What do you want?
Zam. To revel in a scene
Of terror. Wait a minute.
Fran. What d'ye mean?
Zam. You'll see; to make what's coming more terrific
I'll turn the lights down by a charmed specific,
And when the business of the scene requires
I'll heighten the effects with colored fires.

The Stage is darkened. All express terror.

"Phantom Chorus" *Somnambula*

Fran. Oh dear what's coming, strange voices humming?
The stage all dark too, with thunder hark too,
Filling each headful—with notions dreadful.
Oh what shall we do—what shall we do? Oh dear.
Otto. *(going out on tiptoe)*
Now no one's looking I'd best be hooking.
The danger near in—they all appear in
So great a stew with—I've nought to do with. *(exit stealthily)*

At the end of Chorus terrific screams are heard at the back. Frightz and other servants, waiters &c. rush in, in terror. Frightz shuts the folding doors in agony leaning against them.

Fran. What means this early closing resolution?
Is it a bailiff or an execution?
Fri. "Gracious my lord."
Fran. Quick raise thy drooping jaw.
Fri. "I should report that which I say I saw.
But know not how to do't."
Baron. What means the knave?
Fri. Well there's a horrid monster—
Baron. "Liar and slave!"
Fri. Let me endure your wrath if't be not true—
Tall as a giant and as strong as two,
Playing the very deuce.
Baron. As how, you zany.
Fri. Wopping the servants, smashing all the chany;
He broke no end of tumblers cups & plates,
Besides two green grocers in waiting pates,
And pitched the page over the first floor bannisters.

(A rattling of tins outside)

Hark at him now among the tins & canisters.
Baron. Who can it be creating such confusion
By such a "most unwarrantable intrusion"?
Fran. *(aside to Baron)*
Why the fact is, but don't expose me though,
It's that experiment of mine you know,
Which has'nt answered.

Baron. Hah! is that the fact!
Zounds, then your chargeable by the new act
For setting on large bodies to a riot
To the infringement of the public quiet.
In him!

Zam. Hah, now the larks begin!
(A tremendous thump is heard at the door; all look aghast)

Fran. You ain't good looking & you can't come in.

(The door falls in with a crash & the monster appears, blue fire—Ladies scream & faint)

Concerted. The man that could'nt get warm

Mons. I've made a hit beyond a doubt.
Guests. Throw him over, turn him out.
Zam. Few debutantes you read about
So take the house by storm.
Fran. That he'd come out so very strong,
Who would have thought. This festive throng
All quake like him renowned in song,
The man that could'nt get warm.

Chorus. All repeating from Monster.

Shiver and shakey oh! oh! oh!
Crimini crikey, Here's a go—o—o!
That most appalling form.

Fran. You dog, you'll be the death of me you will.
Are'nt you ashamed sir to behave so ill
After the trouble I have been at with you?
You naughty boy! Go home this minute do!
Mons. Hang it! Young minds require occupation
And now and then a little relaxation.
Besides I feel I ought'nt to suppress
My raging organ of destructiveness.
Zam. Of course we wish him not to.
Fran. Pray who's we?
Zam. The Authoress of *Frankenstein* & me.
He knows the sort of thing that we require,
So he'll proceed to set the place on fire.
Fran. Blazes.
Mons. Just so, that's something in my line,
I'm a blaze of triumph long to shine.
To make a night of it my spirit yearns,
Therefore suppose we make it one with Burns.

(Takes a flaming log from the fire)

Baron. Police!
Mons. *(waving his torch)* Just going to light up—Hurrah!
Fran. *(to Zamiel)* Oh! ease him! back him! stop him!
Zam. Hah! hah! hah!

(sinks through trap)
(Undine appears)

Und. Here I'll get up a water rade in aid.
What ho, appear my water fire brigade,
Come from your river beds and stir your stumps,
Dancing attendance with your hose and pumps.

The Walls at the back fall down as if burnt and discover water spirits with firemen's helmets &c. pumping at a Fairy-like engine—guiding hose &c.

Scene 6

A woody Landscape, a crash is heard & screams R. Enter Otto and Tiddliwincz carrying Agatha & Bobinetta fainting.

Otto. Help! Heartshorn! Vinegar, oh some one do.
Tid. Salts and burnt feathers if you please for two.
Otto. Confound the cab, a spill just as my cup
Of joy was full. Come I say do look up.
(to Tid) Put that girl down & try & find some water.
A lady's maid to faint, nice things they've taught her.
The habits of her mistress she's no right
To think of using. Still they're done with quite—
Ha! she recovers. How are you?
Aga. (recovering) Better much.
Bob. (ditto) It's time for me then to behave as such.
Aga. But are you hurt?
Otto. Some trifling sprains & aches.
And you?
Tid. (rubbing himself) A little shaken, no great shakes.
"Bruised worms will turn," I fear that saying's true,
For I suspect I'm turning black and blue.
Aga. But where's the cab?
Tid. Deep in a ditch it lies,
Like Banquo!
Otto. The quotation well applies:
A *Bank* it was our present *woe* produced.
Tid. Pooh! pooh! so runs upon the bank we're used.
Aga. But goodness gracious what is to be done?
We're lost.
Otto. (tenderly) Lost, nonsense dear, we'll soon be one.
Aga. Lor how you talk in such a situation.
Otto. My dear you seem forgetful of our elation.
Remember please, we keep a guardian "genus."
What ho! Undine, my little watery Venus.
Will you be kind enough to step this way?

Fountain appears through gauze behind which Undine rises

Bob. I never.
Tid. Nor I either I must say.
Otto. Well come, you don't your friends long waiting keep,
You can't live far down in the vasty deep.
Und. Why I consider it extremely wrong
When your friends call to keep them waiting long.

Tid. *(admiring Undine)* Oh don't I wish I had a genius.
Bob. *(indignantly)* Do you.
Then such a wish is not becoming to you.
Und. And so you're in a fix.
Otto. Rather a strong one.
Und. Well serves you right—your course has been a wrong one.
Otto. Indeed!
Und. Decidely! instead of running
And the paternal rigour barely shunning,
You should have got the venerable gent
To pledge himself to give you his consent
For some tremendous service you should do—
Running a giant or an ogre through,
Or say a dragon.
Otto. Law how stupid of me,
But I'll redeem my error if you love me.
Tell me where I some monster may fall in with.
Und. There's one you may immediately begin with.
Frankenstein, like so many a thoughtless creature
In blind attempts to better human nature,
Upon the world has let a monster loose,
Who breaks the peace & plays the very deuce.
So there's a chance. Here take this magic flute
And seek him out the most ferocious brute.
Its notes will bring to calm subordination,
It plays a simple tune called Education.
Otto. The very best of music for the million,
To play this monster down then boldly will I on.
Und. Do, and fear not, however savage shows he.
Otto. I understand, just music, play up noisy—

Undine sinks. Exeunt Otto & Agatha. Tiddliwincz admires Undine as she is sinking. Bobinetta draws him away.

Bob. Come here Sir, what's the creature pray to you?
Tid. I wish she'd be our guardian genius too.
Bob. Do you? I don't see that would any good be.
(aside) (I'm not quite sure she's better than she should be)
A man who's fond of spirits cannot make
A steady husband.
Tid. Well the pledge I'll take.
I'll mend my ways, don't let's have any scenes.
Bob. Stop talking about ways—what are your means?
Tid. Sweet thoughtful dear be under no alarm,
I've stocked a comfortable model farm.

SCENE 7

Baron reading paper

A pretty figure I this morning cut,
"Elopement in high life," the wicked slut.
"Startling occurrence," here we are again.

"Our fingers quiver as we hold the pen";
"Monster in human form"; "alarming fire";
Of course what's this, "should anything transpire
"Further particulars in our tenth edition."
Let them alone. A pretty exhibition
They make of anything you want to hush up.
Well is the warrant issued?
Clerk. Yes your wush-up—
Baron. Proof from the printer's come.
Clerk. *(giving bill)*—It's here my lord.
Baron. *(correcting with a pen)*
Let's look at it. "Two hundred pounds reward."
"Absconded," that's all right. "Um-Frankenstein,
"Beard, turned up nose, moustaches, five foot nine
"Whereas said Frankenstein—" yes that'll do,
"Has set a magic monster going—" true,
"By whom the public confidence is shaken."

(Enter Frightz hurriedly)

Fri. My lord the student Frankenstein is taken.
Baron. Off with his—Pshaw what an absurd caprice;
I'm justice not stage tyrant of the piece.
Conduct him hither. *(noise of voices outside)*
But what means this din?
Fri. The sovereign public, sir, they will come in
To hear the prisoner's examination.
Baron. Admit them quick; but stay, on this occasion,
As the proceedings will be interesting,
We'll raise the prices. They won't mind investing.
Charge them for seats, no fear of a denial,
The same as for a first rate murder trial.
Fri. *(going to door)* Walk up, walk up, just going to commence.
Immense attraction—startling new offence—
Most interesting criminal proceedings.
Step forward be in time to hear the pleadings.
(He admits the public gradually, taking money from them)
Baron. Making police courts thus an exhibition
Is rather mean; I make that free admission.
But still are we to blame? No—not at all.
We've great examples for it. Aye! by St. Paul
Bring in the prisoner.
1 Spec. Hats off!
2 Spec. Down in front!
3 Spec. Get off my toes!
4 Spec. Police!
5 Spec. Make Room!
6 Spec. I won't!

Music. Frankenstein loaded with chains led in guarded. An attendant carrying carpet bag & great coat.

Baron. Pris'ner stand forth.

Fran. I shan't, I shall stand first.
Baron. Contempt of court.
Fran. I don't care, do your worst.
By what right am I thus with wrongs environed,
My feelings mangled & my person ironed?

Enter Several peasants.

1 P. Justice great Baron, justice.
Baron. What's the row?
2 P. The monster oh!
Fran. *(aside)* Ah! what's he up to now?
Baron. Tell me the worst, 'tis better I should know it.
Your news.
1 P. Prepare then for a shock.
Baron. Well go it.
1 P. Oh that my tongue such horrors should relate,
He's torn the bell pull off our garden gate.
Baron. Oh monstrous.
2 P. Burnt my rick of hay to cinders.
3 P. Stolen my knocker.
4 P. Broken all my windows.
3 P. Thrashed a policeman.
5 P. Broken down my palings.
2 P. Boned all the pewter pots from all the railings.
Baron. This must be stopped. The justice you demand
You shall obtain. A heavy deed and
I'll lay on him which you of course must pay
As his proprietor. *(to Frankenstein)*
Fran. Oh I dare say
I can't be answerable upon my soul,
He's got completely out of my control.
Why can't you catch him? Hands on the marauder lay.
Fine him five shillings drunken & disorderly.
Baron. Pris'ner or rather student at the bar,
For all his acts responsible you are.
In law he is an infant, yet a minor.
Fran. Well for an infant I never saw a finer.
But take down my defence, I'll soon be showing
I'm not the only man who's set a going
A horrid monster that he could'nt stop.
For precedents across the channel pop.
Otto. *(outside)* Stop the proceedings!
Fran. Here's fresh tidings horrid.

Enter Otto and Agatha, they run across and kneel to the Baron. Tiddliwincz & Bobinetta following.

Otto. *(kneeling)* Your blessing.
Baron. Stop young man your rather for'ard.
Otto. We're married.
Baron. Well but ere you can obtain it,
It's usual to do something first to gain it.

Otto. Then what d'ye say supposing I subdue
And overpow'r the savage monster who
I hear in this immediate neighbourhood
Has just set up as wild man of the wood.
Baron. Yes that's the sort of thing.
Otto. Hurrah I've won it!
Fran. But stop, first catch your monster.
Otto. Well I've done it.
Fran. You have. Oh dear excuse my feelings, pray
I know he's wild wicked I ought to say,
But still my interest in him is such,
I hope you have'nt been and hurt him much.
Otto. Hurt him, oh no, that's not at all the way
We serve offenders in the present day.
The world grows wiser and begins to find
That to its erring sons it should be kind,
And stead of scaring them with jail & fetter,
The proper way is teach them to grow better.
I've tamed him.
All. Ha.
Otto. Yes, by this weapon small,
Whose unobtrusive power would conquer all
The ills that o'er the earth hold domination
If people understood its application.
Behold its charm to soothe the savage breast,
And lull the—everybody knows the rest.

Goes to wing R & commences playing "In My Cottage" very slowly. The monster, neatly dressed à la happy Villager with his hair and moustaches curled, enters smiling & following the music. Otto leads him round the Stage changing his tune to the original Polka. The monster dances pleased.

Fran. Come to my arms you wild young rascal do,
I don't mind saying now I'm proud of you.

Frankenstein & Monster embrace.

And so you'll turn out well at last you dog.
Mon. Yes in reform I go the entire hog.
I've cut my way of life so rough & stormy,
So pr'aps you'll get a situation for me.
Fran. A situation, one I'll quickly send you to,
I've lots of friends that I can recommend you to,

(bringing him to footlights)

Friends who can give you a most glorious berth,
Faith there's no saying what *their* place is worth.
Come here I'll speak for you. *(to Aud)* What d'ye say?
D'ye think you can put something in his way
Spite of his wildness of his past condition?
In the long run (which we by your permission
Hope to enjoy) I really don't mind saying
I think you'll like him.
Baron. *(interrupting)* Stop tho', there's the paying
For all the damages already done. *(Undine enters L)*

Und. Hold, to be blamed for that he's not the one,
The true cause of the mischief I've found out.
Too long this neighbourhood he's prow'll'd about,
But I'm resolved he shall no longer stay.
Notice to quit I've served on him to-day.
Behold him.

(Enter Zamiel very miserably in travelling costume. Ratzbaen carrying Carpet bag and great coats following)

Zam. Can there be no mercy shewn me?
This notice of ejectment's hard upon me.
Und. No words—Sir—Hence—nor dare again be found
Playing your wicked pranks on German ground.
Zam. What, after all these years to be ejected!
In Smithfield vested rights are more respected.
Where can I go to, what am I to do?
Und. Alas for evil spirits such as you
There's generally too much employment jogging.
Zam. There's Austria, it's true; the women flogging,
That's something in my line—but then folks swear
The market's overstocked with demons there.
In California too my chance is small,
There the fiend gold monopolises all
The mischief
Und. Cease, be gone malicious fogey.
Zam. Pity the sorrows of a poor old bogey
Under the influence of an evil star.
Und. Away.
Zam. Good afternoon then.
(very miserably) Hah! Hah! Hah!

(Exit followed by Ratzbaen very lugubriously)

Fran. *(to Und)* Now then.
Und. Now what?
Fran. Why you're the Fairy Queen,
So it's your place to settle the last scene.
Und. I never thought of that the part's so strange
To me. Let's see whom have I got to change
To Clown & Pantaloon.
Fran. That's not the way.
Und. Is'nt it oh! well then suppose we say
I take you all to see me at my quarters
And introduce you to Rhine's fairy daughters.

CURTAIN

John Balderston
Frankenstein
(1930)

Act One Scene One

The living room of Henry Frankenstein, in an old house in Goldstadt. Fire in grate L. front. Mirror above it. Table near fireplace with oil lamp that illuminates only it, leaving book-filled walls in shadow. There is a door R. shut with formidable iron bar. Curtained window R. at an angle, in the rear wall, and in front a large intricate machine—like a galvanic battery. Chairs etc. Door back leading into garden.

Time—1800.

Dr. Waldman is sitting at table, with a book. He is a professor at the University, and a Priest, about fifty years old, benevolent, grey-haired, short and slight. Waldman is clearly disturbed, he lays down book, looks fixedly at closed door R., gets up and walks about worried, then sits down and opens book again.

Knocking at door back. Waldman looks up, startled. More knocks. Waldman goes to door, unlocks it, flash of lightning shows. Waldman opens door few inches.

Waldman. (Gently) Good evening. Do you wish to see Henry Frankenstein? I do not think he can see anyone, tonight.

Figure Without. Dr. Waldman!

Waldman. Victor Moritz! I did not recognize you.

(He is still barring the door)

Victor. Is Henry here, Doctor?

Waldman. Yes—

Victor. May I not come in?

(Waldman hesitates, steps aside)

Waldman. Yes. I . . . I suppose you may.

(Enter Victor, presentable youth in his twenties, normal young man, charm but not particularly intelligent. He shakes rain off cloak)

Victor. What a night. There's a terrible storm over the mountains. Is Henry here?

Waldman. Didn't he ask you to come?

Victor. No, but I only want news of him before I go away. If he won't see me, you can tell me that. He has avoided me for weeks.

Waldman. Were you hurt at his change of manner?

Victor. Of course, until I found he was avoiding everyone. Now I'm too worried to be hurt. Is he all right?

(They are warming their hands by the fire)

Waldman. I'm sure I hope so. I have been worried too. He has shut himself up here alone, dismissed his servant. Tonight he sent me a note.

Victor. But where is he?

Waldman. I don't know. He let me in himself. He said something about not being ready, then he rushed in there—*(Gesture to closed door)*

Victor. But such rudeness to you—Dr. Waldman!

Waldman. He locked that door after him,—both doors.

Victor. There's something wrong.

Waldman. He seemed nervous, hysterical.

Victor. Perhaps I'd better go. What is this machine?

Waldman. I don't know. I never saw it—It's a sort of huge galvanic battery.

Victor. And something like a big lamp. *(Begins to put on cloak)*

Waldman. I wish you'd stay.

Victor. No. He must want to talk to you. You are his priest and his professor too. I can't—

Waldman. You are his boyhood friend.

Victor. But I can't help him in his work and that's all he cares for—except his sister of course and—Amelia.

Waldman. It helps sometimes just to talk to someone else.

Victor. The Confessional, Dr. Waldman!

Waldman. I don't think he sent for me as his priest. As for being his professor, there's no longer anything I can teach him. His experiments in anatomy, chemistry of the tissues, galvanism, have made him the glory of our University. *(Sighs)* They have made his masters feel a little foolish.

Victor. (Forgets in his enthusiasm that he was going, comes down stage toward Waldman). I know nothing of science. The best I can hope is to write his biography when he's famous, if he doesn't kill himself with overwork.

Waldman. (Amused). And what will you say?

Victor. I'll tell how we played together beside the lake at Belrive, how he was always looking for the philosopher's stone, read books on alchemy when he was thirteen and talked about turning base metal into gold.

Waldman. He has deserted his alchemy for the new facts, new experimental truths. They fascinate me as a man of science, though sometimes they terrify me as a priest.

(Victor walks uneasily towards door L. listens. Waldman watches)

Waldman. Something will burst up here. *(Taps head)* unless there is someone to make him lead a more normal life. He studies and works like a man possessed—when is he to marry Amelia—Amelia?

Victor. Amelia Lavenza? *(Flings on cloak suddenly)*

Waldman. Lavenza? But I'd heard YOU were to marry someone of that name—a sister perhaps?

Victor. No, it was Amelia. We had been engaged since we were children—last year she—well she said she loved Henry.

Waldman. (Gently). Are you giving up everything to your friend?

Victor. (Vehemently). NO. Why shouldn't she want him? He has brilliance, he has strength, he will be a great man. I am a weakling—

Waldman. He HAS some uncanny power—

(Noise of bolt shooting in door R., door opens. Enter Henry. Young, thin, nervous, good looking but now at the point of hysteria. He crosses rapidly to them)

Henry (Rudely). Victor! Why have you come here?

Victor. (Much hurt). I didn't know you were engaged. And I'm off to Belrive tomorrow.

Henry. (With sudden change of mood). Forgive me, Victor, I'm a fool. I've got spy-mania, I've been afraid of people prying about, trying to find out things. . . . I do beg your pardon.

Victor. It's all right, Henry. Good-night.

Henry. No, since you're here, stay! Why not? My first childish prattle of science was with you, I should have sent for you, too, I want you to stay, you shall share with me the greatest moment of my life!

(Victor throws off cloak, comes towards table)

Your pardon, Dr. Waldman, I wasn't quite ready.

Victor. Henry, why did you lock yourself up in there?

(Henry's manner makes them both uneasy, they try to humor him)

Waldman. I didn't mind being kept waiting, I was looking through an old book I found here. A treatise, in black letters, on anatomy, with curious drawings by a pupil of Albrecht Durer.

Henry. (Pacing about). The old anatomists lacked our knowledge of detail, but they glimpsed intuitively some truths that you men of today don't understand, Dr. Waldman. You stress detail . . . detail . . . always detail, but you don't see the wood for the trees.

Waldman. No doubt, no doubt.

Victor. Are you going to give a lecture to Dr. Waldman, Henry?

Henry. I am!

Victor. My dear friend, what IS the matter with you tonight?

Henry. Nothing, nothing. Sit down, I want to talk to you.

(Victor, shocked both at Henry's state of hysteria, and at his rudeness to his master, sits down by Waldman. Waldman, placid and calm, lights a pipe. Henry continues to pace about)

Waldman (Lightly). I can see nothing but a black shape pacing about in the shadows, Henry. Does this communication of yours require mystery and firelight? *(Lightning, thunder)* With an appropriate accompaniment from the elements?

(Waldman turns up lamp on table so that his face and Victor's are illuminated. During following scene, as Henry reaches his climaxes he sits at table, peering into their faces, his own lit up, then gets up and walks about again)

Henry Frankenstein, may I say something first? You've been working too hard, and when a MASTER says that to his PUPIL, you may be sure there's something in it.

Henry. Tonight, it is you who are the pupil, I who am the master!

Victor. (Shocked). Really, Henry! Look here—

(Waldman makes pacifying gesture to Victor)

Look at yourself in a mirror! Your people at home are worried about you, you haven't been writing. Your little sister wrote and asked me what was the matter. Go home, Henry, if only for a few weeks!

Waldman. Belrive is less than a day's ride, across the mountains to the lake, isn't it?

(Henry paces about impatiently)

Victor. I don't want to be a busybody, but I also get letters from Amelia. She's worried too, she hasn't heard from you for months.

Henry. (Explosively). Amelia Lavenza can wait!

Victor. Henry! Not even you can talk like that about Amelia to me.

Henry. (More quietly). I love her. I shall make her proud of me. She shall share in the experiment that shall make me famous forever. But I have had no time for anything else.

Waldman. Never mind, Henry, we only want to say that we feel you must have a rest. Your old housekeeper said—

Henry. Yes, I got rid of her, so that she wouldn't say anything. Enough of this please, please. Dr. Waldman, you remember what we talked about, when you came and dined with me here?

Waldman. That was about two months ago, I remember we sat up half the night and that we talked a great deal of nonsense.

Victor. I can't imagine YOU talking nonsense, Dr. Waldman.

Henry. And what sort of nonsense was it?

Waldman. We were discussing the mystery of life, the physical processes of decay in dead matter, even the nature of the vital force that infuses life into matter. And I remember feeling afterwards that we had been very foolish, and perhaps a little wicked.

Henry. Wicked? Why wicked?

Waldman. Because, my friend, it is not for a priest, still less is it for a layman, to probe these mysteries too deeply. We know that life comes from God, from God alone. It is presumption to think the human mind was ever intended to fathom these supreme mysteries—

Henry. On the contrary, it is cowardice that prevents us from solving them.

Waldman. It is presumption, Henry, for us who study anatomy, even for you to whom God has given genius, to push our enquiries so far. We must remember that we can deal only with matter, not with spirit, which is the breath of God.

Henry. You did not have those scruples that night, Doctor. You discussed with me the possibility of destroying life, and creating it again.

Victor. You are nothing if not ambitious, Henry.

Waldman. It was only foolish speculation. We were talking about the curious phenomenon shown by frogs when killed by a galvanic battery. The heart no longer beats, and yet the current makes the limbs move, and there is a semblance of life, although the creature is dead.

Henry. There is more than a semblance of life. For weeks I have worked on that problem, and at last I made a discovery. I have killed toads, and cats and dogs, Dr. Waldman—killed them you understand, and they are now alive in my garden.

Waldman. That is not possible, they only seemed to be dead.

Henry. They WERE dead.

Waldman. (Uneasily). I do not think the Church would approve of these experiments. There is an error—somewhere.

Henry. There is no error. One was dead 14 hours—their hearts ceased to beat—now they are alive.

Victor. Wonderful, Henry. So that's what all this mystery has been.

Henry. Does the man of science, Doctor, ever stop when he is in pursuit of the truth? I did not stop there.

Victor. You don't mean—

Waldman. (On his feet). Your studies have been too much for you. I shall bring a doctor to see you.

Henry. Sit down and listen. You must listen! You are here tonight to share with me my hour of triumph, or to condole with me in my defeat. Between the body of a frog, or a dog and the body of a man, what is the difference? Are we not all animals?

Waldman. Man is not an animal! You speak like a heretic. *(Sternly)* Go on.

Henry. After animals, MAN!

(Both men are up, horrified)

Victor. Henry, you don't mean you've. . . . Oh, forgive me.

Henry. I am no murderer.

Waldman. Then what are you trying to tell us?

Henry. *(Almost unheeding them, as though to himself, as he paces in the shadows).* My task has been horrible, horrible. I have profaned the resting places of the newly dead. With my own hands I have dragged bodies to my workshop.

Waldman. *(Horrified).* What impious perversion of science is this! You have desecrated sacred ground. . . .

Victor. If you were trying to bring the dead to life, we'll keep your secret about the bodies. But of course we must get you away from here. . . .

Waldman. And you must seek absolution and penance from The Holy Church.

Henry. Dr. Waldman, I asked you here not as a priest but as a master of science.

(Strides R.—points through door, turns to them)

Waldman. Henry Frankenstein, what have you in there?

Victor. *(As Henry staggers to table, half collapses).* What is it, Henry? You are ill. . . .

Henry. No, I'm not ill, only tired. I mustn't be tired. I must have the courage of the devil—tonight. Bring me that bottle on the shelf there, pour me out a drink.

(Victor does so and Waldman watches Henry narrowly, Henry half collapses, head in hands on table. Henry revives, rises)

Ah, that's better.

(Waldman takes glass, smells it, shakes head)

Those who died of disease, whose life machine had already run down like a worn out clock, defeated me. Corruption set in too soon. So I failed.

Waldman. Ah!

Henry. I turned to violent death for my experiments.

Victor. *(Horrified, to Waldman).* That thief, who was hanged in chains on the gibbet above Goldstadt!

Waldman. *(Accusingly).* The body disappeared!

Henry. It took me four hours to knock off the chains, I could scarcely drag the corpse up here before daylight.

Victor. But you failed.

Henry. Yes. Strangulation defeated me, but the heart reaction showed I was on the right track. Then—You remember the great storm from the Jura mountains that swept down on the valleys last month?

Victor. Yes, the lightning played all night—

Henry. In the village of Pontoise, that night, a house was struck and a man killed—a young man, doctor, healthy and strong! Dr. Waldman, what was that death, but the same shock from a galvanic battery with which I killed a frog, or a dog?

Waldman. *(Sternly).* You desecrated that man's grave!

Henry. I took my implements, my batteries with me. It took me two days. I hid the body in the woods when it grew light. I went back again at twilight the next night. I brought him to life, there in the forest.

Waldman. Impious! A century ago the Church would have burned you—

Henry. Is he who saves a dying man impious? This young man was dead. If I could give him life, would men regard me as a criminal, or as a saviour?

Waldman. The doctor does not interfere with the *will* of *Heaven*. Henry Frankenstein. He restores the sick BEFORE their souls have gone to God, not afterwards.

Victor. Your studies have been too much for you, Henry. I will help you rebury the corpse.

Henry. You need not bother—I reburied it.

(The men are terrified)

Why are you so horrified, Dr. Waldman? I merely let his life run out. I was simply not interfering with the will of Heaven!

(They remain speechless, Dr. Waldman crosses himself)

I was not interested in his soul, that was no concern of mine. Nor his body, once I had made it breathe. For what was all that but my old experiment with frogs and dogs?

(Rising to a violent pitch)

I did not want to RESTORE, I wanted to CREATE life!

(Goes toward machine)

Waldman. *(Weakly)*. Create?

Henry. Create! From the beginning.

(Voice goes flat but gradually rises towards end of speech)

I had found ways of slowing up corruption but I had to work fast. I knew my way about the graveyard. I stole the key of the dissecting room—I took what I needed as I dared—a leg or a lung or some complicated nerve tissue. I am a sculptor; I moulded a figure and a face.

(To Dr. Waldman)

Do you remember ten days ago when you were dissecting a brain? I took that—some of it! From odds and ends—from charnel house and burying ground, I fashioned a body—I made a man! I have created—

Waldman. A patched-up loathsome thing perhaps—but not Life.

Henry. Tonight we'll see! Victor, will you come with me? *(Smiles down on him ironically)* Are you afraid to come?

(Moves to door R. Victor, trembling, goes after him, passing machine)

Victor. Is this part of your experiment?

Henry. Part of it—Listen—*(With enthusiasm)* Dr. Waldman—what is the highest color in the spectrum?

Waldman. Violet.

Henry. Beyond that—we cannot see it—is another stronger violet—an ultra-violet—In the future its rays will be used for health. Beyond that is still another ray, hotter than ultra-violet—life-giving—even life-creating! In the beginning of the world—of all things—

Waldman. In the beginning was the word and the word was God—

Henry. Perhaps He is a ray—an unseen ray beyond the visible spectrum! You've seen the sun bring primitive forms of life out of nothingness—insects from mud puddles, more complex crawling creatures out of slime—

Waldman. *(Enthusiastic)*. You've found a new electrical force—

Henry. In this machine—all the rays of the spectrum—the ultra-violet, beyond that—and the *great ray* beyond that—which in the beginning brought Life into the world as the hot mass cooled—*(Gesture)* But you would not understand.

Waldman. In the name of Religion, I forbid your experimenting.

Henry. In the name of Science—remain and verify it!

Waldman. *(Sternly)*. Do you believe in the after life, in the soul?

Henry. I am no atheist.

Waldman. Then answer me, when this man in the mountains died, was not his immortal soul summoned to Heaven, to Hell, or to Purgatory?

Henry. *(Impatiently)*. I suppose so.

Waldman. Did God then revoke his irrevocable judgment and send this man's soul from bliss or torment back into his dead body?

Henry. *(Ironically)*. We talked, but I did not inquire!

Waldman. Suppose you succeed now. Your corpse moves and breathes. It seems a man. But can Man exist without soul? Is it then Man? What is It?

Victor. Henry—don't—

Henry. *(To Waldman)*. Wrestle with your theological problems as you choose. I am not interested in souls.

Waldman. The mere attempt is mortal sin.

Henry. Words! Come, Victor!

(Henry goes out R. Victor follows reluctantly)

Waldman. God will not allow it!

(Re-enter Henry and Victor carrying stretcher, covered with sheet, put it down R.C. Victor steps back)

Henry. Dr. Waldman, examine this thing, satisfy yourself and Victor that it is dead.

Waldman. I must see this horror through. You will need the priest, not the master of science, when you come to your senses.

(Approaches stretcher, draws sheet sufficiently on one side to show an arm, pause, lifts hand to feel pulse, puts head down to listen for breathing, steps back)

Of course the thing is dead.

Henry. Look upon its face! *(They hesitate)*

Victor. No, no.

Henry. Then you, Dr. Waldman!

(Waldman with hesitation and loathing, pulls away cloth from face)

Victor. *(Approaches step or two, gazes fascinated)*. It is like a death mask.

Henry. Now is the supreme moment, shall I triumph or shall I fail?

(Attaches wires of galvanic battery to arm, machine, fizzes and gives off queer lights, and sends out sparks. Henry rushes to cupboard, brings out small bottle, and pours contents down throat of the body)

Victor. What is that?

Henry. The Elixir—the Elixir of Life! I found some of the formula in those old black letter books—I worked out the rest for myself. Look—look—both of you. *(They approach fascinated)*

Victor. *(Whispers hoarsely)* In the name of religion, Dr.—no! But in the name of Science—do you want him to succeed?

Waldman. *(Enthusiastically)* Yes! Yes—no! God forgive me, what am I saying? *(Silence)* You have failed Henry, and I thank Heaven for it.

(Pause) (Thunder and lightning)

Henry. *(With a scream)* I have succeeded.

(The body very slowly clenches and unclenches the right hand that has dropped to the side of the stretcher, makes a guttural sound, half a groan, half a breath, lifts right arm stiffly, lifts head a few inches, stares at Henry, then drops back. They all stand motionless)

Henry. *(In wild exaltation)* I have made life, out of matter that was dead!

Waldman. You make yourself equal with God—that was the sin of the fallen angel! *(As Curtain falls—he drops on knees mumbling)* God forgive him, (etc.)

CURTAIN on SCENE ONE

Act One Scene 2

The same room, a few weeks later. Mirror has been removed. It is morning but curtains pulled over the windows keep out most of the light. Some fingers of sunshine come through the chinks in the curtains. Machine has disappeared. Table piled with books, some are spilled on floor.

Voice off stage "Henry!" Knocking on door, handle is turned and Victor enters. Calls again: "Henry! Henry! Where are you?" Crosses to barred door, bangs on it calling again: "Henry!"

Faint rattle of chains off stage. Enter Henry, looking more distracted than in last scene, and quite unkempt.

Henry. Victor! I'm glad you're back. What has happened?

Victor. Your father drove back with me. I couldn't help it.

Henry. Good God! Where is he?

Victor. At the Inn in the square.

Henry. He'll come up here any minute.

Victor. He has to see the horses are put up first, and look after Amelia—

Henry. Amelia! Oh my God, did she come with you too?

Victor. They've been so worried about you. It was your sister who begged Amelia to come.

Henry. What shall I do? I can't see them. I daren't.

Victor. Has it—is it alive?

Henry. Alive! Yes, and growing stronger every day. Nobody knows yet except you and Dr. Waldman.

Victor. Where do you keep it?

Henry. *(Points through barred door).* In the little cellar, under my bedroom. *(There is a faint rattle again)* Chained.

Victor. *(Horrified).* Chained—in eternal darkness! Must you?

Henry. Must you keep a tiger chained?

Victor. He was docile that night. Doesn't he obey you?

Henry. As a beaten cur obeys its master.

Victor. How do you control him?

Henry. Don't ask me that.

Victor. Torture?

Henry. *(Snaps out).* Is a lion-tamer with his whip and his hot iron, a torturer? Besides, what else can I do? There's a devil in him that looks out of his eyes.

Victor. At least he's quiet now. Go in your room, and wash and change your clothes. Your father will certainly be here soon—he'll be angry enough that I ran away the minute we reached the Inn.

(A knock, they both jump slightly. Victor says: "Get in there quickly"—but as the door opens—it is Dr. Waldman)

Waldman. Ah Victor. I saw you in the carriage and guessed whom you were with. So I hurried up here at once.

Victor. Thank Heaven you did. Henry, go make yourself look better, before your father comes.

Henry. (Hysterically). I can't see them. I can't see them.

Waldman. (Gently pushing him through door). Never mind, you needn't just now. We'll think of something. *(Closes door on him)*

Victor. It's alive! We thought it would die when the effects of that Elixir wore off. What is it like?

Waldman. You'll see soon enough. But we must get rid of the Baron, and then quiet Henry and take him down to the Inn.

(The Baron stands in the door: large, red faced country squire, rather angry now)

Victor. Ah—come in, Baron. You found your way here quickly.

Baron. No thanks to you, who turned and ran off while I was back in the stable. You develop queer manners when you return to your university.

Victor. I'm sorry Baron. I thought I'd find Henry and bring him to the Inn to save you walking up the hill.

Baron. You might have said so.

Victor. Permit me to introduce Dr. Waldman, our head professor of Anatomy.

Baron. (Genial at once) I am honored, Dr. Waldman. Henry has spoken a lot of you. But you are the priest I was told to follow. The town people said you'd probably be coming here, that you came every day.

Waldman. Yes,—we've been working a lot together, lately.

Baron. Well, I'm glad to see that, though you may be a professor of anatomy, you are not likely to teach our boys this new, atheistical, scientific nonsense. I hope you see to it that they don't read those books by those scoundrels Rousseau and Voltaire. They started that Revolution in France.

Waldman. (Gently, smiling). You are not in favor of the higher education, Baron?

Baron. I never was. It was his mother's idea, letting the boy stuff his head full of books from the time he was a baby. But where is he?

Victor. He's not here, Baron.

Baron. That's obvious. *(Looks around)* A gloomy place for the lad to kennel himself. What's through there? *(Points to barred door)* It is barred like a strong room *(Knocks)*

Victor. That's his bedroom, and beyond that is his laboratory.

(Baron tries door)

Baron. It's locked. *(Knocks louder)* Then maybe he's in his laboratory and doesn't hear.

(There is a faint rattling of chains, which the Doctor hears for he moves nervously)

Waldman. The windows are shut, I saw them as I came up the hill. I'll find him and bring him to the Inn, Baron, if you'll wait there.

Baron. What, walk down that hill in this heat, when I've just walked up? Thanks, I'll wait here.

(Sits, disgusted—kicks at some books on floor)

Victor. He's probably at a lecture.

Waldman. (Quickly). There's Dr. Kammeren's lecture this afternoon. Henry never likes to miss them.

Victor. Of course, that's where he'd be.

Baron. Lecture? Where is it? Does it mean I have to wait for hours?

Victor. He lectures in the anatomical class room. It's the white building, just beyond the Inn, on the small side street that runs past the stables.

Baron. A rifle shot from where we stopped! I'll go find him there.

(Stops on way to door and looks suspiciously at them)

There's something queer—why did you rush up here without a word to either of us, Victor?

(Victor has no ready reply)

Dr. Waldman, weren't you coming up to see my son?

Waldman. I—I heard Victor was coming up here, I really came to see him.

Baron. *(Laughs jovially).* Oh, you're in for a wigging, are you, my boy? Not so easy to deal with these lazy lads, is it, Doctor, when they get too old to have the cane applied to their tails. Well, I shall see you later at the Inn, Victor. Meantime, tell Henry's servant to get his things packed.

Waldman. *(Agitated, as Baron is going out).* You're not asking him to go home with you, are you, Baron?

Baron. *(Surprised).* Ask him? No, I'm not *asking* him, I'm *taking* him home. *(Looking from one to the other)* What is there so surprising in this? Is the lad never to have a holiday? From all you tell me, he needs one badly.

(As Baron disappears, grumbling, "asking him indeed", Victor & Waldman look at each other in

Waldman. May God forgive me for the lies I have told that man!

(Tension relaxes)

Victor. We're safe for an hour. And Henry had better be got home.

Waldman. Yes, but what about that thing in there?

Victor. Can't it be turned over to the authorities and shut up as an idiot? We could make up some story.

Waldman. The whole secret will come out.

Victor. Isn't that better—than this?

Waldman. *(Knocks on door, calls:)* Henry, your father has gone.

(Door unlocked from inside,—enter Henry, looking just as before—bars door behind him)

Victor. Good Lord, Henry, you can't be taken down to the Inn looking like this. Don't you understand—your father is here and Amelia. They've come to take you home!

Henry. *(With despairing laugh).* Home! I have no home! My home is in there . . . with *that!* How can I go, and leave my monster? The horror of what I have done will ring through all the world when the truth is known by everyone.

Victor. And you thought it would make you famous, you were proud of what you were doing.

Henry. Yes, pride! Pride was the sin of the fallen angel. I might have done great work, and now I have damned myself in life and in death.

Waldman. My son, pray for guidance, as I pray for you.

Henry. I cannot pray.

Waldman. You know that you have sinned, and you repent. That is something. It is much. After sin comes repentance, punishment, I hope expiation.

Henry. Repentance and punishment I have had. At least I can escape.

Victor. How?

Henry. *(To Waldman).* You warned me, and in my mad presumption I would not listen. I usurped the prerogative of God, I tried to make myself His equal.

(Waldman crosses himself)

(Henry continues, challengingly, to Waldman)

God created life, I created life. God gives life and God gives death too! What have you to say to that? Why are you silent?

Waldman. To blasphemy, would you add murder?

Henry. (Suddenly calm, speaks reasonably, quietly). Murder, Dr. Waldman? What is murder? You said, the church says, that man is created in the image of God, but the Church doesn't mean that God has arms and legs like a man, or looks like a man. God gives man part of himself when He breathes into him a soul. Isn't that good theology? Well then, isn't it my crime that I've mocked God by giving life when I cannot give a soul?

Waldman. (Sternly). Thou shalt not kill.

Henry. Does that mean animals, wild beasts, monsters, or does it mean real men, men with souls?

Waldman. Would you atone for one crime by committing another?

Henry. But I'm trying to show you that it wouldn't be as crime. I've performed my experiment, if I end what should never have been begun, destroy my formula, let my satanic secret die with me, have I not made the only atonement possible? Then I can go home, to my father and mother and sister. Not to Amelia, Victor, after this I should never dare look her in the face.

Waldman. Enough of this.

Henry. (Hysterically). You can't have it both ways, priest! If this thing that I made has no soul, is not human, it's a beast, and a beast can be killed without sin!

Waldman. Who am I to know what relation God has decreed between you and this thing that you and the Devil, your rays and your Elixir brought into the world? But it is linked to you more strongly than son to father. And this I know, that it is part of yourself and that you cannot destroy the unholy life that you have dared to breathe into that body.

Henry. Then it will destroy me.

Waldman. (Turns away, Henry's remark strikes him deeply and he seems to agree, as he turns back to Henry). This is in God's Providence.

(Sound of chains and a sudden howl from below. Henry rushes to door, unbars it, goes out. Sounds of blows and groans)

Victor. He'll go mad. He is mad!

(More groans, etc. off)

Waldman. He has been trying to teach him, hoping knowledge would tame him. I come only at night, and the creature sleeps then, for Henry drugs him.

(Re-enter Henry, carrying large whip)

Victor. Henry, *must* you do this?

Henry. He could pick me up and break me in half, if he knew his strength. I can only handle him through Fear.

Victor. What does he want?

Henry. What every caged beast wants—freedom. He heard our voices.

Victor. Bring him in here, Henry.

Henry. Are you not afraid?

Victor. We are three men to one—you can't keep him chained up always!

Henry. Very well, you shall see Frankenstein!

Victor. Frankenstein!

Henry. (Ironically again). Yes—Frankenstein—I made him, I gave him life, he's the emanation of my brain—isn't it appropriate that I call him Frankenstein. *(Goes to door—turns)* Remember, he has never been loose before and is inhumanly strong.

(Exit Henry. Grunts, uncouth noises, crack of whip, noise of chains, heard off stage)

Waldman. *(Crossing himself)*. Are you not afraid? You are about to behold an insult to the majesty of God—the living fruit of a sin against the Holy Ghost—

Victor. It's Henry I'm thinking about and Amelia.

(Re-enter Henry, carrying whip, stops at door—speaks in harsh tones of command)

Henry. Frankenstein! Come here!

(Pause. Noise of shuffling and chain, grunts and whimpers)

Frankenstein! *(To others)* He is afraid of the light.

Victor. *(To Waldman)*. Think of it, Doctor, a creature who has never seen the sun!

Henry. Come! *(Cracks whip)*

Victor. *(Looking in awe and horror)*. God!

Waldman. He moves like something blind.

(Frankenstein shambles in; half-clothed in coarse rags, matted hair, slightly stumbling, walks half-crouching, like an ape, shielding his bloodshot eyes with his hands)

(Waldman throws back curtains from window, admitting sunlight. Frankenstein, terrified, scuttles back out of light like a scared animal, crouches on floor, then as he looks up and sees the sun, drags himself into the sunlight and kneels holding up his hands like a savage in prayer to the sun, muttering gibberish)

Waldman. *(Shocked)*. He is praying to the sun!

Henry. Of course! Sun worship—fire worship—he is going through all the instinctive processes of primitive man—both in religion and behavior. Growing children do it too. *(To Frankenstein)* Fire! Great fire!

(At word "fire" Frankenstein shows terror, jumps up and cringes)

Victor. Why does he do that?

Henry. There was once—he was in a rage, I could not tame him with the whip, I was afraid he'd break his chains, I had to use a—hot iron.

(Frankenstein is mumbling in terror "fire" and repeatedly touches his side)

Waldman. *(Soothingly)*. Good fire. Great fire.

Henry. Not burn. Not hurt.

(Frankenstein again looks up to sun)

Waldman. Bright, soft fire.

(Frankenstein gets up, goes to window, holds out arms again, draws deep breaths)

Henry. That is my garden. Say it! Garden!

Frankenstein. Gar-den.

(Frankenstein points, eager questioning in his motions and his grunts)

Henry. Trees.

Frankenstein. Trees!

Henry. Flowers.

Frankenstein. Flow-ers! *(Looks up, pointing above, with similar gesture)*

Henry. Great soft fire, the sun. Sun.

Frankenstein. Sun.

Henry. The blue Heaven, the—sky.

Frankenstein. Sky. *(He continues to gaze, panting, excited, enraptured)*

Henry. Come here! *(Frankenstein turns, reluctantly)* Kneel! No, further off, there! *(Frankenstein kneels)* What is this? *(Puts out hand)*

Frankenstein. Hand.

Henry. (Points to Frankenstein's hand) And that?

Frankenstein. (Raises hand) Hand. *(Looks from his hand to Henry's)* Like . . . like . . .

Henry. (Hastily). What is your name?

Frankenstein. Fran-ken-stein.

Henry. What am I?

Frankenstein. Man.

Henry. Yes, man. What else?

Frankenstein. Mas-ter. *(Mumbles to himself)* Fran-ken-stein, mas-ter. *(Gets up, holds out arms again to the world without)* Sun—sky—trees.

(Turns to door, starts for door. Henry bars way, holding whip)

Henry. No, back!

Waldman. It is light and air that he wants, like any animal, like any plant.

Henry. (Imperiously). Be careful, Dr. Waldman, before this slave here there must be only command, blind obedience, no discussion.

Victor. But surely, Henry, of course you must be stern, but not cruel.

Frankenstein. (Eagerly questioning). Cru-el?

Henry. You have not seen him in his rages, my way is the only way. Frankenstein, you shall go out there in the garden, when it is dark.

Frankenstein. Dark?

Victor. When the sun goes down.

Waldman. When the great fire goes—no more fire.

Frankenstein. (Piteously). No more . . . great fire.

Waldman. The great fire will come again. It is begun again . . . every day.

Frankenstein. Be-gun?

Victor. Born.

Frankenstein. Born? Born? *(Thinks, asks as question)* Fran-ken-stein—born?

Henry. (Angry). No more of this, I beg you not to put ideas . . .

Waldman. There is something stirring there. *(To Frankenstein)* There is BEAUTY in the garden, in the world outside, that's why you want to go out there.

Frankenstein. Beau-ty.

Waldman. Sun, flowers, trees, the mountains around us, all that is—beauty.

(Frankenstein gazes outside, drinking in his first sight of the world)

Henry. He's thinking, I can't stand it when he thinks! Frankenstein, speak! What are your thoughts?

Frankenstein. Thoughts?

Henry. Yes, talk, speak, use the words I have taught you.

Frankenstein. (Gestures to Waldman and Victor) Men . . . mas-ters . . . like—*(Gestures to Henry)*

Waldman. Yes, I see what he means, he's never seen anyone but you, he thought you were the only other man—

Frankenstein. Other-er?

Henry. The only MAN, you mean.

Frankenstein. Man . . . other man. But Fran-ken-stein—*(Gives it up)*

Henry. Well, go on.

Frankenstein. Man talk. Fran-ken-stein talk. *(Looks at hand)* Hand like . . . *(Looks at their hands)* hand. Fran-ken-stein not . . . man.

Henry. Of course not. You are not a man . . . a master . . . you must never think such thoughts or I shall punish you. *(Frankenstein cringes)*

Waldman. You are not a man, but you are like a man.

Frankenstein. (Eagerly). Like? Like?

Henry. (Feverishly drawing Waldman aside). Doctor, you must not say such things. There is no mirror in this house, I have destroyed them all. He doesn't know that he's like US—if he did! Don't you see it's hard enough to control him?

Waldman. You cannot keep this up, Henry. There is Mind there. And remember, though he has every right to hate you, you have none to hate him.

Frankenstein. (Overhearing). Hate? Hate? *(They turn and are silent)* Hate . . . hurt . . . *(Glaring at Henry)* hurt Fran-ken-stein.

Victor. (Turning to window). God, I can't stand this.

(Frankenstein slouches down in chair, face to audience)

Henry. (Wildly). You see how impossible it is. I know I oughtn't to hate him, Dr. Waldman, but he's part of me and I hate myself. He oughtn't to exist. It would be no sin, no sin I tell you, and it's the only way . . .

(Grasps Frankenstein's throat from behind, chokes him)

(Screams)

He's worse than a corpse, a corpse mustn't walk and talk, a corpse mustn't THINK—

(Victor from window, Waldman from fireplace, rush on Henry, shouting, but before they reach him, Frankenstein grasps his wrists, throws him off and almost to floor and rises—fully erect for first time. Henry staggers to feet)

His hands are like steel, he could kill us all.

Frankenstein. (Fiercely, questioning but questioning triumphantly) Kill? KILL? KILL!!

Henry. (Recovering himself, picks up whip, strikes Frankenstein violently with butt) Slave; dog! How dare you throw me down?

(Frankenstein steps back, shrinks a little but does not cringe as before)

Frankenstein. Throw down! *(Touches himself, points to master and then to floor)* Mas-ter! Down! *(He pulls himself up as others watch him fascinated and alarmed)* Hand! Like Man and . . . arm—*(Feels his arms and body, looking at them, feels his chest, measures the others with his eyes and he slowly realizes his own size and strength)*

Henry. (Raising whip) Down—down on the ground!

(Frankenstein, looks at him with hate, meditating defiance, then crouches slowly, unwillingly, like lion before trainer)

(Noise of horses outside)

Victor. There's a carriage!

Waldman. The Baron!

Henry. (Hastily). Go in there, Frankenstein *(Frankenstein rises sullenly, turns to window)*

Frankenstein. Fire, great fire—sun.

(Henry raises whip, pointing)

(Cowering)

No . . . dark.

(Henry strikes him)

(Snarling)

Sun. Beau-ty.

(Henry raises whip again, Frankenstein with renewed snarls and looks of hate shambles off. Henry hastily locks and bars the door and throws whip in corner as Baron enters)

Waldman. Ah. Baron, your son has come back.

(Baron stops, horrified, as Henry turns to him)

Baron. My God!

Henry. Father—

Baron. *(After long look, turns on Waldman)*. And this is what you make of your students, Dr. Waldman! A fine healthy lad I sent you, and now, the boy looks like a maniac.

Victor. I said he'd—he'd been overworking, Baron.

Baron. *(Turning on Victor)*. I went to that lecture place where you told me Henry had gone, and an old professor with whiskers said—*(Imitates German accent)* he hadn't been near his classes in weeks and spends all his time up here. *(To Henry)* Where were you this morning, Sir?

Henry. I was reading, father.

Baron. But that door was locked, and Dr. Waldman here said you weren't here. *(To Waldman)* If you'd let me give that door a few healthy kicks I'd have saved myself a walk down that confounded hill. *(To Henry)* Why do you have your rooms barred with that great thing as though it were a strong-box?

Henry. To prevent myself being disturbed . . . students, you know—

Baron. What in the devil is this great whip doing here?

(Picks up whip)

(Waldman and Victor alarmed)

Henry. It belongs to a carter, who has been doing some odd jobs about the house. He forgot it when he left. *(Baron drops whip)*

Baron. Dr. Waldman, are you sure you didn't know the poor lad was here all the time? Were you trying to keep his father from seeing him?

Henry. I was asleep, father, I was enjoying a most refreshing sleep.

Baron. You look it. *(To Waldman)* It seems to me, Sir, that when a father comes all this distance to visit his son, he's not to be fobbed off and lied to because the lad's asleep.

Waldman. I was at fault, Baron, I owe you an apology.

Baron. *(To Henry)*. But you said just now you were reading!

Henry. Yes, I had been asleep, then I picked up a book.

Baron. My reception here seems a little strange.

Henry. Father, there was no discourtesy intended. Tell me the news from home. How are mother and Katrina?

Baron. Little thought you've given to your mother and sister—you might have cheered Katrina with a letter. She was sure you were ill, she gave me no rest until I agreed to drive over with Victor. But are they the only people at Belrive you care to ask after?

Henry. I hope Amelia is well.

Baron. Much you seem to care about that too! Thirty miles to Belrive and you've never been back once in five months to see her—or us. This damned University has played the devil with you. But I'm here to take you home and let you lead a normal quiet life—

Henry. Father, I'd give anything—to go back home with you, but I can't. Not now.

Baron. And why not, Sir?

Henry. I have most important work to do. It's impossible.

Baron. *(Enraged, to Waldman)*. You've made a nervous wreck of my boy in this damned pest hole, you've taught him lying and deceit by your own example. Is this how you teach him obedience? He's coming home with me, not for a rest but to stay there, and may God forgive you for what you've done to him in Goldstadt! *(To Henry)* Sir, I give you five minutes to pack your things, the horses and carriage are outside. And there's someone else outside whom I'd never have permitted to come here had I known of the filthy mess you've made of yourself. So this is what they call the new learning—this is education—

Henry. (Hysterical). Why do you come here to torture me, why do you talk of home and happiness and the peace I've thrown away?

Waldman. Baron, if I might speak with your son alone—

(Knock at door rear—they all turn. Enter Amelia)

Amelia. May I come in? *(Silence) (Shocked at his appearance)* Henry! Henry!

Henry. (Speaking quietly). Father, don't judge me, don't judge my friends. You cannot understand. I beg one thing, since you have brought Amelia here, leave me alone with her!

Waldman. (Taking Baron's arm). Baron, I understand your very justified indignation, but the truth is experiments in natural science have overwrought your son. We have all done our best to get him to take a rest, I myself a few weeks ago was urging him to go home, etc. . . .

(Walks Baron out L.)

(Victor looks from Amelia to Henry and to door R. anxiously)

Amelia. Go after them, Victor, help to calm the Baron.

(As Victor hesitates)

Do go!

(Exit Victor L. after last look at door R.)

(Pause. They look at each other)

Amelia. (At length) Henry . . .

Henry. Nothing's the matter with me, Amelia. I've been working too hard, that's all.

Amelia. (Looking at him). Something HAS happened to you here, something terrible.

Henry. (Coming a little closer). Nothing has happened to you, you're just the same—just as lovely as when we said goodbye by the lake at Belrive.

Amelia. That was five months go.

Henry. Five months! It was five years ago, it was five centuries ago. Oh, God, Amelia, why did you come here? *(Turning from her)*

Amelia. (Choking back tears). I'm sorry that I came, Henry, the Baron thought you would be glad to see me.

Henry. No, I'm not glad to see you, Amelia, you're like an angel from heaven who comes to a soul in hell, to remind him in his torment of the heaven he has thrown away.

Amelia. (Comes up to him, gently insistent). What has happened to you, Henry?

Henry. Don't ask me, I could never tell you.

Amelia. We always told each other everything.

Henry. I've done something that can't be told.

Amelia. You have suffered a great deal.

Henry. Nothing compared with what I suffer now, when I see before me all that I love and all that I have lost.

Amelia. You do still love me, then?

Henry. I am a man who must never speak of love.

Amelia. Henry, I love you, always.

Henry. Don't, Amelia, please, please! *(Cries)*

Amelia. You need me, Henry, now. You never did before.

Henry. You must never see me again, you must forget me.

Amelia. Henry, you remember that morning by the lake?

Henry. Why do you torture me with that?

Amelia. When I said I loved you—I meant that I loved you for life—whatever happened.

Henry. Yes, but I can't drag you down into the pit with me. When I came here full of ambition, my work was all for you, my experiments were all for you, I wanted to be famous for you, to do great things so you would be proud of me—

(She embraces him, he sobs on her breast)

I've wrecked my own life, but I've decency enough not to wreck yours.

Amelia. (Gently). We'll go back with the Baron, and then we'll go down to our old place by the lake, where you used to show me how far you could throw pebbles when you were a little boy,—you were so proud because you could throw so far,—and you'll tell me then, and we'll face it together.

Henry. Amelia, I know that if you don't give me up, I shall destroy you as well as myself.

(Banging on barred door from within. Frankenstein's hoarse cry is heard. Amelia steps back in alarm. Henry, steps R. shouting, furious)

Silence! Stop that, go back! *(More banging on door)*

Amelia. (Imperatively). Who is in there?

Henry. Amelia, go, go at once, go to my father, leave me, go back to Belrive. Go, go, for God's sake! *(More banging)*

Amelia. No, THIS is your horror, this is what has changed you! Henry, WHO IS BEHIND THAT DOOR?

(With one final smash from within, the locks burst, the bar breaks its fastenings, and the door crashes open, Frankenstein stumbles in. Frankenstein, catching sight of Amelia, stands still staring at her as she stares at him. Henry turns back stage, picks up whip)

Henry. Back, back!

(Raises whip to Frankenstein who pays no attention but continues to stare at Amelia)

Amelia. (With horror). Henry! He looks like you!

(Henry overcome at this, drops whip, staring at Frankenstein)

Frankenstein. Like . . . Mas-ter? *(To Amelia)* You . . . not man. *(Vague questioning sounds meaning 'what are you?')*

(Frankenstein advances slowly, shambling towards Amelia who stands fascinated and horror struck like a bird before a snake)

Fran-ken-stein want—*(Puts out hands)*

Amelia. (Repeats with amazement and horror) Frankenstein!

Henry. (Coming out of his daze). Back, you vile creature, you dare to speak to a woman—

Frankenstein. (Triumphantly). Wo-man! WO-MAN! . . . beau-ty . . . wo-man . . .

Henry. (To Amelia). Go, go, for God's sake.

(Hits Frankenstein with butt of whip on head, Frankenstein unheeds this, but continues to gaze hungrily at Amelia who runs through outer door)

(Screaming)

Down, down at my feet. *(Frankenstein contemptuously flings him off)*

Frankenstein. Wo-man . . . Frankenstein want—

Henry. Flame—at your master's feet.

(Frankenstein looks at him unmoved. Henry, afraid, starts toward door. Frankenstein, with sudden leap, catches and drags him back)

Frankenstein. Master! Where is the woman?

(Shakes him. Henry gasps almost inaudibly, "down at your master's"—)

(Frankenstein ironically, fiendishly)

Master! Master! I am YOUR master now.

(Shaking him as curtain falls)

CURTAIN

Act Two

Scene: Main hall of the Baron's house at Belrive. Folding windows rear, look out on balcony, treetops and distant view of lake and mountains. Doorway R. open to stairs. Door closed L. Couch R. Cage with three doves at Rear window, table with bowl containing water L. rear, chairs, etc.

Time: Several weeks later.

Amelia and Victor are standing at window rear looking out over lake.

Amelia. (Turning, coming down) She loves you.

Victor. (Following) But dear Amelia, it's you I want to talk about, you and Henry. Today of all days . . .

Amelia. Katrina loves you.

Victor. I love her too, everybody loves her. But she's too good for just ordinary life, she's different from other people, it's impossible to think about things like marriage, and children.

Amelia. While you and Henry were at the University she grew up. You don't realize that. She's not a child.

Victor. It seems to me she'll always be a child, or an angel. At any rate, not a woman.

Amelia. She adores Henry so, too. Now I am taking him away and she'll only have her father and mother.

Victor. It will be lonely for her. But YOU'LL come HERE. SHE'LL visit YOU. I think you're playing a trick on me, with all this.

Amelia. What do you mean?

Victor. You began to talk about Katrina to stop my talking about Henry.

Amelia. Well, what have we to say about Henry? *(Nervously)* He's still your best friend, don't you want me to marry him?

Victor. Of course, if you are happy. I'm not going to bring up MY love, my feelings for you. You wanted him before when he was strong and ruthless and could command your love; you want him now when he is weaker than I was and more dependent on you.

Amelia. AREN'T you bringing up your feelings?

Victor. I'm sorry. Only—

Amelia. Only what?

Victor. Well, this marriage has come up so suddenly. You were going to wait six months. Then you write to Goldstadt and tell me it is at once . . . it came as a sort of shock.

Amelia. That was last week, and the wedding is today. If you've anything to say against Henry, you've waited rather to the eleventh hour, haven't you?

Victor. (Hurt) How could I have anything to say against Henry?

Amelia. (Slightly hysterical) Of course I know what it IS. This . . . this mystery. Victor, let me tell you I don't want to find out things from you, though I know that you know them. I'm proud enough not to want to know anything about Henry that he doesn't want to tell me.

Victor. (Giving her a little hug) It will be all right. All THAT is over.

Amelia. All that . . . no, I'm not asking you, don't say anything.

Victor. I only meant that insane spell of work, that broke down his nerves, and his health.

(Enter Baron, shooting coat, gun etc., and Katrina R. Katrina, 19, grave, childlike, fair, fragile, walks with slight limp)

Baron. (Genially) (Puts gun & game bag in corner) Well said Victor Moritz! That nest of lunatics and priests would poison anybody's mind, and I take some small credit to myself for going back there with you and getting him out of their clutches.

Victor. (Laughs) Goldstadt never did me any harm, Baron.

Baron. You! Their devilment rolled off YOU like water off a duck's back. I know the reason. You don't read their books, and you never listen to their infernal lectures. *(Goes up to Amelia, kisses her, arm around her)* This is what my boy needs, and now he's going to get it. You should see what they're doing to our old church, in your honor!

Katrina. They are filling it with flowers, masses of them! Mother is showing the women how to arrange everything. They are making a bower for you and Henry to stand under, and garlands round the pillars. I've never seen anything so beautiful.

Amelia. (Touched) You are being so good to me, even your village women. And I am taking Henry away from you.

Katrina. Not so very far away. And we'll be busy looking after each other, father and mother and I.

(Enter Henry L., no longer the wild dishevelled youth of Act One, properly dressed and comparatively calm)

Baron. (Who senses something strange about Henry but misunderstands it) Cheer up, my boy, getting married isn't like being hanged.

Amelia. (Laughing) A gallant speech, Baron.

Baron. (To Amelia) Men are all like this. There's something inside us that makes us all dread the altar. Have you ever seen how an ox pulls back on the rope when you try and drag him into the slaughter house.

Katrina. (Slightly shocked) You know father's little ways, Victor.

(Henry crosses to Amelia, puts arm around her)

Baron. Ah—our love birds. Well, I must change my coat for the wedding. Are you coming, Victor?

(Exit Baron and Victor)

(Henry remains standing, arm around Amelia R. Katrina L. Katrina looks at them)

Katrina. I've been so busy at the church, and now I'm afraid they'll be waiting for me with the dress. There were two more little things I told them not to do until I came, and then you are to come and try it on.

Amelia. But we need not dress just yet.

Katrina. I know. But I must be sure it is perfect. Everything must be perfect for Amelia. *(Exit L.)*

Henry. Then come back and let me see you!

Amelia. Oh no, I think it ought to be a surprise for you. You won't know your country Amelia at the altar, dressed up like a great lady from Versailles or Vienna. The trouble Katrina has taken—the stuffs from Paris—the consultations—

Henry. Then you MUST come back. Too many people will be in the church, I shan't be able to admire you. I'll be too nervous, anyway. Besides, I want to tell Katrina how beautifully she has done it.

Amelia. Henry, she's worked so hard, with those two old seamstresses—as though it were to be her own wedding dress. She wouldn't even let me help. She—Henry, I've been talking to Victor.

Henry. (Quickly) What about?

Amelia. Katrina. He does love her, but I wish he loved her differently. He thinks of her as something scarcely human.

Henry. I know, Amelia. *(Going to cage)* Nothing would make me so happy, but it will never be. She's not a woman to him, I think she never will be to any man. She's—like one of her own doves.

Amelia. But that's wrong. Life can't be like that. She loves him.

Henry. Katrina, as a wife? Victor idealizes her.

Amelia. But—? I'm glad I'm not your ideal.

Henry. My wife, today, this afternoon, in a few hours. *(Kisses her)*

Amelia. Happy?

Henry. Terribly.

Amelia. Not afraid?

Henry. Not of anything.

Amelia. Neither am I. *(Kiss)* And there are to be no more of those terrible studies?

Henry. *(Agitated)* No, never. Don't talk about them, Amelia, I can't bear it.

Amelia. Of course I won't. But you're sure you'll be happy, just with me?

Henry. Only with you, only with you. There can be no other happiness, no other life, I couldn't live without you. That's a thing lovers say, but it was never so true before.

Amelia. Somehow I can't think of you as a little country squire, settling down on the place the Baron has given us, with a squire's small interests, hunting and cattle and tenants.

Henry. It will be peace, it will be heaven. We shall have each other. And there will be books; poetry, romance, history. But no science, no SCIENCE! And in the years to come, we shall have our children.

Amelia. Yes.

Henry. You're sure you're not still worried, about . . . that time?

Amelia. No.

Henry. You came back and saved me, but for you I should have gone out of my mind.

Amelia. Even though it happened four months ago, I still wake up at night and see that man. Sometimes he is looking at me, in your rooms, and sometimes groping past me as I stood behind the wall before Victor found me.

Henry. Don't, don't, please.

Amelia. It doesn't matter now. Let's go down to the lake, where you first told me you loved me. There will be so much excitement as soon as we leave here—you won't seem to belong to me at all.

Henry. Until we are alone again tonight.

(Enter Katrina with flowers)

Amelia. Oh, the dress—I can't go.

Katrina. *(Smiles at her)* You may, for a few minutes. Then come up to my room.

(She begins arranging flowers in bowl. Knock without, enter Maid with Dr. Waldman. He is talking)

Waldman. But it is *Henry* Frankenstein I wish to see, pray do not disturb—

Katrina. I am Henry's sister. Can I do anything?

(Exit Maid)

Waldman. You are the little Katrina?

Katrina. And you are Dr. Waldman—You want to see Henry?

Waldman. Please. Where is he?

Katrina. He has just gone down to the lake.

Waldman. Alone—is he alone?

Katrina. Amelia is with him.

Waldman. Is the wedding over?

Katrina. No, it is this afternoon, you are just in time.

Waldman. Thank Heaven.

(Victor comes in)

Victor. Dr. Waldman.

Waldman. Victor Moritz!

Victor. You look exhausted. Katrina, send Helene with some wine.

Katrina. I'll bring it. *(Exits R.)*

Victor. Let me take your cloak. Have you ridden today from Goldstadt?

Waldman. Goldstadt, without a halt.

Victor. You wrote Henry you couldn't come. What has—

Waldman. They must not be married, my son.

Victor. Why not? Do you mean—

Waldman. They must not be married.

Victor. But it's too late, everything is arranged. Father, even if what Henry did was a mortal sin, as you think, there must be forgiveness. They love each other.

(Enter Katrina with tray, bottle of wine and glasses—which she puts on table)

Katrina. Now I'll go find Henry for you, Dr. Waldman.

(Exits on balcony. Victor pours glass of wine for Dr., which he sips, sitting exhausted in chair)

Waldman. How much have you told Henry of what has been going on these past four months? If it comes to that, how much do you know?

Victor. Only what you told me about these attacks and murders. But there has been no conclusive evidence.

Waldman. There is evidence enough now. I have just learned more. Have you told him that this monster is still alive, preying upon innocent—

Victor. It would send him out of his head. They have been trying, with Amelia's help, to bring him back to health, to make him forget.

Waldman. Amelia's parents are dead. You love her too, therefore the responsibility for her fate is partly yours. *Forget!* while this monster lives.

Victor. God cannot be the Old Testament tyrant you think Him. God is Love, God is mercy.

Waldman. He is also just. Sin must be punished.

Victor. You loved Henry, once.

Waldman. I love him now. But a curse is on him, he must not bring upon an innocent girl the sin that is his own burden.

Victor. But this monster may be dead! You said he was living in glaciers among the mountains. Then he cannot get food. This horror cannot last, Dr. Waldman.

Waldman. I am afraid that this horror is just beginning.

(Conversation heard as Henry, Amelia and Katrina come up the invisible balcony steps)

Victor. *(Hands to lips)* Amelia and Henry! Have mercy!

(Enter Henry and Amelia from balcony)
(Henry stops in surprise and violent agitation, which he tries to conceal)

Henry. Dr. Waldman! So you did come? I'm glad.

Waldman. My dear Henry! *(Takes his hand)*

Amelia. Dr. Waldman, do you remember me? I saw you for a moment in Henry's rooms. This is a great compliment, we never supposed you could have spared the time. *(Waldman kisses her hand. She senses tension, looks from one to the other. Seems about to speak, then hesitates and says at length)* Is anything wrong?

Henry. Of course not, darling, what could be wrong?

Katrina. (After a pause) Come dear, it's time for you to dress. *(They go out)*

Henry. (Pleadingly, agitated) It's most kind of you to come, Dr. Waldman. You HAVE come for the wedding, haven't you? I mean, there isn't any bad news, is there?

Waldman. My poor Henry, you know before you ask.

Henry. The creature has come back to Goldstadt?

Waldman. Victor Moritz seems to have told you nothing.

Henry. I dared not ask. I hoped he was dead.

Waldman. He has become a scourge of God, a terror, a destroyer.

Henry. But where is he, how does he live, what does he do?

Waldman. He lives anywhere, in the mountains, among the glaciers. For food, he preys upon the remote cabins of woodcutters, seizes their beasts, tears them to pieces and devours them, without fire, like an animal.

Henry. Did you know this, Victor?

Victor. I heard stories. I couldn't be sure it was the same.

Henry. Perhaps then it will live as an animal, die as an animal, never show itself where men and women live . . .

Waldman. You have not heard the worst.

Victor. (Pleads) He is being married today, and there is nothing he can do, NOTHING.

Waldman. (Unheeding) In secluded valleys, on lonely hills, in remote hamlets beyond Goldstadt, there have been murders.

Henry. (Aghast) Murders!

Waldman. Committed by a monster, of inhuman strength and incredible ferocity. The first one was only two weeks after you left. The legend grew, slowly, of this abominable horror in the mountains. No one believed, at first as only a few peasants had seen. Superstition, the authorities thought. But after the third killing, gendarmes were sent. But what could they do? Scale precipices, live in the eternal snows? He has been seen to go up the overhanging sides of Mount Saleve, which no man has ever climbed. This creature's nerves and sinews are of steel, your elixir has given him the strength of ten men. I guessed, I knew. By day and night I prayed for you, Henry. I have talked to the peasants, I have gone to the scenes of some of his crimes.

Henry. (With hoarse cry) MY crimes, MINE.

Waldman. I wondered, could the thing remain an animal, or would it go on developing a MIND? I wondered, but I knew, for even at Goldstadt it was beginning to learn.

Henry. Yes. But who could have taught him since that day when he escaped?

Waldman. Who indeed, when every peasant who has seen him has run in terror? That I cannot tell you. But he has been learning, at least he has developed cunning.

Henry. What am I to do? Oh, Amelia, Amelia!

Waldman. There is something else.

Henry. There can be nothing worse.

Waldman. All the early crimes were committed in the mountains near Goldstadt, but last week there were two attacks, one half way between Goldstadt and Belrive, the second . . . you must have heard of it.

Henry. The wood-chopper who was strangled last week near Borck . . . could that have been . . . then he's near HERE, can he be coming to ME?

Victor. Of course not, that's an absurd idea, he couldn't possibly know where you live.

Waldman. Would it not be natural, that the creature should come and seek out its creator?

Henry. Amelia must never know. He saw Amelia in my rooms. Doctor . . . I didn't tell you, he was chasing her but she hid from him . . . promise me that whatever happens, she shall never know!

Victor. But this is impossible! I'll prove that to you! Since the monster can't talk, ask questions, or read, then how can he ever learn where you live?

Waldman. I don't know, perhaps his movements towards Belrive are coincidence. But even animals have strange instincts. Can a cat ask questions, or read, yet cannot a cat find its way . . . home?

Henry. (With wild laugh) Home!

Waldman. (Sternly) And have you thought that GOD might guide him here?

Henry. That's true. It is my duty. I can force him to obey, I am his master.

(Before he has finished, Frankenstein bursts in door, tattered clothes, covered dirt and mud, shaggy hair, they look at him petrified. He has overheard and now, after glaring at them, he suddenly bursts into a mocking laugh, pointing at Henry)

Frankenstein. Master! *(Laughs again)*

(Frankenstein draws himself up. Henry threatens to strike him, Frankenstein raises hands to strangle Henry, Victor seizes Henry and pulls him back. Henry throws Victor off and advances on Frankenstein again)

Henry. What do you want here?

Frankenstein. Wo-man.

(Henry turns away in horror, Victor whispers to him)

Victor. The servants?

Henry. The men are all in the village, or at the church. *(Victor goes quickly L. & picks up gun) (To Waldman)* My power over him is broken.

Frankenstein. (Imperiously, to Henry) The wo-man! Where is the woman?

Henry. There is no woman here.

Waldman. Frankenstein, mortal woman is not for you.

(Victor L. has Baron's gun, which he raises as Frankenstein, attracted by noise of doves, turns to cage. He watches doves, makes clucking imitative sounds during following scene)

(Waldman throws himself on Victor)

Waldman. In the name of God, I forbid!

Henry. (Crossing to them) Give it to me, this is my task.

(They talk fast, in low voices, repeatedly glancing at Frankenstein)

Waldman. Would you do murder?

Henry. (Hysterically) Murder! I told you at Goldstadt, you can't have it both ways, Dr. Waldman, it is murder to kill man, not a monster without a soul.

Waldman. You cannot give life, and then take it away—

Victor. Then let ME do it. There is no other way, it will save the lives of others.

Waldman. And get you hanged. Who would believe this story?

Victor. (Puts gun down) We are three against one.

Waldman. No, no, you do not know his strength. Remember what he did to Henry. We must keep him with us, somehow, not let him get away into the hills, until he sleeps. Then chains. These murders can be brought home to him; he will be judged mad, confined in an asylum.

Victor. Yes, that's the best way, we must try that.

(Frank, turning away from cage, remembering, threateningly)

Frankenstein. Wo-man, my mas-ter!

(Enter Baron L. Stops amazed seeing Frankenstein)

Baron. *(Sputtering)* Who . . . what . . . who is this fellow? And my old friend the priest, from Goldstadt.

Waldman. I rode over to see my old pupil, Baron.

Baron. We're getting him out of your clutches for good, Sir, and I think you'll agree that a normal, healthy life at home—*(Looking at Henry)* Henry, what the devil's the matter with you? And who let this lout in here? *(Advancing on Frankenstein)* What do you want, fellow?

(Frankenstein glares at him, does not answer, Baron raises his stick. Frankenstein raises his hands in strangulation gesture, as the others leap forward)

Waldman. Baron!

Henry. Father! You don't understand, this man is our friend!

Baron. *(Lowers stick, turns astonished)*. Your friend?

Victor. Yes, Baron, at the University, at Goldstadt.

(Baron looks from Frankenstein to others and bursts out into hearty laughter)

Baron. So, an old school-fellow! *(His instincts of hospitality struggle with his amazement and disgust, but he manages to speak with fair civility to Frankenstein)* Your pardon, Sir, I see there has been some mistake. You are welcome to my house, as a friend of my son.

(Frankenstein stares at him, he turns away uneasily and impatiently)

(To Henry)

Well, am I not to have the honor of an introduction?

Henry. Pardon, Father, this is . . . this is . . .

Baron. Well, don't you know his name? *(To Frankenstein)* What is your name, Sir?

Frankenstein. Fran-ken-stein!

Baron. Frankenstein! *(To Henry)* What the devil does he mean? I ask him his name and he says Frankenstein . . .

Frankenstein *(Suddenly moving about wildly)* Drink, drink!

(Baron watches him amazed, others anxious)

(Frankenstein looks about, sees flowers in bowl, takes them from bowl, dashes them on floor, picks up bowl, drinks greedily. Puts bowl down)

Baron. *(Laughs)* Come, Sir, no guest in my house drinks water!

(Takes glass and bottle from tray, pours out glass, walks up to Frankenstein holds him out glass with slight bow. Frank clumsily takes glass, spilling a little, sniffs it suspiciously, drinks it, with lightning movement grabs bottle from Baron's other hand and drinks that down. Baron angrily retreats and turns to others)

Henry. *(Involuntary—ejaculation of rebuke)* Frankenstein!

Baron. *(Losing temper)* Is this some jest at my expense, gentlemen? Are those the manners of the young gentlemen at the University, Dr. Waldman? *(To Frankenstein)* And what the devil do you mean, Sir, by bellowing out "Frankenstein" when I ask you who you are? Haven't you got a tongue in your head? *(Turning to Henry)* And you, sir, did I not hear you call him "Frankenstein" just now?

Victor. Let me explain, Baron. *(Walking him away, speaking quietly)* This poor fellow is a lout who attached himself to Henry at Goldstadt. He's a little touched—*(Tapping forehead)* People call him Frankenstein's man, so that's why he calls himself Frankenstein.

Baron. Hasn't he got a name?

Victor. No one knows who he is. He's evidently followed Dr. Waldman here.

Baron. Then I shall thank Dr. Waldman to take him away. *(Looking at Frankenstein closely)* God, what a monster . . . He looks like a man who's been dead and turned half rotten.

(Waldman crosses himself)

(Frankenstein who has been holding bottle, throws it out of window, begins lurching about)

Frankenstein. Good. *(Advances on Baron)* More!

Baron. Oh, no, my friend, one bottle of THAT drink is more than sufficient.

Frankenstein. (Questioning) Drink? Drink is . . . wa-ter.

Victor. That was wine.

Frankenstein. (Fiercely to Baron). Wine! More wine! *(A little maudlin, but with commanding force to Baron)* Wine! *(To Henry)* Wo-man!

Baron. WOMAN? What does he mean? Where does he think he is? he may treat my house as a tavern if he likes, but now he's going a little too far. Wine—wo-man—song, eh, my beautiful? *(To Dr. Waldman)* You'll stay for the wedding, of course, and lend a little ecclesiastical reinforcement to our village priest. *(To Frankenstein)* Come now, you whatever your name is, you must clear out of here and go back to Goldstadt, and don't call yourself Frankenstein, do you hear me? It's my name and my son's, not yours, and it's an old name too, do you see those coats of arms up there? *(Points to escutcheon on wall)* If you haven't got a name, make one up for yourself.

(Frank glares at him malevolently and advances, Baron withdraws a step)

Victor. Please, Baron, you mustn't cross him. I'm afraid he's . . . dangerous.

Baron. Dangerous, eh? Well, I fancy there are enough of us here to handle him.

Waldman. Baron, believe me, his strength is superhuman.

Baron. Well I don't want all the furniture smashed up and all the women in the house upset, but what in God's name are we going to do with him?

Frankenstein. (With sudden cry) Where is the woman?

Baron. (In rage) How dare you?

(Rushes at him—general scuffle. Frankenstein looks about him cunningly, pauses, as though making up his mind, then turns and rushes out R.)

Victor. Come, come, we must not lose sight of him!

(Henry, Victor, and Waldman go out hurriedly R.)

(Enter Katrina L.)

Katrina. Father! What's all the noise about?

Baron. Some lout who followed that old priest here—they say he's a little gone in the head and that he attached himself to Henry, at Goldstadt. Apparently at that university they breed not only mad professors and atheists, but idiots as well. Nearly knocked me over. They've run out to catch him.

Katrina. (She is untying boxes, removes wedding wreath from one) Oh poor fellow. What will they do to him?

Baron. Lock him up until after the wedding I suppose. I'd better help them. Don't let our bride see him, she might get nerves.

Katrina. (Laughs) Oh, but don't you remember the old legend, Father, that an idiot at a wedding brings good luck?

(Baron goes off. Katrina following. Frankenstein appears, climbing over balcony. Searches room with swift motions like a panther, finally stops before cage of doves. Is interested again, looks from them to birds outside in sky, roughly pulls open door takes one (the artificial one) carries it to balcony, crushing it in great hands, throws it in the air)

Frankenstein. Fly, bird, fly, fly! *(To his astonishment it falls) (Pointing down)* Bird fall! Water! Shining water!

(Turns gazes puzzled at birds in cage.)

(Enter Katrina; who goes up to him and touches his arm gently)

(After pause, wonderingly)

You . . . not fear?

Katrina. Who are you?

Frankenstein. Fran-ken-stein.

Katrina. (Misunderstanding) Yes, that is our name. You didn't mean to frighten them.

Frankenstein. (Shakes head) Frighten? Fear?

Katrina. I knew that! Why have you come to us?

Frankenstein. Mas-ter . . .

Katrina. Master? Do you mean Henry, my brother?

Frankenstein. Man . . . mas-ter . . . not mas-ter now. *(Draws himself up half-laughing, raising hands in strangling motion) (Wonderingly, as She does not show terror)* all men fear . . . *(Touches his breast)*

Katrina. Why should I fear you?

Frankenstein. Other wo-man fear.

Katrina. What other woman—Amelia? Have you seen her? *(In distress)* Oh, you must not frighten her today. If I could only make you understand. *(He waits dumbly)* It's just that you don't understand, and I'm so sorry for you.

Frankenstein. Sorry?

Katrina. Don't you know what sorry means? *(He shakes his head)* Oh dear, how can I make you understand? *(Holds out her hand to him,—He touches it and then the other wonderingly, holds them an instant)*

Frankenstein. No man touch Frankenstein—fear. Hit Frankenstein. Master beat—not *now.* I kill! You woman, you not hate?

Katrina. You mean people hate you?

Frankenstein. Hate Frankenstein. All people. Hurt Frankenstein.

Katrina. I don't hate you, my poor friend.

Frankenstein. Friend?

Katrina. Don't you know what friend is either? Somebody one's fond of. I should like to help you.

Frankenstein. You woman, you beauty like . . . like garden. Like sky. No pain like . . . like other woman.

Katrina. I don't understand you.

Frankenstein. (He is almost on his knees) Help Frankenstein.

Katrina. Of course I will. If only you could go away a little while, just until after the wedding.

Frankenstein. Wedding?

Katrina. Yes, Henry's wedding. Didn't you know? My brother, your friend, he's going to marry Amelia.

Frankenstein. Marry? Other woman? Hate?

Katrina. Yes.

Frankenstein. (Savagely) No.

Katrina. Yes, today.

Frankenstein. No! Frankenstein master now. Frankenstein mate. Frankenstein woman.

(As he moves about Katrina suddenly sees cage)

Katrina. (With little cry) Oh, my dove! How did it get out? *(To Frankenstein)* There were three, the cage door was shut.

(Frankenstein points to cage, points outside)

I see, you took it, you let it fly. You wanted to be kind, but I'm afraid some wild bird will kill it.

Frankenstein. (Walking to balcony) Not fly. *(Points down)*

Katrina. It fell down?

Frankenstein. (Looking) Wa-ter . . . shin-ing wa-ter.

Katrina. You mean it floated along the water? Oh, I see, you didn't mean to, but your hands are so strong. *(Cries)* It's all right, I know you meant no harm.

Frankenstein. (With lateral motion of hand, conveys picture of dove floating) On Wa-ter. Like leaves. Beau-ty. Shin-ing wa-ter. *(Looks at her)* Eyes . . . wa-ter.

Katrina. Tears. I am so fond of my doves.

Frankenstein. Tears? *(Fingers to his own eyes)*

Katrina. Then you are sad sometimes, too? *(Frankenstein nods)*

Frankenstein. Wa-ter. Tears. Pain. *(Turns again, looks down from balcony)* Bird—wa-ter—*(Repeats floating gesture)* That beau-ty too.

Katrina. You saw it floating on the water. Perhaps it's not dead but only hurt.

Frankenstein. Hurt.

Katrina. Perhaps I could find it—*(Goes towards balcony and stops)* Where did it fall? *(He makes vague downward gesture)* You must come with me, down to the lake.

Frankenstein. Lake . . . water.

Katrina. (Half distracted) Yes. Don't you understand? I cannot leave you here. Amelia is putting on her wedding gown, she's coming down here any moment. She mustn't see you—if she's frightened of you. And if the men come back and find you here—there'll be a lot of noise.

Frankenstein. (Wondering) Frankenstein . . . with you?

Katrina. (Holds out her hand with a smile) Yes of course. We'll find my dove and then you must stay away until after the wedding. *(As they go off)* See there's my little boat, we'll take that, it can't have floated far. *(She walks along the balcony out of sight)*

Frankenstein. (Looks down at lake) Wa-ter . . . bird . . . beau-ty . . . friend.

(Exit Frankenstein, following Katrina)

(Baron marshals in Waldman & Victor, R., talking as they enter. He is in jovial mood, laughing and amused by the adventure)

Baron. No, no, no, I won't have you wandering all about the place looking behind every boulder, like that mad son of mine. Where the devil is Henry now, and what sort of stories do you think will get about the neighbourhood? Do you suppose I want all Belrive to think that an escaped lunatic has terrified me and my whole household? *(Goes to door L. calls loudly)* Amelia! Katrina!

(Amelia's voice: "Yes, Baron")

(Victor & Waldman look at each other, disturbed)

(Baron crosses and calls R.)

Helen! Where the devil is everybody? Helen! *(Pause, he calls to her as he sees her, off)* Bring more wine and some glasses! *(Turns to them)* Can't you see what's happened? Your pet maniac has had enough of us and has gone back to your abode of the higher learning, Dr. Waldman, where you'll find him when you get there. And scaring all the peasants out of their wits along the road. I must say I'd rather you had him on your hands than me.

(Helen enters with tray, puts it down—exits. Baron pours out three glasses)

Thanks Helen, now go find Master Henry. One last glass to toast the bridegroom before we leave.

(Baron & Victor drink—Waldman pretends to)

Tell me, Dr. Waldman, what do you think of our Henry now we've got him away from the University?

Waldman. (Courteously). He looks much better, Baron.

Baron. Better!

Waldman. He was suffering from over-work.

Baron. (Explosively) Overwork! I think you're all mad, over there in Goldstadt. Do people faint from overwork? There he was, in a dead faint on the floor of his lodgings. And in comes Amelia in hysterics, with Victor. Well, the plain uneducated countryman put them all in the carriage and drove straight back here to Belrive.

Waldman. (With great effort) Baron, about this marriage—

Baron. Yes, what about this marriage? Where is the bridegroom? We must be down in the Village in less than an hour. We mustn't keep my wife waiting for us at the Church. A simple country wedding, Doctor, just our own parish priest, a few neighbors will be driving over, and all the village people and the tenants . . . *(Victor gets up restlessly and sits again)* What's the matter with you, boy?

Victor. Nothing, Baron, nothing at all, that strange creature upset me a little, perhaps.

Baron. Good God, I should think he had. You too, Dr. Waldman, you might be a pair of mourners at a funeral. Come, another glass, Father.

Waldman. No thank you.

Baron. Victor? *(Victor shakes his head) (He pours himself more wine)* You'd better go and find Katrina and see if the girls are ready. These women take so much time over last minute frilling and God knows what . . .

Victor. (Rising alarmed) Where is Katrina?

Baron. She started out with me, then went back to Amelia.

(Victor starts out L. door, stops as Maid crosses stage quickly from R. to balcony)

Maid (In great alarm) Oh master, master, I saw him—with something white—

(What she sees from the balcony makes her recoil horrified with scream. She retreats into room)

Baron. What's the matter?

(Enter Frankenstein from balcony carrying the drowned Katrina, her body dripping water. He steps into the room, stands looking about him bewildered, dazed)

(The men rush up to him, Victor pulls out couch, they take body and put it down. Waldman kneels by body testing it for sign of life, crosses himself)

Oh God, no—not that! Oh, my child!

Waldman. Go to your mistress, don't let her come in. *(Exit Maid L. crying)*

Baron. Can nothing be done?

Waldman. My poor friend!

Baron. (Sobbing) My child. *(Stumbles towards door R., stops, turns on Frankenstein)* How did this happen?

(Frankenstein looks at him dumbly, makes no answer)

Victor. There's no use asking him now, he doesn't understand.

Baron. I must go to the Church—to my wife—my poor wife—

(Exit Baron, R.)

(Enter Henry, running R., almost colliding with Baron as he comes in)

Henry. I saw him with Katrina in his arms, what has he done to her, what has he done to her?

(Flings himself by body)

(Frankenstein standing dumbly begins to cry)

(Henry looks up)

Can nothing be done? *(Waldman shakes his head)*

Victor. (To Frankenstein) How did this happen?

Frankenstein. Not speak . . . why?

Henry. *(Looking up fiercely)* What did you do to her, fiend, devil?

(Waldman turns away, kneels by corpse in prayer)

Frankenstein. She touched . . . *(Holds out hand)* we go . . . wa-ter . . .

Victor. You were in the boat with her?

Frankenstein. *(Shakes head) (Makes motion of pushing)* Boat float . . . like leaves . . . like bird . . shin-ing wa-ter . . . *(With gesture of picking her up)* She beau-ty—I want her float—on shin-ing wa-ter . . she not float. Cry. *(Gesture picking her up)* Not speak.

Henry. You murderer, you killed my sister.

Frankenstein. Kill? No, this kill! *(Bringing up hands in gesture of strangling)*

Victor. You drowned her! She's dead, dead! *(Waldman rises)*

Frankenstein. Dead? Fran-ken-stein . . . kill—friend? *(Wildly appealing to Waldman)* Hurt . . . hurt . . . pain . . . *(Hand to head)* Not tell me shin-ing wa-ter kill. She touch . . . she not hate me—

(Breaking down—with wild sobs, sinks beside body)

(Henry crosses to gun, takes it up. Waldman follows, slight struggle. Victor joins. The two force gun away from Henry—Waldman unloads it and throws cartridges out over balcony)

Victor. He didn't know.

Waldman. *(Sternly)* Vengeance is Mine, saith the Lord.

Henry. Yes, but why her, her? Why not me, it was my sin! I am the one who should be punished!

Waldman. You are being punished, my son.

Henry. *(Rushing at Frankenstein . . . kicks him, strikes him)* Get away, you devil.

Waldman. *(To Victor)* Take her to her room. Leave me alone with him.

Victor. We can't do that, Dr. Waldman.

Henry. Go, go, it was God who sent this thing to find me here—this thing that I made, this thing that has never been born, that I let loose upon the world. You would not let me kill him, then let him kill me!

(Frankenstein scrambles up from floor, snarls at Henry)

Frankenstein. I . . . kill mas-ter!

Henry. *(To Waldman)* It's not his murder, it's mine! Take her away, for God's sake take her away. Take her to her room.

(Waldman & Victor pick up body and carry it off L.)

Henry. Go to Amelia, Dr. Waldman. But tell her it was an accident.

(Frankenstein makes few steps after body, dashing tears from eyes)

Frankenstein. *(To himself)* Kill . . . kill beau-ty . . . kill friend. Why did you not tell me the shining water could kill?

(In following scene Henry has to drag out of Frankenstein the content of his mind because Frankenstein can't talk, but Frankenstein shows that he understands most of what is said to him)

Henry. Frankenstein!

Frankenstein. *(Forgetting Katrina, sidles up to him, menacingly, speaks with savage irony)* Mas-ter! Fran-ken-stein find mas-ter!

Henry. How have you found me? How did you know? *(Frankenstein gives a horrid laugh)* That doesn't matter now. What do you want?

Frankenstein. Find Mas-ter . . . find the wo-man.

Henry. *(Wildly)* Every woman would flee from you in horror, except my sister whom you murdered.

Frankenstein. Fran-ken-stein saw . . . wo-man above—up there.

Henry. That woman is not for you—there can be *no* woman for you.

Frankenstein. Man . . . wo-man. Man . . . mate.

Henry. But you're not a man. Don't you understand that? *(Frankenstein nods)* You know!

Frankenstein. *(Pointing accusing finger)* You . . . you . . . *(With other hand taps his breast)*

Henry. *(Hysterically)* Yes, you know! God gave life to all men, but I, a man, gave life to you! How can you know this?

(Frankenstein with triumphant laugh, takes papers from pocket, hands them to Henry)

(Takes them, looks at them)

My notes. That—that's—my coat. You came back, you stole my clothes, you found these papers—the notes of my experiments, my dissecting, my filthy work—*(Pause, Frankenstein looks at him)* But you have learned to *read*—you *understand* what I did—

(Frankenstein shakes his head)

(Victor returns—says aside to Henry: "She wants to come. I told her not to." Henry nods)

How do you know what these notes are?

Frankenstein. Man read . . . man make Fran-ken-stein know.

Henry. Who was it? What man read my notes?

Frankenstein. Man in field—I make him tell. *(Gesture of hands to throat)*

Henry. Then my secret is known. Who was he? Where did he go? *(Frankenstein makes gesture of throttling something, and then tossing it aside)* *(Understanding)* After he told you, you killed him? *(Frankenstein gurgles and chuckles assent)* *(Looking at papers)* A letter from Amelia—*(Looking at it)* It speaks of our house at Belrive. Then the man told you where I live, how to get here, before you killed him! *(Frankenstein nods)* *(Jamming papers in pocket)* Why do you commit these crimes? You're a beast, not a man, but even a beast kills only for food . . .

Frankenstein. Hate!

Victor. What do you mean?

Frankenstein. Men hate—*(Beating breast)* I hate men.

Henry. You needn't hate men, hate me, it is I whom you should kill. But if all men flee from you except those you killed, how have you learned to understand so much? You filthy mass that moves and talks, who taught you?

Frankenstein. I learn . . . I know . . . man, wo-man, lit-tle men *(Indicating children by holding out hand to show their height)* run . . . Find . . . high up . . . moun-tain . . . house. They not see . . . I see, I hear.

Henry. But how could you see and hear, if they didn't see you?

Frankenstein. Fran-ken-stein . . . out. Men—wo-man—in—not see.

Victor. I can't understand you.

(Frankenstein lies down on floor, shows by pantomime looking through hole in wall, then puts ear to wall)

Henry. I understand. But how could you learn so much?

Frankenstein. *(Getting up)* Great fire come . . . great fire go. *(Holds out hands, ticks off his fingers many times, twelve or fifteen, in effort to count, then stops)*

Henry. For weeks you watched. You heard these people, who didn't suspect the horror that was listening, talking about their daily life, you saw how men eat and sleep, ideas came to you—*(Frankenstein picks up book from table, opens it, looks at it)* Yes, you saw a man reading.

Frankenstein. Man looked . . . spoke words . . . after great fire go . . . then sleep.

Henry. You heard a man reading the Bible to his family . . .

Frankenstein. *(Nods)* Bible! All on knees . . . speaks to man not there . . . great man.

Henry. Evening prayers to God!

Frankenstein. (Nods) Prayer. Who is God?

Henry. You never could understand, He's man's God, not a God of beasts. I made your life with an elixir and a magnetic spark. I am your God, Frankenstein.

Frankenstein. You, my God!

(After a pause Frankenstein indicates by bending with hand to eyes, but without getting down again to floor, his looking through into hut)

I saw man . . . wo-man . . . man . . . mate, bed. You Fran-ken-stein's God . . . Fran-ken-stein pray—God give mate.

Henry. You—pray, to me! I hate you and yet I made you, you are mine, you are part of me. I know how God felt when he made man, and man turned out a filthy mess. He must have hated us and yet . . . we were His responsibility.

Frankenstein. Man . . . mate. Fran-ken-stein . . . al-one.

Henry. But I can't give you a mate.

Frankenstein. Make me mate.

Henry. No.

Frankenstein. Then I kill.

Henry. (Laughs wildly) Kill, that's what I want you to do. Kill me! What have I got left? You've killed my sister—that's practically killing my mother and father. Do you think I can marry Amelia now? Kill me, that's what I want!

(Goes up to Frankenstein, who makes motions of strangling, then stops—looks cunning)

Frankenstein. Kill first, then take your wo-man.

Victor. Good God! Have you thought of that?

Henry. She's not here.

Frankenstein. Yes, here, Frankenstein saw her . . .

Henry. And if I do—what you say—

Frankenstein. Then I take mate . . . go away men who hate . . . mountains . . . sleep leaves . . . No hate . . . not kill you . . . not kill men.

Henry. If I do this . . . you will go away now, keep away from Amelia, from that woman. *(Frankenstein nods)* You will go away now? *(Frankenstein nods cunningly)*

Frankenstein. Go with master. Watch master.

Henry. Victor, I must do it, if it will save her. It will take months! And I might not succeed again.

Frankenstein. Then I kill.

Henry. I can't work any more in Goldstadt, I must get my—God, that charnel house of mine at Goldstadt! Where is the formula? *(Searches through papers—taken from Frankenstein's pocket, finds what he wants)* I must go up into the mountain—*(Frankenstein nods)*

Frankenstein. You go get horses now.

Victor. My God you can't do it again.

Henry. All I can do is get him away from here—to the mountain. Get me that gun. *(Victor slips it to him)* I have cartridges at Goldstadt. In the mountains I can kill him—shoot him—poison—somehow!

Frankenstein. Go! *(Henry staggers. Victor throws arm around him to support him)* You on horse—I follow! *(Frankenstein goes out on balcony)*

Henry. Amelia—

Victor. Dr. Waldman is with her.

(They go out. Frankenstein appears on balcony—waits a second, then gently slides door shut and locks it, starts for door L. Amelia's voice heard calling "Henry". Frankenstein jumps to balcony

and waits crouched half hidden from door L., which She enters, door closing behind her. She is in bridal dress and veil, without wreath, weeping. Starts for balcony calling, "Henry, where are you going?" Meets Frankenstein and jumps back, too terrified to scream)

Frankenstein. Woman!

Amelia. You! What do you want here?

Frankenstein. You! Woman!

Amelia. No! *(Tries to reach balcony, calling, "Henry,"—He catches and holds her back)*

Frankenstein. Master gone—away.

Amelia. I know, I saw him. Let me go, I must follow him.

Frankenstein. No! •

Amelia. I must, oh, don't you see Katrina's dead—*(His hands drop, and she jumps back free, but unable to move by the horror of her discovery.)* You—you are this mystery. You—did you drown Katrina? Victor said it was an accident. Who are you?

Frankenstein. (Draws himself up arrogantly) I—I Frankenstein master. Send him away. *(Suddenly—almost humble)* Wait . . . for you.

(She tries to run, but He seizes her. She screams "Victor, help!", in the struggle He tears off her bridal veil and the top of her dress.

Amelia. Go away. You disgust me, you fill me with horror. Victor, help!

(Between her screams can be heard His whinings and pleadings: "woman" "Mate" "Frankenstein mate". Victor's voice calling "Amelia" in answer to her screams. Someone shakes the locked door R., Victor's voice calls again: "Amelia, let me in." Amelia tears herself away, half dressed and flees through door L. Frankenstein stands half in stupor. Victor again shakes door. Sound of feet on stairs above, and slamming door. Frankenstein rushes out L. sound of heavy feet on stairs and of smashing blows at door above. At this point Victor rushes in balcony window and across to door L. and Baron can be heard knocking and shaking the locked door R. as

THE CURTAIN FALLS.

Act III

Six months later. A hut in the Jura mountains, bare and rough in appearance. There is a window in the wall R., and a large double window waist high in the rear wall, through which are seen mountains and moonlight, later obscured by clouds and lit up by flashes of lightning.

Both doors are in the L. wall. One, backstage, leads into hallway, the other, front, into Henry's bedroom.

Table and two stools L., a lamp on the table, closed chest in alcove R. rear, brazier in which charcoal fire glows R., a number of bottles, papers, retorts, etc. on table. Against the recessed wall R., placed crossways, is a low couch or bier on which lies an inanimate form covered by drapery. Electric machine in shadows against back wall.

The curtain discovers Henry working over a liquid in a retort on the table. He is in rags, long tangled hair, emaciated, at last stages of exhaustion.

He staggers to chest R., takes out papers, returns to table, adds few drops from bottle to elixir in retort, goes back, replaces papers in chest. Then comes to table again and tries to go on working, but sinks on stool, head in hands, then staggers to feet, registers exhaustion and drags himself into his bedroom thru door L. front.

Frankenstein is seen peering through rear windows. Not seeing Henry, he shakes windows in rage, then disappears L., and crash is heard off L. as of outer door being forced. Frankenstein enters thru door L. rear. His hair is longer, his appearance even more frightful than in preceding acts, the same clothes as he wore in Act II, but much torn and ragged. He looks about. Uttering inarticulate sounds of anger. Goes to form in alcove, lifts corner of sheet, looks, makes inarticulate noises. (The audience at no time sees the figure.) Then goes off L. into Henry's room, drags Henry back on stage, points to retort and bottles on table and to covered form in recess.

Henry. Do you want to kill me before I've done it? I'm a man not a monster, I must sleep sometimes. I thought you were a dream, only another filthy dream!

Frankenstein. (In tone of menace and command) Work!

Henry. (Hysterically) Get out. I must have rest, I'm exhausted, I can't go on.

Frankenstein. (Near corpse, makes vague gestures over it) To-night!

Henry. No, not tonight, tomorrow—I'll give her to you tomorrow—

Frankenstein. You say—to-night.

Henry. What difference do a few hours make—I must have rest, my nerves must be steady for the final act—

Frankenstein. To-night . . . her, mate—we go—

Henry. Yes, go with her, forever, you have sworn it, away from me, away from all mankind. *(Frankenstein nods)* All right, demon.

(Starts tinkering with vials on table, goes to chest, takes out bottle, drinks)

Frankenstein. (Advancing on him) Drink!

(Snarling, starts to take bottle, Henry pours out remainder of contents on floor, throws bottle in corner, Frankenstein snarls at him, raises hands in strangling motion)

Henry. (Laughs) Go on, kill me! I wish you would, before I do this thing—*(Frankenstein drops hands)*

Frankenstein. Don't forget—the woman.

Henry. (Sullenly) Get out and I will finish. Then I shall be free, no more your slave—

(Frankenstein shambles towards door R. rear, pauses)

Frankenstein. Fran-ken-stein watch!

Henry. You always watch. When I tried to escape you dragged me back, you tracked me down like a blood-hound—

Frankenstein. When you tried kill me, I took away gun. *(Pausing near body)* No more . . . a-lone. Her . . . no hate . . . no hor-or. *(Draws himself up threateningly, pointing)* WORK! *(Exit)*

(Henry follows him off, can be heard shutting outer door—re-enters, examines liquid in retort, fusses with wires of machine which fizzes and gives off light as before, only more quietly. Goes to chest again, opens it, but as he is taking out paper there is a rap at the window R.)

(Henry starts violently, goes to window, sees Dr. Waldman's face, indicates by sign he is to go to door. Holds up light as he goes towards door, which opens. In rushes Amelia, followed by Waldman and Victor—all cloaked—Her hair blown by wind, all exhausted and excited)

Henry. Are you ghosts?

Amelia. Henry! Henry!

(Goes to him, but draws back, she cannot embrace him. Waldman takes one hand, Victor throws an arm around him)

Henry. My friends. My friends. *(Almost weeping)* How did you find me?

Amelia. Henry. Poor Henry. We searched everywhere. It was the Doctor who finally—

Waldman. No, it was Amelia. She guessed some of the truth. We told her the rest.

Amelia. Poor, Henry. Poor Henry. We went to Goldstadt to find you after—after we buried Katrina.

Waldman. I rode at once to Goldstadt. But you had already gone. Then I went back to them at Belrive—

Henry. But how did you find me? I thought this was the loneliest spot in the Jura Mountains.

Victor. We thought you were out of your mind with grief. We were nearly out of ours.

Amelia. But I knew you'd never leave—your parents—or me—unless there was some, some terrible reason.

Victor. We went everywhere.

Waldman. I heard tales, when at last I reached the little valley below you here, of a strange wild young man who had staggered up the mountain with sacks of books, of instruments.—A mad student, they told me.

Victor. There were other stories—

Henry. About him?

Victor. Yes, the herdsmen had seen him, from the other mountain peaks.

Henry. Yes, he stays near me, he watches me. He has even tried to help. He carried up my books and my machine.

(They stare about them, horrified—Doctor goes near bier)

Waldman. Henry, what are you doing?

Henry. It doesn't matter now. *(He is holding tightly one of Amelia's hands)* It is so good to see you. I have been mad—for months.

Amelia. Poor Henry. Who wouldn't be?

Henry. But how did you come? It takes days!

Waldman. When I was sure, I told them. Then we took horses—Amelia insisted on coming. We've climbed all day—there's a herdsman's hut a few miles below here—

Henry. Old Peter, I've seen him sometimes from a distance. He's a lunatic too, like me. But harmless.

Amelia. Henry, don't talk so.

Henry. . . . And a cripple, so he can't climb up here.

Amelia. Henry, when I guessed, and when they told me, about—about Frankenstein, I wanted to find you. And when—that machine was gone and your books, I knew—what you were doing, and that you were doing it for me—for my safety. So I made Victor bring me.

Henry. Why?

Amelia. Because, if—if it is me he wants, I'd rather—I'd rather he had his way—*(From Henry & Victor at once: "No")* than that you should do again—make again—*(Gesture towards bier)* commit that sin over again. Don't you see it? You can't—you can't—people the world with a race of monsters like him.

Henry. What else can I do—but bring this thing to life? I've tried escape; he catches me, and then tortures me. I've tried to make him kill me, he tells me of the crimes he'll commit and of—My God, if he comes back and sees you here! Get back there—by the door, out of sight of the windows. *(Pushes her towards bedroom door)* I've tried to kill him—he breaks my traps and laughs at me, he took my gun, he carries my knife. He sleeps in some place I cannot find—if he sleeps at all. He never eats food near here, for I have also tried poison. But he watches me every hour.

Amelia. Henry, poor Henry!

(The moonlight has gone—there is faint thunder)

Henry. Having committed some crime, Dr. Waldman, I have no choice but to commit another, perhaps a worse crime. Tonight!

Waldman. What do you mean?

Henry. Amelia has told you—there is the woman; I promised her to him tonight. You saw my first experiment, when I was filled with pride and elation. Now, on another night almost like that, with only despair and horror in my heart *(Breaks down. Amelia soothes him)*

Waldman. *(Simply)* It was God that guided us up here tonight.

Henry. For what? To see the finish of my work? For now I must complete it—he'll find you, he'll kill us—and then—Amelia—

Amelia. It is better than—to set loose on the world a race of—Frankensteins.

(A howl outside)

Henry. Oh God, why did you come? Victor, you'll help me—take Amelia in there, that is my bedroom. Stay there with her, the shutters are barred, he can only enter it through here. He must know someone is with me—you can stay here, Dr. Waldman. *(Exit Amelia reluctantly, and Victor)* Don't you see? There is no other way. *(Takes bottle of fluid, holds it over test tube)* You shall see the last rites—or is it the first? Look! *(Pours one colorless fluid into another colorless one, they burn a bright color. Holds up tube)* My Elixir! *(Flashes and thunder and Frankenstein's face through the window)*

Waldman. My son, you are Satan, the Anti-Christ.

Henry. I have become so.

Waldman. Suppose you fail? You say he will kill us all. Suppose you succeed? Will he keep his word to you, and go away—with his mate—and live gently, doing no harm?

Henry. I do not know. It is my only chance—Amelia's only chance—

(Frankenstein bursts in through window, shattering of glass—more lightning)

Frankenstein. The woman is here. The woman—

Henry. There is your woman—*(Points to bier)*

Frankenstein. No. Not now. The woman—in there—*(Starts towards door. Waldman places himself before it)*

Henry. Your promise—to go away—tonight! *(Frankenstein, towering over Waldman, is about to enter door. Henry raises hand with elixir in it, pours it on brazier. Sharp sudden flash)*. I'll break my promise too!

(Tears up formula, throws bits away. Picks up a heavy bar, smashes at machine. Frankenstein leaps at him, throws him over table, struggle, one quick twist and he throws him to the floor—dead)

(Waldman comes to body, kneels, prays, holding crucifix. Amelia and Victor have rushed in—Amelia clings to Victor. Suddenly Frankenstein throws himself down by body too, sobbing)

Frankenstein. Master—master—not mean kill. Master—not hate you! Woman—no woman for Frankenstein. Alone—*(Beating breast)* Alone.

(Waldman has risen, standing before Victor and Amelia. Frankenstein gets up goes to him—raises arms menacingly. Waldman stands perfectly calmly, facing him)

(Astonished) You . . . not fear . . . You . . . man . . . Frankenstein kill. Hate all men. Master dead . . . You . . . *(Again raises arms—Waldman remains calm, crucifix in hand)* Men fear death . . . I am death.

Waldman. Kill me, if it is God's will. I am not afraid. *(Bows head over crucifix, clasped in hands)*

Frankenstein. What that? I saw—like that—in hut. Man hang on wall.

Waldman. That is the son of God. He was killed—by men who hated him. He died to save all men from death.

Frankenstein. All men. I not man.

Waldman. I don't know what you are. When you killed Katrina you felt pain.

Frankenstein. Yes, pain—pain. Why he not tell me shining water kill. Love Katrina—not like that—love—*(Points towards Amelia)*

Waldman. Pain—that kind of pain is not felt by animals, it comes from the soul. Even when you killed him, you felt pain—*(Points to corpse on floor)* Yet you—I do not understand.

Frankenstein. Soul—what is soul?

Waldman. It is the part of God He gives to every man who lives. It is the part of man God calls back to himself after man dies. *(Frankenstein murmurs: "not man.")* That's why I'm not afraid to die. You can kill the body, but not the soul. Katrina is with God; I think that after all he has suffered, Henry's spirit is with God too.

Frankenstein. Where is God? I thought he—*(Points to Henry)* God—my God.

Waldman. *(Holds crucifix up)* No—God is there. Here—everywhere.

Frankenstein. Your God hate—

Waldman. God loves the birds, the beasts, as well as men.

Frankenstein. Love Frankenstein?

Waldman. Yes. Whatever you are, you have taught me, a priest, something about God. He loves you.

Frankenstein. He—friend?

Waldman. Yes.

Frankenstein. Show—way to Him. Not want . . . kill . . . more.

LIGHTNING

Waldman. I cannot do that. I can only tell you—that you must ask him yourself. Ask His forgiveness for your murders.

Frankenstein. *(Flash of old ferocity)* Men hate me.

(LOUDER THUNDER)

Waldman. Katrina did not hate you. You killed Katrina.

Frankenstein. *(Suddenly sobs loudly, backs towards window, holds up hands)* Katrina . . . Friend . . . God! *(Stretches up arms)* God help me.

(Lightning strikes hut—some of which crumbles. Lamp goes out—darkness but for brazier. Frankenstein falls, dead, face near brazier, look of peace. Amelia screams)

Amelia. Victor. Take me away. Take me away. Victor, don't leave me, don't ever leave me.

(They go out. Waldman lays cross on breast of Frankenstein and slowly follows them)

CURTAIN

Appendix
Music from
Vampire's Victim
(1887)

Richard Butler and H. Chance Newton

Frankenstein; or, The Vampire's Victim (1887)

UNDER THE pseudonym "Richard Henry," Richard Butler and H. Chance Newton, respectively the editor and the theatrical correspondent of *The Referee,* wrote the libretto of *Vampire's Victim.* William Meyer Lutz, who became the musical director of the Gaiety in 1868, composed the music. The text of *Vampire's Victim* exists in two forms: a typescript located in the British Library (LC 53392 B) and a musical score.

The typescript was licensed for performance by the Office of the Lord Chamberlain on 19 December 1887. The text was typed by the International Type Writing Office and consists of 84 leaves in three acts. This total includes four preliminary leaves: one preceding Act 1, on which is typed the list of dramatis personae; one preceding Act 2, on which is typed "'FRANKENSTEIN.' | ACT II.", followed by a stamp that reads: "International Type Writing Office, | 127 Strand, London, W.C."; and two preceding Act 3, the first of which bears a stamp, reading: "International | TYPE WRITING | AND | COPYING CO. | 127, Strand, W.C."; the second leaf bears in type "'FRANKENSTEIN.' | ACT III.'" followed by the same stamp placed on the preceding page of Act 2. Each of the three acts is independently paginated: Act 1: [i] 1–34; Act 2 [i] 1–25; Act 3 [i–ii] 1–21. Typing appears on the rectos only, black ribbon being used for every page except pages [i] and 11 to 27 of Act 2, which are typed with a blue ribbon. Stage directions are underlined in red pencil. The leaves (254 × 206 mm) are of a rough texture and beige in color. They are composed of unwatermarked laid paper with wirelines occurring 17 per 20 mm and vertical chain lines occurring ten to the leaf. Running down the left-hand side of the margin is a vertical line approximately 40 mm wide. This line separates dialogue (on the right) from the character names (on the left). The typescript is bound in a beige cover that bears a white licensing stamp (71 × 59 mm) on which is written an inventory number (273), the title and a description of the play ("Frankenstein | Burlesque &c | 3 acts"), the theatre of debut and the date of licensing. The cover also bears the title: FRANKENSTEIN. | OR | THE VAMPIRE'S VICTIM. | ACT I. The upper right edges of the document are charred, suggesting that it had at least one serious brush with a fire.

C. Jefferys published Lutz's musical score in 1888 (see figure). I have located three copies in the following libraries: Cambridge and Oxford University Libraries, and the Allen O. Brown Collection of the Boston Public Library. The score contains forty-three pieces of music: thirteen solos, two duets (both involving the Creature, one sung with Frankenstein and one sung with the vampire Visconti), one quartet, five choral pieces, three finales (one for each act), and nineteen musical interludes. The musical interludes are as short as a few notes, or as long as several bars. Many interludes serve to set the tone for a character's entrance. Tartina's entrance in Act 1 is announced by two brief measures:

No. 2. MELOS.

The music for an entrance by Frankenstein in Act 2 is similarly brief:

No. 23. FRANKENSTEINS ENTRANCE.

In Act 1, when Frankenstein steps on stage for the first time, the music functions not only to introduce him, but to set the tone of the entire

PERFORMED AT THE GAIETY THEATRE. LONDON.

FRANKENSTEIN

BURLESQUE MELODRAMA,

WRITTEN BY

RICHARD HENRY,

WITH INCIDENTAL SONGS

BY

Robert Martin,

THE MUSIC

BY

W· MEYER LUTZ.

PRICE FIVE SHILLINGS NET.

LONDON.
C. JEFFERYS, 67, BERNERS STREET.

scene. The typescript reads: *"FRANKENSTEIN, appears on mountain. CHORD."* The music for the entrance reads:

Chance and Newton obviously composed their libretto with the intention of wedding it to the music of Lutz at a later date. Thus, the entrance of Frankenstein's servant, Schwank, is followed by the notice, *"SONG SCHWANK,"* below which half of the page has been left blank. (The song, entitled "Oh! what a remarkable mission is mine," appears in Jefferys.) Similarly, the typescript indicates that Frankenstein sings a song entitled "The Magicians" (followed by three-quarters of a blank page), whereas in the score Lutz substituted a song entitled "It's a funny little way I've got" (reproduced below).

Chance and Newton also generalized their stage directions to enable changes in the script. Thus Act 3 opens at the Vampire's Club, with a stage direction that reads: "Short recitative for MONDELICO, now the Vampire's Secretary &c. &c. as thus . . .

> Come bustle-bustle-also look alive
> For very soon our members will arrive."

The actual recitative as published by Jefferys presents a soprano who sings:

To the Vampire Club we all belong
Here we meet to sing a song . . .
We smile and play till dawn of day
Quick and clever sportsmen we.

This song leads in the score to a solo by Frankenstein, entitled "One of the boys." In contrast, the typescript indicates that the song of Mondelico is followed by Maraschino's solo. (A space appears in the typescript for the insertion of the lyrics.) In turn, Frankenstein sings a song with the chorus, followed only then by "One of the boys."

As a consequence of the vagueness of stage directions and of the willingness of the composer and playwrights to allow the play to develop itself freely, songs rarely bear any relevance to the dramatic action. Thus, after a woman is abducted by two Spanish bandits, Frankenstein breaks out in the following song:

I'm a boy that's merry when the chance I get,
I'm vivacious, very always gay, you bet!
If oppres'd by trouble, soon I form a plan
For giving it the double, quick as e'er I can;
And whenever people say, how can you thus defy
All woes and worries day by day, this is my reply.
It's a funny little way I've got,
It's a chummy little way I've got,
It's a funny little, chummy little, rummy little way,
It's a funny little way I've got.

Or in Act 3, after avoiding his Vampire wife, the Creature steps on stage to sing "Sworn in," the music for which is reproduced below.

Obviously then, the songs and musical interludes are intended as set pieces of comedy, individual jewels whose sole purpose is to delight and to entertain the audience rather than to advance the plot. Hence, each act of the play functions as an independent unit. Plot, in the sense of an ordered structure of action, degenerates into the mere juxtaposition of comic scenes without reference to integrity or logical progression. Thus Act 1 concludes when the Creature abducts Frankenstein in Germany, but Act 2 opens in Spain with Frankenstein as first the prisoner and then the leader of two Spanish bandits. Act 2 concludes when the Creature attempts to stab Frankenstein and Visconti, but Act 3 opens at the Vampire Club with the Creature and Visconti leagued against Frankenstein. The finale of each act leads not to a climax of dramatic action, but to a musical number in which the chorus—the pretty Gaiety Girls—and the main characters join in a rousing musical number. I therefore include the Finale of Act 3 of *Vampire's Victim* in which Tartina celebrates her rescue by Frankenstein and a sun goddess.

NOTE

Reproductions of the score derive from a copy at Cambridge University and are made with permission. The British Library reportedly possesses a copy of the score, but efforts on my part failed to locate it. Apparently, the score never returned from the bindery where it was sent in 1981.

both you and me
Allegro moderato
Frank:
now are free
Frank - en - stein your he - ro

Prays that you will make
Send him down to ze - ro
Now so far he's

got
To fur - ther my in - ven - tion, this mon - ster which I've

made I hope your kind at - ten - tion will of - ten then be

Tempo di Polka
paid For to wish to get ap-plause a lot It's a fun-ny lit - tle way I've

got T'is a fun-ny lit - tle sun-ny lit - tle rum-my lit - tle way It.s a

Monster:
fun-ny lit-tle way we've got Bri-tan-nia rules the waves And

I have all my staves so now quite gay I'll march a-way If
3
3

Repeat for Chorus
you ap-prove my piece. And we all hum-bly crave You'll let this show long

End of Third Act

Bibliography

Albert, Maurice. *Les Théâtres des boulevards (1789–1848)*. Paris: Société Française, 1902.

Aldiss, Brian. *Billion Year Spree: The True History of Science Fiction*. New York: Doubleday, 1973.

Aldridge, Owen A. "The Vampire Theme: Dumas Père and the English Stage." *Revue des Langues Vivants* 39 (1973–74): 312–24.

Anoble, Richard J. *Frankenstein*. New York: Universe Books, 1974.

Astle, Richard Sharp. "Structures of Ideology in the English Gothic Novel." Dissertation, University of California, San Diego, 1977.

Bailey, J. O. *Plays of the Nineteenth Century*. New York: Odyssey, 1966.

Baker, Michael. *The Rise of the Victorian Actor*. London: Croom Helm, 1978.

Bancroft, Squire. *The Bancrofts—Recollections of Sixty Years*. New York: Dutton, 1909.

Barker, H. Barton. *The London Stage from 1576 to 1888*. London: 1889. Vol. 2.

———. *Our Old Actors*. London: 1878.

Bassin, Henry. "The Gothic Transformation: Developments in the British Gothic Romance, 1764–1887." Dissertation, Indiana University, 1979.

Bates, Al. "Thomas Edison Created a Monster: Edison's *Frankenstein* is Found." *Clouds* 21 (1979): 8.

Bedford, Paul. *Recollections and Wanderings of Paul Bedford*. London: Routledge, 1864.

Bennett, Betty. *The Letters of Mary Wollstonecraft Shelley*. Baltimore: Johns Hopkins University Press, 1981. Vol. 1.

Bloom, Harold. "Frankenstein; or, The Modern Prometheus." *The Ringers in the Tower: Studies in Romantic Tradition*. Chicago: University of Chicago Press, 1971. 119–29.

———. "The Internalization of the Quest Romance." *The Ringers in the Tower*. 13–35.

Booth, Michael. "East End Melodrama." *Theatre Survey* 17 (1976): 57–67.

———. *English Melodrama*. London: Jenkins, 1965.

———. *Prefaces to English Nineteenth-Century Theatre*. Manchester: Manchester University Press, 1981.

Boujart, Michel. *Frankenstein*. Levallois-Perret: Cercle du Bibliophile, 1969.

Bowerbank, Sylvia. "The Social Order vs. the Wretch: Mary Shelley's Contradictory-Mindedness in *Frankenstein*." *ELH* 3 (1979): 418–31.

Boyd, Alice Katherine. *The Interchange of Plays Between London and New York, 1911–1939*. New York: King's Crown, 1948.

Brantlinger, Patrick. "The Gothic Origins of Science Fiction." *Novel* 14 (1980): 30–43.

Buchen, Irving. "*Frankenstein* and the Alchemy of Creation and Evolution." *Wordsworth Circle* 8 (1977): 103–12.

Bud, Robert, and Gerrylynn K. Roberts. *Science versus Practice: Chemistry in Victorian Britain*. Dover: Manchester University Press, 1984.

Callahan, Patrick. "*Frankenstein,* Bacon, and the 'Two Truths'." *Extrapolation* 14 (1972): 39–48.

Clarens, Carlos. *An Illustrated History of the Horror Films*. New York: Putnam's, 1967.

Clinton-Baddeley, V. C. *The Burlesque Tradition in the English Theatre After 1660*. London: Methuen, 1952.

Clubbe, John. "Mary Shelley as Autobiographer: The Evidence of the 1831 Introduction to *Frankenstein*." *Wordsworth Circle* 12 (1981): 102–06.

Conger, Sydney McMillen. "A German Ancestor for Mary Shelley's Monster: Kahlert, Schiller, and the Buried Treasure of *Northanger Abbey*." *Philological Quarterly* 59 (1980): 216–32.

Connor, Edward. "The Saga of *Frankenstein*." *Screen Facts* 1 (1963): 15–30.

———. "*Frankenstein*—1910." *Famous Monsters of Filmland* 23 (1963): 44–45.

———. "The First Frankenstein." *The Monster Times* 21 (1973): 15.

Conolly, L. W., and J. P. Wearing. *English Drama and Theatre, 1800–1900: A Guide to Information Sources*. Detroit: Gale, 1978.

Cosslett, Tess. *The "Scientific Movement" and Victorian Literature*. Sussex: Harvester, 1982.

Crouch, Laura. "Davy's *A Discourse, Introductory to a Course of Lectures on Chemistry:* A Possible Source of *Frankenstein*." *Keats-Shelley Journal* 27 (1978): 35–44.

Cude, Wilfred. "Mary Shelley's Modern Prometheus: A Study in the Ethics of Scientific Creativity." *Dalhousie Review* 52 (1972): 212–25.

Degen, John. "A History of Burlesque-Extravaganza in Nineteenth-Century England." Dissertation, Indiana University, 1977.

Dircks, Phillis T. "James Robinson Planché and the English Burletta Tradition." *Theatre Survey* 17 (1976): 68–81.

Donohue, Joseph. "Burletta and the Early Nineteenth-Century English Theatre." *Nineteenth Century Theatre Research* 1 (1973): 29–51.

Duffy, Michael. *The English Satirical Print, 1600–1832*. Cambridge: Chadwyck-Healy, 1986.

Dunn, Richard J. "Narrative Distance in *Frankenstein.*" *Studies in the Novel* 6 (1974): 408–17.

Dussinger, John A. "Kinship and Guilt in Mary Shelley's *Frankenstein.*" *Studies in the Novel* 8 (1976): 38–55.

Ellis, Kate. "Monsters in the Garden: Mary Shelley and the Bourgeois Family." Levine, *Endurance* 123–42.

Evans, Bertrand. *Gothic Drama from Walpole to Shelley.* 1947. Millwood, N.Y.: Kraus, 1977.

Fleck, P. D. "Mary Shelley's Notes to Shelley's Poems and *Frankenstein.*" *Studies in Romanticism* 6 (1967): 226–54.

Florescu, Radu. *In Search of Frankenstein.* Boston: New York Graphic Society, 1975.

Florey, Robert. *Hollywood d'hier et d'aujourd'hui.* Paris: Editions Prisma, 1948.

Forry, Steven Earl. "The Hideous Progenies of Richard Brinsley Peake: *Frankenstein* on the Stage, 1823–1826." *Theatre Research International* 11 (1985).

———. "Dramatizations of *Frankenstein,* 1821–1986: A Comprehensive List." *English Language Notes* (1988).

Foust, R. E. "Monstrous Image: Theory of Fantasy Antagonists." *Genre* 13 (1980): 441–53.

Frank, Frederick. "Mary Shelley's *Frankenstein:* A Register of Research." *Bulletin of Bibliography* 40 (1983): 163–87.

Gaskell, Elizabeth C. *Mary Barton.* 1958; rev. ed. (ed. Stephen Gill) Harmondsworth, Middlesex: Penguin, 1984.

George, M. Dorothy. *Catalogue of Political and Personal Satires Preserved in the Department of Prints and Drawings of the British Museum, 1828–32.* London: Trustees of the British Museum, 1954.

Gifford, Dennis. *Movie Monsters.* London: Dutton, 1969.

Gilbert, Sandra M., and Susan Gubar. *The Madwoman in the Attic: The Woman Writer and the Nineteenth-Century Literary Imagination.* New Haven: Yale University Press, 1979.

Gilmer, Walter. *Horace Liveright: Publisher of the Twenties.* New York: David Lewis, 1970.

Ginisty, Paul. *La Féerie.* Paris: Louis-Michaud, 1910.

Gladstone, William. *The Gladstone Diaries,* ed. M. R. D. Foot. Oxford: Clarendon, 1968.

Glut, Donald F. *The Frankenstein Catalog.* Jefferson, N.C.: McFarland, 1984.

———. *The Frankenstein Legend.* Metuchen, N.J.: Scarecrow, 1973.

Godwin, William. Letter to Mary Shelley. 22 July 1823. Huntington Library. HM 11634.

Goldberg, M. A. "Moral and Myth in Mrs. Shelley's *Frankenstein.*" *Keats-Shelley Journal* 8 (1959): 27–38.

Goodman, Walter. *The Keeleys on the Stage and at Home.* London: 1895.

Gosse, Dalton, and Mary J. H. Gosse. "Grimaldi." *Notes and Queries* 226 (1981): 403–04.

Gotlieb, Howard B. *William Beckford of Fonthill.* New Haven, Conn.: Yale University Press, 1960.

Granville-Barker, Harley. "Exit Planché—Enter Gilbert." *London Mercury* 25 (1931): 457–66; 558–73.

Gray, Douglas. "Frankenstein and the Development of the English Novel." Dissertation, University of Dallas, 1979.

Gregorio, Mario A. di. *T. H. Huxley's Place in Natural Science*. New Haven, Conn.: Yale University Press, 1984.

Griffin, Andrew. "Fire and Ice in *Frankenstein*." Levine, *Endurance*. 49–73.

Gross, Dalton, and Mary J. H. Gross. "Joseph Grimaldi: An Influence on *Frankenstein*." *Notes and Queries* 226 (1981): 403–04.

Gryllis, R. Glynn, *Mary Shelley: A Biography*. London: Oxford University Press, 1938.

Hartog, Willie G. *Gilbert de. Pixérécourt: sa vie, son mélodrame, sa technique et son influence*. Paris: Champion, 1913.

Henderson, Mary C., ed. *Performing Arts Resources, Vol. 5: Recollections of O. Smith, Comedian*. New York: Theatre Library, 1978.

Hill, J. M. "*Frankenstein* and the Physiognomy of Desire." *American Imago* 32 (1975): 335–58.

Hirsch, Gordon D. "The Monster was a Lady: On the Psychology of Mary Shelley's *Frankenstein*." *Hartford Studies in Literature* 7 (1975): 116–53.

Hitchens, Gordon. "Breathless Eagerness: Historical Notes on Dr. Frankenstein and his Monster." *Film Comment* 6.1 (1970): 46–52.

Hoehn, Douglas William. "The First Season of *Presumption!; or, The Fate of Frankenstein*." *Theatre Studies* 26–27 (1978–81): 79–88.

Hollingshead, John. *Gaiety Chronicles*. London: 1898.

———. *"Good Old Gaiety": An Historiette and Remembrance*. London: Gaiety Theatre, 1903.

———. *My Lifetime*. London: 1895.

Horn-Monval, Madeleine. *Répertoire bibliographique des traductions et adaptations françaises du théâtre étranger du XVe siècle à nos jours*. Paris: C N R S, 1958.

Howard, Cecil, ed. *Dramatic Notes: A Yearbook of the Stage*. London: 1888.

Hume, Robert. "Gothic Versus Romantic: A Revaluation of the Gothic Novel." *PMLA* 84 (1969): 282–90.

Huss, Roy, and T. J. Ross. *Focus on the Horror Film*. Englewood Cliffs, N.J.: Prentice-Hall, 1972.

Irving, Laurence. *Henry Irving: The Actor and His World*. London: Faber, 1951.

Jensen, Paul. "Paul Jensen on Frankenstein." *Film Comment* 6.3 (1970): 42–46.

Jones, Frederick L., ed. *Mary Shelley's Journals*. Norman: University of Oklahoma Press, 1947.

Jones, Michael Wynn. *The Cartoon History of Britain*. New York: Macmillan, 1971.

Joseph, Gerhard. "Frankenstein's Dream: The Child as Father of the Monster." *Hartford Studies in Literature* 7 (1975): 97–115.

Kemnitz, Thomas Milton. "Matt Morgan of 'Tomahawk' and English Cartooning, 1867–1870." *Victorian Studies* 19 (1975): 5–34.

Ketterer, David. *Frankenstein's Creature: The Book, The Monster, and Human Reality*. English Literary Studies, no. 16. Victoria, B.C.: University of Victoria, 1979.

———. "Mary Shelley and Science Fiction: A Select Bibliography Selectively Annotated." *Science-Fiction Studies* 5 (1978): 172–78.

Klein, Michael, and Gillian Parker. *The English Novel and the Movies*. New York: Ungar, 1981.

Knoepflmacher, U.C. "Thoughts on the Aggression of Daughters." Levine, *Endurance*. 88–119.

Kreymborg, Alfred. *Troubadour—An American Autobiography*. New York: Sagamore, 1957.

Lauritzen, Einar, and Gunnar Lundquist. *American Film Index, 1908–1915*. Stockholm: Film-Index, 1976.

LaValley, Albert. "The Stage and Film Children of Frankenstein: A Survey." Levine, *Endurance*. 243–89.

Leathers, Victor. *British Entertainers in France*. Toronto: University of Toronto Press, 1959.

Lee, Walt. *Reference Guide to Fantastic Films: Science Fiction, Fantasy and Horror.* Los Angeles: Chelsea-Lee, 1973.

Lennig, Arthur. *The Count: The Life and Films of Bela "Dracula" Lugosi*. New York: Putnam's, 1974.

Leslie, Fred. *Recollections of Fred Leslie*. London: 1894.

Levine, George. "*Frankenstein* and the Tradition of Realism." *Novel* 7 (1973): 14–30.

———. *The Realistic Imagination: English Fiction from Frankenstein to Lady Chatterley*. Chicago: University of Chicago Press, 1981.

Levine, George, and U. C. Knoepflmacher, ed. *The Endurance of Frankenstein: Essays on Mary Shelley's Novel*. Berkeley: University of California Press, 1979.

Lyles, W. H. *Mary Shelley: An Annotated Bibliography*. New York: Garland, 1975.

Macqueen-Pope, W. *Gaiety—Theatre of Enchantment*. New York: Greenburg, 1949.

MacMillan, Dougald. *Catalogue of the Larpent Plays in the Huntington Library*. San Marino, Ca.: San Pasqual Press, 1939.

———. "Planché's Early Classical Burlesques." *Studies in Philology* 25 (1928): 340–45.

———. "Some Burlesques with a Purpose, 1830–1870." *Philological Quarterly* 8 (1929): 255–63.

Mank, Gregory William. *It's Alive! The Classic Cinema Saga of Frankenstein*. New York: Barnes, 1981.

Massey, Irving. *The Gaping Pig: Literature and Metamorphosis*. Berkeley: University of California Press, 1976.

Mathews, Anne, ed. *Memoirs of Charles Mathews, Comedian*. London: Bentley, 1838–39.

Mathews, Charles. Letter to O. Smith. 21 August 1827. Enthoven Collection, Victoria and Albert Museum.

Mayer, David. *Harlequin in His Element: The English Pantomime, 1806–1836*. Cambridge, Mass.: Harvard University Press, 1969.

Mays, Milton. "*Frankenstein,* Mary Shelley's Black Theodicy." *Southern Humanities Review* 3 (1969): 146–53.

Meisel, Martin. "Political Extravaganza: A Phase of Nineteenth-Century British Theatre," *Theatre Survey* 3 (1962): 19–31.

Miles, Alfred. *The Poets and Poetry of the Nineteenth Century: Charles Kingsley to James Thompson*. London: Routledge, 1905.

Millhauser, Milton. "The Noble Savage in Mary Shelley's *Frankenstein*." *Notes and Queries* 190 (1946): 248–50.

Miyoshi, Masao. *The Divided Self: A Perspective on the Literature of the Victorians.* New York: New York University Press, 1969.

Morley, Henry. *The Journal of a London Playgoer from 1851 to 1866.* London: 1866.

Mortion, Peter. *The Vital Science: Biology and the Literary Imagination, 1860–1900.* London: George Allen, 1984.

Murray, E. B. "Shelley's Contribution to Mary's *Frankenstein*." *Keats-Shelley Memorial Bulletin* 29 (1978): 50–68.

Murray, John. *A Handbook for Travellers in Sicily.* London: 1864.

Nelson, Lowry Jr. "Night Thoughts on the Gothic Novel." *Yale Review* 52 (1963): 236–57.

Nichols, Harold. "The Acting of Thomas Potter Cooke." *Nineteenth Century Theatre Research* 5 (1977): 73–84.

Nicoll, Allardyce. *A History of English Drama: 1660–1900.* 6 vols. Cambridge: Cambridge University Press, 1955.

Nitchie, Elizabeth. *Mary Shelley: Author of Frankenstein.* New Brunswick, N.J.: Rutgers University Press, 1953.

Niver, Kemp. *Motion Pictures from the Library of Congress Paper Print Collection, 1894–1912.* Berkeley: University of California Press, 1967.

Odell, George C. *Annals of the New York Stage.* New York: Columbia University Press, 1927. Reprint, AMS Press, 1977.

Ozolins, Aija. "Recent Work on Mary Shelley's *Frankenstein*." *Science-Fiction Studies* 3 (1976): 103–12.

Palacio, Jean de. *Mary Shelley dans son oeuvre*. Paris: Editions Klincksieck, 1969.

Peake, Richard Brinsley. Letter to Charles Mathews. 10 December 1824. Enthoven Collection, Victoria and Albert Museum.

Pixérécourt, Gilbert de. *Théâtre choisi de G. de Pixérécourt*. Paris: 1842.

Planché, James Robinson. *The Extravaganzas of J. R. Planché*. London: 1870.

———. *Recollections and Reflections*. London: Tinsley, 1872.

Prawer, S. S. *Caligari's Children: The Film as Tale of Terror.* Oxford: Oxford University Press, 1980.

Praz, Mario. Introduction. *Frankenstein; or, The Modern Prometheus*. By Mary Shelley. 1969. Harmondsworth, Middlesex: Penguin, 1978.

Quackenbush, Robert. *Movie Monsters and Their Masters. The Birth of the Horror Film*. Chicago: Whitman: 1980.

Rahill, Frank. *The World of Melodrama*. University Park: Pennsylvania State University Press, 1967.

Reynolds, Ernest. *Early Victorian Drama (1830–1870)*. New York: Blom, 1936.

Rhodes, R. Crompton. "The Early Nineteenth-Century Drama." *Library* 4th ser. 16 (1936): 91–112; 210–31.

Rieger, James. "Dr. Polidori and the Genesis of *Frankenstein*." *Studies in English Literature* 3 (1963): 461–72.

Robinson, David. *The History of World Cinema*. New York: Stein, 1973.

Robinson, Henry Crabb. *The London Theatre 1811–1866: Selections from the Diary of Henry Crabb Robinson*. Ed. Eluned Brown. London: Society for Theatre Research, 1966.

Rowell, George. *The Victorian Theatre: 1792–1914*. Cambridge: Cambridge University Press, 1978.

Sadoul, Georges. "Georges Meliès." *Cinéma d'aujourd'hui*. Paris: Editions Seghers, 1961.

Schug, Charles. "The Romantic Form of Mary Shelley's *Frankenstein*." *Studies in English Literature* 17 (1977): 608–19.

Scott, Clement, ed. *The Theatre: A Monthly Review of the Drama, Music, and the Fine Arts*. London: 1894.

Seed, David. "*Frankenstein*—Parable of Spectacle." *Criticism* 24 (1982): 327–40.

Shelley, Mary. *Frankenstein: or, The Modern Prometheus*. Ed. James Rieger. 1974. Chicago: University of Chicago Press, 1982.

Shaw, George Bernard. *Fabian Essays in Socialism*. London: 1889.

———. *Frankenstein; or, The Modern Prometheus*. Ed. M. K. Joseph. London: Oxford University Press, 1971.

Sherwin, Paul. "*Frankenstein:* Creation as Catastrophe." *PMLA* 96 (1981): 883–903.

Spark, Muriel. *Child of Light: A Reassessment of Mary Wollstonecraft Shelley*. Hadleigh, Essex: Tower Bridge, 1951.

Stephens, John Russell. *The Censorship of English Drama 1824–1901*. Cambridge: Cambridge University Press, 1980.

Sterrenburg, Lee. "Mary Shelley's Monster: Politics and Psyche in Frankenstein." Levine, *Endurance* 143–71.

Stevenson, Robert Louis. *Dr. Jekyll and Mr. Hyde*. New York: Bantam, 1981.

Stoker, John. *The Illustrated Frankenstein*. New York: Sterling, 1980.

Tannenbaum, Leslie. "From Filthy Type to Truth: Miltonic Myth in *Frankenstein*." *Keats-Shelley Journal* 26 (1977): 101–13.

Tennyson, G. B. "British Fiction: Recent Books." *Nineteenth-Century Fiction* 40 (1985): 117–22.

Thompson, *The Making of the English Working Class*. 1963; rev. ed. Harmondsworth, Middlesex: Penguin, 1983.

Thorp, Willard. "The Stage Adventures of Some Gothic Novels." *PMLA* 43 (1928): 467–86.

Titterton, W. R. *From Theatre to Music Hall*. London: Swift, 1912.

Tolles, Winton. *Tom Taylor and the Victorian Drama*. 1940. New York: AMS, 1966.

Trewin, J. C. *The Theatre Since 1900*. London: Dakers, 1951.

Tropp, Martin. *Mary Shelley's Monster: The Story of Frankenstein*. Boston: Houghton, 1976.

Trussler, Simon, ed. *Burlesque Plays of the Eighteenth Century*. London: Oxford University Press, 1969.

Varma, Devendra P. *The Gothic Flame, Being a History of the Gothic Novel in England: Its Origins, Efflorescence, Disintegration and Residuary Influences*. London: Barker, 1957.

Vasbinder, Samuel Holmes. "Scientific Attitudes in Mary Shelley's *Frankenstein*." Dissertation, Kent State University, 1976.

Vincent, W. T. *Recollections of Fred Leslie*. 2 vols. London: 1894.

Wallack, James William. *A Sketch of the Life of James William Wallack (Senior), Late Actor and Manager*. New York: 1865.

Walls, Howard Lamarr. *Motion Pictures, 1894–1912*. Washington, D.C.: U.S. Library of Congress, 1953.

Watson, Ernest Bradlee. *Sheridan to Robertson—A Study of the Nineteenth-Century London Stage*. Cambridge, Mass.: Harvard University Press, 1926.

Watt, William W. *Shilling Shockers of the Gothic School: A Study of Chapbook Gothic Romances*. Cambridge, Mass.: Harvard University Press, 1932.

Weissman, Judith. "A Reading of *Frankenstein* as the Complaint of a Political Wife." *Colby Library Quarterly* 12 (1976): 171–80.

Wexelblatt, Robert. "The Ambivalence of *Frankenstein*." *Arizona Quarterly* 36 (1980): 101–15.

Wilt, Judith. "*Frankenstein* as Mystery Play." Levine, *Endurance* 31–48.

———. *Ghosts of the Gothic: Austen, Eliot, and Lawrence*. Princeton, N.J.: Princeton University Press, 1980.

Wolf, Leonard. *The Annotated Frankenstein*. New York: Potter, 1977.

Yates, Edmund. *Recollections and Experiences*. London: 1884.

Yeo, Richard. "Science and Intellectual Authority in Mid-Nineteenth-Century Britain: Robert Chambers and *Vestiges of the Natural History of Creation*." *Victorian Studies* 28 (1984): 5–31.

Ziolkowski, Theodore. "Science, Frankenstein, and Myth." *Sewanee Review* 89 (1981): 34–56.

Zirker, Joan. "The Gothic Tradition in English Fiction, 1764–1824." Dissertation, Indiana University, 1974.

Index

HIDEOUS PROGENIES